SPEECHES FROM ATHENIAN LAW

THE ORATORY OF CLASSICAL GREECE

Translated with Notes • Michael Gagarin, Series Editor

VOLUME 16

SPEECHES FROM ATHENIAN LAW

Edited by Michael Gagarin

 UNIVERSITY OF TEXAS PRESS, AUSTIN

This book has been supported by an endowment dedicated to classics and the ancient world and funded by the Aretē Foundation; the Gladys Krieble Delmas Foundation; the Dougherty Foundation; the James R. Dougherty, Jr. Foundation; the Rachael and Ben Vaughan Foundation; and the National Endowment for the Humanities.

First edition, 2011

Library of Congress Cataloging-in-Publication Data

Speeches from Athenian law / edited by Michael Gagarin. — 1st ed.
　　　p.　cm. — (Oratory of classical Greece ; v. 16)
　　Includes bibliographical references and index.
　　ISBN 978-0-292-72638-3
(pbk. : alk. paper)
　　1. Forensic orations—Greece—Athens.　2. Trials—Athens—History—Sources.　I. Gagarin, Michael.
　　KI81.S68　2011
　　340.5'385—dc22　　　　　　　　　　　　　　　　　2010026801

　　ISBN 978-0-292-78652-3 (E-book)

CONTENTS

〰〰〰〰〰〰〰〰〰〰〰〰〰〰〰〰〰〰〰〰〰〰〰〰〰〰〰〰〰〰〰〰〰〰〰〰〰

PREFACE

The selection of speeches in this volume is primarily intended to illustrate some of the main features of Athenian law. My aim is to provide teachers of Athenian law and students and scholars wishing to learn about Athenian law with a useful selection of primary sources. The speeches also present a kaleidoscope of life in classical Athens, and so the volume can also serve as a resource for those with other interests. As with any selection, space limitations have forced me to omit speeches I would have liked to include; others would undoubtedly have chosen differently.

The translations of each speech together with their introductions and notes are taken directly from volumes of *The Oratory of Classical Greece* (University of Texas Press 1998–). Except for minor corrections and stylistic changes, I have not changed the translations; as a result, they are not fully consistent: for example, the *dikastai* who comprised Athenian juries are translated "judges" or "jurors," or transliterated as "dicasts," according to the preference of the translator. This and other Greek words do not correspond exactly to a single English term, and although the inconsistency may be awkward at first, it also alerts the reader to some of the important differences between Athenian law and our own. I have edited the introductions and notes to each speech more extensively, primarily to provide a sharper focus on law by reducing or eliminating material that is purely historical or otherwise nonlegal. I have also fixed cross-references where necessary and have reorganized material to reduce the amount of repetition.

That said, the different translators have somewhat different interests and emphases and may even on occasion take different positions on a matter. I have not tried to eliminate such discrepancies, preferring to let the reader see that some features of Athenian law (indeed of any legal system) can be understood in different, even opposed, ways.

This volume contains the work of many contributors. I am particularly grateful to all the translators, both for their original translations and in some cases for corrections and revisions made in the preparation of this volume. David Mirhady and Mark Sundahl read the entire manuscript and gave me a great deal of useful feedback. And the staff at the University of Texas Press was friendly and efficient, as always, and a great pleasure to work with. In particular, Jim Burr, Lynne F. Chapman, and Nancy Bryan were most helpful with this volume.

EDITOR'S NOTE ON ABBREVIATIONS, CURRENCY, AND DATES

ABBREVIATIONS

Orators

Aes. = Aeschines
Is. = Isaeus
And. = Andocides
Hyp. = Hyperides
Isoc. = Isocrates
Ant. = Antiphon
Lys. = Lysias
Dem. = Demosthenes

Other

Ath. Pol. = Aristotle (?), *The Constitution of the Athenians* (*Athenai/ ōn Politeia*)
IG = Inscriptiones Graecae

CURRENCY

The main unit of Athenian currency was the drachma; this was divided into obols, and larger amounts were designated minas and talents.

1 drachma = 6 obols
1 mina = 100 drachmas
1 talent = 60 minas (6,000 drachmas)

It is impossible to give an accurate equivalence in terms of modern currency, but it may be helpful to remember that a drachma was the daily wage of some skilled workers; thus, it may not be too misleading to think of a drachma as worth about $50–$100 (or £30–£60) and a talent about $500,000 or £300,000.

DATES

The Athenians assigned to each of their years the name of the (eponymous) Archon for that year—"in the archonship of X." Since the Athenian year began in late summer, a date like 404/3 designates the year that began in 404 and ended in 403.

SPEECHES FROM ATHENIAN LAW

INTRODUCTION

~~~~~~

Oratory and Law at Athens

One of the many intriguing (and unique) aspects of Athenian law is that our information about it comes very largely from speeches composed for delivery in court. These date to the period 420–320[1] and reflect in part the high value the Greeks in all periods placed on effective speaking. Even Achilles, whose fame rested primarily on his martial superiority, was brought up to be "a speaker of words and a doer of deeds" (*Iliad* 9.443). Great Athenian leaders such as Themistocles and Pericles were accomplished public speakers; epic poetry, tragedy, comedy, and history all made frequent use of set speeches. The formal pleadings of the envoys to Achilles in *Iliad* Book Nine, the messenger speeches in tragedy reporting events like the battle of Salamis in Aeschylus' *Persians*, and Pericles' funeral oration in Thucydides' *History* are but a few indications of the Greeks' never-ending fascination with the spoken word, and with formal public speaking in particular, which reached its height in the public oratory of the fifth and fourth centuries.

I. ORATORY

Originally, oratory[2] was not a specialized subject of study but was learned by practice and example. The formal study of oratory as an "art" (*technē*), which we call rhetoric, began, we are told, in the middle

---

[1] All dates in this volume are BCE unless the contrary is indicated or obvious.

[2] For a good brief introduction to oratory and the orators, see Edwards 1994. Usher 1999 has a brief but useful discussion of each surviving speech.

of the fifth century in Sicily with Corax and his pupil Tisias.[3] These two are scarcely more than names to us, but another Sicilian, Gorgias of Leontini (ca. 490–390), developed a dazzling new style of speech and argument. Gorgias initiated the practice, which continued into the early fourth century, of composing speeches for mythical or imaginary occasions. This tradition of "intellectual" oratory was continued by the fourth-century educator Isocrates and played a large role in later Greek and Roman education.

By contrast, "practical" oratory—speeches delivered on real occasions in public life—had been practiced throughout Greece for centuries. Athenians, in particular, had been delivering speeches in the courts and public assemblies since the days of Draco and Solon (late seventh and early sixth centuries), if not longer, though these speeches were not put in writing and thus not preserved. But as the participation of citizens in political and legal institutions increased during the fifth century, so too did the importance of oratory. The practice of writing down speeches for use in court began with Antiphon, a fifth-century intellectual sometimes included (with Gorgias) in the group we call the Sophists.[4] Antiphon contributed to the intellectual oratory of the period with his Tetralogies (sets of four fictional speeches each), but he also had a strong practical interest in law. Although he mostly avoided direct involvement in legal or political affairs, he gave advice to others who were engaged in litigation. Probably around 430, Antiphon began writing entire speeches for litigants to memorize and deliver in court. Thus began the practice of "logography"—writing speeches for others—and because these speeches were written, they could be preserved. Logography was a particularly appealing career for those like Lysias who were not Athenian citizens and who were thus barred from active participation in public life, and the practice continued through the fourth century and beyond.[5]

Antiphon and others also began to write down speeches they would themselves deliver in court or (occasionally) in the Assembly. One other type of practical oratory was the special tribute delivered

---

[3] For differing accounts of these two figures, see Kennedy 1963: 26–51; Gagarin 2007.

[4] See Gagarin 2002.

[5] See further Todd 2005.

on important public occasions, the best known being the funeral oration. These three types of oratory were later classified by Aristotle (*Rhetoric* 1.3) as forensic (for the courts), deliberative (for the Assembly), and epideictic (for display). The speeches in this volume are all forensic.

II. THE SPEECHES

We know almost nothing about the "publication" of speeches at this time, but there was an active market for books in Athens, and some speeches may have achieved wide circulation.[6] An author may have circulated copies of his own speeches to advertise his talents or in political cases to make his views more widely known. Booksellers may have collected and copied speeches in order to make money. With the foundation of the great library in Alexandria early in the third century, scholars began to collect and catalogue texts of many classical authors, including orators.

These scholars selected the ten best orators and gathered all their speeches, though among the hundreds of speeches they collected, many were undoubtedly written by other authors of the same period and misattributed. Only a small percentage of these speeches survived to the modern era in manuscript form; a few more have been recovered from ancient papyrus remains. Today the corpus of Attic Oratory consists of about 150 speeches and letters, about 100 of which are forensic speeches. These cover many subjects: important public issues, crimes, business affairs, lovers' quarrels, inheritance, citizenship, and others; the twenty-two speeches in this volume are only a sample.

III. THE ORATORS

In the period 420–320, dozens of now unknown orators and logographers composed speeches for delivery in court. Most of them are now lost, but speeches have survived from the ten authors considered

---

[6] Dover's discussion (1968) of the preservation and transmission of the works of Lysias is fundamental for all the orators, though his stylistic criteria of authenticity and his theory of shared authorship have found few followers (see Usher 1976).

the best by later scholars. The authors represented in this volume are:[7]

- AESCHINES (ca. 390–ca. 322) rose from low origins to become a major political figure and a bitter enemy of Demosthenes. His speeches all concern public issues. He went into exile after losing the case "On the Crown" (Aes. 3) to Demosthenes in 330.

- ANTIPHON (ca. 480–411), in addition to writing speeches, was one of the leaders of an oligarchic coup in 411. The democrats quickly regained power, and Antiphon was tried for treason, convicted, and executed.

- DEMOSTHENES (384–322) is generally considered the greatest Greek orator. His father died when he was a boy, and guardians mismanaged his estate, probably stealing much of it. After turning eighteen, he sued them and won, but despite repeated suits (Dem. 27–31), he never fully recovered the estate. He wrote speeches for others and also for his own use in court and in the Assembly. In the 340s and 330s he vigorously opposed the growing power of Philip of Macedon, and after Athens' defeat he successfully defended this policy against Aeschines in his most famous speech *On the Crown* (18), delivered in 330.

- APOLLODORUS (ca. 394–335?) was probably the author of six or seven of the speeches attributed to Demosthenes (including Dem. 59). His father Pasion was a slave but was later freed and eventually obtained Athenian citizenship.

- HYPERIDES (390–322) was a political leader and logographer. With Demosthenes, he led the Athenian resistance to Philip and Alexander and was condemned to death after Athens' final surrender. None of his speeches survived in manuscript form, but all or most of six speeches and parts of others have been recovered from papyrus remains.

- ISAEUS (ca. 415–ca. 340) is said to have been a pupil of Isocrates and the teacher of Demosthenes. He wrote speeches on a wide

---

[7] For more information about these authors, see Edwards 1994 and the Introductions to volumes of *The Oratory of Classical Greece.*

range of topics, but the eleven that survive in full all concern inheritance.

- ISOCRATES (436–338) was a philosopher and educator. He came from a wealthy family that lost most of its property in the Peloponnesian War (431–404). He took up logography but abandoned it about 390 in favor of writing and teaching; six court speeches survive from this period. He taught a broad mixture of statesmanship, public speaking, and practical philosophy, attracting pupils from the entire Greek world and greatly influencing education and rhetoric in the Hellenistic and Roman times.

- LYSIAS (ca. 445–ca. 380) was a metic—a noncitizen resident (see below, IVB). Much of his property was seized by the Thirty during their brutal oligarchic coup in 404/3. He wrote speeches for others on a wide range of subjects and may have delivered one himself, on the murder of his brother (Lys. 12). He is particularly known for his engaging narratives, his realistic characters, and his lucid and vivid prose style.

IV. GOVERNMENT

A. Officials

The Athenian political system was a direct democracy, not the representative form of democracy common today.[8] All significant policy decisions were made by the Assembly, in which all citizens could participate (a quorum was 6,000); a small payment for attendance enabled the poor to attend. A Council of 500, 50 from each tribe selected annually by lot, prepared material for and made recommendations to the Assembly; each tribal group of 50 served as an executive committee, the Prytany, for one-tenth of the lunar year (35 or 36 days). The tribe holding the Prytany carried out all the administrative duties of the Council.

All important officials other than military commanders were

---

[8] Hansen 1991 is the best short account. Much of our information about the legal and political systems comes from *The Athenian Constitution* (*Ath. Pol.*), attributed to Aristotle but probably written by a pupil of his (translated with notes by Rhodes 1984).

selected annually by lot, and most offices could be held only once. Thus, many citizens held public office at some point, but almost none served for an extended period of time. The most important officials were the nine Archons (lit. "rulers"): the (eponymous) Archon after whom the year was named, the Basileus ("King" or "King Archon"), the Polemarch, and the six Thesmothetae. The Archons oversaw the courts and had various other duties. The Archon supervised family and inheritance cases, the Basileus was in charge of homicide and religious cases, the Polemarch heard cases involving metics and others who were not Athenian citizens, and the Thesmothetae oversaw political trials. Most private cases were heard by the Forty, four tribal judges from each tribe to whom cases were allocated according to the tribe of the defendant.

All officials and members of the Council underwent a "scrutiny" (*dokimasia*) before taking office, and officials submitted to a final accounting (*euthynai*) at the end of their term. Others also underwent scrutiny, among them boys before being granted full citizenship at the age of eighteen and the poor who wished to receive public welfare (see Lys. 24). At the scrutiny, any citizen who wished could challenge a person's fitness for his new position or privilege. The accounting examined the conduct of officials during their term of office in two phases, the first devoted to their financial accounts, the second to their general conduct; at the second stage, it was open to anyone to lodge a complaint.

B. The People

Participation in the political and legal systems was restricted mostly to Athenian citizens, that is, adult male citizens. This restriction applied to holding office, voting in the Assembly, and serving on a jury. Determining citizen status was sometimes difficult (see Lys. 23). In 507 Cleisthenes organized Athens into ten tribes and 139 demes (precincts). Citizenship lists were kept by the demes. Membership was hereditary, and fathers registered their sons in their deme at the age of eighteen. Every citizen also belonged to the tribe to which his deme was assigned. Pericles' citizenship law, enacted in 450, restricted citizenship to those whose parents were both citizens. Although this requirement seems to have been neglected during the Peloponnesian

War (431–404), it was reinstated in the archonship of Eucleides in 403/2.

Women citizens could not participate in this system, though they had important roles in many religious rituals and festivals. Their commercial life was also limited. There was apparently a law (Is. 10.10) that women (and children) could not enter into a contract for more than a *medimnos* of barley (about 1½ bushels), but we also have evidence that seems to violate this restriction. In financial matters or in court, a woman would normally be represented by her *kyrios* ("guardian"), usually her husband, brother, father, or son.

Besides citizens, the resident population consisted of metics and slaves. Metics were foreigners residing permanently in Athens. They had to register and pay a metic tax each year and serve in the military. They were not allowed to own real property, but otherwise they could participate fully in the economic life of the city. Many practiced trades, and some became quite rich. Metics could appear in court in certain kinds of cases. They could become citizens only by a vote of the Assembly; this was rare and normally was granted as a reward for special benefactions.

The number and condition of slaves in Athens is a matter of dispute. Many citizens and metics seem to have had one or two slaves helping in the house or in the fields, but apparently even the rich did not have a large number of slaves for these tasks. Small workshops regularly were staffed by slaves; the two owned by Demosthenes' father (Dem. 27), with twenty and thirty slaves respectively, were larger than most. Publicly owned slaves performed some functions in the city but were primarily used in the silver mines, where their lives were extremely hard. Slaves could sometimes earn money for themselves and could occasionally buy their freedom or be freed by their master. Freed slaves had the status of metics.

C. The Liturgy System

Politicians gained influence not by election to office but by their ability to sway the majority of citizens in the Assembly to vote for their policies. Success was often temporary, as victory on one policy issue could quickly be followed by defeat on another. Leading politicians, who were often very wealthy, also gained prominence by undertaking public service in the form of "liturgies" (*leitourgiai*). Except for occasional war taxes (*eisphora*), levied on the richest citizens, the Athenians avoided direct taxation, relying instead on a system of liturgies, which were required of the wealthiest citizens on a rotating basis.

The two most important and costly liturgies were the *chorēgia* and the trierarchy. In the former, a *chorēgos* organized and paid for the training of a chorus either for the dithyrambic contests (see Ant. 6) or for the dramatic competitions. A trierarch equipped a warship (trireme) and paid its expenses, and often commanded it for a year. Shared trierarchies appear to have been introduced in the final years of the Peloponnesian War to cope with financial strains among the Athenian elite. Many litigants refer to their own liturgies to create a favorable impression with the jury. A person liable to a liturgy could challenge a richer man either to undertake the liturgy in his place or else to exchange properties with him: this exchange was called an *antidosis*. Details are unclear, but it seems most likely that the speaker often accepted the exchange and that disputes then arose about the content or value of the properties.

V. ATHENIAN LAW

A. History

The legal system[9] was an integral part of this political system. The first written laws were enacted by Draco (ca. 620) and Solon (ca. 590), and new laws were regularly added. By the end of the fifth century these laws were in a rather chaotic state, and so an appointed commission examined all the laws. They removed conflicting or obsolete laws and reinscribed the valid laws that remained, although whether this project was completed is uncertain. A new procedure was instituted for enacting laws: before a new law could be voted on by the Assembly, a group of Lawgivers (*Nomothetai*) had to certify that the proposed law did not conflict with any existing law.

---

[9] The books on Athenian law by MacDowell 1978 and Todd 1993 are most accessible to beginners; Harrison 1968–1971 and Lipsius 1905–1915 provide more details. Boegehold 1995 is a full collection of the material evidence for Athenian courts and trial procedures.

After 403 the Athenians distinguished formally between laws (*nomoi*) and decrees (*psēphismata*), with laws having greater authority. When a decree was proposed in the Assembly, any Athenian who wished could bring suit against it and its proposer by means of a *graphē paranomōn*, or "indictment for illegal [proposals]." A conviction in the case meant that the decree would be rescinded, and its proposer could be fined.

B. Judicial Organization

At the heart of the Athenian judicial system were the popular courts (*dikastēria*). Most trials were held in these courts before juries that numbered between 201 and 501 citizens but in important cases could be as large as 1501. The older, aristocratic Council of the Areopagus also heard cases, but after 462, its jurisdiction was confined to homicide and some religious cases. It was composed of all former Archons, and would thus have numbered around 200. Trials and the procedures leading up to them were supervised by one of the Archons or one of the Forty (see above, IVA). The role of these officials was purely administrative; they had no professional training and were in no way equivalent to modern judges.

Officials alone decided private cases involving ten drachmas or less, but private disputes concerning larger amounts went first to a public arbitrator; every citizen was required to serve as an arbitrator during the year he turned sixty. At the arbitration hearing, the two litigants presented their cases. The arbitrator collected all the documentation for the case, and he could question either litigant. The arbitrator then rendered a decision that, if accepted by both sides, was final; but either party could reject this decision and take the case to court. In public suits, a preliminary hearing was also held at which documentation was similarly collected. The documents presented at these hearings were sealed in a jar and kept for the trial, and litigants could use only these documents in the trial.

C. The Trial

A trial consisted of one speech by each litigant, beginning with the plaintiff; in some private cases each side gave a second, rebuttal speech.

A litigant normally presented his own case. If he could afford it, he could enlist the help of a logographer, who probably gave advice in addition to writing a speech. In addition, one or more friends could serve as a supporting speaker (*synēgoros*), presenting part or all of the case, but payment for this service was prohibited.

Speeches were timed by a water clock (*klepsydra*) to ensure an equal hearing for both sides,[10] and all trials were completed within a day. During his pleading, a litigant could have the clerk read out a document such as a law, a witness deposition, or a contract; in private cases, the water clock stopped for this. Most of these documents no longer survive, except for a notation in the text, such as "[LAW]." In some cases, documents are preserved in the manuscripts, but these are often (not always) later forgeries.

Jurors (*dikastai*)[11] were selected by lot from those citizens, who registered each year and who appeared for jury duty that day; only males aged thirty or older were eligible, and as with the Assembly, a small payment allowed the poor to serve. At the beginning of the year, all 6,000 jurors empanelled for that year swore an oath whose clauses included promises to vote according to the laws and the decrees of Athens or—in default of a law—according to "their most just opinion," to give both sides a fair hearing, to cast their vote specifically on the subject under dispute, and to take no bribes. It is common for speakers to remind the jurors of the oath, either in general or with reference to specific clauses.

After both sides spoke, the jury voted immediately, without formal deliberation, in a secret ballot; the litigant with the majority of votes won (a tie favored the defendant). This meant that all the issues in the case, substantive and procedural, were decided in one vote. In some cases in which the penalty was not fixed, after a conviction the jurors voted again in an "assessment" (*timēsis* or *timēma*) of the penalty, choosing between the penalties proposed by each side. A famous example of this is in Plato's *Apology*. Penalties were typically monetary fines, although litigants could propose other types of penalties, including death.

---

[10] For the water clock, see Boegehold 1995: 31, 77–78, 226–230, and plate 13.

[11] Because the Athenian *dikastai* combined the roles of judge and juror in modern legal systems, *dikastēs* can also be translated "judge."

D. Witnesses

In the fifth century, witnesses[12] gave their testimony in person. Early in the fourth century, a system of written depositions was introduced. The litigant drafted the deposition for the witness, who merely affirmed the statement after it was read out by the clerk. Witnesses could be sued for false witness (*pseudomartyria*); three convictions on this charge resulted in the loss of civic rights. A witness who objected to the deposition prepared for him could take an oath of disclaimer (*exōmosia*) to the effect that he had not been present at the incident in question or did not know that the facts were as stated. If he refused to testify or swear this oath, he was subject to a summons (*klēteusis*), with a penalty of 1,000 drachmas for failure to respond.

E. Types of Procedure

The traditional form of procedure was a *dikē* ("suit") in which the injured party (or a relative in a homicide case) brought suit against the offender. When the victim was a woman or a slave, the suit was brought by the woman's *kyrios* (see above, IVB) or the slave's master. Strictly speaking, a *dikē* was a private matter between individuals, though it could have public dimensions. The other main form of procedure was a *graphē* ("indictment") in which any citizen who wished could prosecute. This procedure was instituted by Solon, probably to allow prosecution of offenses against victims who were unable or unlikely to bring suit themselves, such as orphans,[13] but the use of *graphai* soon increased to cover many types of public offenses. Other more specialized forms of prosecution, such as *eisangelia* ("impeachment") used in cases of treason, also depended on prosecution by volunteers. The existence of multiple procedures sometimes meant that different procedures were available for the same offense, but this does not appear to have been a problem (see Dem. 54.1–2). Rather, the system was intended to be flexible so that citizens could easily find a procedure by which to bring their complaints to court.

---

[12] See further Thür 2005.

[13] In Greek, an "orphan" (*orphanos*) is someone whose father had died; his mother might still be alive.

The system of volunteer prosecutors meant that Athens never had a public prosecutor. By the end of the fifth century the system was apparently being abused by "sykophants" (*sykophantai*), who, perhaps with trumped-up evidence, brought or threatened to bring suits against rich men, either to gain part of the fine that would be levied or to induce the accused to settle out of court. It is impossible to gauge the true extent of this problem, but many litigants accuse their opponents, usually in rather vague terms, of being sykophants. The Athenians took steps to prevent sykophancy, for example, by subjecting a plaintiff who dropped the case or failed to obtain one-fifth of the jury's votes to a fine of 1,000 drachmas. In any case, litigation was common in Athens and was seen by some as excessive.

F. Laws

Litigants often cite or refer to laws in their pleadings, and they (or their logographer) could read the laws either on public inscriptions or, by the fourth century, in an archive. Statutes were generally written in ordinary, nontechnical language, and offenses were designated by broad terms ("damage," "assault," "impiety") without further precision. Plaintiffs would select an appropriate category and then specify the particulars of the alleged offense. There was no need for specialists to interpret the law, and as a result, Athens had no lawyers, no trained judges, and no authoritative interpreters of the law (such as jurists). Religious "exegetes" (cf. Is. 8.39 below) could be consulted on legal matters that had a religious dimension, such as the prosecution of a homicide, and these opinions could be reported in court, but they had no official authority. Thus, litigants could assert whatever interpretation of the law they wished, sometimes adducing the lawgiver's (presumed) intent in support. In such cases, jurors had to decide for themselves whether to accept the litigant's account.

VI. CONCLUSION

The Athenian legal system operated without professional oversight or control. Until recently, this lack of professional control led most scholars to judge Athenian law quite harshly. For critics like Plato (437–327), who argued against many aspects of Athenian culture (including poetry), democracy was essentially the tyranny of the masses, and the Athenian legal system was capricious and depended entirely on the rhetorical ability of litigants, who had no regard for truth or justice. Scholars often note that Athenian law was closely interwoven with politics and did not have the autonomy it later achieved in Rome and continues to have, at least in theory, in most modern legal systems. Many recent scholars, however, conclude that the aim of Athenian law was a fair and orderly procedure that enabled any citizen to have his grievance heard in court by a group of his peers, and to have it heard quickly and cheaply without the need for special training or professional help. In this it clearly succeeded, and despite several wars and two short-lived oligarchic coups, Athenian democracy and the Athenian legal system remained relatively stable for almost two centuries (508–320).

PART I HOMICIDE AND ASSAULT

〰〰〰〰〰〰〰〰〰〰〰〰〰〰〰〰〰〰〰〰〰〰〰〰〰〰〰〰〰〰〰〰〰〰〰〰〰〰

Athens appears to have been a relatively nonviolent society. Men did not normally carry weapons and at most might pick up a stone or piece of broken pottery to aid in a fight. Nonetheless, assaults and homicides did occur and are the subject of several surviving cases, including Antiphon's three Tetralogies, speeches composed for imaginary cases; the First Tetralogy (Ant. 2) is included here. Several kinds of homicide could be prosecuted, including unintentional, as in Antiphon 6; this speech also sheds light on some of the pretrial maneuvering that could occur in legal cases. In Antiphon 1 the speaker accuses a woman of plotting to poison her husband. In Antiphon 5 the defendant is accused of murdering a man whose body was never found; in addition to maintaining his innocence, he objects to the unusual procedure used by the prosecution. Finally, the defendant in Lysias 1 argues that his killing of an adulterer caught in bed with his wife was legally justified.

The next three cases concern assault. All three occur in the course of long-running disputes between the parties involved. In Demosthenes 54 a man claims to have been beaten within an inch of his life by Conon and his sons with whom he has clashed in the past, and Isocrates 20 contains similar accusations of violent assault. In both speeches the charge was probably simple assault (*dikē aikeias*), but both speakers argue that the assault could also be considered *hybris*, a kind of aggravated assault, and could have been prosecuted by a *graphē hybreōs*, a procedure with more serious consequences. In Lysias 3 an older man defends himself against a charge of "wounding with intent to kill" in an ongoing dispute with a rival for the sexual favors of a young man.

ANTIPHON 2. FIRST TETRALOGY

INTRODUCTION

The Tetralogies are artificial exercises illustrating different types of argument in homicide cases. Each has four speeches, two on each side, as in actual homicide cases.[1] Because the focus is on argument, the narrative portion is omitted or reduced to the minimum necessary to understand the case, and no witnesses are called to testify. The arguments can become rather complex, as each is answered by a counter-argument, which is then answered in turn.

The issue of pollution for homicide is prominent in the prologues and epilogues of all three Tetralogies. Both sides argue that a killer is polluted and his pollution also pollutes the whole city. Both sides claim a religious duty to see that the true killer is tried and convicted. Convicting an innocent man or not convicting the true killer will bring pollution on whichever litigant errs and perhaps also on the jurors. If the killer goes free, moreover, the whole city will suffer: its sanctuaries will be defiled and its crops ruined. Pollution is much less prominent, however, in Antiphon's other speeches (cf. 5.81–83) and does not seem to have been very important in actual Athenian homicide law.

The First Tetralogy concerns a question of fact: did the accused do it? A man and his servant have been killed in the street late at night. When the crime was discovered, the man was already dead, but his servant, before dying, allegedly identified the accused as the murderer. This direct evidence is disputed (the servant would be biased), and

---

[1] We never have the second speech from actual homicide trials, probably because in most cases the logographer wrote only the first speech.

additional arguments are elaborated, most of which take the form of arguments from likelihood or probability (*eikos*): no one else is likely to have killed the man; or, the accused had a strong motive; or, his previous dealings with the victim made him more likely to avoid killing him. This type of argument was especially favored by the two figures traditionally credited with inventing rhetoric, Corax and Tisias.[2] Another commonplace argument is the citation of previous service to the city. Toward the end of his second speech (2.4.8) the defendant offers an alibi; if confirmed, this would provide strong evidence in his favor, probably strong enough to decide the case, but the issue is not developed.

ANTIPHON 2. FIRST TETRALOGY

2.1

[1] It is not difficult to obtain a conviction for crimes planned by ordinary people, but when those with natural ability and previous experience commit a crime at that point in their lives when their mental faculties are at their height, it is difficult to get any knowledge or proof of it. [2] Because of the great risk involved, in their planning they pay close attention to security and do not undertake anything without first guarding against all possible suspicion. You should be aware of this, and even if you accept a point as only likely (*eikos*), you should have confidence in it. For our part, in bringing this homicide case we are not letting the guilty one go free in order to prosecute an innocent man. [3] We know that the whole city is polluted by the killer until he is prosecuted and that if we prosecute the wrong man, we will be guilty of impiety, and punishment for any mistake you make (in convicting him) will fall on us. Since the entire pollution thus falls on us, we will try to show you as clearly as possible from the facts at our disposal that he killed the man.

[4] <Common criminals[3] are not likely (*eikos*) to have killed the

---

[2] See the Introduction, I.

[3] The first part of this sentence is missing in the manuscripts of Antiphon, but words to this effect must have been there originally. "Common criminals" translates the Greek word *kakourgoi*, which occurs in the defendant's response to this

man,> for no one who went so far as to risk his life would abandon the gain he had securely in hand; and yet the victims were still wearing their cloaks when they were found. The killer wasn't someone who was drunk, for he would have been identified by his fellow drinkers. He wasn't killed in a quarrel, for they were not quarreling in the middle of the night in a deserted place. And no one would have killed him by accident when aiming at someone else, for then his attendant wouldn't have been killed too. [5] So all other suspicions are removed, and the circumstances of the death show that it was deliberately planned. Who is more likely to have attacked him than someone who has already suffered great harm from him and expects to suffer even more? That person is the defendant, who is his old enemy and has prosecuted him many times on serious charges but never gained a conviction. [6] In turn, he was prosecuted even more often and on more serious charges, and since he never once won acquittal, he has lost most of his property. Most recently the defendant was indicted by him for theft of sacred property with a penalty of two talents.[4] He knew full well he was guilty, he knew his opponent's ability from previous experience, and he harbored resentment from the earlier incidents. In all likelihood, therefore, he formed this plan, and in all likelihood he killed the man to defend himself against this hostile action. [7] Desire for revenge made him unmindful of the danger, and fear of impending disaster fired him with greater eagerness to attempt the crime. He hoped by this action to kill the man without being caught and to be free from that indictment, since without a prosecutor the case would be dropped.[5] [8] Even if he should be caught, he thought it more

---

argument (e.g., 2.4.5–6). *Kakourgoi* were subject to the legal procedure of *apagōgē* or "summary arrest" (see Ant. 5 below). Originally, *kakourgoi* designated common street criminals, such as thieves and muggers (cf. Ant. 5.9 below). The most serious street crime in Athens was *lōpodusia* or the theft of a cloak, a cloak being normally the most valuable possession a man had with him in public.

[4] Theft of sacred property (*hierosylia*) usually involved stealing public funds or other valuables from a temple. The fine is equivalent to perhaps $600,000.

[5] Theft of sacred property was a public action (a *graphē*), so that any citizen who wished could prosecute (see the Introduction, VE). But such cases were often brought by the accused's political enemies, and the speaker reasons that with the defendant's main enemy dead, no one else would prosecute.

honorable to gain his revenge and suffer the consequences than to be a coward and do nothing but let himself be destroyed by the impending prosecution. He was quite certain he would be convicted in that case; otherwise, he would not have thought this trial offered him a better chance. [9] These considerations forced him to commit this unholy crime. As for witnesses, if many had been present, we would have presented many here. But since only his attendant was present, those who heard him speak will testify. For he was still breathing when we picked him up and questioned him, and he said he recognized this man alone among those who attacked them.

Since, then, his guilt is established both by arguments from likelihood and by those who were present, there is no way his acquittal could be just or advantageous. [10] For it would be impossible to convict those who plan crimes if they cannot be convicted either by the testimony of those present or by arguments from likelihood; and it is harmful to you if this polluted and unholy person should enter the precincts of the gods and pollute their holiness or share the tables of innocent men and infect them with this pollution. Acts such as these cause harvests to fail and affairs in general to miscarry. [11] So make this man's punishment your own concern: attribute his impiety to him alone, and you will insure that his misfortune remains his alone and the city remains untainted by it.

2.2

[1] I don't think I'm wrong to consider myself the most unfortunate of all men. Others suffer misfortunes, but if their troubles are caused by a storm, these cease when good weather returns; if they fall sick, the danger passes when they recover their health; and if some other misfortune assails them, a reversal of conditions brings relief. [2] But in my case, when this person was alive, he was ruining me and my family, and now that he is dead, even if I am acquitted, he has caused me considerable pain and anxiety. For my bad luck has reached the point that showing my decency and innocence will not be enough to save me from ruin. Unless I can also find the true killer and prove his guilt—something they in their quest for revenge are unable to do—then I will be judged guilty of murder and wrongly convicted. [3] They claim that my cleverness makes it hard to establish my guilt,

but they also accuse me of foolishness when they argue that my actions show that I did the deed. For if the enormous hostility between us leads you now to consider me the likely suspect, then it was even more likely that before committing the crime I would foresee that I was going to be the obvious suspect, and far from committing the murder myself and willingly incurring the obvious suspicion, I would even prevent others from killing him if I learned they were planning to do so.[6] For if the deed itself showed that I was the killer,[7] I was doomed, and even if I escaped detection, I was quite certain I would incur this suspicion. [4] I am thus in this miserable position: I am forced not only to defend myself but also to reveal the true killers. Still, I must try, for it seems that nothing is more bitter than necessity. I have no other way to proceed than with arguments the prosecutor used when he absolved others of the crime and claimed that the circumstances of the death show that I am the murderer. For if making them seem innocent makes the crime appear to be my doing, then it is only right that making them suspect should make me seem innocent.

[5] It is not unlikely, as they claim, but likely that someone wandering around in the middle of the night would be killed for his cloak. That his cloak was not removed proves nothing. If the killers didn't remove it in time but left it there because they were frightened by others approaching, then they were acting prudently; they were not crazy to prefer their own safety to considerations of profit. [6] If he wasn't killed for his cloak, perhaps he noticed others committing some crime and was killed so he wouldn't report it. Who knows? There are also many others who hated him almost as much as I did; surely one of these is more likely to have killed him. It was clear to them that I would be suspected, and I was quite certain I would be blamed instead of them. [7] As for the attendant's testimony, how can you believe it? Terrified by the danger, it is not likely that he recognized the killers, but it is likely he was persuaded to agree with his masters. Since the testimony of slaves in general is untrustworthy—otherwise we wouldn't

---

[6] This type of argument—because a person is likely to commit a crime he is in fact unlikely to do so because he knows he will be the obvious suspect—can be termed "reverse-*eikos*." It is attributed to both Corax (Aristotle, *Rhetoric* 2.24.11) and Tisias (Plato, *Phaedrus* 273a–c).

[7] He probably means "if I was caught in the act."

torture them[8]—how can it be right for you to believe this witness' testimony and destroy me?

[8] If anyone thinks arguments from likelihood carry as much weight against me as the truth, by the same reasoning he should consider it more likely that in planning I would watch out for my own safety and would take care not to be present at the crime rather than let this man recognize me as he was being killed. [9] Unless I was out of my mind, I did not think this crime presented less danger than the indictment I was facing, but rather far more, as I will show. If I was convicted in that case, I knew I would lose my property, but I wouldn't lose my life or my city. I would survive, and even if I had to borrow money, I wouldn't have faced total destruction. But if I am convicted now and put to death, I shall leave a foul disgrace for my children; or if I go into exile, an old man without a country, I'll be a beggar in a foreign land. [10] Thus, all their accusations are unconvincing. If it is likely but not a fact that I killed the man, then it is only just that I be acquitted. I was clearly defending myself against an enormous injustice; otherwise, it wouldn't seem likely that I killed him. Your proper task, however, is to convict killers, not those who have a reason to kill.

[11] Since I am absolved of the charge in every way, I will not defile the holiness of the gods if I enter their sacred precincts, and I will not offend them if I persuade you to acquit me. But the prosecution, who charge me, an innocent man, but let the guilty one go free—they are the ones to blame for the failure of harvests. They urge you to offend against the gods, and they should suffer all the punishment they say I deserve. [12] That's what they deserve, so don't believe their arguments. If you consider everything I have done, you will know that I didn't make plots or seek anything improper. On the contrary, I have contributed generously to many special levies, outfitted many triremes, produced splendid choral performances, lent money to many friends, and guaranteed many large debts as well.[9] I have acquired my

---

[8] See below, Ant. 1.6n.

[9] For service to the city in the form of special levies (*eisphorai*) and "liturgies," see the Introduction, IVC. The last two services listed are common private ways of helping friends. Here the defendant claims to have undertaken every possible service as often as possible, but speakers normally mention only some of them.

property, moreover, by hard work, not litigation;[10] I have performed sacrifices and obeyed the laws. That's the way I am, so don't convict me of anything unholy or disgraceful. [13] If the victim were still alive, I would not only be defending myself but would also show that he and his helpers have no concern for justice but are bringing this case only for their own profit. I pass over these matters out of decency rather than justice. So I implore you, gentlemen, since you judge and oversee the greatest matters, take pity on my misfortune and cure it. Do not join their attack and let them subject me to this lawless and godless destruction.

2.3

[1] He wrongs misfortune when he tries to use her to mask his crimes and remove his pollution. But he deserves no pity from you; he brought disaster on the unwilling victim but willingly got himself into this danger. In my earlier speech I showed that he killed the man; I will now try to refute the claims he made in his defense.

[2] If the killers had seen others approaching and had fled, leaving the victims there without removing their cloaks, then those who discovered the victims would have gotten a clear story from the servant, who was still conscious when they found him even if his master was already dead, and they would have reported the culprits to us so that this man would not be blamed. Or if others had been seen committing a crime and had killed the victims so that they wouldn't be identified, then the other crime would have been reported at the same time as this murder, and suspicion would have fallen on those others. [3] And I don't know how those who were in less danger would have plotted against him more readily than those who had more to fear. For the latter, fear and the great wrong they had suffered overcame their caution, whereas for the former, the danger and disgrace of the crime outweighed their dispute and moderated the vehemence of their spirit, if they even contemplated such action. [4] They are wrong to say you should not believe the attendant's evidence. For evidence like that we don't torture slaves, we free them. In cases where they deny a theft or conspire with their masters to conceal a crime, then we consider their

---

[10] I.e., he was not engaged in sykophancy (see the Introduction, VE).

testimony truthful only under torture. [5] And the accused is no more likely to have been absent than present: he would run the same risk absent as present, since anyone captured at the scene would have confirmed that he was the planner;[11] but the execution of the crime would have suffered, since none of his agents would be as eager for it as he. [6] I will also show that he thought the indictment[12] posed not a smaller but a far greater risk than this trial. Let's assume he had the same expectation of conviction or acquittal in each case. He had no hope of avoiding trial on the indictment as long as this man was alive, for he would never agree to a settlement; but in this case he hoped to avoid trial, since he thought he could kill the man without being caught. [7] If he thinks you should not suspect him because he's the obvious suspect, he is wrong. If the risk of suspicion was enough to deter this man from attacking when he faced the gravest danger, then no one would have planned the murder; anyone in less danger would be even less likely than he to attempt the crime, since the fear of incurring suspicion would still outweigh the danger he was facing. [8] The special levies and choral productions are a good indication of his prosperity but not of his innocence. On the contrary, fear of losing this prosperity makes it likely that he committed this unholy murder. And when he says that murderers are not those who are likely to have killed but those who actually did kill, he is correct about those who killed, if it were clear to us who his actual killers were. But if the actual killers have not been revealed, then since his guilt is proven by the arguments from likelihood, this man and no other would be the killer; for such things are not done in the presence of witnesses but secretly. [9] Since from his own defense it is clearly proven that he killed the man, his plea is nothing more than a request that you transfer his pollution onto yourselves.[13] We, on the other hand, ask for nothing; we simply tell you that if neither likelihood nor witnesses can convict this man, then no defendant can any longer be convicted. [10] If you acquit him wrongly, the dead man's spirit will not seek revenge from us but will

---

[11] For the "planner" of a homicide, see the Introduction to Ant. 6.

[12] I.e., the indictment for theft of sacred property brought by the dead man (2.1.6).

[13] I.e., if the jurors fail to convict the killer, they themselves will, in effect, be the killers and will be polluted.

weigh on your consciences. You know quite certainly how he died, you know that the tracks of suspicion lead to this man, and you have the attendant's reliable testimony; how in all justice can you acquit him? [11] With this in mind, assist the victim, punish the killer, and purify the city. You will achieve three good results: fewer men will plot crimes,[14] more men will observe their religious duties, and you will free yourselves from this man's pollution.

2.4

[1] Look! I willingly entrust myself to misfortune,[15] which they say I am wrong to blame, and to these enemies of mine: although I fear the enormity of their slander, I have confidence in your intelligence and in the truth of my actions. If they prevent me from even lamenting my present misfortune before you, I don't know where else to seek refuge. [2] Their slanderous accusations are pure invention—or should I call them evil intention? They pretend to be prosecuting and punishing a case of murder, but they reject all valid suspicion and call me the murderer simply because they don't know who really killed him. Their duty is to punish the killer, but their goal is evidently just the opposite, to kill me unjustly. [3] My proper course is only to defend myself against the attendant's testimony, for I am not obliged to reveal or convict the true killers, only to answer the charge against me. Nonetheless, I must do more if I am to make it entirely clear to you that these men are plotting against me and that I am free of all suspicion. [4] So I ask that my misfortune, which they use to criticize me, be turned to good fortune and that you delight me with an acquittal rather than pity me after a conviction.

They assert that anyone who happened on them during the attack would be more likely to investigate exactly who the killers were and report them when they reached home than to run away. [5] But I don't think any man is so brave or reckless that if in the middle of the night

---

[14] That a conviction will deter others from committing crimes is a commonplace in prosecution speeches.

[15] Apparently an allusion to the rule that the defendant in a homicide case is allowed to go into exile before delivering his second speech. This may suggest that Antiphon considers the defendant's case fairly strong.

he came upon corpses still quivering, he wouldn't turn and run away rather than risk his life trying to learn the identity of the criminals. And since they surely preferred to do what was reasonable, it would be unreasonable to let those who killed them for their cloaks go free. Thus, I am no longer a suspect. [6] Whether or not any other crimes were reported at the same time as the murder, who knows? No one took the trouble to look into this. So, since nothing is known of any such report, it is not implausible that he was killed by these criminals. [7] And why should you believe the attendant's testimony rather than that of free men?[16] If it is determined that the latter have testified falsely, they lose their civic rights and are fined, but since this man furnished no proof and was not tortured, how will he be punished?[17] Indeed, what proof could there be? Since he faced no danger in testifying, it's not surprising he was persuaded by his owners, my enemies, to lie about me. But it would be a sacrilege if this untrustworthy testimony should cause you to destroy me. [8] They also assert that it is more plausible that I was present at the scene of the murder than absent, but I shall prove my absence not as a matter of likelihood but as a fact. I offer you all my slaves for torture, male and female;[18] if it becomes clear that I was not at home in bed that night or that I went out anywhere, then I admit I am the murderer. It was no ordinary night, for the man died the day of the Dipolieia.[19] [9] As for their

---

[16] There is, of course, no testimony from free men in this case. For the testimony of slaves under torture, see Ant. 1.6n. A free witness could potentially face a suit for false witness; see the Introduction, VD.

[17] In this case, the slave is already dead, and so the question of his punishment is moot. But Antiphon includes the generic argument that slaves have no reason to provide true testimony except under torture, perhaps to demonstrate its use.

[18] According to the rules, challenges to torture a slave had to be issued before the trial, though occasionally one is issued during a trial (Aes. 2.126–128). Antiphon's purpose in not mentioning this alibi until nearly the end of the Tetralogy may be to illustrate that facts (*erga*) produce a more powerful argument than likelihood (*eikos*); it was the absence of facts, of course, that necessitated the *eikos* arguments in the first place (2.3.8). Note that the alibi, if accepted, proves only that the defendant was not at the scene of the murder; he could still have been the "planner" (cf. 2.3.5) and enlisted an agent to commit the crime.

[19] An annual festival in honor of Zeus Polieus in the month Scirophorion (roughly June); see Parke 1977: 162–167. The inclusion of this detail would help confirm an alibi.

claim that it is likely that I killed him because I was afraid of losing my prosperity, the situation is just the opposite. It is those in misfortune who stand to gain by stirring up trouble,[20] since in a time of change their own impoverished state can be expected to change. Those who are prosperous, on the other hand, stand to gain from preserving stability and protecting their present prosperity, for when conditions change, their fortune becomes misfortune. [10] Although they claim to establish my guilt on the basis of likelihood, they then assert that I am the man's killer not in likelihood but in fact. But it has been shown that the likelihood is on my side; moreover, the witness' testimony against me has been proven to be unconvincing, and it cannot be tested. Thus, I have shown that the evidence supports me, not him, and that the tracks of the murder lead not to me but to those who are being set free by my opponents.

Since their entire case has proven unconvincing, my acquittal would not mean that criminals cannot be proved guilty, but my conviction would mean that no one facing prosecution can present a successful defense. [11] Their prosecution is unjust; they claim to be pure while seeking to murder me in unholy fashion and then calling my actions unholy though I urge only that you respect the gods. Since I am innocent of all charges, for myself I implore you to respect the righteousness of those who have done no wrong; I remind you that the dead man needs retribution, and I urge you not to convict an innocent man while you let the guilty go free. For if I am put to death, no longer will anyone search for the actual killer. [12] With these considerations in mind, acquit me in accordance with the laws of gods and men. Do not wait until later to change your mind and recognize your mistake, for later regret is no cure for such mistakes.

---

[20] The verb *neoterizein* means "innovate," often with the implication "make a revolution." The general point that the rich do not foment change is irrelevant to the prosecution's argument about motive, but the implication that the rich do not engage in this sort of street crime may carry some weight.

ANTIPHON 6. ON THE CHORUS BOY

≈≈

unintentional homicide

INTRODUCTION

The speech *On the Chorus Boy* was delivered by an unknown Athenian who in 419 was assigned the important (and expensive) liturgy (Introduction, IVC) of training a boys' chorus to compete at the Thargelia, a festival held in the late Spring. As the choregus ("chorus producer"), he recruited the fifty boys needed for the chorus, which represented two of the ten tribes, and provided room in his house for them to train. Being busy with his other affairs (so he tells us), he assigned the duty of training the boys to his son-in-law and three other men. One day during his absence, a boy named Diodotus was given a drug to drink, perhaps to remedy a sore throat. Instead it caused his death. Two days later the boy's brother Philocrates formally charged the choregus with unintentional homicide—specifically with "having killed the boy by planning his death" (6.16; see below)—but the Basileus, the official in charge of homicide cases (Introduction, IVA), refused to accept the suit. Almost two months later a new Basileus took office, and Philocrates resubmitted his case to him about six weeks after that. This time it was accepted, leading to a trial at the Palladium, the court that heard cases of unintentional homicide, for which the penalty was exile.

The choregus advances three main lines of argument: (1) he did everything required of him and more in overseeing the chorus' training; (2) he had nothing to do with Diodotus' death and was not even present when he died; (3) the prosecutor brought this case only because he was bribed by the choregus' political enemies, whose motive was to force him to abandon the legal case he was bringing against them. The details and supporting arguments provided in the speech suggest that all three points may be valid; nonetheless, the prosecution could attack these claims in a number of ways, and their main arguments probably focused on some different issues. We may speculate that (1) they criticized the choregus for not supervising the training himself and perhaps presented some evidence of specific faults or shortcomings in the arrangements or the people assigned to supervise the boys; (2) they probably did not challenge the choregus' claim that he was not present at Diodotus' death, since this fact could easily have been proved, but they presumably argued that as choregus, he was responsible nonetheless, and they may have alleged that he told others to give the boy a drug; (3) they may have argued that the choregus persecuted them for political reasons and forced them to countersue in self-defense.

The charge of "planning an unintentional homicide" on the surface seems self-contradictory. As early as Draco, the planner was held legally responsible for a homicide just like the actual killer, but this provision was almost certainly intended to be used for the planner of an intentional homicide. Antiphon 6 is the only case we know in which the charge is planning an unintentional homicide. Presumably the charge designates some degree of involvement in an accidental death, but any attempt to determine its precise meaning or to set clear guidelines for its use is futile. We do not know, and the Athenians themselves probably could not say, precisely what circumstances would make someone legally liable for the actions of his subordinates. Rules for such cases can only be inferred from regular practice, not from the outcome (if we knew it) of one or two cases. Athenian law allowed considerable leeway in adapting existing procedures to different circumstances (as we see in Ant. 5), and a strict or "narrow" interpretation of a statute would be difficult in any case, given the generality of the language of Athenian statutes. All we can say is that in this case the charge of planning an unintentional homicide was plausible enough for a Basileus to allow the case to proceed, and the choregus takes the accusation seriously and does not question the legitimacy of the charge.

On the other hand, not much weight should be put on the first Basileus' refusal of the case or on the second Basileus' acceptance of it. The Basileus' legal duties were administrative and probably included making the initial proclamation, arranging the trial, holding preliminary hearings (*prodikasiai*), running the trial itself, and perhaps declaring the verdict (*Ath. Pol.* 57). When Philocrates first presented his accusation, the Basileus rejected it on the ground that it was necessary to hold three preliminary hearings in three different months (6.41–42) and that his term of office would end in less than two months. Philocrates protested but did not accuse the Basileus of misconduct at his accounting at the end of his term (Introduction, IVA). Six weeks into the next year Philocrates presented the case again, and the new Basileus accepted it. The first Basileus probably had the legal right to reject the case, but it is not clear that he was required to reject it; the law may have required three hearings but not necessarily by the same Basileus; or it may have been vague on the matter. It is possible that the first Basileus rejected the charge out of political friendship with the choregus, as the prosecution probably argued; but the second Basileus probably had no choice but to accept the case.[1]

Each side may have presented a strong case. The prosecution's attempt to hold the choregus responsible for the death might be loosely compared (to use a modern analogy) to a parent's attempt to hold the owner of a day-care center responsible for the death of a child at the center even if the owner was out of town that day and the drug was given by an employee without the owner's knowledge. If the owner could be depicted as irresponsible, the case might succeed. Moreover, if the choregus' picture of this case as part of a series of suits and countersuits is accurate, it may have mattered little to the prosecution if their chances of securing a conviction were small; the accusation in itself would have the desired effect of forcing the choregus to withdraw from the case he was about to bring against his opponents.

In his defense, the choregus presents strong arguments on all three of his main points, and the jurors might well wonder whether someone who had taken such thorough precautions to ensure that the boys would be well cared for and was not even in the house at the time could be held liable for an accidental death. The picture he paints of his opponents' political opportunism and Philocrates' vacillation, moreover, would raise strong doubts about whether this case should have been brought in the first place. All in all, the speech appears to be an effective response to the challenge of a novel and complex situation.

The prologue (1–6) is followed by a preliminary attack on the pros-

---

[1] See further below, 6.42n.

ecution (7–10). The narration of events leading up to the death (11–14) leads to arguments that the choregus is not responsible for it (15–19), which is followed by a further narrative (20–22) and by the choregus' challenge that the prosecution interrogate his slaves (23–32). Narrative and argument are then mixed together in the discussion of the first Basileus' rejection of the case and Philocrates' second, successful attempt to prosecute (33–50). A very brief epilogue (51) concludes the speech.

ANTIPHON 6. ON THE CHORUS BOY

[1] The sweetest thing a human being could have is a life free of danger to his person; that's what he would pray for in his prayers. If forced to confront danger, I think the best thing is a clear conscience that one has done nothing wrong. But if some misfortune should actually occur, one would hope it resulted from chance, not crime, without wickedness or shame. [2] Everyone would agree in praising the laws governing these matters as the finest and most righteous of laws. They are the oldest established laws in this land and have always remained the same, which is the best sign of well-enacted laws, for time and experience teach people the faults in things.[2] Therefore, you should not learn from the prosecutor's words whether the laws are good or not, but rather let the laws instruct you whether or not the prosecutor's words present a correct legal account. [3] This trial is of greatest importance for me, the defendant and the one facing danger. But I think it's also important for you, the jurors, to decide homicide cases correctly both for your own sake and especially out of respect for the gods. Only one verdict is given in such cases,[3] and if it is wrong,[4] it overpowers justice and truth. [4] When you convict someone, even

↳ RELIGION

---

[2] Solon (ca. 590) enacted new laws on many subjects, but for homicide he kept Draco's law (see the Introduction, VA). Draco's homicide law was republished in 409/8, and a damaged copy survives today. This passage is repeated in almost the same words in Ant. 5.14.

[3] This is perhaps a reference to "assessable" cases (Introduction, VC), in which the jurors take a second vote to decide the penalty.

[4] Much of the text from here to the end of 6.6 also occurs in Ant. 5.87–89; there are significant differences, however, indicating that the thought has been specifically adapted to the context of 6.3–6.

if he is not the murderer and has no responsibility for the crime, he is forced to submit to justice, and he is banned from the city, its shrines, its trials, and its sacrifices—those greatest and most ancient of human institutions. Indeed, the law has such power that even if someone kills a person under his control and there is no one to avenge his death, from fear of the gods and human custom he purifies himself and stays away from the places mentioned in the law, hoping thus to have the best future.[5] [5] For the greater part of life for humans depends on hope, and dishonoring the gods or violating their laws deprives a person of that very hope, the greatest good humans have.|No one would dare disobey a verdict rendered in court just because he was confident of his own innocence, nor would he dare not submit to the law if he knew he had committed such a crime. He must yield to the verdict even if it goes against the truth, and he must yield to the truth especially if the victim has no one to avenge his death. [6] For these reasons the laws, oaths, sacrifices, proclamations, and aspects of procedure in homicide cases are very different from other cases, because it is of the highest importance to determine the facts correctly when so much is at stake. When they are decided correctly, the victim has his vengeance; but if an innocent man is convicted of murder, it is a mistake and a sin against the gods and the laws. If the prosecutor brings an incorrect accusation, this is not the same as you jurors rendering an incorrect verdict. Their accusation is not now final but depends on you and on the trial; but if you give an incorrect verdict in the trial, there is no way to escape the blame by assigning it elsewhere.

[7] I have a rather different idea about my defense than the prosecution does about their case. They say they are prosecuting for piety and justice, but in fact their entire prosecution has been aimed at slander and deception. This is the most serious violation of justice in human affairs. They don't want to prove that I did something wrong so they can punish me with justice, but only to slander me, even if I have done nothing wrong, so that they may punish me with exile from this land. [8] My view, however, is that I should first be judged on the specific charge and recount for you all that happened in connection

---

[5] If an Athenian killed a slave, the slave's master would normally take action, but if he killed his own slave there would be no one to bring suit and (apparently) there would therefore be no legal consequences. We may doubt that everyone in such circumstances behaved as Antiphon recommends.

with it; then, if you like, I'll willingly defend myself against all their other accusations, for I think these will benefit me and my reputation and will cast shame on those who accuse and slander me. [9] It's a terrible thing indeed, gentlemen: if I had done any wrong to the city in training the chorus or in anything else, they had the opportunity to make this known and prove it, punishing one of their own enemies and helping the city at the same time, but none of them was ever able to prove that I had committed any crime, large or small, against you, the people; on the other hand, in this trial, when they are prosecuting me for homicide and the law requires them to stick to the crime itself,[6] they are conspiring against me by inventing falsehoods and slandering me for my public activities. For the city, if it really has been injured, they offer an accusation but no punishment, but for themselves they think they should get private satisfaction for wrongs they say were done to the city. [10] For these accusations they don't deserve to be thanked or trusted: they are not earning the city's thanks by prosecuting a crime for which the city would gain satisfaction, if it had been wronged; and he surely does not deserve your trust, but rather your disbelief, when in a case like this he directs his accusation to charges other than those that are the subject of his prosecution. I am fairly certain you would not convict or acquit someone for any reason other than the crime itself, which is the only way consistent with righteousness and justice. Having said all that, I will begin.

[11] When I was appointed choregus for the Thargelia[7] and was allotted the poet Pantacles and the tribe Cecropis in addition to my own, I performed my duties in the best and fairest way I could. First I equipped the most suitable room in my house as a training room, the same one I used when I was choregus for the Dionysia.[8] Then I gathered the best group of boys I could without levying any fines or forcing

---

[6] See below, Ant. 5.11n.

[7] A festival honoring Apollo on days 6 and 7 of the month Thargelion, the next to last month in the Attic year (roughly equivalent to May). Five choruses of boys and five of men competed, each representing two of the ten Attic tribes. The speaker could recruit boys from either his own tribe (the Erechtheid) or the Cecropid tribe.

[8] The most important annual festival at which most tragedies and comedies were first performed. The speaker is clearly a man of wealth and importance, who regularly undertakes these costly liturgies.

anyone to provide guarantees[9] and without making any enemies; everything was done in the most pleasant and most suitable way possible for both of us, I making my requests and they sending their sons of their own free will. [12] When the boys first arrived, I did not have the time to be there and attend to matters, for I happened to be engaged in a legal action against Aristion and Philinus, and as it was an impeachment (*eisangelia*),[10] I considered it very important to prove the case to the Council and the Athenian people correctly and fairly. Since I was giving this case my full attention, I put Phanostratus in charge of whatever might be needed for the chorus. He is from the same deme as these prosecutors and a relative of mine (he married my daughter), and I thought he would give the best supervision. [13] I also appointed two others, Ameinias, from the Erechtheid tribe—I thought him a fine man, and the tribal leaders had selected him each time to collect and supervise choruses—and the other man from the Cecropid tribe; he too used to recruit choruses each time from that tribe. I also appointed a fourth man, Philippus, who was in charge of purchasing whatever the poet or anyone else might want so that the boys might receive the best training and not lack anything just because I was busy. [14] These were my arrangements for the chorus. And if I am lying to justify my behavior, the prosecution can refute me in their second speech on any point they wish. But this is the situation, gentlemen; many of these onlookers[11] have precise knowledge of all that happened, and they listened to the administrator of oaths and are paying attention to my defense. In their eyes I should like to appear true to my oath and truthful in persuading you to acquit me.

---

[9] A choregus could require a boy to serve in the chorus and could fine a parent who would not let his child serve unless he had a valid excuse, in which case the parent was required to post surety, which would be forfeited if the excuse proved invalid.

[10] *Eisangelia* cases (Introduction, VE) were heard by the Council or the Assembly.

[11] Since the choregus was a well-known public figure, his trial would presumably attract a large crowd, including some who were present at the time of the death. Some of the jurors may also have known of the events, but this would not prevent them from serving.

[15] I will first show you that I did not order the boy to drink the drug, I did not force him to drink, I did not give him the drink, and I was not even present when he drank. And I'm not emphasizing these points in order to absolve myself and put the blame on someone else.[12] No, I blame no one, except fortune, who I think is also to blame for the deaths of many others, and whose course no one, not I or anyone else, could alter from what it must be for each of us.[13]

[WITNESSES]

[16] You have heard the witnesses testify to the facts, gentlemen, as I promised you. From these you must examine what each side swore and decide which of us was more truthful and swore more correctly. They swore[14] that I killed Diodotus by planning his death,[15] but I swore I did not kill him either by my own hand or by planning. [17] They base their accusation on the argument that whoever ordered the boy to drink the drug or forced him to drink or gave it to him is responsible; but I will use this same argument to show that I am not liable to the charge, since I did not order or give or force. And I will add to these that I was not present when he drank it. So, if they say it's a crime if someone orders, I did nothing wrong, for I gave no order. And if they say it's a crime if someone forces, I did nothing wrong, for I used no force. And if they say that someone who gives the drug is responsible, then I'm not responsible, for I did not give anything. [18] Anyone who wants can make accusations and level false charges,

---

[12] It appears that none of the subordinates were prosecuted for homicide. Blaming someone else might have helped the speaker's case, but it would surely hurt his standing in the community if he helped convict an associate of homicide.

[13] In Antiphon's Second Tetralogy, the defendant avoids blaming fortune, and the plaintiff argues (3.3.8) that even if the death was caused by fortune, the blame still falls to the accused. The difference may be that the defendant in that case was directly involved in the boy's death and so could be held responsible even for an accident; the choregus may have been less inclined to blame fortune if he had given the drink himself.

[14] These oaths would be sworn at a preliminary hearing and would contain each side's case in a nutshell. Thus, a litigant would know the precise words of an oath beforehand.

[15] For the notion of "planning," see the Speech Introduction.

for these things are in each person's control. But I don't think their
words can make it so that something happened that did not happen,
or that someone committed a crime who did not, but these depend on
justice and truth. Now when a murder is planned in secret[16] and there
are no witnesses, you are forced to reach a verdict about the case on
the basis of the prosecutor's and defendant's words alone; you must be
suspicious and examine their accounts in detail, and your vote will
necessarily be cast on the basis of likelihood rather than clear knowledge. [19] But here, in the first place the prosecution themselves admit
that the boy's death did not result from any intent or design, and
second, the entire event occurred openly in front of many witnesses,
men and boys, free and slave, who would have made it very clear if
anyone had committed a crime and would have provided a sure test if
someone should accuse an innocent man.

[20] It is worth considering two things, gentlemen, my opponents'
motives and the way they have handled this matter. From the beginning, their behavior toward me has been completely different from
mine toward them. [21] On the day of the boy's funeral, Philòcrates
here came to the court of the Thesmothetae[17] and said that I had killed
his brother while he was in the chorus by forcing him to drink a drug.
When he said this, I went to the court and told the same jurors that
by accusing and slandering me in court Philocrates was using the law
unjustly to protect certain people. I intended to bring legal action
against Aristion and Philinus the next day and the day after,[18] and this
was the reason he was making these statements. [22] It was easy to
prove that his accusations and slanders were lies, since a great many
people knew the facts—slave and free, young and old, more than fifty
in all, who knew what had been said about the drinking of the drug
and everything else that was said and done.

[23] I said this in court, and also issued him a challenge[19] then and

---

[16] For this point, cf. Ant. 2.1.1–3 above.

[17] The choregus' *eisangelia* against Aristion et al. was presented to the Council
(6.12n), but such cases were often referred to the courts, since the maximum
penalty the Council could levy was a fine of 500 drachmas. For the Thesmothetae,
see the Introduction, IVA.

[18] According to Athenian law, each defendant had to be tried separately.

[19] For the challenge to interrogation under torture (*basanos*), see below,
Ant. 1.6n.

there, and again the next day before the same jurors. I told him he should go and question those who had been present (and I named each one of them), taking with him as many witnesses as he wanted. He should examine the free men in a manner befitting free men,[20] for they would give a true account of what had happened for their own sake and for justice; and he should also examine the slaves, if he thought they were answering truthfully. If not, I was ready to hand over all my slaves for examination under torture, and if he wanted any slaves belonging to someone else, I agreed to get their master's permission to allow him to interrogate them however he wanted. [24] I issued this challenge openly in the court, where the jurors and many other private citizens were present as witnesses, but they were unwilling to accept this just procedure either right then and there or any time since. They are well aware that this test would not provide support for their case against me but for my case against them, since their accusation was both unjust and untrue. [25] You know, gentlemen, that compulsion is the greatest and strongest force in human life, and proofs derived from it are the clearest and most reliable guide to justice when there are many free men and slaves who know the facts. Then you can compel the free men to tell the truth by means of oaths and pledges, which have the greatest importance for free men, and you can use a different compulsion on slaves, which will compel them to tell the truth even if their information will lead to their death, for an immediate compulsion has more effect on everyone than one in the future. [26] I challenged them on all these matters, so that every means we humans have of learning truth and justice were available to them, and they had no excuse left. In other words I, the one who was accused and committed a crime, as they say—I was ready to provide them with the most just confirmation of the case against me; but they, the ones who make this accusation and claim they have been wronged—they were unwilling to prove they had been wronged.

[27] Now,[21] if I had refused to reveal who was present when they issued me a challenge, or to hand over servants when they asked for them, or had rejected any other challenge, they would treat these

---

[20] I.e., without using torture. Free witnesses could later be prosecuted for giving false testimony (Introduction, VD).

[21] The argument in 6.27–28 is termed a "hypothetical role-reversal"; it is common in Antiphon (1.11–12, 5.38, 5.74, 5.84).

refusals as very strong evidence that the charge against me was true. So when I issued a challenge and they were the ones avoiding the test, surely it is only fair that this same refusal be evidence on my side that the charge they are bringing against me is not true. [28] I also know this, gentlemen, that if the witnesses[22] who were present were giving testimony on their side against me, they would consider this very strong evidence, and they would display the testimony of these witnesses against me as clear confirmation of their case. But when these same witnesses testify that what I say is true and what they say is not true, they now tell you not to trust the witnesses who are testifying and say you should trust the arguments they make instead, though if I made such arguments without witnesses, they would accuse me of lying. [29] It's strange if the same witnesses should be trustworthy when they're testifying on their side but untrustworthy when testifying on my side. If no witnesses at all had been present and yet I were presenting witnesses, or if I were not presenting the witnesses who had been present but others instead, then these men's words would likely be more trustworthy than my witnesses. But when they agree that witnesses were present, and I am presenting those who were present, and from the first day both I and the witnesses have clearly been saying just what we are now saying to you, what other means than this, gentlemen, can I use to make you believe what's true and not believe what's not true?

[30] If someone should tell you with words what happened without presenting any witnesses, you would say his words are in need of witnesses; and if someone should present witnesses without providing any arguments in support of the witnesses, you could make the same objection, if you wanted. [31] But I am now presenting you with a plausible account, with witnesses who support this account, with facts supporting the witnesses, and with arguments derived from these very facts, and in addition to all this, with my two greatest and strongest arguments: the prosecutors, who are refuted by themselves and by me, and I myself, who am acquitted by them and by myself. [32] For when I was willing to be tested concerning their accusation but they were not, then they did wrong, and they absolved me, surely, for they

---

[22] I.e., the free witnesses. Much of this section is similar or identical to Ant. 5.84.

became witnesses testifying against themselves that their accusation was both unjust and untrue. So, if I have presented my opponents themselves as witnesses in addition to my own witnesses, what other evidence or what arguments could I possibly introduce to show that I am acquitted of the charge?

[33] From what has been said and demonstrated, I think it only right that you should acquit me, knowing that nothing in this accusation concerns me. But to give you an even better understanding of the case, I'll add a few words to show you that the prosecutors are the most perjured and unrighteous of men. Because of this case they deserve not just my hatred but the hatred of all of you and the rest of the citizens. [34] I say this because on the first day, when the boy died, and on the following day when his body was laid out, they did not think to accuse me of any crime whatsoever in this affair, but they spent time talking with me. On the third day, however, the day of the boy's funeral, they were persuaded[23] by my enemies, and they prepared an accusation and a proclamation banning me from the places prescribed in the law.[24] Who persuaded them? And why were they so eager to persuade them? I must explain this to you. [35] I was about to go to trial before the Council in my impeachment case against Aristion, Philinus, Ampelinus, and the scribe of the Thesmothetae, who was their partner in embezzlement. Given the facts in the case and the seriousness of their crimes, they had no hope of acquittal, but they thought if they could persuade these men to register their case and make a proclamation banning me from the places prescribed in the law, this would make them safe, and they would be rid of the whole affair. [36] For the law says that when someone is inscribed as the accused in a homicide case, he is banned from the places prescribed in the law; and I would not be able to proceed with my prosecution if I was banned from the places prescribed in the law, while they would easily be acquitted and would pay no penalty to you for their crimes,

---

[23] The implication is that they were bribed. Since only the victim's relatives could bring a homicide case, others would have to "persuade" the boy's relatives to do so.

[24] Although the relatives made a proclamation naming the killer, only registration of the case with the Basileus, who then made his own proclamation, had the legal consequence of barring the accused from public places (see above, 6.4).

since I was the one who had brought the impeachment and knew the facts, and I would no longer be prosecuting them. I was not the first person Philinus and the others used this scheme against; they also used it against Lysistratus earlier, as you yourselves have heard.

[37] Thus, they were anxious to register me immediately, the day after the boy was buried, even before purifying the house and conducting the proper rites; for they knew that was the day set for the trial of the first of them, and they wanted to prevent me from prosecuting even one of them and revealing their crimes to the court. [38] But the Basileus read them the laws and showed them that there wasn't enough time to register the case and issue all the necessary summonses;[25] and I brought those who were behind this plot to trial and convicted them all, and, as you know, they were assessed fines. When these men here found they could not give them the assistance they had originally been paid to give, at that point they approached me and my friends asking for reconciliation and saying they were ready to make amends for their mistakes. [39] My friends persuaded me to agree, and we were reconciled during the Dipolieia[26] in front of witnesses at the temple of Athena.[27] Afterwards we spent time together and talked in shrines, in the agora, at my house, at their house, and everywhere else. [40] To top it all off, by Zeus and all the gods, in the Council-house in front of the Council, Philocrates here joined me on the podium, and with his hand on my arm he talked with me, calling me by name, and I did the same. Naturally, the Council thought it pretty strange when they later learned that a proclamation banning me from the places prescribed in the law had been issued by the same people they had seen talking with me the day before.

[41] Now, pay close attention and think back, gentlemen, for not only will I prove this from witnesses, but when you hear what they did, you will easily understand that I am speaking the truth. First, they accuse the Basileus of refusing to register the suit because of my efforts, but this is evidence against them and shows they are lying. [42] After he had registered a suit, the Basileus had to hold three preliminary hearings in three months and then hold the trial in the fourth month,

---

[25] The choregus explains this constraint in more detail below (6.42).

[26] For this festival, see above, Ant. 2.4.8n.

[27] The Parthenon.

just as we're doing now; but he only had two months left in his term of office, Thargelion and Scirophorion.[28] Obviously he would not be able to conduct the trial during his own term, and he is not allowed to pass on a homicide case to his successor; indeed, no Basileus in this country has ever passed on a homicide case. Since he could not hold the trial or pass it on to anyone, he decided not to register the case in violation of your laws.[29] [43] The strongest evidence that he did them no wrong is that Philocrates here shook down and blackmailed other officials when they presented their accounts, but despite accusing the Basileus of terrible crimes, he brought no charges against him during his accounting.[30] What stronger evidence could I present that Philocrates was not wronged by me or the Basileus? [44] When this present Basileus took office on the first day of the month of Hecatombaion, they could have registered the case on any day they wanted, thirty days in all, but they never did. Then in the month of Metageitnion they could also have registered the case on any day they wanted from the beginning, but they still did not register it but passed up twenty days of this month. Thus, they had more than fifty days[31] under this Basileus in which to register the case but did not. [45] Anyone else who cannot proceed with the same Basileus because of the time limit registers[32] his case as soon as the new Basileus takes office. But these men knew the law well and saw me entering the Council-house as a Councilor—and in the Council-house there stands a shrine to Zeus of the Council and Athena of the Council, and the Councilors go and pray in it, and I was one of the ones who did this, and I entered all the other shrines with the Council, and I sacrificed and prayed on behalf of this city; and

---

[28] The last two months in the Athenian year; Hecatombaion and Metageitnion (6.44) are the first and second months. The term of annual offices ended at the end of the year.

[29] The choregus' language is carefully crafted to suggest that legally the Basileus had no other choice, but see Speech Introduction.

[30] For the accounting, see the Introduction, IVA. It may seem significant that Philocrates did not lodge a protest at the Basileus' hearing, but at that time he and the choregus had apparently been reconciled.

[31] Since thirty and twenty add up to exactly fifty, either "more than fifty" is an exaggeration or the text is corrupt.

[32] Something is clearly missing from our manuscripts; I give the general sense that seems to be required by the context.

furthermore, I served as a member of the first Prytany[33] for all but two days, supervising the sacred rites and offering sacrifices for the democracy, and I directed the voting on issues and stated my views on the highest and most important public matters, and all this was done in public view. [46] These men were in town and present at these events; they could have registered the case and banned me from all these events, but they decided not to. Surely if they had really been wronged, it was a serious enough matter that they would remember and be concerned about it, for their own sake as well as the city. Then why didn't they register it? Why were they spending time talking with me? They were spending time with me because they didn't think I was a murderer, and they did not register the case for the same reason, that they didn't think I had killed the boy or was liable for a charge of homicide, or that I had anything to do with the matter.

[47] How could people be more wicked or have less regard for the law than these men, who think they can persuade you of something when they cannot persuade themselves, and who ask you to convict when their own actions have spoken for acquittal? Other men test arguments against the facts, but these men are trying to use their arguments to make you disbelieve the facts. [48] If I have not said or shown you anything else, and if I have presented no witnesses but have only demonstrated this, that when they were getting money to attack me they leveled charges and made a proclamation,[34] but when no one was giving them money they spent time talking with me, this in itself would be sufficient to make you acquit me and judge them the most perjured and unrighteous of all men. [49] These men! Is there any litigation they would not bring to court, is there any court they would not try to deceive, is there any oath they would hesitate to transgress? After all, they took thirty minas from the Revenue Managers, the Supervisors of Public Resources, the Debt Collectors,[35] and the secretaries who work for them to bring this case against me, forcing me out of the Council-house and swearing fearful oaths, all because when I was in the Prytany, I had learned of terrible crimes they had committed and had brought a case against them to the Council and had

---

[33] The first tenth of the year; see the Introduction, IVA.

[34] I.e., naming the (alleged) killer (6.28).

[35] The *Poristai*, the *Pōlētai*, and the *Praktores*; these all managed public funds.

shown that the matter warranted investigation and prosecution. [50] Now the whole affair has been brought to light, and they and their accomplices with whom the money was deposited are paying for their crimes—crimes so outrageous that even if they wished, they could not easily deny them.

[51] Is there then no court they would not enter intent on deceiving it? Is there no oath they would hesitate to swear, these ungodly villains? They know you are the most righteous and just jurors in Greece, and yet they come before you intent on deceiving you if they can, despite the mighty oaths they have sworn.

Half brother representing the mother.

ANTIPHON 1. AGAINST
THE STEPMOTHER

against his case: why did he wait
Points for essay:
- *intentional homicide - thought love potion - unintentiona[l]*
- *lack: witnesses*

INTRODUCTION

This speech is delivered by a young man who is prosecuting his stepmother for poisoning his father. She is defended by another son, the speaker's half-brother.[1] The death occurred when the speaker was a boy (1.30); he must have turned eighteen, the minimum age for bringing a legal case, a few years earlier, because his younger half-brother must also have turned eighteen.

The "facts" are set forth in a vivid narrative (14–20), whose details must have come largely from the speaker's imagination. There is no real evidence and little argument other than the allegation of an earlier attempt at a similar poisoning. Modern scholars have tended to accept the analysis of a similar (the same?) case in the Aristotelian treatise *Magna Moralia* (1188b29–38), in which a woman accused of poisoning her husband is acquitted because her intent was to secure his love, not to kill him; but the speaker seems to ignore this consideration, emphasizing instead his own loyalty to his father and his brother's and stepmother's corresponding disloyalty, and drawing parallels with the story of Clytemnestra (17), who treacherously killed her husband Agamemnon and was in turn killed by their son Orestes. The appeal to stereotypical behavior of women as a continual threat to men—plotting, using drugs, concerned primarily with love—may have been more effective with the male jurors than an argument that she acted out of love, since even if the stepmother did not intend to kill, the

---

[1] Lit. "brother from the same father" (*homopatrios*). This must be the victim's son from a previous marriage; the speaker's mother probably died when he was very young (perhaps in childbirth), and his father remarried very soon.

sacreuge   *Orestes.*

jurors may have concluded that her behavior so threatened her husband's authority and the stability of the family that she deserved punishment.

The case was tried before the court of the Areopagus, which heard cases of intentional homicide. As usual, we do not know the verdict and know nothing of the defense's arguments beyond what we can surmise from this speech. The date is unknown but is usually placed in the period 420–411.

innocent and well behaved

ANTIPHON 1. AGAINST THE STEPMOTHER

[1] I am still so young and inexperienced in legal matters,[2] gentlemen, that I face a terrible dilemma in this case: either I fail in my duty to my father, who instructed me to prosecute his murderers, or, if I do prosecute, I am forced to quarrel with people who should least of all be my opponents—my own half-brothers and these brothers' mother. [2] But fortune and these opponents themselves have forced me to bring this case. It would be more reasonable for them to seek vengeance for the dead man and assist my prosecution, but they did just the opposite: they opposed my suit and are thus murderers themselves, as I and my indictment both state. [3] If I show that their mother murdered our father intentionally and with premeditation, and indeed that she was caught in the act of contriving his death not just once but many times before, then I beg you, gentlemen, take vengeance, first for your laws, which you received from the gods and your ancestors, for you convict people by these laws just as they did; second, avenge the dead man, and at the same time help me who am left all alone. [4] You are now my family while they, who ought to avenge the dead man and help me, have become his murderers and my opponents. Where can one turn for help? Where can one take refuge except with you and with justice?

[5] I am amazed at my brother. What is he thinking in opposing my case? Does he think piety consists simply in not forsaking his mother? Well, I think it is much more of a sacrilege to abandon ven-

---

[2] The plea of inexperience may already be a rhetorical *topos* ("commonplace"), but there is no reason to doubt that the speaker is young (see the Speech Introduction).

① *suck up & bring gods into mix*

geance for the dead man, especially since he died as the involuntary victim of a plot, whereas she killed with full intention and foreknowledge. [6] How can he say he is "quite certain"[3] that his mother did not kill our father? When he had the opportunity to gain certain knowledge through an interrogation of slaves,[4] he refused, but he was eager to try methods that could not produce information. However, he should have been eager for the proposal I made in my challenge, so that the truth of the matter could be fully examined. [7] If the slaves did not agree with me, he could have eagerly defended himself against me with certainty, and his mother would be entirely free of the charge. But since he was unwilling to put the facts to a test, how can he know things he wasn't willing to investigate? Surely then, jurors, it isn't likely that he knows things when he didn't accept the truth about them. [8] What defense will he make? Since he was quite certain he couldn't save her by interrogating the slaves, he thought safety might lie in avoiding an interrogation; that way, he thought, the facts might disappear. How then can he have truly sworn an oath that he is "quite certain," when I wanted to carry out a completely fair interrogation, but he was unwilling to obtain certain knowledge about the matter? [9] I wanted to interrogate their slaves, for they knew that on a previous occasion this woman—the mother of these men—had contrived our father's death by poisoning, that he had caught her in the act, and that she had not denied it, except to claim she was giving the drug as a love potion, not to kill him. [10] I therefore wanted to conduct an interrogation about these facts as follows.[5] I wrote down the accusa-

---

[3] The speaker is quoting directly from his opponent's preliminary oath (see 1.28).

[4] The interrogation of slaves under torture (*basanos*) was the only means of introducing the testimony of slaves in court. It could normally occur only if agreed to by both parties, usually after one litigant had "challenged" the other to allow certain slaves to be interrogated (see further, next note). The challenge is normally rejected by the other litigant; but this provides the challenger with the rhetorical opportunity (as here) to tell the jurors what the slaves would have said had they been interrogated (see Gagarin 1996; Mirhady 2006b). In criminal investigations an interrogation could take place without a challenge (see Ant. 5.29–42).

[5] The speaker's conduct, as he presents it, conforms to the proper rules of the challenge: the challenger determines (and here writes down) the questions to be asked, which generally require simple yes-or-no answers.

tion I was making against the woman and asked these men to conduct the interrogation in my presence; this way, the slaves would not be forced to say what I asked them, for I was satisfied if they used the written questions. I think I am justified in taking this as evidence that I was prosecuting my father's murderer justly and correctly. If the slaves should deny or disagree with my assertions, the interrogation would force the accusation to conform to the facts, for it forces even those who are prepared to lie to make true accusations. [11] Now, I am quite certain that if they had approached me[6] the moment they heard the news that I was going to prosecute my father's murderer and had offered to hand over their slaves for interrogation and I had refused to accept them, they would be presenting this as the strongest possible evidence that they were innocent of the murder. So since I am the one who wanted to conduct the interrogation myself, at first, and then asked them to conduct it instead, it is only reasonable that these same considerations should be evidence for my side that they are guilty. [12] If they were willing to hand over slaves for interrogation and I had refused them, this would be evidence for their side. In the same way, then, consider it evidence for my side that they refused to hand over their slaves when I wanted to put the matter to the test. It seems to me a terrible thing if they are trying to persuade you not to convict them, when they did not see fit to become jurors in their own case by handing over their own slaves for interrogation. [13] In this matter, then, it is clear that they were trying to avoid a clear investigation of the facts; they knew that their own wickedness would become apparent, and so they wanted to let the matter rest in silence without an interrogation. But not you, gentlemen; I am quite certain you will make things clear. But enough about that. I will now try to give you a true account of what happened, and may justice be my guide.

[14] Our house had an upstairs room in which Philoneus, a true gentleman and a friend of our father, used to stay when he was in Athens. Now, Philoneus had a mistress[7] whom he was going to set up as a prostitute. Learning of this, my brother's mother became friends with her. [15] She realized that Philoneus was treating the woman wrongly, and so she summoned her and, when she arrived, said she too

---

[6] For this form of argument ("hypothetical role-reversal"), see above, Ant. 6.27n.

[7] The status of this mistress (*pallakē*) is disputed, but she is probably a slave.

ng counts as murder.
reakness relying on other peoples info.

was being treated wrongly by our father. If the woman followed her instructions, she said, she was capable of renewing Philoneus' love for her and my father's love for herself. She added that her job was to contrive the plan; the woman's was to carry it out. [16] She asked the woman if she was willing to help, and she agreed—without hesitation, I think. Some time later it was time for Philoneus to attend to the sacrificial rites of Zeus Ctesius in Piraeus,[8] and since my father was about to sail for Naxos, Philoneus thought it would be an excellent idea to accompany his good friend, my father, to Piraeus and on the same trip entertain him after celebrating the rites.[9] [17] Philoneus' mistress accompanied them to help with the sacrifice. When they reached Piraeus, Philoneus carried out the sacrifice in the proper manner. When he had finished, the woman began planning how she should give them the drug: should it be before or after dinner? Finally, following the advice of Clytemnestra—this man's mother—she decided it would be better to give it after dinner. [18] It would take too long for me to tell and for you to hear the details of the dinner, but I will try to relate the rest of the story about the giving of the drug as briefly as possible. When they had finished dinner, one of them celebrating a sacrifice to Zeus Ctesius and entertaining his guest while the other was preparing to sail and was dining with his friend, they naturally began pouring libations and adding frankincense to them. [19] But while Philoneus' mistress was pouring the libations, and the men were uttering prayers that would never be fulfilled, at the same time, gentlemen, she was pouring in the drug. And she also thought she would be clever and put more into Philoneus' cup, on the theory that if she gave him more, he would love her more. She didn't realize she had been deceived by my stepmother until the evil was already done. She gave my father a smaller amount. [20] When the men had poured out the libations, each took hold of his own murderer and drank it down—his last drink. Philoneus died immediately, and our father became sick and died from the illness twenty days later. For this deed

---

[8] Zeus Ctesius ("Zeus, god of property") was naturally honored by the wealthy. Philoneus is apparently a merchant who lives in Piraeus, the port of Athens, a few kilometers from the city; he stays with the speaker's father when he is in the city.

[9] Presumably a ritual prayer for good sailing.

Both parties have to be present.

the woman who assisted with it has the reward she deserves, even though she was not to blame; she was tortured on the wheel and then handed over to the executioner.[10] And the woman who was really responsible and who thought up the plan and carried it out,[11] she will have her reward too, if you and the gods are willing.

[21] Consider now how much more just my request is than my brother's. I am asking you to avenge this man's wrongful death for all time; he asks for nothing for the dead man, though he deserves your pity and help and revenge for the impious and infamous way he departed this life before his appointed time, victim of those who should least of all have done this. [22] Instead, he will make requests for the killer that are immoral, unholy, impossible, and unworthy of consideration by you or the gods; for he asks you not to punish her for a crime she could not persuade herself to avoid. You are here not to assist murderers but their victims who have been intentionally killed— killed by those who should least of all have killed them. So now it is in your hands to decide this case correctly. Be sure to do so.

[23] My opponent will plead for his mother, who is still living despite her thoughtless and godless act of murder, and will try to persuade you that she should not pay the penalty for her crime. But I plead for my father, who is dead, that she should pay the penalty to the fullest. And your task, the reason you are jurors and have that name,[12] is to bring criminals to justice. [24] I am prosecuting her with this speech so that she will pay the penalty for her crime and I will gain revenge for our father and for your laws, and I deserve help from all of you if I speak the truth. He is doing just the opposite, helping her escape punishment for her crime, even though she disregarded the laws. [25] Does justice require punishment for a person who kills

---

[10] The torture was probably punitive, since if the woman had also been interrogated under torture, the speaker would probably report what she said. Her involvement in the death was great enough to justify her punishment even if she was not the main instigator.

[11] Strictly speaking, the servant carried out the crime, and many editors move the words "and carried it out" to the preceding sentence. But since the speaker's strategy is to shift all the responsibility to the stepmother, he would want to exaggerate her role.

[12] "Juror" (*dikastēs*) is derived from "justice" (*dikē*).

intentionally or not? Whom should we pity more, the dead man or the killer? The dead man, in my view, since that would be in accord with justice and righteousness, both human and divine. So again I ask you: just as she showed no pity and no mercy in killing him, so she should herself be put to death by you and by justice. [26] She killed him willingly and with premeditation; he died unwillingly and violently. Surely, gentlemen, he did die violently.[13] He was about to sail abroad and was being entertained by one of his friends; she sent the poison and gave orders that it be given to him to drink, thus killing our father. How could she deserve any pity or respect from you or anyone else, when she herself didn't think to show pity for her own husband but destroyed him without shame or respect? [27] You know it's right to show pity for involuntary suffering rather than for willing and intentional crimes and errors. Just as she destroyed him, with no respect and no fear for gods or heroes or humans, so she would receive the just punishment she most deserves if she is put to death by you and by justice, without respect or pity or sympathy.

[28] I am amazed at my brother's audacity. He swears he is "quite certain" that his mother did not do these things; but how could someone be quite certain of something that happened when he wasn't there himself? Surely those who plot the murder of their close friends and relatives do not contrive their schemes and make their preparations in front of witnesses but in the greatest possible secrecy so that no one else will know. [29] The victims of plots know nothing until the evil is already done and they understand the destruction that has come on them. Then, if they can and have enough time before their death, they summon their friends or relatives as witnesses, tell them who is causing their death, and direct them to take vengeance for the wrongs they are suffering. [30] This is just how my father directed me, though I was

---

[13] The prosecution may have a problem because the law on homicide (see Dem. 23.22) treats poisoning as murder "if one gives the poison oneself," implying perhaps that someone who only supplied the poison is not guilty of homicide. By asserting that his father died a "violent death" (though nothing indicates that it actually was violent), the speaker may be trying to present this as an ordinary case of murder, and not just a poisoning. In ordinary homicide, an accomplice (the "planner") was considered just as responsible as the actual killer (see the Introduction to Ant. 6).

why did he not call more witnesses.
why put it on underage son.

AGAINST THE STEPMOTHER 51

just a boy, when he was suffering his terrible last illness. If victims lack these means, they write things down, and they summon their own servants as witnesses and reveal to them who is causing their death. Young as I was at the time, [my father revealed these matters to me and gave instructions to me, not to his slaves.]

[31] I have told my story and have come to the help of the dead man and the law. It is up to you by yourselves to consider what remains to be done and decide in accordance with justice. The gods below, I think, are concerned about the victims of crime.

- wants slaves come forward as shes tried it before.
- story telling- very hypothetical.
- Estate → divided between brothers.
- what is his intention?
    even if mother guilty doesnt mean step brothers loose inherit.

- He was not allowed interrogate slave

who tortured the slave girl- phrenous as its his slave
why didnt phrenous family push trial
prosecutor- 20% of vote if notfired.

- 20 days - why did it take him 20 day die but his friend only a day

- how can his brother be quite sure.
- claims intent & with premeditation but flicks to unintent.

ANTIPHON 5. ON THE MURDER OF HERODES

INTRODUCTION

Antiphon's longest surviving speech, *On the Murder of Herodes,* was regarded in antiquity as one of his best. Modern commentators generally agree, noting the vividness of the narrative, the creativity of the arguments from probability, and the effectiveness of the procedural arguments. However, our ignorance on several important issues makes any assessment of the argument difficult. Being a defense speech, it can be selective in its narration of events, for the jurors would already have been given an account by the prosecution. The mixture of substantive and procedural issues also complicates any assessment.

The speech was delivered about a decade after the Mytilenean revolt in 427. As reported by Thucydides (3.1–50), Mytilene, the main city on the island of Lesbos and one of Athens' most powerful and important allies in the Peloponnesian War, rebelled against Athenian dominance. Athens put down the revolt, executed its leaders, and sent in Athenian settlers ("cleruchs"), who divided up the territory. The Mytileneans continued to farm the land, paying an annual rent. It is a reasonable guess that Herodes was one of these Athenian settlers. The defendant is a young Mytilenean, whose name, according to a late source, is Euxitheus. His father had played some part in the revolt (5.74–80) and is now living in voluntary exile in Thrace. The Athenian jurors would undoubtedly remember the revolt and might be biased against any Mytilenean, though it is impossible to know how this would have affected their verdict.

The prosecution's account of events, as best we can reconstruct it, was as follows: Euxitheus was traveling on the same boat as Herodes from Mytilene to Thrace, when they were forced by a storm to put in at a small harbor on the north shore of Lesbos. There they waited out the storm, drinking, on another boat in the harbor, one with a roof. Sometime during the night Herodes disappeared and was not seen again. A search was made, but no body was ever found. Euxitheus then continued to Thrace, but when he later returned to Mytilene, he was accused of murdering Herodes. In his absence, Herodes' relatives had interrogated a slave who initially denied any knowledge of the crime but later, under torture, confessed to assisting Euxitheus in the murder. His story was that they had killed Herodes on shore, striking him with a rock, and had dumped his body at sea from a small boat. The prosecution also presented an incriminating note, allegedly written by Euxitheus to a certain Lycinus. Both men had previously had dealings with Herodes. It is not clear what specific motive, if any, the prosecution gave for the crime. Euxitheus was then brought to Athens for trial.

In his defense, Euxitheus first argues vehemently against the procedure used to prosecute him (see below). He then disputes the facts, claiming the events that night happened by chance and could not have been planned, and pointing to several contradictions in the prosecution's case. Euxitheus also emphasizes that the slave's story was extracted from him by torture when he was absent, and the prosecution then put the slave to death, their purpose being (he says) to prevent Euxitheus from questioning the man and exposing the truth. Another witness, a free man, had given different testimony, also under torture, stating that Euxitheus never left the boat that night. Euxitheus also accuses the prosecution of planting the note to Lycinus and claims, moreover, that neither he nor Lycinus had any motive for killing Herodes. He concludes that the prosecution do not know who killed Herodes, and he accuses them rather vaguely of manufacturing the case against him for their own profit.

The procedural issue is thorny. The regular procedure for a homicide case was a *dikē phonou* ("suit for homicide"), which would be tried before the Areopagus. The accused was banned from most sacred and public places until the trial but was not otherwise constrained (see Ant. 6.34–36). Special rules applied to these cases: not only litigants (as in regular trials) but also witnesses had to swear a special oath, the *diōmosia*, and indeed nobody could be called as a witness who had not previously so sworn. There was in addition at least formally an obligation on litigants not to introduce irrelevant material into their speeches, though there was no separate means of enforcing this rule. Moreover, the accused could voluntarily go into exile any time before his second speech.

Euxitheus came to Athens expecting to face a *dikē phonou,* but instead he was arrested by a special procedure, *apagōgē,* normally used against common criminals (*kakourgoi;* see Ant. 2.1.4n). It could also be used against a killer caught in a place from which he was banned, but according to Euxitheus, it had never before been used for an ordinary case of homicide. Apparently the prosecution argued that this was legitimate, since homicide was a great evil (*kakourgēma;* 5.10), and the officials in charge of *apagōgē,* the Eleven, accepted the case.[1] The prosecution did not allow Euxitheus to post sureties, as was normally done, and so he was imprisoned until trial. He is being tried in one of the popular courts (where most trials took place) before a jury of ordinary citizens, rather than before the Areopagus. The reason the prosecution used this irregular procedure may have been to ensure that he did not leave Athens before the trial. Since his father was living in Thrace, voluntary exile would probably not be much of a hardship for him. But the prosecution may have had other motives as well.

The prologue (1–7) is followed by arguments about the proper procedure for prosecution (8–19). Then comes the narrative, which includes some argument (20–24); arguments from likelihood (*eikos,* 25–28); the interrogation and testimony of the prosecution's witnesses (29–42); more arguments from likelihood (43–45); further discussion of the interrogation of the witnesses (46–52); and briefer discussions of the note to Lycinus (53–56), alleged motives (57–63), the need for certain proof (64–73), Euxitheus' father and the Mytilenean revolt (74–80), and signs from heaven (81–84). The epilogue (85–96) largely reiterates the procedural issues discussed in 8–19. The verdict is unknown.

---

[1] The Eleven were the officials who supervised prisons, executions, and certain other matters, such as *apagōgē* cases. It is not clear on what grounds they could refuse to accept a case. In Lysias 13 the Eleven forced the prosecutor to modify the wording of his indictment before they would accept it.

ANTIPHON 5. ON THE MURDER OF HERODES

[1] I wish I had the ability to speak and the experience in practical matters equal to my recent troubles and misfortunes,[2] but my experience of the latter goes beyond what is proper, while my deficiency in the former leaves me at a disadvantage. [2] For when I had to endure physical suffering because of an improper accusation,[3] my experience was no help, and here, when my salvation lies in stating the facts truthfully, my inability to speak hurts me. [3] Before now, many who lacked speaking ability were unconvincing in telling the truth and were destroyed for this very reason, that they were unable to make the truth clear; but many others who had speaking ability were convincing with their lies and were saved precisely because they lied. Thus, someone with little experience in legal contests is forced to address himself to the prosecution's words rather than the actual events and the truth of what happened.[4] [4] So, gentlemen, I will not make the usual request that you pay attention, which is what most litigants ask who have no confidence in themselves and assume you will be unjust—for it's a reasonable expectation among good men that even without requesting it, the defendant will have your full attention, just as the prosecution did without requesting it. [5] So this is my request: if I make any mistakes in speaking, forgive me and realize that the error was caused by inexperience, not wickedness, but anything I say correctly is spoken with truth rather than cleverness. It is not right for someone who goes wrong in his actions to be saved by words or for one who has been correct in his actions to be ruined by words. A word is only a mistake of the tongue, but a deed is a mistake of the mind. [6] A man who faces personal danger cannot avoid making some mistake, since he must consider not only his speech but his whole future; everything that is now unclear is more in the hands of fortune than foresight, and this will necessarily unnerve someone already in danger. [7] I have observed that even those with much experience in court do not speak

---

[2] For the *topos* of inexperience, cf. Ant. 1.1.

[3] Euxitheus refers to the use of the wrong procedure against him (see 5.8–19).

[4] For the dichotomy of words (*logoi*) and deeds or events (*erga*) in connection with "the truth of what happened," cf. Antiphon's Second Tetralogy (3.2.3, 3.3.1).

as well as usual when they face danger, but when there is no danger, they are more successful. So, my request, gentlemen, is both legally and morally right—in accordance with your justice no less than my own. I shall now answer each of the charges in turn.

[8] First, I will demonstrate to you that I was brought to this trial by highly illegal and violent methods. It's not that I would avoid trial by you, the people:[5] even if you were not under oath or subject to any law, I would entrust my life to your verdict, since I am confident I have done no wrong in this matter and that your decision will be guided by justice. But I want you to treat this violent and illegal behavior as evidence of their treatment of me and their conduct in general. [9] My first point is that I was denounced[6] as a common criminal (*kakourgos*), though in fact I'm on trial for homicide, something no one in this land has ever experienced before. The prosecution themselves bear witness that I am not a common criminal and am not subject to the law concerning them. That law concerns thieves and cloak-snatchers, and they have not shown that these are relevant to my case. So at least as regards this arrest (*apagōgē*), they have shown that both law and justice require my acquittal. [10] Then they say that homicide is surely a great crime. I agree; it's the greatest. But so are temple robbery and treason, and yet there are separate laws for each of these. In my case, the prosecution have in the first place caused the trial to be held in the agora,[7] the very place that is proclaimed off-limits for others on trial for homicide; and they have also made the case assessable,[8] when the law stipulates that the killer should be killed in turn. They did this not for my benefit but for their own profit, thereby giving the dead man less than the law provides. You will learn their reasons for this in the course of my speech.[9]

---

[5] I.e., by the popular court as opposed to the court of the Areopagus.

[6] The prosecution first issued an *endeixis* ("denunciation") requesting that the Eleven arrest Euxitheus by *apagōgē* (see the Speech Introduction).

[7] Where the popular courts were located; the Areopagus met on a hill nearby. He was probably tried in the Parabyston, where the Eleven presided (Boegehold 1995: 178–179).

[8] For the process of assessing the penalty, see the Introduction, VC. The penalty in an *apagōgē* was normally death, but some cases may have been assessable.

[9] This promise is never fulfilled; it is not clear just how the prosecution would profit.

[11] Second, as I think you all know, all courts judge homicide cases in the open air, for the simple reason that the jurors won't be together with someone with impure hands and so that the prosecutor of a homicide won't be under the same roof as the killer. You have evaded this law and done the opposite from others. Also, you ought to have sworn the greatest and strongest oath, calling down destruction on yourself, your family, and your entire household and swearing to confine your case to this murder alone.[10] Thus, I would not be convicted for anything besides this act, even if I had committed many other crimes, and I would not be acquitted for my good deeds, no matter how many I had accomplished. [12] But you have evaded these rules: you invent laws for yourself, you prosecute me without swearing an oath, and your witnesses testify without swearing, though they ought to testify against me only after swearing the same oath as you with a hand on the sacrificial victims. And then you ask the jurors to convict me of homicide on the evidence of unsworn witnesses, whom you have proven untrustworthy by your own violations of the established laws. You must think your illegal conduct should take precedence over the laws themselves! [13] You say that if I had been freed, I would not have awaited trial but would have departed, as if you compelled me to come to this land unwillingly;[11] but if being banned from this city was of no concern to me, I could equally well have not come when summoned and lost the case by default, or I could have made my defense but left after my first speech. This course is available to everyone, but you have enacted your own private law, trying to deprive me alone of something all other Greeks have.

[14] I think everyone will agree that the laws governing these matters are the finest and most righteous of all laws. They are the oldest established laws in this land, and their main points have always remained the same,[12] which is the best sign of well-enacted laws; for time and experience teach people the faults in things. Therefore, you should not learn from the prosecutor's words whether the laws are good or not, but rather let the laws instruct you whether or not the prosecutor's words give an accurate account of the situation. [15] Thus, the laws on homicide are the finest, and no one has ever dared change

---

[10] For the special rules for homicide cases, see the Speech Introduction.

[11] Euxitheus came willingly because he expected to face a *dikē phonou*.

[12] Cf. the nearly identical section in Ant. 6.2 (with note).

them. Only you have had the audacity to become a legislator and make them worse, seeking to ruin me unjustly in violation of these laws. Your violations are themselves the greatest evidence in my favor, for you are well aware that you would not have anyone testifying against me if they had had to swear the homicide oath.

[16] Moreover, you did not have enough confidence in your case to set one conclusive trial on the matter, but you left room for further dispute and argument; evidently you lack confidence in these jurors as well. As a result, even an acquittal will do me no good, since you can say that I was acquitted of being a common criminal but not on the charge of homicide; on the other hand, if you win, you'll demand the death penalty on the ground that I was convicted of homicide. Could there be a more clever trap than this? If you persuade these men once, you'll have what you want, but if I am acquitted once, I'll still face the same danger! [17] There is more, gentlemen: my imprisonment was the most illegal act ever committed. I was willing to post three sureties,[13] as the law allows, but they would not let me do so. No other foreigner who was willing to post sureties has ever been imprisoned; and the officials in charge of cases of common criminals abide by this same law. So once more this law that applies to all other men fails to benefit me alone. [18] This was to their advantage, of course: first, I would be unprepared, since I could not attend to my own affairs, and second, I would suffer physically, and because of this my friends would become more willing to testify falsely on their side than to tell the truth on mine. They have also disgraced me and my family for the rest of our lives. [19] So, I have come to trial at a disadvantage with regard to your laws and justice. Even so, I'll try to demonstrate my innocence, though it is indeed hard to refute on the spot lies that have been carefully plotted for a long time now; one cannot take precautions against the unexpected.

[20] I made the journey from Mytilene in the same boat as Herodes, the man they say I killed. We were sailing to Aenus,[14] I to visit my

---

[13] A standard way of guaranteeing any promise, such as a debt, was to have friends stand surety (see Socrates' offer in Plato's *Apology* 38c; also Isoc. 17.12). The prosecutor's refusal to accept sureties is unusual but probably not illegal.

[14] Aenus was a Greek commercial city in Thrace about 200 kilometers from Mytilene; the journey would take about three days in normal conditions. From

father—for he happened to be there at the time—and Herodes to ransom prisoners to some Thracians. Also on the same boat were the prisoners who were to be ransomed and the Thracians who were going to pay the ransom. I present witnesses to these facts.

[WITNESSES]

[21] This was the reason we each had for the trip. We happened to encounter a storm, which forced us to put in to shore at a spot in the territory of Methymna.[15] Another boat was anchored there, and Herodes transferred to it before he died (as they say). But first consider this: these events took place by chance, not prearrangement, for no one has shown that I persuaded the man to sail with me. No, he made the journey on his own, for his own private business; [22] and I too clearly had sufficient reason of my own to make the journey to Aenus. Putting in to shore was also unplanned and resulted from necessity. Then, after we anchored, there was no contrivance or deceit in the transfer to the other boat, but this too was necessary because of the rain, for the boat we were sailing in did not have a covered deck, but the one we transferred to did. I present witnesses to these facts.

[WITNESSES]

[23] When we crossed over to the other boat, we began drinking. It's clear that Herodes left the boat and did not return again, but I did not leave the boat at all that night. The next day the man was missing, and I helped in the search no less than the others; for this was as much a concern to me as to anyone. And I was responsible for a messenger being sent to Mytilene; for on my advice we decided to send him. [24] When no one else from the [roofed] boat or from those sailing with Herodes was willing to go, I was willing to send my own attendant, though surely I did not deliberately want to send someone who would inform against me. When the man could not be found in

Mytilene one would sail north along the coast and then west perhaps as far as Methymna, then directly north to Asia Minor and to Aenus—never out of sight of land. It is likely that the boat left Mytilene early in the day and encountered a storm in the early evening.

[15] Probably the small harbor of Skala Sikaminias, about 50 kilometers from Mytilene by road.

Mytilene or anywhere else and good sailing weather had returned and all the other boats were putting out to sea, I too sailed off. I present you with the witnesses to these facts.

[WITNESSES]

[25] These are the facts; now consider the conclusions that can reasonably be drawn from them. First, before I left for Aenus, when the man was missing and these men had already heard the news, no one accused me, or else I never would have sailed away. At that moment, truth and the facts were more powerful than their accusation, and also I was still there. But when I sailed away and these men conspired and contrived their plot against me, then they made their accusation. [26] They say the man died on land when I hit him on the head with a stone, but I did not leave the boat at all. And they have precise information about this, but they cannot give any plausible account of the man's disappearance. Clearly this probably happened near the harbor; the man was drunk and left the boat at night, so he probably could not control his actions, and someone wishing to lead him far away at night would not have had a plausible excuse to do so. [27] They searched for the man for two days, both in the harbor and away from it, but they could not find anyone who had seen him or any blood or any other sign of him. So should I accept their account, even though I have witnesses that I did not leave the boat? Even if I definitely left the boat, there's no reasonable explanation how the man could disappear and not be found unless he went a long way from the sea. [28] But they say he was thrown into the sea. In what boat? Clearly the boat must have come from the harbor; why wouldn't they find it? There would probably be some evidence in the boat, if a dead man was thrown overboard at night. In fact, they said they found evidence in the boat where he was drinking and then left—where they agree he did not die; but they have not found the boat from which he was thrown into the sea or any sign of it. I present you with the witnesses to these facts.

[WITNESSES]

[29] When I sailed off to Aenus, the boat on which Herodes and I were drinking reached Mytilene. The first thing they did was go on

board and search the boat, and when they found the blood, they said the man had been killed there. But when this possibility was eliminated and they discovered that it was the blood of sheep,[16] they abandoned this line of argument, and instead they seized and interrogated the men under torture. [30] The man[17] they interrogated immediately said nothing bad about me, but the other they interrogated many days later, after keeping him to themselves in the interval, and they <u>persuaded him</u> to <u>accuse me falsely</u>. I present you with the witnesses to these facts.

[WITNESSES]

[31] You have heard testimony that the man was interrogated long afterwards. Now, consider carefully the nature of this interrogation.[18] In the slave's case, since they probably promised him his freedom and had the power to put an end to his suffering, he was probably persuaded to give <u>false testimony</u> by both factors, hope of freedom and desire for immediate release from the torture. [32] ⌊I think you know that those who are interrogated normally testify in favor of those who have most control over the interrogation and say whatever will be pleasing to them; they will benefit most in this way, especially if those they are falsely accusing don't happen to be present.⌋ If I ordered him put on the rack for not telling the truth, this alone would probably make him recant his false accusations. As it was, the interrogators calculated their own self-interest. [33] So, as long as he was hopeful of benefiting from his false accusation, he stuck to this story; but when he realized he would be put to death, then he began telling the truth

---

[16] The sheep may have been sacrificed in gratitude for escaping the storm.

[17] Euxitheus is (perhaps deliberately) vague about the identities of these men. The first is a free man, probably a Mytilenean of low standing, since he was tortured, perhaps Euxitheus' attendant (5.24); the second, a slave, cannot have belonged to Herodes, whose relatives had to purchase him (5.47), or to Euxitheus, who presumably would not have sold him.

[18] Strict rules applied to an interrogation that resulted from a challenge by one litigant to the other (Ant. 1.6n), but these rules did not apply to interrogation during a criminal investigation, especially when the slave was suspected of involvement in the crime. Nonetheless, Euxitheus' complaints may raise doubts about the prosecution's motives.

and admitted that he had been persuaded by these men to lay false charges against me. [34] But neither his persistent attempts to give false evidence nor his subsequent statement of the truth helped him at all; they took the man and killed him. Now they base their case against me on this informer, though everyone else treats informers in just the opposite way, rewarding free men with money and slaves with their freedom. But they rewarded this informer with death, despite the entreaties of my friends that they should not kill the man before I returned. [35] Clearly they had no need for his person, only his story. If the man were alive and I carried out the same interrogation, he would provide evidence of their plotting, but now that he's dead, his absence makes it impossible to prove the truth, while his false words live on as the truth and destroy me. Call witnesses to these facts.

[WITNESSES]

[36] In my view, they should have presented the informer here in person[19] and convicted me by this means, presenting the man publicly and asking me to interrogate him, not killing him. But tell me, which of his stories are they using now? The one he told first or the later one? And which is true? When he said I did the deed or when he denied it? [37] If we consider what is likely, his later account appears truer: he lied for his own benefit, but when his lies were about to ruin him, he thought he would save himself by speaking the truth. There was no one there to defend the truth, since I was the only ally of his later true statement and I happened to be away; others were there, however, who were going to put away his earlier false statements[20] so that they could never be corrected. [38] Men who are incriminated by informers may steal them away and eliminate them, but these men arrested this informer against me and carried out their investigation and then eliminated him. Of course, if I had eliminated the man, or had refused to hand him over, or avoided some other test, they would consider these actions most significant and would treat them as important evidence against me. So now that they themselves refuse this test when my friends challenged them, then surely these same actions ought to be

---

[19] Slaves did not normally appear in court themselves.

[20] The exact sense is unclear; this may mean "put away for safe keeping."

evidence against them that the accusation they brought against me is false. [39] They also say that during the interrogation, the fellow agreed that he helped kill the victim, but I disagree: he did not say this but only that he led the victim and me off the boat and then, after I had killed Herodes, helped pick him up and put him in the boat, and then threw him into the sea. [40] Consider this too: at first, before being put on the wheel where he faced extreme compulsion, the man was guided by the truth and cleared me of the charge; but when he was put on the wheel, he was now guided by compulsion and testified falsely against me, hoping to be released from the torture. [41] Then when the torture stopped, he stopped accusing me of any of these things, and at the end he cried out that both of us were being ruined unjustly. He was not doing this for my sake—how could he? After all, he had falsely accused me. No, he was compelled by the truth to reaffirm the truth of his first statement. [42] Furthermore, the other man—the one sailing on the same boat, who was present to the end and was with me[21]—was subjected to the same interrogation and agreed that the first and last statements of the man were true, since he absolved me to the end. But he disagreed with the story the slave gave while on the rack, which he told under compulsion, not for the truth; for the slave said I left the boat and killed the man and that he helped me pick up the body when it was already dead, but the other said I did not leave the boat at all.

[43] Likelihood is also my ally, for I was surely not so deluded that I planned the man's murder all by myself in order to have no accomplice (for this was the only real danger for me), but then, when it was all done, I enlisted the help of witnesses and co-conspirators. [44] Furthermore, the man was killed very near the sea and the boats, or so their story goes; but wouldn't someone being killed by just one man either cry out or somehow draw the notice of people on land or in the boat? You can hear something at much greater distance at night than in the daytime, on a beach than in the city, and they say people were still awake when the man left the boat. [45] In addition, he was

---

[21] "The same boat" must be the boat in which Euxitheus and Herodes set out from Mytilene; "was present to the end" must mean until the end of the events in the harbor.

killed on land and put into the boat, but there was no blood or any sign of this either on land or in the boat, although he was killed and put in the boat at night. Do you really think that under such circumstances a man could scrape away the traces on land and wipe them off the boat, when even someone in full control of himself with nothing to fear and working during the day could not make them completely disappear? How likely is this, gentlemen?

[46] Consider this in particular—and don't be upset if I repeat these points several times, since I face great danger: if you decide correctly, I am saved, but if you're at all deceived by their lies, I am destroyed—so don't let anyone make you forget this: they killed the informer and did all they could to prevent his appearing before you and to make it impossible for me to take him and interrogate him when I returned, although this would have been to their advantage. ·
[47] But no, they purchased the man who was their informer and killed him, entirely on their own, though the city did not vote for this, and the man was not the actual killer. They should have tied him up and guarded him, or released him to my friends with guarantees, or handed him over to your officials so that you could vote on him. Instead, they themselves convicted him of the man's murder and killed him. Even a city cannot inflict the death penalty without the Athenians' permission.[22] And now you ask these jurors to judge his statements, though you yourselves have already judged his deeds.
[48] Even slaves who kill their masters and are caught in the act are not put to death by the victim's relatives but are delivered to the officials according to your ancestral laws. If a slave is allowed to testify against a free man in a murder case, and a master who wishes can bring a case on behalf of his slave, and a verdict can be rendered equally for the murder of a slave and a free man, then surely it was reasonable that

---

[22] I.e., without a decision by an Athenian court. Treaties between Athens and its allies often specified that those accused of capital crimes be tried in an Athenian court, but such provisions probably did not apply to slaves. In Ant. 1.20 the servant is turned over to officials for execution, but we do not know if this was required. The reference to "your ancestral laws" in 5.48 suggests that specific rules may have been lacking, and, in any case, rules may have been different in Mytilene.

he should be given a trial and not be killed by you without trial. Indeed, there would be more justice if you stood trial for this than in this unlawful trial I now face.

[49] Now consider, gentlemen, the justice and likelihood in the statements of each of the tortured men. The slave gave two accounts: once he said he had done the deed; once he denied it. But the free man,[23] who was subjected to the same interrogation, hasn't yet said anything bad about me. [50] They could not persuade him by holding out promises of freedom, as they could the other. He was willing to risk suffering whatever was necessary, when he too knew where his own advantage lay: that he would stop being tortured the moment he said what they wanted. So, which is likely to be more trustworthy, the one who always gave the same account to the end, or the one who said one thing then denied it? Even without torture, those who always give the same account of the same matters are more trustworthy than those who contradict themselves. [51] Also, an equal share of the slave's statements favors each side: his assertions favor them, his denials, me; similarly, of the two men who were tortured, one said I did it, the other denied it to the end. Of course, equality favors the defendant rather than the prosecutor, since if the number of votes is equal, this helps the defendant rather than the prosecutor.[24]

[52] On the basis of this sort of interrogation, gentlemen, they say they are quite certain I killed the man. But if I had had a guilty conscience or had done any such thing, I would have gotten rid of the two men when I had the opportunity either to take them with me to Aenus or to drop them off on the mainland; I wouldn't have left behind informers who knew of the crime.

[53] They say that in the boat they found a note, which I sent to Lycinus saying I killed the man. But why did I need to send a note since it was my accomplice who carried the note? He would have given a clearer account in person of what he did, and there was no need to hide things from him. People generally use writing for messages the messenger is not supposed to know. [54] Also, someone would need

---

[23] For this man's identity, see 5.29n.

[24] A tie vote resulted in acquittal: the "vote of Athena" (see Aeschylus' *Eumenides*).

to write down a very large message so the messenger would not forget it on account of its length. But this was a short message, namely, that the man was dead. Consider this point too: the note differed from the man's testimony, and the man differed from the note, for when tortured, he said he himself killed him,[25] but the note, when opened, indicated that I was the killer. [55] So which should we believe? They did not find the note the first time they searched the boat, only later, for at that time they hadn't yet devised their plot; but when the first man to be tortured said nothing that incriminated me, then they dropped the note into the boat so they would have evidence for this charge against me. [56] When the note was read and the second man under torture disagreed with the note, they could not make what had been read disappear. If they had thought from the beginning they could persuade the man to testify against me, they would never have contrived the message in the note. Call my witnesses for these matters.

[WITNESSES]

[57] What motive did I have for killing the man? There was no hostility between him and me. They go so far as to say I killed the man as a favor; but who has ever done such a deed as a favor to someone else? I don't think anyone has. Anyone intending to do this must have great hatred, and it would be abundantly clear that he's plotting a crime. But there was no hostility between us. [58] Well then, did I fear for my life, thinking he might do the same to me? A person could be forced to commit this crime for such a reason. But I had no such feelings toward him. Well, was I going to get money if I killed him? No, he didn't have any. [59] Why, I could more reasonably and truthfully ascribe this motive to you, that you are trying to kill me for money, than you could ascribe it to me. And you could much more justly be convicted of homicide by my relatives, if you kill me, than I could by you and that man's relatives, for I have shown clearly your intentions against me, but you are trying to destroy me with an unclear account. [60] I tell you this, jurors, because he has no motive for me to kill the man; so it seems I must defend not only myself but Lycinus too and

---

[25] This is a direct contradiction of 5.39, perhaps intended to confuse the jurors.

show that their charge against him is also improbable. I can tell you that he is in the same situation as I am: there was no way he could get money if he killed this man, and there was no danger he could avoid if this man died. [61] Here is the best evidence that Lycinus did not want to kill him: if he had had any previous score to settle, he had the opportunity to bring Herodes into court on a very dangerous charge and destroy him in full accordance with your laws, and in so doing he would have served his own interest and would have earned the gratitude of your city by pointing out his crimes; but he decided not to and took no legal action, even though this would have been a more honorable course.

[WITNESSES]²⁶

[62] Since on that occasion he let him go, do you really think that on this occasion, when he would have to endanger both himself and me, he hatched this plot, even though he knew that carrying it out would lead to my banishment into exile and his banishment from all that is sacred and holy and of the highest value among men? Moreover, if Lycinus definitely wanted to kill him (and here I adopt the prosecution's argument) but did not want to carry out the murder himself, would he ever have persuaded me to commit this crime instead of him? [63] Was it that I was physically able to handle this very risky business, while he had enough money to pay me to take risks? Surely not, for I had money, but he had none. Quite the contrary: in all likelihood he would more readily have been persuaded by me to do this than I by him, since when he was in default on a debt of seven minas, he couldn't pay it, but his friends paid it for him. And this is the best evidence that relations between Lycinus and me were not so friendly that I would do everything he wanted: since I did not pay his debt of seven minas when he was suffering in prison,²⁷ surely I did not take so great a risk as to kill a man on his account!

---

²⁶ The manuscripts indicate a break here for witnesses, but there is no indication of witnesses in the text just before or after the break, there is no evident reason for the testimony of witnesses at this point, and 5.62 follows directly from the end of 5.61.

²⁷ Debtors could be imprisoned until they paid their debt; otherwise, imprisonment as a penalty was rare.

[64] I have demonstrated as best I can that I am not guilty of the deed, nor is he. Their strongest argument is that the man has disappeared, and perhaps you are anxious to hear about this. Now, if you want me to speculate about it, then you jurors are in the same situation, since you're not guilty of the deed any more than I am. But if we are supposed to find the truth, then I suggest they ask one of those who did it, for he would be best able to tell them. [65] In my case, since I did not do it, the fullest answer I can give is simply that I didn't do it; but the person who did do it could easily demonstrate what happened, or if not demonstrate, at least give a plausible account. Those who commit crimes also devise explanations for the crime at the same time, but it's difficult for someone who did not do it to speculate about the unknown. I think any one of you, if someone asked you about something you didn't happen to know, would just say you didn't know; then if someone told you to say more, I think you would be quite perplexed. [66] So don't put me in this quandary, which even you could not easily escape from, and don't think my acquittal should depend on how well I can speculate. It should be quite enough for me to demonstrate my own innocence in the matter, and I should be judged innocent not because I am able to discover how the man disappeared or died but because I had no reason to kill him.

[67] I know from reports that in the past, killers or their victims have sometimes not been found, and it would not be right if those who were with them at the time were blamed. But many men have received the blame for other people's crimes and have been put to death before the facts became clearly known. [68] For example, the murderers of your fellow-citizen Ephialtes[28] have never yet been found. Now, if someone thought that those who were with him[29] should speculate about the identity of his killers, and if they didn't, they should be held responsible for the murder, that would not be right for those who were with him. Moreover, those who killed Ephialtes did not try to get rid of the body and by so doing run the risk of exposing

---

[28] Ephialtes, a prominent associate of Pericles, was murdered in 461, perhaps because of the reforms he carried out in 463.

[29] The expression "those who were with him" could also mean "his associates," who would presumably be the least likely to kill him.

the crime—as the prosecution say I did, alleging that I let no one help me with plotting the crime but enlisted help in lifting the body. [69] Then, not long ago a young slave, not twelve years old, tried to kill his master, and if he hadn't become frightened at the victim's cries and run off leaving his dagger in the wound but had had the courage to remain, all the servants in the house would have been put to death. No one would suspect the boy would dare commit such a crime. As it was, however, he was arrested and later confessed.[30] And then there were your Hellenotamiae,[31] who were blamed for financial wrongdoing, although like me now they were not guilty. They were all put to death in anger without any deliberation, except for one. Later the facts became clear. [70] This one man—they say his name was Sosias—had been sentenced to death but not yet executed, and when it was revealed in the meanwhile how the money had been lost, this man was rescued by you, the people, though he had already been delivered to the Eleven. The others had already been put to death, though they were innocent. [71] I think you older jurors remember these events, and the younger ones have heard about them, as I have. They show how good it is to put things to the test of time. Perhaps this question too, how Herodes died, might become clear later. So don't wait till later to decide that you executed me when I was innocent, but come to the right decision sooner and not in anger or prejudice; for there could not be worse advisers than these.

[72] It is impossible for an angry man to make good decisions, for his anger destroys the faculty he uses in planning, his judgment. Day succeeding day is a great thing, gentlemen, for restoring judgment in place of anger and for discovering the truth of what happened. [73] You can be quite certain that I deserve pity from you rather than punishment. It's reasonable to punish criminals but to pity those who

---

[30] We know nothing of this event besides what is said here. The point seems to be that if the boy had not panicked, he would have succeeded in the murder and would not have been identified; even though he would presumably have been put to death with the other servants, the crime would remain unsolved.

[31] A group of ten (later twenty) officials who oversaw the finances of the Delian League. This episode, which is not mentioned in any other source, probably occurred in the 450s or 440s.

are unjustly in danger, and your power to save me justly should always be stronger than my enemies' desire to destroy me unjustly. By delaying, you'll still be able to do the terrible things the prosecution requests, but by acting immediately, you'll leave no opportunity at all for correct deliberation.

[74] Now I must also defend my father, even though it would be more reasonable for him to defend me, since he's my father. He's much older than my affairs are, but I'm much younger than his.[32] Of course, if I were giving evidence against the prosecutor here concerning a matter I wasn't certain about but knew only from hearsay, he would say I was treating him terribly. [75] But he doesn't think it's terrible to compel me to defend myself on matters that are much older than I and that I know only by word of mouth. Nevertheless, I will tell you as much as I know so my father will not be unjustly maligned before you. I might perhaps slip up and not give a completely correct account of everything he did so correctly, but that's a risk I must take. [76] Before the revolt of Mytilene[33] he showed his loyalty to you by his actions; but when the whole city wrongly decided to revolt and failed to meet your expectations, he was compelled to join with the whole city in that failure. Even during these events his feelings toward you remained the same, but he could no longer demonstrate the same loyalty, since he could not easily leave the city. His children and his property held him there like bonds, and while he remained there, it was impossible for him to act with confidence. [77] But ever since you punished the leaders of the revolt, which clearly did not include my father, and allowed the rest of the Mytileneans to live on their own land without reprisal, my father has not done anything wrong. He's done everything required of him and has not neglected any of the special needs of either city, yours or Mytilene, but he has sponsored choral productions[34] and paid his taxes. [78] If he likes to live in Aenus, his intent is not to avoid any of his obligations to the city. He hasn't become a citizen of any other state as I see others doing, some going to the mainland to live

---

[32] The sense of this puzzling sentence is clarified in 5.75.

[33] In 427. In what follows, "you" (jurors) pointedly suggests also "you Athenians."

[34] For this "liturgy," see the Introduction, IVC.

among your enemies while others bring suits against you under treaties, and he's not trying to avoid your courts; his only reason is that,
like you, he hates sykophants.[35] [79] It isn't right for my father to be
punished as an individual for things he did together with the whole
city under compulsion, not by choice. All Mytileneans will remember
forever the mistake they made then. They exchanged great happiness
for great misery and saw their own homeland devastated. Don't believe
the slanderous charges these men have leveled against my father personally; for they have contrived this whole case against us for the sake
of money. Many factors help those who want to get hold of other
people's property; he's too old to assist me, and I'm much too young
to be able to protect myself as I should. [80] Help me, then, and don't
teach these sykophants to be more powerful than you are. If they come
to you and get what they want, the lesson will be that people should
come to an agreement with them and avoid your court; but if they
come to you and are judged to be scoundrels who will get nothing,
then honor and power will be yours, and justice will be done. Help
me, then, and help justice too.

[81] You have now heard everything that can be demonstrated by
human evidence and witnesses; but before casting your vote, you
should also look just as much to the evidence of signs from the gods.
You rely on these especially in managing the public affairs of the city
safely, in times of danger and other times too; [82] you should also
consider these signs important and reliable in private affairs. I think
you know that before now, many who have embarked on a ship with
unclean hands or with some other pollution have themselves perished
together with others who led devout lives and fulfilled all their obligations to the gods.[36] Others who did not perish were subjected to life-
threatening dangers because of such people. And many others attending sacrifices were shown to be unholy and were prevented from
completing the proper rites. [83] With me, however, it's just the opposite in every case. Those I sailed with have enjoyed the finest voyage,

---

[35] For sykophants, see the Introduction, VE. This implies that his father is
wealthy.

[36] For the idea that the killer's pollution can affect others, see the Introduction
to Ant. 2.

and at the sacrificial rites I have attended, the sacrifice has never been anything but the finest. I think this is important evidence that the prosecution's accusations against me are untrue. Witnesses please.

[WITNESSES]

[84] I also know this, gentlemen of the jury, that if witnesses were giving testimony against me that something unholy had happened on a ship or at a sacrifice when I was present, they would consider this very strong evidence and would display these signs from the gods as clear proof of their accusation; but now that the evidence goes against their claims and the witnesses testify that my case is true and their accusation is false, now they say you should not trust the witnesses, but you should trust their arguments. Well, other men test arguments (*logoi*) against the facts (*erga*), but these men are trying to use their arguments to make you disbelieve the facts.

[85] I have now answered as many of the charges as I can remember, and I ask you to acquit me. For me, acquittal means salvation; for you, it is right and in accord with your oath, for you swore to judge the case according to the laws. And though no longer subject to the law under which I was arrested, I can still be tried lawfully by the proper procedure for this charge. If this results in two trials instead of one, it's the prosecutor's fault, not mine. So just because my worst enemies subject me to two trials, surely you impartial arbiters of justice will not prematurely convict me of homicide in this trial. [86] Don't do this, gentlemen; but give time a chance, for time lets those who wish discover the precise facts most accurately. I should think, gentlemen, that in such matters a trial should be held according to the laws, while according to justice the case should be tested as often as possible. In this way you would reach a better decision, for repeated trials are the ally of truth and the enemy of slander. [87] In a homicide case the verdict, even if wrong, overpowers justice and truth, and if you convict me, I am forced by necessity to submit to justice and the law, even if I am not the murderer and have no responsibility for the crime. No one would dare disobey a verdict rendered in court just because he was confident of his own innocence, nor would he dare not submit to the law if he knew he had committed such a crime. He must yield to the verdict, even if it goes against the truth, and he must yield to the truth

especially if the victim has no one to avenge his death.[37] [88] For these reasons, the laws, oaths, sacrifices, proclamations, and other aspects of procedure in homicide cases are very different from other cases, because it is of the highest importance to determine the facts correctly when so much is at stake. When they are decided correctly, the victim has his vengeance; but if an innocent man is convicted of murder, it is a mistake and a sin against the gods and the laws. [89] If the prosecutor brings an incorrect accusation, this is not the same as you jurors rendering an incorrect verdict. Their accusation is not final but depends on you and on the trial; but if you give an incorrect verdict in the trial, there is no way someone could undo your mistake by appealing it elsewhere. [90] How then might you decide this case correctly? By letting these men swear the established oath before presenting their case and by letting me defend myself on the issue itself.[38] And how will you do this? By acquitting me now. I won't be free of your judgment, since you'll be the ones voting on me there too.[39] If you spare me now, you'll still be able to do what you want with me then, but if you destroy me, you won't be able to deliberate about me again. [91] If you have to make a mistake, it would be more righteous to acquit someone unjustly than to destroy someone unjustly; the former is just a mistake, but the latter is also a sacrilege. When you're about to do something incurable, you need to consider it very carefully. It's a less serious mistake to become angry and yield to prejudice if your actions can later be remedied, since you could change and reach a correct decision later. But where there is no remedy, changing your mind and recognizing your mistake later does more harm. Some of you have already condemned someone to death and then changed your mind; but when deception leads you to change your mind, surely those who deceived you should be put to death. [92] Unintentional errors, moreover, deserve pardon, but not those that are intentional. For an unintentional error, gentlemen, happens by chance; an intentional error, by choice. Now, how could there be a more intentional error than if

---

[37] Much of 5.87–89 is repeated in Ant. 6.4–6; see 6.4n.

[38] I.e., in a *dikē phonou*, in which litigants would have to stick to "the issue itself"; see the Speech Introduction.

[39] I.e., before the Areopagus, where in fact the jurors would be different.

someone immediately does what he plans to do? And killing someone with your hand or with your vote has the same effect. [93] You can be quite certain I would never have come to this city if such a crime had been on my conscience. But I came trusting in justice, and there is nothing more valuable for a man on trial than knowing he has done nothing wrong and has not sinned against the gods. In such a situation, even when the body gives up, it can be rescued by a spirit that has a clean conscience and will endure anything. But a guilty conscience in itself is your worst enemy; your body is still strong but your spirit leaves, assuming this bad conscience is punishment for the crime. I come before you with no such guilt on my conscience.

[94] That the prosecution are slandering me is hardly surprising; that's their business. But it's your business not to be persuaded to do what's wrong. If you believe me, you can still change your minds and cure your mistake by punishing me the second time; but there is no cure if you believe them and do what they want. It's just a short time until you can legally do what the prosecution are trying to persuade you to do illegally by your verdict. The matter requires proper deliberation, not haste. In this case you are just fact finders; next time you will be judges of the witnesses; now you just have opinions; then you will judge the truth. [95] It is the easiest thing to give false testimony against a man on trial for murder. If they persuade you just for the moment to sentence him to death, he loses his life and any possibility of revenge. Even friends will not seek revenge for someone who is dead, and if they want to, what good will it do the dead man? [96] So, acquit me now. These men will then swear the customary oath and prosecute me by the regular procedure for homicide. You will judge me by the established laws; and if I come to any harm, I can no longer argue that I'm being ruined illegally. That is my request; I have not overlooked your piety, and I am not depriving myself of justice; my salvation too lies in your oath. Put your trust in whichever of these you will, and acquit me.

LYSIAS 1. ON THE DEATH OF ERATOSTHENES

INTRODUCTION

At first sight, this appears to be a speech about adultery,[1] but in fact the case concerns homicide. Euphiletus, the speaker, has killed Eratosthenes, who was in the act of committing adultery with his wife, and pleads that the killing was justified. Trials for justifiable homicide came before the court of the Delphinium, and it is possible (though not certain) that they were heard by a specialist panel of Ephetae, rather than by a regular dicastic court consisting of ordinary citizens selected by lot. As usual, we do not know the result of the case, but the speaker will be declared guiltless if the court decides in his favor. If they decide for his opponents (who are presumably the dead man's relatives), he will be convicted of deliberate homicide and punished accordingly.

Euphiletus cites three laws in his support (at 1.28, 1.30, and 1.31). Scholars have plausibly identified one of these with a law on justifiable homicide attributed to Draco, which is quoted at Demosthenes 23.53: "If somebody kills a man after finding him next to his wife or mother or sister or daughter or concubine kept for producing free children, he

---

[1] There has been considerable dispute in recent scholarship (based partly on this speech) over the meaning of *moichos* ("adulterer"). The most detailed treatment of the subject is by D. Cohen (1991: 98–132), who argues that *moichos* meant specifically "somebody who has sex with a married woman," and this view has won some support. Other scholars, however, adhere to the traditional view that the important factor was that the woman was a citizen—i.e., wife, mother, or daughter of an Athenian citizen; see Cantarella 2005: 241 note 14, with references.

shall not be exiled as a killer on account of this." In law, therefore, Euphiletus' action in killing the adulterer would seem justified. Lysias' problem is that by this date (ca. 400), it was probably rare to kill an adulterer, and the act thus creates suspicion. We know nothing about the opponents' arguments except what we can infer from Euphiletus' speech. They have evidently claimed that Euphiletus had enticed his victim into the house with the intention of killing him (cf. 1.37) and that the adulterer had not finally been captured in bed but had succeeded in escaping to the hearth of the house (1.27), thereby throwing on Euphiletus the sacrilege of removing him by force. It is not clear that either of these claims would undermine the legal basis of Euphiletus' case, but the prosecution presumably expects the court to regard his action in such circumstances as an improper (and therefore unlawful) exercise of his statutory rights.

We have already noted that the speaker's name is Euphiletus: this information arises from a chance remark he reports in 1.15. Otherwise, nothing more is known about him than can be inferred from his speech, and one of the main attractions of the speech is the extraordinarily vivid picture of Euphiletus' domestic circumstances. He is evidently a farmer, living either in the city or in one of the surrounding villages (his neighbors are mentioned at 1.14, but cf. also 1.10n and 1.23n) and walking out to his fields (1.11, 1.20). The unexpectedness of his return from the countryside in 1.11 suggests that he has been spending some days there. Presumably this is what he does at peak agricultural seasons, and he will have a hut or a shed where he can sleep. It is unlikely that he has a second house: we hear of only one domestic slave, who helps Euphiletus (not his wife) with the shopping, takes her turn minding the baby, and is (as usual) sexually available to her master. Euphiletus' wife at first sight appears dominated by her husband, but she is nowhere blamed for the affair, and she is quite capable (at least, as Lysias represents her) of outwitting her husband in private conversation (1.12–13).

Euphiletus' victim Eratosthenes is named several times.[2] He cannot

---

[2] After naming Eratosthenes in the introduction, Lysias takes considerable care throughout the preliminary narrative to refer to him as "this man," etc., rather than by name. This may be designed to support the claim that Euphiletus knew nothing of the affair until the news was broken to him in 1.16.

be firmly identified, but the name is very rare in Athens. The only other classical Athenian known to us with the same name is the member of the Thirty Tyrants who is accused by Lysias in Speech 12 of having killed Lysias' brother Polemarchus. It has been suggested that the two are either the same Eratosthenes (in which case, of course, the dead man in Lysias 1 must previously have been acquitted of killing Polemarchus) or that they are closely related (Greek names tend to run in families). There are considerable problems with such an identification (most notably, why the connection with the Thirty is never mentioned),[3] but lingering hatred of the Thirty would provide a motive for Euphiletus' unparalleled action and would also suggest an attractive answer to one of the most puzzling problems behind this speech: how could a man like Euphiletus, from a one-slave family, afford to commission a speech from a (presumably expensive) orator like Lysias, unless Lysias had particular reasons for waiving his fees?

One of the most striking features of this speech is the absence of reference to events outside the domestic sphere. For this reason, it cannot be dated more narrowly than the broad confines of Lysias' career. However, the world that Lysias creates for us here, in what is perhaps his finest short speech, is extraordinarily vivid. There is some use of detailed legal argument, in particular that adultery is a more serious offense than rape (1.32–33).[4] For the most part, however, it is the narrative that dominates the speech, creating a version of the story that makes Euphiletus' behavior appear to be what the laws "order" (whereas in fact they merely "permit") and turning the case from a prosecution of Euphiletus for homicide into a prosecution of Eratosthenes by "the laws" for adultery.

I am not convinced by Usher's insistence (Edwards and Usher 1985) that Euphiletus is portrayed as a man whose response to adultery

---

[3] A possible explanation might be that to attack the Thirty would be to admit a motive and that Lysias is leaving the opposition with the opprobrium of bringing up this subject if they dare.

[4] The argument relies on selective quotation, because Lysias fails to mention that there were other laws available that allowed for less severe penalties against adulterers and that the law of *hybris* (which could result in a death sentence) may have been available against rape. (Both Harris [1990] and Carey [1995b] agree on this point, though differing on much else.)

adultery - brings shame on family & corrupt whos the dad.

would be anger. A modern pleader would tend to play this case as a crime of passion, but what is striking is the atmosphere of terrible calm in which Euphiletus represents himself not as outraged individual but as quasi-judicial representative of the city (this point is well made by Carey 1989: 62). See further Todd 2007.

LYSIAS I. ON THE DEATH OF ERATOSTHENES

[1] I should be very glad, gentlemen, if in this case you are the same sort of judges towards me as you would be towards yourselves, if you had suffered what I have. For I know full well that if you held the same opinions about others as you do about yourselves, there would not be a single one of you who would not be angry at what has happened; instead, you would all regard as trivial the penalties for those who do things like this. [2] Indeed, this verdict would be shared not only by you, but throughout Greece: this is the only crime for which both democracy and oligarchy give the same right of revenge to the powerless against the most powerful, so that the lowliest citizen has the same position as the greatest. Clearly therefore, gentlemen, everybody believes this is the most terrible outrage. [3] I am sure you all agree about the level of the penalty. Nobody rates the matter so lightly as to think that those responsible for such offenses ought to be pardoned or that they deserve only a trivial punishment. [4] As far as I can see, gentlemen, my job is to demonstrate the following: that Eratosthenes committed adultery with my wife; that he corrupted her, disgraced my children, and humiliated me by entering my house; that there was no prior hostility between us except for this; and that I did not do what I did for the sake of money, to become rich instead of poor, or for any other reward except for the vengeance permitted by law. [5] So I shall tell you everything I did from the beginning, leaving nothing out, but telling the truth. This in my opinion will be my only refuge, if I can tell you everything that happened.

[6] After I decided to get married, men of Athens, and brought my bride home, for a while my attitude was not to trouble her too much but not to let her do whatever she wanted either. I watched her as best I could and gave her the proper amount of attention. But from the moment my child was born, I began to have full confidence in her and placed everything in her hands, reckoning that this was the best rela-

sees self as defending law

tionship.[5] [7] In those early days, men of Athens, she was the best of women: a good housekeeper, thrifty, with a sharp eye on every detail. But my mother's death was the cause of all my troubles. [8] For it was while attending her funeral that my wife was seen by this fellow and eventually corrupted by him: he kept an eye out for the slave girl who did the shopping, put forward proposals, and seduced her.

[9] Now before continuing, gentlemen, I need to explain something. My house has two stories, and in the part with the women's rooms and the men's rooms, the upper floor is the same size as the floor below.[6] When our baby was born, his mother nursed him. To avoid her risking an accident coming down the stairs whenever he needed washing, I took over the upstairs rooms, and the women moved downstairs. [10] Eventually we became so used to this arrangement that my wife would often leave me to go down and sleep with the baby, so that she could nurse it and stop it crying. Things went on in this way for a long time, and I never had the slightest suspicion; indeed, I was so naive that I thought my wife was the most respectable woman in Athens.

[11] Some time later, gentlemen, I returned unexpectedly from the country. After dinner, the baby began to cry and was restless. (He was being deliberately teased by the slave girl, to make him do this, because the man was inside the house: I later found out everything.) [12] So I told my wife to go down and feed the baby, to stop it crying. At first she refused, as if glad to see me home after so long. When I became angry and ordered her to go, she said, "You just want to stay here and have a go at the slave girl. You had a grab at her once before when you were drunk." [13] I laughed at this, and she got up and left. She closed the door behind her, pretending to make a joke out of it, and bolted it.[7] I had no suspicions and thought no more of it, but gladly went to

---

[5] Or "reckoning that our relationship was as secure as it could be."

[6] Or perhaps, "the upper floor (i.e., the women's rooms) is the same size as the lower floor (i.e., the men's)."

[7] It is not linguistically clear whether this is a lock from which she can remove the key, or a bolt that remains on the outside of the door, and both are archaeologically attested. A bolt (unlike a key) would imply that she is concerned simply to prevent her husband getting at the slave girl, rather than the slave girl getting in.

innocence isn't the strongest position.

bed, since I had just returned from the country. [14] Towards morning, she came and unlocked the door. I asked her why the doors had creaked during the night, and she claimed that the baby's lamp had gone out, so she had to get it relit at our neighbors'. I believed this account and said no more. But I noticed, gentlemen, that she had put on makeup, even though her brother had died less than a month earlier. Even so, I did not say anything about it but left the house without replying.

[15] After this, gentlemen, there was an interval of some time, during which I remained completely unaware of my misfortunes. But then an old woman came up to me. She had been secretly sent, or so I later discovered, by a lady whom this fellow had seduced. This woman was angry and felt cheated, because he no longer visited her as before, so she watched until she found out why. [16] The old woman kept an eye out and approached me near my house. "Euphiletus," she said, "please do not think that I am being a busybody by making contact with you. The man who is humiliating you and your wife is an enemy of ours as well. Get hold of your slave girl, the one who does the shopping and waits on you, and torture her: you will discover everything. It is," she continued, "Eratosthenes of the deme Oe who is doing this. He has seduced not only your wife but many others as well. He makes a hobby[8] of it." [17] She said this, gentlemen, and left. At once I became alarmed. Everything came back into my mind, and I was filled with suspicion. I remembered how I had been locked in my room, and how that night both the door of the house and the courtyard door had creaked (which had never happened before), and how I had noticed that my wife had used makeup. All these things flashed into my mind, and I was full of suspicion. [18] I returned home and told the slave girl to come shopping with me,[9] but I took her to the house of one of my friends and told her that I had found out everything that was going on in my house. "So it is up to you," I said, "to choose the fate you prefer: either to be flogged and put out to work in the mill and never have any rest from such sufferings; or else to admit the whole truth and suffer no punishment but instead to be

---

[8] *Technē*, lit. "craft-skill," almost "profession."

[9] Lit. "to accompany me to the agora."

revenge

forgiven for your crimes. No lies now: I want the full truth." [19] At first she denied it and told me to do whatever I pleased, because she knew nothing. But when I mentioned the name Eratosthenes to her and declared that this was the man who was visiting my wife, she was astonished, believing that I knew everything. She immediately fell at my knees and made me promise she would suffer no harm. [20] She admitted,[10] first, how he had approached her after the funeral, and then how she had eventually acted as his messenger, and how my wife had in the end been won over, and the various ways he had entered the house, and how during the Thesmophoria,[11] when I was in the country, my wife had attended the shrine with his mother. She gave me a full and accurate account of everything else that had happened. [21] When she had finished, I said, "Make sure that nobody at all hears about this; otherwise, nothing in our agreement will be binding. I want you to show me them in the act. I don't want words; I want their actions to be clearly proved, if it is really true." She agreed to do this.

[22] After this there was an interval of four or five days, as I shall bring clear evidence to show.[12] But first, I want to tell you what happened on that last day. There is a man called Sostratus, who was a close friend of mine. I happened to meet him, at sunset, on his way back from the country. I knew that if he arrived at that time, he would find none of his friends at home, so I invited him to dine with me. We returned to my house, went upstairs, and had supper. [23] After he had had a good meal, he left, and I went to bed. Eratosthenes entered the house, gentlemen, and the slave girl woke me at once to say he was inside. I told her to take care of the door, and going downstairs, I went out silently. I called at the houses of various friends: some I discovered

---

[10] Lit. "accused," which has a slightly stronger flavor and prefigures the way in which Euphiletus constructs himself as the judge of Eratosthenes' case at 1.26.

[11] A women's festival in honor of Demeter, celebrated in the autumn. Men were excluded, and women camped out together for three days (as in Aristophanes' *Women at the Thesmophoria*).

[12] He does not in fact produce such evidence, nor is it obvious why he should wish to do so. Many scholars suspect that some words have dropped out of the text between "days" and "as."

were out, and others were not even in town. [24] I gathered as many as I could find at home and came back. We collected torches from the nearest shop and made our way in; the door was open, because it had been kept ready by the slave girl. We burst open the door of the bedroom, and those of us who were first to enter saw him still lying next to my wife. The others, who came later, saw him standing on the bed naked. [25] I struck him, gentlemen, and knocked him down. I twisted his arms behind him and tied them, and asked why he had committed this outrage against my house by entering it. He admitted his guilt, and begged and entreated me not to kill him but to accept compensation. [26] I replied, "It is not I who will kill you, but the law of the city. You have broken that law and have had less regard for it than for your own pleasure. You have preferred to commit this crime against my wife and my children rather than behaving responsibly and obeying the laws."

[27] So it was, gentlemen, that this man met the fate that the laws prescribe for those who behave like that. He was not snatched from the street, nor had he taken refuge at the hearth, as my opponents claim. How could he have done so? It was inside the bedroom that he was struck, and he immediately fell down, and I tied his hands. There were so many men in the house that he could not have escaped, and he did not have a knife or a club or any other weapon with which to repel those coming at him. [28] I am sure you realize, gentlemen, that men who commit crimes never admit that their enemies are telling the truth, but instead they themselves tell lies and use tricks to provoke their hearers to anger against the innocent. So, first of all, please read out the law.

[LAW]

[29] He did not dispute it, gentlemen. He admitted his guilt, he begged and pleaded not to be killed, and he was ready to pay money in compensation. But I did not accept his proposal. I reckoned that the law of the city should have greater authority; and I exacted from him the penalty that you yourselves, believing it to be just, have established for people who behave like that.

Will my witnesses to these facts please come forward.

[handwritten: didn't accept money, took law into own hands]

[WITNESSES]

[30] Read me this law also, the one from the inscribed stone on the Areopagus.[13]

[LAW]

[handwritten: accusations : he didn't kill him in the act]

You hear, gentlemen, how the court of the Areopagus itself (to which the ancestral right of judging homicide cases belongs, as has been reaffirmed in our own days) has expressly decreed that a man is not to be convicted of homicide if he captures an adulterer in bed with his wife and exacts this penalty from him. [31] Indeed, the lawgiver was so convinced that this is appropriate in the case of married women that he has established the same penalty in the case of concubines, who are less valuable. Clearly if he had had a more severe penalty available in the case of married women, he would have imposed it; but in fact he was unable to find a more powerful sanction than death to use in their case, so he decided the penalty should be the same as in the case of concubines. Read me this law as well.

[handwritten right margin: [Bottom] → street walkers ↓ Brothal escorts mistress [top]]

[LAW]

[handwritten: judge homocide. levels of prostitution]

[32] You hear, gentlemen: if anybody indecently assaults a free man or boy, he shall pay twice the damages; if he assaults a woman (in those categories where the death sentence is applicable), he shall be liable to the same penalty. Clearly therefore, gentlemen, the lawgiver believed that those who commit rape deserve a lighter penalty than those who seduce: he condemned seducers to death, but for rapists he laid down double damages. [33] He believed that those who act by violence are hated by the people they have assaulted, whereas those who seduce corrupt the minds of their victims in such a way that they make other people's wives into members of their own families rather than of their husbands'. The victim's whole household becomes the adulterer's, and as for the children, it is unclear whose they are, the husband's or the seducer's. Because of this, the lawgiver laid down the death penalty for them.[14]

---

[13] For the Areopagus, see the Introduction, VB. For the identification of the law cited here with the one quoted in Dem. 23.53, see the Speech Introduction.

[14] For the argument, see the Speech Introduction.

[handwritten: wife, girlfriend]

[handwritten: seduces = death. Rape = double / large fine. all about inheritance.]

[34] In my case, gentlemen, the laws have not only acquitted me of crime but have actually commanded me to exact this penalty. It is for you to decide whether the law is to be powerful or worthless. [35] In my opinion, every city enacts its laws in order that when we are uncertain in a situation, we can go to them to see what to do, and in such cases the law commands the victims to exact this penalty. [36] So I ask you now to reach the same verdict as the law does. If not, you will be giving adulterers such immunity that you will encourage burglars to call themselves adulterers too. They will realize that if they describe adultery as their object and claim that they have entered somebody else's house for this purpose, nobody will dare touch them. Everyone will know that we must say good-bye to the laws on adultery and take notice only of your verdict—which is the sovereign authority over all the city's affairs.

[37] Please consider, gentlemen: my opponents accuse me of having ordered my slave girl on the day in question to fetch the young man. In my view, gentlemen, I should have been acting within my rights in capturing in any way possible the man who had corrupted my wife. [38] Admittedly, if I had sent her to fetch him when words alone had been spoken but no act had been committed, then I would have been acting unlawfully; but if I had captured him, whatever my methods, when he had already done everything and had repeatedly entered my house, then I would regard myself as acting properly. [39] But consider how they are lying about this as well, as you can see easily from the following argument. As I told you before, gentlemen, Sostratus is a close friend of mine. He met me around sunset on his way home from the country, he had dinner with me, and when he had eaten well, he left. [40] But just think for a moment, gentlemen. If I had been laying a trap that night for Eratosthenes, would it not have been better for me to dine somewhere else myself, instead of bringing him back home for dinner and so making the adulterer less likely to risk entering my house? And secondly, does it seem plausible to you that I would send away the man who had had dinner with me, and remain behind alone and unaccompanied, instead of asking him to stay and help me punish the adulterer? [41] Then again, gentlemen, do you not think I would have sent messages during the day to my acquaintances, asking them to meet at a friend's house—whichever

ideal argucment made that he was
setting a trap.
wasnt premedicated. ON THE DEATH OF ERATOSTHENES 85

was nearest—rather than running around during the night the moment I heard the news, not knowing who I would find at home and who would be out? In fact I called on Harmodius and on another man, who were out of town (I had no reason to expect this), and I found out that others were not at home; but I went around and gathered everybody I could. [42] And yet if I had planned it all in advance, do you not think I would have gathered some slaves together and warned my friends: then I could have entered the bedroom with complete safety (how was I to know whether he too might be armed?) and could have exacted the penalty with the maximum number of witnesses? But in fact I knew nothing of what was going to happen that night, so I took with me those I could find.

My witnesses to these facts will please come forward.

[WITNESSES]

[43] You have heard the witnesses, gentlemen. Examine the affair in your own minds as follows. Ask yourselves if there had ever been any enmity between Eratosthenes and myself except for this. You will not find any. [44] He had not maliciously brought a public prosecution against me, he had not tried to expel me from the city, he had not brought a private prosecution, and he did not know of any offense of mine that I would kill him for, out of fear that it would become public knowledge. And if I had succeeded, I had no hope of receiving any money (some people do admittedly plot the deaths of others for this purpose). [45] So far from there being any dispute or drunken brawl or other disagreement between us, I had never even seen the man before that night. What was I hoping for, then, by running so great a risk—if I had not in reality suffered the most terrible of injuries at his hands? [46] And why did I commit this impious act after summoning witnesses, given that if I had wanted to make away with him illegally, I could have prevented them all from knowing about it?

[47] So, gentlemen, I do not accept that this penalty was exacted privately on my own behalf. Instead, it was for the sake of the whole city. If men who commit this sort of offense see the rewards that await such crimes, they will be less eager to commit them against other people—provided they see you holding fast to the same opinion. [48] Otherwise, it would be much better to erase the existing laws and

why do you not torture the slave girl.
↳ counter argucment.

enact others, which would impose penalties on men who guard their own wives, and grant total impunity to those who commit offenses against married women. [49] It would be far more just to do this than to let citizens be trapped by the laws: for the laws instruct the man who catches an adulterer to treat him in any way he pleases, whereas the court turns out to be far more dangerous to the victims than to the men who break the law and dishonor other people's wives. [50] For I am now on trial for my life, my property, and everything else—simply because I obeyed the laws of the city.

why does he kill him.
   protect his pride & masculinity.

laws on homicide.
   can hurt/kill him without knife

if go court and find guilty.
   → humiliate the indiv

wife. if kill someone due adultery must
   divorce wife.

divorce- dowry. doesn't spoil reputation
divorce was amicable in that time.

DEMOSTHENES 54. AGAINST CONON

[handwritten annotation:] defendant
battery aikeia
referred to as hybris.

INTRODUCTION

From antiquity until the present day, *Against Conon* has been one of the favorite speeches of the Demosthenic corpus. Moderns are amused by its vivid portrayal of drunken brawling in an army camp and in the streets of Athens itself, as well as the other forms of shocking behavior the speaker describes. There is, moreover, much interest in the speaker's discussion of the choices available to a man contemplating a lawsuit and his account of an arbitration hearing.

If we are to believe Ariston, the speaker, there was no enmity between himself and Conon until he had the bad luck to find himself bivouacked near Conon's sons, who for no good reason directed what we can term frank anal aggression against Ariston's slaves. The hostilities continued and escalated when Ariston returned from military duty. This time (so we are told) Conon, the defendant, not only actively participated in the abuse but took the lead. The actual charge is battery (*aikeia*), but Ariston repeatedly refers to *hybris*. The Athenian law of *hybris* has generated much debate in the recent past. The word itself is difficult to pin down but seems to designate both a state of mind combining overconfidence and arrogance, and conduct (often but not necessarily violent) either designed to humiliate others or showing reckless contempt for the rights and status of others.[1] As an offense under the laws, *hybris* overlaps with crimes of violence (assault, rape), but scholars are not agreed on the degree to which the law

---

[1] The matter is highly controversial; see Fisher 1992. For *hybris* as an undefined term, see Dem. 21.47. For a short discussion of Athenian legal terminology, see Todd 1993: 61–62.

speaker is prosecuting

might be applied to nonviolent conduct. In Aeschines 1.15, Aeschines argues that hiring a free boy for sex is *hybris,* but the addition of "I imagine" (*pou*) betrays an attempt at persuasive definition.

Neither the date of the events Ariston describes nor the date of the trial can be confidently ascertained.

DEMOSTHENES 54. AGAINST CONON

[1] I was assaulted,[2] gentlemen of the jury, and at the hands of Conon, the man here, I suffered injuries so severe that for a very long time neither my family nor any of the doctors expected I would survive. But when I unexpectedly recovered and was out of danger, I initiated this private case for battery (*dikē aikeias*) against him. All the friends and relatives whom I asked for advice said that for his deeds Conon was liable to summary arrest (*apagōgē*) as a cloak stealer[3] and to public suits for *hybris* (*graphai hybreōs*). But they advised me and urged me not to involve myself in greater troubles than I could handle; and also, not to be seen to complain more than a young man should about what was done to me. I have acted accordingly and, because of those advisers, have instituted a private case, but I would, with the greatest pleasure, men of Athens, have put him on trial on a capital charge. [2] You will all forgive this feeling, I'm sure, when you hear what I suffered. You see, shocking as the assault was, his brutality afterward was no less terrible. I say it is right, and I ask you all without distinction, first, to listen sympathetically to my account of what I suffered, and second, if it seems that I have been wronged and treated illegally, to help me—as is just. I will tell you from the beginning how each of the events happened, in as few words as I can.

[3] Two years ago I went out to Panactum when we were assigned guard duty there. The sons of this man Conon pitched their tent near us—I wished they hadn't. You see, that is where the hatred and the clashes between us first began: you will hear what it started from. These men regularly spent the day drinking, starting right off at their

---

[2] Lit. "subjected to *hybris*." See the Speech Introduction.

[3] This would have been understood as a crime committed not to acquire a valuable object but to humiliate the victim; see above, Ant. 2.1.4n.

first meal, and they went on doing this for as long as we were on guard duty. We, on the other hand, behaved while away from the city just as we are accustomed to do when here. [4] When the others had their dinner, these men were already drunk and abusive, mostly to the slaves who were attending us, but finally to us ourselves. You see, using the excuse that while they were cooking, our slaves were aiming the camp-fire smoke in their direction, or that every word our slaves spoke to them was an insult, these men beat them, emptied out their latrine buckets on them, urinated on them, and indulged in every sort of brutal and outrageous behavior. When we saw this, it bothered us, and at first we objected, but when they mocked us and would not stop, we reported the matter to the general—all of us messmates going to him as a group, not I apart from the others. [5] He rebuked them and reprimanded them not only for treating us roughly but also for their general conduct in the camp. But far from stopping or feeling shame, as soon as it got dark that very evening, they burst in on us. They started with verbal abuse but ended up actually hitting me; and they raised such yelling and uproar at the tent that both the general and the tribal detachment leaders (*taxiarchai*) came and also some of the other soldiers; they kept us from suffering irreparable injury or doing the same in retaliation when attacked by these drunkards. [6] The business came to such a point that when we returned to Athens, we naturally felt anger and hatred for one another over what had happened. But by the gods, I really did not think that I should bring a suit against them nor take any account of what happened, but instead, I simply resolved to take precautions in the future and to guard against getting near men like this. So first I want to present witnesses to the events I have mentioned and after that to explain what I suffered at this man's hands, so that you know that the man who ought to have condemned the first wrongdoings, this very man, was the first to commit crimes much more shocking.

[DEPOSITIONS]

[7] These are the events I thought I should ignore, but not long after, while I was taking a stroll, as was my custom, in the evening in the agora with Phanostratus of the deme Cephisia, a man of my own age, Conon's son Ctesias came by, drunk, along by the Leocorion, near

Pythodorus' shops.[4] He saw us, yelled out, and said something to himself, as a drunk will do, so you can't understand what he's saying, and then went up toward Melite.[5] There they were drinking, as we later learned, at the shop of Pamphilus the fuller: Conon here, a fellow named Theotimus, Archebiades, Spintharus the son of Eubulus,[6] Theogenes the son of Andromenes, and many fellows whom Ctesias incited as he made his way into the agora. [8] It happened that we encountered these men as we were turning away from the temple of Persephone[7] and were walking back, just about at the Leocorion. In the mêlée, one of them, a man I didn't know, rushed Phanostratus and pinned him down, and Conon here and his son and the son of Andromenes fell on me. First they pulled off my cloak, then tripped me and threw me down in the mud, jumped on me and hit me so hard they split my lip and made my eyes swell shut. They left me in such a state that I could not get up or speak. And as I lay there, I heard them saying many shocking things. [9] Generally it was filthy stuff, and I hesitate to repeat some of it before you, but I will tell you something that is evidence of Conon's insolence and indicates that the whole business came about at his instigation. You see, he sang out, imitating victorious fighting cocks, and his cronies urged him to flap his elbows against his sides, like wings. Afterward, passersby took me home, naked,[8] and these men went off with my cloak. When I got to my door, my mother and the serving women cried and shrieked and only with difficulty got me into a bath, washed me off all around, and showed me to the doctors. I will present witnesses of these events to show that I am telling the truth.

[WITNESSES]

[10] Now it happened, gentlemen of the jury, that Euxitheus of the deme Cholleidae, this man here, a relative of mine, together with

---

[4] The topography of this stroll is uncertain.

[5] The deme southwest of the agora, taking in the Areopagus and the Pnyx.

[6] In all likelihood, Spintharus' father is the prominent politician.

[7] Probably to the west of the agora, towards the Acropolis.

[8] Not literally; the speaker probably means that he was left wearing only his tunic.

Meidias,[9] met me on their way back from dinner somewhere. I was already near my house, and they accompanied me as I was carried to the bath and were present there when people were bringing in a doctor. I was in such poor condition that to spare me being carried a long way to my house from the bath, those who were present decided to take me to Meidias' house for the night, and so they did. [*To the clerk*] Take their depositions too, so you will learn that many men know how I was abused by these men.

[DEPOSITIONS]

[*To the clerk*] Also take the doctor's deposition.

[DEPOSITION]

[11] My condition then as the immediate consequence of the blows and abuse I suffered was as you hear, and all those who saw it right after have given you their testimony. Afterwards the doctor said he was not too worried by the swellings on my face and my cuts, but continuous fever followed and pains, terrible pains throughout my body, but especially in my sides and belly, and I lost my appetite. [12] And as the doctor said, if I hadn't spontaneously lost a great deal of blood—I was already suffering intense pain and in despair—I would have died from an abscess. But this loss of blood saved me. [*To the clerk*] Read out the depositions of the doctor and my visitors to show that what I say is true, that my illness, a result of the blows I suffered at their hands, was so severe that I nearly died.

[DEPOSITIONS]

[13] I think it has become clear in many ways that the blows I suffered were not ordinary or insignificant, but that I was in extreme danger because of abuse and brutality of these men, and I have instituted a suit far less severe than appropriate. But I suppose that some of you are wondering what Conon will possibly dare say in answer to this. I want to tell you in advance that I have learned he is prepared to turn the issue away from the assault and the deeds that were done and try to reduce it to laughter and ridicule. [14] He will say that there are

---

[9]Not the defendant in Dem. 21.

many men in the city, sons of gentlemen (*kaloi kagathoi*), who play around as young men will, giving themselves nicknames; some they call "*ithyphalloi*," others "*autolēkythoi*,"[10] and some of them are in love with *hetairai*[11] and in point of fact his own son is one of them, and he is often getting into fights over a *hetaira*. And that's the way of young men. And Conon will paint me and all my brothers as violent drunks but also as hardhearted and sour. [15] Gentlemen of the jury, though I feel resentful about what I have been put through, I would be just as indignant and would consider myself as no less abused, if I may say so, if this man Conon comes across as telling the truth about us, and there is an ignorance so deep among you that whatever character someone claims for himself, or whatever a neighbor charges him with, you will believe him to be as described, and no benefit whatsoever comes to decent people from their daily lifestyle and practices. [16] You see, we have never been seen by anybody engaging in drunken behavior or treating people insultingly, and we think we are doing nothing hardhearted if we think it is right, for wrongs done to us, to seek justice in conformity with the laws. To this man's sons we concede the titles "*ithyphalloi*" and "*autolēkythoi*," and I pray to the gods that this business and all activities like it recoil on Conon and his sons. [17] You see, these are the men who initiate each other with the *ithyphallos* and do things of the sort that decent people are very embarrassed even to mention, let alone do.

But what does this have to do with me? I for one, am amazed if any excuse or pretext has been found in your court that would allow someone who is proven to have assaulted and beaten another to escape

---

[10] Neither of these compound words bears an entirely transparent meaning. The straightforward sense of the first is "with erections," but it is very likely that the word was chosen for its association with various cults known to have been celebrated with raucous obscenity. The second element of the second word is "oil flask," but the force of the first element is less clear. Some scholars believe the word suggests "carrying one's own oil flask," i.e., impersonating a poor man and therefore not having a slave in attendance to carry the vessel and witness his owner's disreputable behavior; others believe that this word too carries a phallic connotation.

[11] Expensive and relatively elegant prostitutes; see further Aes. 1.42n.

laws against slander
prevent people from actual
fighting   AGAINST CONON 93

paying the penalty. To the contrary, to prevent escalating violence, the laws have anticipated pleas based on necessity.[12] For example—you see, because of this man I have been forced to do research and learn about these things—there are private suits for slander (*dikai kakēgorias*). [18] People say that these suits come about for this reason, that men who verbally abuse each other will not be incited to physical violence. Also, there are suits for battery (*aikeia*), and I hear that they serve this purpose, that a man who is getting the worst of it won't defend himself with a stone or anything else of that type but instead will wait for the legal process. Also, there are public suits for wounding (*graphai traumatos*) to prevent homicides when men are wounded. [19] In my view, there is provision for the least important of these acts, verbal abuse, to avoid the final and worst, homicide, from happening and to prevent the escalation by small steps from verbal abuse to blows, from blows to wounds, and from wounds to death; instead, the laws provide a legal action for each of these, instead of letting these actions be decided by the individual's anger or desire.   ②   *men homosexuality*

[20] That is how it is in the laws, but if Conon says, "We are a group of fellows called the '*ithyphalloi* club,' and when we have love affairs, we punch and we throttle whomever we want," then are you really going to laugh and let him go? I don't *think* so! None of you would have laughed if you happened to be there when I was being dragged around, stripped, and abused. I left my home in one piece and came back on a stretcher, and my mother rushed out when she saw me, and in the house the women were shrieking and crying so much, as if someone had died, that some of the neighbors sent people to us to ask what had happened. [21] In general, it is the right thing, gentlemen of the jury, that in your court there be no such excuse or impunity available for anybody that would make it possible for him to engage in abuse. Now, if someone *is* to have such excuse or immunity, it is right that those men who do something because of their youth win indulgence of that sort, but even for them, the indulgence should not mean escaping the penalty but that they pay a penalty milder than the expected one. [22] But when a man over fifty is in the

---

[12] A "plea of necessity" might take the form, "Since X insulted me, I *had* to retaliate."

when men have sex one needs be submissive
not like this older man fancying a younger.
If you get paid be submissive could loose
citizenship.

company of younger men, especially his sons, and not only does not divert them or stop them but in fact is himself their leader, initiates their action and is the most repulsive of them, what penalty might he pay that would match his acts? For my part, I don't think even death would be sufficient. For in fact, if Conon had committed none of these acts, but merely stood by while his son Ctesias did the same things as he blatantly has done, he would deserve your hatred. [23] For if he trained his sons in such a fashion that they commit offenses in his presence—some of which are punishable by death—without fear or shame, what punishment do you think would be unreasonable for him to suffer? I think this is evidence that Conon had no respect for his own father, since if he had honored and feared *him,* he would have demanded the same from his own sons.

[24] [*To the clerk*] Please take the laws, both the one on assault (*hybris*) and the one on clothes-stealers. You will see that these men are in fact liable under both. Read them out.

[LAWS]

For his deeds, this man Conon is liable under both these laws, since he committed assault and stole a cloak. If we chose not to punish him by reference to these laws, we would rightly be seen as respectable people minding our own business, but he is evil all the same. [25] And if something had happened to me,[13] he could have been charged with homicide and the most severe consequences. The father of the priestess at Brauron,[14] at any rate, was sent into exile by the Areopagus, and rightly so, for inciting a crime though it was admitted that he had not touched the dead man—because he encouraged the assailant to strike him.[15] You see, if those who are present, instead of preventing men who have set their hand to committing a crime, whether in drunkenness or anger or for some other cause, encourage them, there would be

---

[13] A euphemism for "if I had died."

[14] Brauron, a town east of Athens, was the center of a cult of Artemis.

[15] The precise charge against the priestess' father is unclear. Some scholars have thought it was *bouleusis* ("planning") of intentional homicide; others, that it was intentional wounding. Gagarin (1990) argues that *bouleusis* was not a technical legal term for planning a homicide and that the charge was simply for homicide (*phonou*).

no hope of survival for someone who fell in with brutal men, but they would have license to go on with their assault until they got tired. And that is just what happened to me.

[26] I want to tell you what they did during the arbitration meeting,[16] since from that you will observe their brutality. You see, they stretched things out past midnight, refusing to read out their depositions or to provide copies, just bringing out witnesses, one by one, to the stone,[17] putting them under oath and writing out irrelevant depositions—the boy was Conon's son by a *hetaira* and this and that had happened to him—things that, by the gods, gentlemen of the jury, everyone present criticized and found disgusting, and in the end they disgusted themselves. [27] Anyway, when they finally had enough of that business and let it go, for the sake of delay and to prevent the document holders from being sealed,[18] they issued me a challenge, stating their willingness to hand over slaves whose names they wrote down to testify about my wounds.[19] And I suppose that the majority of their arguments will center on this. But I think you should all consider this point, that if these men had issued the challenge to have the interrogation under torture actually take place, and if they had put trust in this means of proof, they would not have issued the challenge at night when the arbitrator's decision was already being announced and they had no excuse left. [28] Instead, they would have done so from the first, before bringing the suit, when I was lying wounded, not knowing whether I would survive, and I was declaring to all who came to visit that Conon was the first to strike me and had inflicted most of the abuse I suffered. He would have come to my house right away with many witnesses, and on the spot he would have offered to hand over his slaves and would have called in some members of the Areopagus. I say Areopagus, since if I had died, the trial would have taken place in that court. [29] If perhaps he was ignorant of this, and so did not

---

[16] For public arbitration in private suits, see the Introduction, VB, and *Ath. Pol.* 53.

[17] A stone marked the spot where the arbitration was conducted. See *Ath. Pol.* 55.5.

[18] The documents were sealed in jars; see the Introduction, VB. The jars could not be sealed in this case until the new challenge could be included.

[19] On slave testimony, see above, Ant. 1.6n.

prepare for such a great danger, although he had this means of proof available, as he will now say he did, then at least as soon as I got up from my sickbed and summoned him, at the beginning of the arbitration, he would have openly offered the slaves: but he did not take any of these steps. To show that I am telling the truth and that his challenge was issued as a delaying tactic, [*To the clerk*] read out this deposition, since it will be clear from this.

[DEPOSITION]

conon calls in his fellow buddies who will lie to protect a friend

[30] So on the subject of the interrogation under torture, remember this, what time it was that he issued the challenge, his motive for doing it—to stall for time—the first opportunities he had to issue the challenge, when he clearly did not want to use this means of proof, as he neither proposed the challenge nor demanded an interrogation. But since he was proven at the arbitration to have done all the same things he is now proved to have done, and he was clearly shown to be liable to all the charges against him, [31] he throws in a false deposition and has inscribed in it as witnesses the names of men whom I suppose you too will recognize if you hear them: "Diotimus son of Diotimus of the deme Icaria, Archebiades son of Demoteles of the deme Halae, Chairetius son of Chairimenes of the deme Pithus testify that while returning from dinner along with Conon, in the agora they came across Ariston and Conon's son fighting, and Conon did not hit Ariston"—[32] as if you will immediately believe them and not take account of the truth, first, that Lysistratus, Paseas, Niceratus, and Diodorus, who have explicitly testified that they saw me being struck by Conon, having my cloak ripped off, and all the other abusive acts that I suffered, are men who did not know me and were present only by chance; that they would not have been willing to perjure themselves, unless they saw me suffering those insults. Further, if he had not treated me in this way, I myself would never have let off those who are acknowledged by these men themselves to have beaten me and would never have chosen to prosecute first a man who did not even touch me. [33] Why would I have done that? No, the man who struck me first and dealt me the worst abuse, he is the one I am suing, and whom I detest, and whom I am prosecuting. And everything I am saying is true and plainly so. But if Conon had not offered these wit-

nesses, he certainly would have had no argument but would have been convicted on the spot, without saying a word. But as this man's drinking companions, men who shared in many acts of that sort, they naturally gave false testimony. If things are to be like this, if some people lose all shame and dare to give blatantly false testimony, and there is no advantage in telling the truth, then it will be a most shocking state of affairs. [34] But no, by Zeus, they're not like men of that sort! But many of you, I think, know Diotimus and Archebiades and Chairetius, this man here who's turning gray, men who during the day wear sullen expressions and say that they follow Spartan fashion and wear light cloaks and thin sandals, but when they get together and enjoy each other's company, they indulge in everything foul and disgusting. [35] And this is their sparkling, young man's talk: "What, we're not going to testify for each other? Isn't that what pals and friends do? Really, what terrible charge will Ariston bring against you? Do some people say they saw him being beaten? We'll testify that he wasn't even touched. His cloak was pulled off? We'll say that others did this first. His lip was stitched? We'll say that your head or some other part of you was broken." [36] But I am presenting doctors too as witnesses. Gentlemen of the jury, this is evidence these men do not have. Aside from what they produce themselves, they have no witness to bring against us. By the gods, I could not tell you how ready they are to do anything at all. But so you know what sorts of acts they go around doing, [*To the clerk*] read them these depositions here, and [*to the man in charge of the water clock*] you, stop the water.

[DEPOSITIONS]

[37] Do you suppose that men who break into houses and who beat people they encounter would hesitate to give false testimony for each other on a scrap of paper, these partners in viciousness, wickedness, shamelessness, and brutality so foul and extreme? You see, I think all that is part of their actions. Yet there are other things they have done, even worse than that, though we would not be able to find all their victims. [38] I think it better to tell you in advance about the most shameless thing that, I hear, he is going to do. People say that he will gather his children around him and swear on their heads and will call down certain dreadful, cruel curses, so awful that the man who heard

them and reported them to us was amazed. Gentlemen of the jury, these acts of daring are impossible to resist, since I suppose that the best men who are least likely to lie themselves are most susceptible to being fooled by men of this character. But you must believe what you see of their lifestyle. [39] I will tell you of Conon's contemptuous attitude towards things like this. You see, I have been forced to learn about it. I hear, gentlemen of the jury, that a certain Bacchius, who was executed by your court, and Aristocrates, the man with the bad eyes, and others of this sort, and Conon, the man here, were friends as young men and had the nickname "Triballoi."[20] These men would regularly gather offerings to Hecate[21] and also pig testicles, the ones used for purification when there is going to be a public meeting, and dine on them every time they got together, and they swore oaths and perjured themselves as casually as can be. [40] Conon, a man of this sort, is certainly not to be believed when he takes an oath, far from it. Rather, the man who of his own free will makes no oath, not even an honest oath, and would not even dream of swearing an oath on his children's heads, which is not sanctioned by your custom, but would suffer anything rather than do that—if an oath is in fact necessary—he is more to be believed than a man who swears by his children, even going through fire.[22] Thus, Conon, I, a man who in every respect would more properly be trusted than you, was willing to swear these oaths; and my purpose would not be like yours, to avoid punishment for my crimes, all along committing any act whatever; rather, I would do it for the sake of the truth and so as not to suffer further abuse, with the aim of not losing my case because of Conon's perjury. [*To the clerk*] Read out my challenge.

[CHALLENGE]

[41] That is what I was willing to swear to then, and now too I swear by all the gods and all the goddesses, for your sake, gentlemen

---

[20] The name was taken from a Thracian tribe that in the Athenian view was uncivilized and belligerent in the extreme.

[21] A goddess associated primarily with magic.

[22] The text and precise meaning of this phrase are uncertain. It might refer to the ritual of burning victims as part of the oath taking, or it might be a metaphorical expression indicating willingness to endure any consequences.

of the jury, and the sake of the spectators,[23] that I did suffer at Conon's hands the insults of which I accuse him. I was dealt those blows, and my lip was split so badly that it needed to be stitched, and for this abuse I am suing him. And if I am swearing honestly, may I reap many benefits, and may I never suffer such a thing ever again, but if I am perjuring myself, may I myself be completely ruined, as well as anything I possess or will possess. But I am *not* perjuring myself, not even if Conon explodes with indignation. [42] So I ask you, gentlemen of the jury, since I have explained all my legitimate claims and have added an oath to them, that just as each of you, if you are injured, would hate your assailant, that you feel the same anger at this man Conon for my sake; and I ask you not to regard any affair of this sort as a private matter, even if it should happen to another man, but no matter who the victim is, to help him and give him justice and hate those men who before they are accused are brash and reckless but at their trial are wicked, have no shame, and give no thought to opinion or custom or anything else, except for escaping punishment. [43] But Conon will beg and wail. Do consider who is more to be pitied, the man who suffers the sort of things I have suffered at his hands if I leave the courtroom with an added insult and do not attain justice, or Conon, if he is punished? Is it to your individual advantage that it be permitted to hit and commit assault or not? I, for my part, think not. Well, if you acquit Conon, there will be many men like that; if you punish him, fewer.

[44] There is much I could say, gentlemen of the jury, about how we have been useful to the city, I and my father, as long as he was alive, serving as trierarchs[24] and as soldiers and doing what was assigned, and useful as neither Conon nor his sons have been. But there isn't enough time, and the argument isn't about these matters. You know, if it happened that we were, admittedly, more useless than these men and more evil, we should not on that account be beaten or insulted. I don't know what more I should tell you, since I think you understand everything that has been said.

---

[23] Bystanders seem to have been common at Athenian trials and important to the process: see Lanni 1997.

[24] The trierarchy was an important and expensive public service (Introduction, IVC).

LYSIAS 3. AGAINST SIMON

wounding with premeditation

INTRODUCTION

Lysias 3 concerns a case of "wounding with premeditation (*pronoia*)," which apparently meant with the intention of killing, or what we might call attempted murder. This offense at Athens was subject to the same special procedural rules as murder itself (for which see the Introduction to Ant. 5). It is not clear on what substantive basis (if any) premeditated wounding was differentiated from simple assault, but there is a hint at 3.28 that possessing a weapon could be represented as a significant criterion.

Lysias 3 concerns a quarrel and a series of fights arising out of disputed possession of a live-in rent boy. The latter's name is Theodotus, and he is described as a young man (*meirakion*) from Plataea.[1] The significance of his status as a Plataean is disputed. Plataea had been an ally of Athens and had offered unique military assistance at the battle of Marathon in 490 BC. When Plataea was destroyed by Thebes in 427 (it was not rebuilt until 386), the Plataeans were offered the special privilege of Athenian citizenship if they chose to register for it.[2] It seems unlikely, however, that Theodotus' family was registered as Athenian citizens, not least because the speaker envisages the possibility of his having to give evidence under torture (3.33), which was never applied to citizens. It is possible that Theodotus was a Plataean slave, but on the other hand he is assumed to be capable independently of entering into an agreement to provide sexual services (3.22–26). More

---

[1] The word *meirakion* denotes a male in his late teens.

[2] The continuing existence of Plataean émigré community, and the status of its *bona fide* members as Athenian citizens, forms the background to Lys. 23 (below).

on the border · Athens

probable is the suggestion that he was part of a[...] of free Plataeans who had not bothered to register [...] status was indeterminate.

Nothing is known about the parties to the dispute, apart fro[...] can be gleaned from the speech. The speaker is the defendant. He d[...] not give his name, but the claim that he has performed many liturgies (Introduction, IVC) implies that he is wealthy (3.47), and his hints about jealousy (3.9) suggest that he is portraying himself as a politically active member of the elite. This may, however, be an exaggeration, because part of his tactic throughout the speech is to simulate embarrassment by portraying himself as too respectable and too old to have wanted to make the matter public by initiating litigation—despite the fact that (according to his own version of events) injuries had been suffered on all sides, and the real provocation had come from his opponent. We have only the speaker's side of the story, but reading between the lines, we may suspect that there was more provocation from the speaker than he claims: for instance, when he placed Theodotus at the house of Lysimachus (3.10), which, as he promptly admits, was close to the house that Simon had rented (3.11).

Simon, the prosecutor, is represented as a much poorer man, but there are hints that he is lying about his wealth (3.21–26). It is continuously implied that Simon has overstated the seriousness of his injuries, and there is a comic flavor in the speaker's account of the fighting at 3.15–18. Simon is also repeatedly characterized as violent and lawless, notably in the one anecdote in the speech that can be dated (3.45): the expedition to Corinth and the battle of Coronea took place in 394 BC, and so the speech must be some time (but we do not know how long) after that date.

Useful recent books that deal with aspects of violence at Athens are Fisher 1992; D. Cohen 1995; and Herman 2006. On the details of the speech, see further Todd 2007.

LYSIAS 3. AGAINST SIMON

[1] I already knew many disreputable things about Simon, members of the Council,[3] but I did not expect him to reach such a level of audacity that he would bring a prosecution, pretending to be the vic-

---

[3] The Council of the Areopagus.

eserves to be punished, and that
...earing such a great and serious
...ng to decide my case, I would be
...now that carefully prepared tricks
...oduce wholly unexpected outcomes
...am appearing before you, I remain
...tice. [3] I am particularly upset, mem-
...rced to speak about matters like this in
...nistreatment, because I was ashamed at
...e knowing all about me. But Simon has
pu...   ...that I shall tell you the full story without
hiding any...   ...ave done anything wrong, members of the
Council, I do not exp... ...any mercy, but if I can show that I am not
guilty of any of the charges that Simon has stated on oath, even though
it is obvious that I have behaved rather foolishly towards the young
man, given my age, I shall ask you to think no worse of me. You know
that desire affects everybody and that the most honorable and
restrained man is the one who can bear his troubles most discreetly. In
my case Simon here has prevented all this, as I shall show you.

[5] We were both attracted, members of the Council, to Theodotus,
a young man from Plataea. I expected to win him over by treating him
well, but Simon thought that by behaving arrogantly and lawlessly he
would force him to do what he wanted. It would be a lengthy task to
list all the wrongs that Theodotus suffered at his hands, but I think you
should hear the offenses he committed against me personally. [6] He
found out that the young man was staying with me, and came to my
house drunk one night. He knocked down the doors and made his way
into the women's rooms, where my sister and my nieces were—women
who have been brought up so respectably that they are ashamed to be
seen even by relatives. [7] Simon, however, reached such a level of
arrogance (*hybris*) that he refused to leave, until the men who were
present, together with those who had accompanied him, realized that
by entering the rooms of young orphaned girls he was behaving unac-
ceptably, and threw him out by force. Far from apologizing for this
outrageous conduct, he found out where I was having dinner and did
something that was extraordinary and (unless you know his criminal

---

[4] The *diōmosia* (the special oath in homicide cases).

insanity) unbelievable. [8] He called me out of the house, and as soon as I came out, he immediately tried to hit me. I defended myself, so he moved off and threw stones at me. He missed me but hit his own companion Aristocritus with a stone, injuring his forehead. [9] For my part, members of the Council, I felt this was appalling treatment, but as I said earlier, I was embarrassed by the experience and decided to put up with it. I preferred not to bring legal action over these offenses, rather than appear foolish to my fellow-citizens. I knew that the affair would be seen as typical for a criminal like him but that my misfortunes would be laughed at by many of those who are always jealous of anybody who tries to play a responsible role in the city. [10] I was so unsure how to react to his lawlessness, members of the Council, that I decided it would be best to leave Athens. So I took the young man—you need to know the whole truth—and left the city. When I thought that enough time had passed for Simon to forget him and to be sorry for his earlier offenses, I returned. [11] I went to live in Piraeus,[5] but my opponent immediately heard that Theodotus had returned and was staying with Lysimachus, who lived close to the house he himself had rented. He called on some of his friends to help him. They began eating and drinking, and set a lookout on the roof, so that they could seize the young man when he came out. [12] It was at this moment that I arrived from Piraeus, and since I was passing, I called at Lysimachus' house. After a little while we came out. These men, who were by now drunk, jumped on us. Some of those present refused to join this attack, but Simon here, together with Theophilus, Protarchus, and Autocles, began dragging the young man off. But he threw off his cloak and ran away. [13] I reckoned he would escape, and they would be embarrassed and give up the chase as soon as they met anybody, so I went away by a different route. You see how carefully I tried to avoid them, since I thought everything they did was trouble for myself. [14] So where Simon claims the battle occurred, nobody on either side had his head broken or suffered any other injury. I will produce those who were present as witnesses for you.

---

[5] The timing and purpose of this visit are left vague, perhaps deliberately. Theodotus remains at the house of Lysimachus, which is evidently in Athens itself, and it is striking that this just happens to be close to where Simon is living (see the Speech Introduction).

chance? Really unlikely and not plausable.

[WITNESSES]

[15] Those who were present, members of the Council, have testified that he was the one who intentionally attacked me, not the other way around. After this, the young man ran into a fuller's shop, but they charged in and started to drag him off by force. He began yelling and shouting and calling out for witnesses. [16] Many people rushed up, angry at what was happening, and said that it was disgraceful behavior. My opponents ignored what they said but beat up Molon the fuller and several others who tried to protect Theodotus. [17] I was walking along by myself when I happened to meet them in front of Lampon's house. I thought it would be a terrible disgrace just to watch this lawless and violent assault on the young man, so I grabbed him. I asked why they were acting so illegally towards him, and they refused to answer. Instead, they let go of the young man and started hitting me. [18] A fight developed, members of the Council. The young man was throwing things at them and defending himself. They were throwing things at us and were still hitting him, because they were drunk. I was defending myself, and the passersby were all helping us, because we were the ones being attacked. In the course of this melee, we all got our heads cracked. [19] As soon as they saw me after this episode, the others who had joined Simon in this drunken assault asked my forgiveness—not as victims but as wrongdoers. Since then, four years have passed, and at no time has anybody brought a prosecution against me. [20] My opponent Simon, who was the cause of all the trouble, kept the peace for a while because he was afraid. However, when he heard that I had lost some private cases arising from an *antidosis*,[6] he grew contemptuous of me and recklessly forced this trial on me. To show that here too I am telling the truth, I shall produce those who were present as witnesses of this for you.

[WITNESSES]

[21] You have heard what happened, both from me and from the witnesses. For my part, members of the Council, I could wish Simon shared my opinions, so that you could hear both of us tell the truth

---

[6] For the *antidosis* (exchange of properties), see the Introduction, IVC.

and then easily make the right decision. But since he pays no attention to the oath he has sworn, I shall also try to explain to you the ways in which he has lied. [22] He had the nerve to claim that he gave Theodotus three hundred drachmas and made an agreement with him, and that I plotted to turn the young man against him. But if this were true, he should have called for support from as many witnesses as possible and dealt with the matter according to the laws. [23] However, it is clear that he has never done anything of the sort. Instead, in his insolence[7] he beat up both of us, took part in a *kōmos*,[8] battered down the doors, and entered by night into the presence of freeborn women. You should regard this, members of the Council, as the strongest evidence that he is lying to you. [24] Look at what he said, which is quite unbelievable: he has valued his entire property at two hundred and fifty drachmas[9]—but it would be incredible if he hired somebody to be his boyfriend for more money than he actually possesses. [25] He has become so reckless that it was not enough for him simply to lie about having paid the money, but he even claims to have recovered it. And yet how can it be plausible that at one moment we should have committed the offense of which he has accused us—the alleged plot to defraud him of three hundred drachmas—but that after winning the fight we should have given him back the money, when we had received no formal release from legal charges and were under no obligation to pay? [26] In fact, members of the Council, he has devised and constructed the whole story. He says he paid the money, so that he would not appear to be treating the young man so outrageously in the absence of an agreement. But he claims to have got it back, because it is evident that he never brought a prosecution to claim the money and in fact made no mention of it.

[27] He alleges that I beat him up in front of his house and left him

---

[7] Lit., "he committed *hybris*," a form of aggravated assault so outrageous that it was the subject of a special public prosecution; see the Introduction to Dem. 54.

[8] A *kōmos* is a kind of moving drinking party; in Plato's *Symposion*, for example, Alcibiades arrives at the symposium with a group of "revelers" (*kōmastai*, 212c).

[9] It is difficult to imagine a context for this valuation unless Simon also has been involved in a challenge to undertake a liturgy (cf. 3.20n above).

half mile.

in a terrible state. But it appears that he pursued the young man for more than four stades[10] from his house without any difficulty. More than two hundred people saw him, but he denies it.

[28] He says we came to his house carrying a piece of broken pottery and threatened to kill him—and that this constitutes "premeditation." In my opinion, however, members of the Council, not only you (who are experienced in examining cases like this) but everybody else can easily see he is lying. [29] Would anybody think it credible that in a premeditated plot I came to Simon's house in daytime with the young man, when so many people were gathered there?—unless of course I had so lost my mind that I was eager to fight alone against so many, particularly when I knew he would be pleased to see me at his doors. This is the man who came to my house and entered it by force, who dared to search for me without consideration for my sister or my nieces, and who called me out and attacked me after discovering where I was dining. [30] On that occasion, I kept quiet and tried to avoid notoriety, in the belief that his wickedness was simply my misfortune. Can I really (as he claims) have developed a passion for notoriety later on? [31] If the young man were living with him, there would be a certain logic in his false claim that I was compelled by passion to behave in an improbably stupid way. As it is, however, Theodotus was not even on speaking terms with him but hated him more than anyone and was living with me instead. [32] So do any of you think it credible that I previously sailed away from the city taking the young man with me to avoid fighting with my opponent, but when I came back I took him to Simon's house, where I was bound to run into trouble? [33] And is it credible that I was plotting against him, given that I arrived at his house so unprepared that I could not call on any friends or slaves or anybody else for help—except this child[11] who could not give me any assistance, but was capable of denouncing me under torture if I did anything illegal? [34] Was I so stupid that while

---

[10] About half a mile. (A stade is the length of a running track, about 200 yards.)

[11] Only here is Theodotus described as *paidion* (small child) rather than *meirakion* (teenage boy)—presumably an attempt to minimize his age. The significance of this passage for determining his civic status is discussed in the Speech Introduction.

hypothetical

emphasizes youth

plotting against Simon not only did I not watch to see where he could be found alone, either by night or by day, but in fact went where I was bound to be seen by lots of people and get beaten up—as if I were premeditating against myself, so that my enemies would be most able to carry out their aggravated assault?[12]

[35] Another point to consider, members of the Council, is that simply from the details of the fight it is easy to recognize he is lying. As soon as the young man realized what was happening, he threw off his cloak and ran off. My opponents pursued him, while I left by a different route. [36] So who should you consider responsible for what happened: those who ran away or those who tried to catch them? In my view, everybody knows that those who are afraid run away, whereas those who pursue want to do something wrong. [37] If my account sounds reasonable, what actually happened was no different. They seized the young man and began dragging him forcibly off the street. When I happened to meet them, I did not touch them but simply grabbed hold of the young man, whereas they continued dragging him off by force and began beating me up. This has been affirmed by witnesses who were present. So it would be terrible if you decide I premeditated this affair, when they have behaved in such a disgraceful and lawless fashion. [38] What would have been my fate if the opposite of what happened had taken place? What if I, together with many friends, had met Simon, and had fought him, beaten him, chased after him, caught him, and then tried to drag him off by force—given that now, when my opponent has behaved like this, I am the one who is facing this trial, in which I risk losing my fatherland and all my property? [39] And here is the strongest and clearest proof: he claims that I have wronged him and plotted against him, but he did not venture to take any legal action[13] for four years. Other people who are in love, and are deprived of what they desire, and are beaten up, immediately seek revenge while they are angry. This man does it much later.

[40] I think it has been clearly demonstrated, members of the Council, that I am not responsible for any of what has happened. My attitude towards disputes like this is that although I had often been abused and assaulted by Simon, and had even had my head broken,

---

[12] *Hybris*: cf. 3.23n above.

[13] Lit. "bring an *episkēpsis*" (preliminary denunciation), similarly in 3.40.

doesn't make sense

nevertheless I did not venture to take legal action. I thought it dreadful to try to throw people out of their fatherland simply because of a quarrel over a boy. [41] I also thought there could be no premeditation in wounding if somebody wounded without intent to kill: for who is so naive that he premeditates long in advance how one of his enemies will be wounded? [42] Clearly our lawgivers also did not think they should prescribe exile from the fatherland for people who happen to crack each other's heads while fighting—or else they would have exiled a considerable number. On the other hand, they did establish such severe penalties for those who plot to kill others, and wound but do not succeed in killing. The lawgivers thought that those who have plotted and premeditated ought to pay the penalty: even if they did not succeed, nevertheless they had done their best.[14] [43] And indeed, on many previous occasions you have given the same verdict about premeditation. So it would be a terrible thing if you were to impose such severe penalties, including expulsion of citizens from their fatherland, when people are wounded while fighting because of drunkenness or quarreling or horseplay or insults or over a courtesan (*hetaira*)—the sorts of things that everybody regrets when they recover their senses.

[44] I am very confused about my opponent's character. Being in love and being a sykophant[15] do not seem to me compatible: the first is characteristic of simple people, the second of those who are particularly unscrupulous. I wish I were allowed to demonstrate his wickedness by referring to other events. That way, you would recognize that it would be far more just for him to be on trial for his life than to put other people in danger of exile. [45] I shall omit everything else, but mention one episode I think you should hear about, as evidence of his outrageous audacity. At Corinth, arriving after the battle against the enemy and the expedition to Coronea,[16] he had a fight with Laches his commander and beat him up. When the army marched out in full force, he was judged an insubordinate criminal and was the only Athenian to be publicly censured by the generals.

---

[14] I.e., "even if the lawgivers did not succeed in preventing all such cases." Or it may refer to the assailants: "Even if they did not succeed (in killing), nevertheless they had done the best they could (to kill)."

[15] Malicious prosecutor. See the Introduction, VE.

[16] In 394 (see the Speech Introduction).

drunken play or highlighting / how exile would be extreme

attacking his character / public service.

[46] I could tell you many other things about him, but since it is unlawful to mention irrelevant material in your court,[17] please bear this point in mind: my opponents are the ones who enter our houses by force; they are the ones who pursue us; they are the ones who drag us off the street by force. [47] Remember this, and deliver a just verdict. Do not let me be unjustly expelled from my fatherland, for which I have faced many dangers and performed many liturgies. I have never been responsible for any harm to the fatherland, nor have any of my ancestors; instead, we have brought many benefits. [48] So I rightly deserve pity from you and from others, not only if I should suffer the fate that Simon intends but simply because I have been compelled by these events to undergo such a trial.

---

[17] For this rule in homicide cases, which the speaker has of course just violated, see the Introduction to Ant. 5.

jurors swear an oath saying that they will only listen / judge you on relevant information to the trial, however they disregard this all the time

law suits in Athens · lot of building of character & sometimes used show a pattern of crime → all things have done against you. Background - why might be bringing false claims

ISOCRATES 20. AGAINST LOCHITES

INTRODUCTION

It is commonly believed that the beginning of this speech, which would have contained the narrative of events, has been lost. But it is possible that the speaker, who makes a point of his poverty, was able to afford only this short, prepared speech. The testimony of witnesses, together with his own improvised connecting comments, may have provided the bulk of the narrative. The function of this text, then, was only to underline the importance of the affair. The speaker seems to attempt to obscure whether the speech arose from a *graphē hybreōs* (a public suit for *hybris*, "wanton violence") or a *dikē aikeias* (a private suit for assault).[1] The emphasis at the beginning of the speech on who struck the first blow and the later reference (19) to the prosecutor's receiving personal compensation suggest that this case was a *dikē*, but most of his arguments deal with *hybris*.

There are several interesting arguments in this speech; some of them would shock a modern jurist. It opens with a discussion of the importance of legislation restricting physical assault (1–3), touching at several points on the intent of the legislators. It also casts an eye on the recent tyranny of the Thirty, "the oligarchy" (4, 11), which helps to date the speech to ca. 402–400. The speaker anticipates his opponent's argument concerning the seriousness of the case by arguing that even minor transgressions are indications of serious moral depravity and that it is for the latter rather than the former that Lochites should be punished (5–9), a surprising legal principle indeed, as if simply being

---

[1] See the Introduction to Dem. 54, where the same types of cases are discussed.

depraved, without acting out that depravity, were punishable. He then restates this argument, substituting the character of those involved with the tyranny for the seriously depraved, even though Lochites is too young ever to have been involved with the Thirty (10–14). The rest of the speech develops an argument about equality in justice, in which the speaker attempts to make the judges identify with him (15–22).

ISOCRATES 20. AGAINST LOCHITES

[1] That Lochites did indeed strike me and started the fight[2] all who were present have testified to you. You must not think this wrong similar to others, nor should you assign equal punishment for injuries to the person as for property damage. You know that the body is the most personal concern for all people: we have established laws and we do battle over its freedom; we desire democracy and we do everything else in life for its sake. Therefore, it is reasonable to restrain with the greatest punishment those who do wrong in this regard, which you take very seriously.

[2] You will find that those who have enacted our laws have been especially mindful about our bodies. First, they have created both private and public suits[3] without a preliminary deposit for this wrong alone, so that to the extent that each of us may be able and willing, he may punish those who injure him. Next, while in other charges the wrongdoer is liable to prosecution only by the victim, in a case of violent assault (*hybris*), inasmuch as it is a matter of public concern, any citizen who wishes may bring a *graphē* to the Thesmothetae[4] and come before you. [3] The legislators thought that the act of striking each other was so terrible that even for verbal abuse they enacted a law requiring those who say something forbidden to owe damages of five hundred drachmas. Indeed, what degree of punishment must be inflicted on behalf of victims of physical abuse, when you appear to be so angered on behalf of victims of mere verbal abuse?

[4] It is amazing if you believe those who committed *hybris* during

---

[2] "Started the fight" is an archaic legal expression found in Draco's law, more than two centuries earlier.

[3] *Dikai* and *graphai;* see the Introduction, VE.

[4] For the Thesmothetae, see the Introduction, IVA.

[handwritten notes at top: "crous reigme, throwing people / out of Athens, comparing to 30 tyrants / oppressive / bloody reigme"]

...serve death, but you let those doing the same things
...ocracy go unpunished. They should rightly receive a
...ient, for they are showing their depravity more clearly.
...s transgress the laws now when it is not tolerated, what
...done then when those in control of the city were even
...who committed such wrongs?

[5] Perhaps Lochites will try to make light of the matter, disparaging my prosecution and saying that I suffered nothing serious from the blows, that I am making more of a fuss about what happened than it deserves. If there had been no *hybris* attached to what he did, I would not have come to you. But as it is, I have come to obtain justice from him not for any injury resulting from his blows but for the outrage and indignity he inflicted. [6] About these matters, free people should be especially indignant and inflict the greatest retribution. I see that when you condemn someone for temple robbery or theft, you do not set the penalty according to the size of what they take. You condemn all alike to death and believe it just that those who attempt the same acts should be restrained by the same punishments. [7] Surely you must hold the same principle regarding those committing *hybris*: examine not whether the beating was severe, but whether the law was broken; punish them not just for what happened to result in this case, but for their entire behavior; take into consideration that small pretexts have often resulted in great evils, [8] and that because of those who dared to strike blows in the past, some people have become so angry that they have resorted to assaults, killings, exiles, and the greatest misfortunes. None of these things happened in this case, not because of the man defending it—for his part, they were all done—but nothing irrevocable occurred because of luck and the strength of my character.

[9] I think that you would be properly angered at this act if you went through for yourselves how much greater this crime is than others. You will find that other acts of injustice do harm to only a part of life, but *hybris* degrades all our activities. Many homes have been destroyed and many cities ruined because of it. [10] But why must I spend time talking about others' misfortunes? We ourselves have twice seen the democracy destroyed, and we have twice been robbed of freedom,[5] not by those guilty of other forms of depravity but because

---

[5] In 411/10 and 404/3.

intent(?)

of men who despised the laws and wished to be enslaved to the enemy and to commit *hybris* against their fellow citizens. [11] Lochites happens to be one of these. Even if he is younger than those who held power then, he has the character of that government. These were the natures that betrayed our empire to the enemy, razed the walls of our homeland, and executed fifteen hundred of our citizens without trial.

[12] It stands to reason that you should recall those events and punish not only those who harmed us then but also those who now wish to treat the city in this way. Just as those who are expected to be depraved are more dangerous than those who have already done wrong, it is better to discover how to avert future crimes than to obtain justice for those already committed. [13] Don't wait until they have banded together and seized upon a crisis in order to harm the entire city, but when they are handed over to you on a pretext, punish them for this in the belief that when you arrest someone demonstrating his complete depravity in a minor incident, you've had a piece of good luck. [14] It would be best if some sign or other were affixed to base people so that they might be restrained before they injured any citizen.[6] But since they cannot be recognized before they victimize someone, when they are discovered, then everyone must hate such people and regard them as public enemies.[7]

[15] Consider too that the poor have no share in threats to property, but everyone has the same interest in outrages to the body, so when you punish thieves, you benefit only the wealthy, but when you check those committing *hybris*, you are helping yourselves. [16] For this reason, these must be thought the most important of trials, and while in other private dealings the penalty must be only as much as the prosecutor deserves, for *hybris* the defendant must pay enough that he will stop his present brutality. [17] If you take away the property of those who act like young thugs toward citizens, and if you believe that no punishment is sufficient for those who commit bodily harm but suffer only a monetary fine, then you will do everything that good judges must. [18] And in the present case, you will decide correctly, you will

---

[6] This image recalls a similar sentiment expressed in Euripides' *Medea* 516–519.

[7] The legal principles expressed in this paragraph go far beyond anything else expressed in Greek law.

make the other citizens more orderly, and you will make your own lives more secure. It is characteristic of judges who have good sense to vote justly with regard to other people's affairs and at the same time to determine their own affairs well also.

[19] Let not even one of you think it right to reduce the award because you have observed that I am poor, one of the many.[8] It is unjust to make the penalty less for little-known victims than for the famous, to think that the impoverished are worse than those who have much. You would be dishonoring yourselves if you thought such things about citizens.

[20] Moreover, it would be most terrible of all if in a democratic city all people should not enjoy the same good fortune, if we thought that we all deserved to hold office yet robbed ourselves of justice under the laws, if we were willing to fight and die for our constitution yet allotted more in our voting to those who have property. [21] If you listen to me, you will not treat yourselves this way. You will not teach the young to despise the mass of citizens. You will not suppose that trials concern only others, but each of you will cast his vote as if he were judging on his own behalf. Those who dare to transgress this law, which was established on behalf of your bodies, do injustice to everyone alike. [22] Therefore, if you are sensible, call on one another and signal your anger to Lochites. You know that all such people despise the established laws but believe that these decisions of yours are the real laws.[9]

I have said what I can about the case. If someone present has something to say on my behalf, let him come up here and speak.

---

[8] We may wonder whether this argument is not disingenuous inasmuch as most of the judges would also have been relatively poor. But it seems likely that Athenian judges, like modern jurors, were probably slightly intimidated by wealth. The speaker thus makes a circuitous attempt to make the judges identify and sympathize with him.

[9] This argument not only contains a rhetorical commonplace but identifies a reality of the Athenian legal system, that the panel of judges was free to decide issues of both fact and law without any accountability.

PART II STATUS AND CITIZENSHIP

For male Athenians, citizenship depended primarily on membership in a deme (small "precincts" established by Cleisthenes in 508 that were originally territorial) but also presumed membership in a phratry—older, larger groups based on an assumed ancient kinship (see below, Dem. 57.23n). A father normally acknowledged his son's paternity before witnesses soon after his birth and introduced him to his phratry as an infant. But the most important step appears to have been registration in the deme at the age of eighteen; every year deme members conducted a scrutiny (*dokimasia*) of all boys who turned eighteen that year and formally approved those who were of age, were free persons, and had two Athenian parents. Demes kept written lists of citizens, but these were often unreliable, and tampering with the lists was often suspected. Enrollment in a deme could later be challenged, as in the case in Demosthenes 57. Women were citizens by virtue of being born of two Athenian parents but were not formally inscribed in any citizen lists. Citizenship could also be awarded by a vote of the Assembly, though this was rare and reserved for special benefactors.

Other Athenian residents included slaves and metics—free resident aliens (see the Introduction, IVB). Metics needed a sponsor (*prostatēs*), though it is not entirely clear what his role was. Freed slaves assumed the status of metics.

A person's status could be difficult to determine, and both Lysias 23 and Demosthenes 59 involve questions about status. But the Athenians guarded the privilege of citizenship closely and expected high standards of behavior from their citizens, especially those engaging in public life; Aeschines 1 accuses a man of violating these standards by, among other things, prostituting himself.

DEMOSTHENES 57. APPEAL
AGAINST EUBULIDES

〰〰〰〰〰〰〰〰〰〰〰〰〰〰〰〰〰〰〰〰〰〰〰〰〰〰〰〰〰〰〰

INTRODUCTION

This speech revolves around the issue of Athenian citizenship. The stakes were very high: it is no exaggeration when in the opening section the speaker equates conviction with ruin, for he was to be sold into slavery if he lost the case (though at 57.65 it appears that an unsuccessful appellant might be expected to leave Attica before that happened).

A man named Euxitheus came before an Athenian court to appeal the decision of his deme, Halimus, to strike him from its official register of deme members. Although the trial arises from an appeal (*ephesis*), the deme takes the role of prosecutor, represented by Eubulides and four other elected deme officers, an exception to the general rule that prosecution in the Athenian judicial system lay in private hands. Euxitheus had been removed from the register in the course of a review in which the status of each member was confirmed by the vote of all members present. He claims that he meets the requirement of citizenship—descent from an Athenian mother and father—and that Eubulides, the man responsible for his expulsion, acted out of personal enmity. The procedure and penalties relevant to this case are known from internal evidence, *Ath. Pol.* 42 and the *hypothesis* (summary) of the speech provided by Libanius (fourth century AD).[1] This hypothesis also supplies the speaker's name. If we believe Euxitheus, the evidence against him was flimsy and mean-spirited: his father's

---

[1] In Isaeus 12, which also concerns the denial of citizenship during the same review, the procedure is rather different.

dialect and his mother's humble employment, selling ribbons and working as a wet nurse.

The case arises from a review of deme registries that was conducted in 346/5 and mandated by a decree of the Assembly. The speech is likely to have been delivered about a year later.

For a general treatment of demes in Athenian society and government and discussion of some individual passages in this speech, see Whitehead 1986 and Jones 1999.

DEMOSTHENES 57. APPEAL AGAINST EUBULIDES

[1] As Eubulides has made many false accusations against us, and made defamatory statements that are neither fitting nor just, I will try, gentlemen of the jury, by telling what is true and just, to show both that we have a share in the city[2] and that I myself have been treated badly by this man. I ask all of you, gentlemen of the jury, and I beseech you, and I implore you, to take account of the enormity of the present trial and the shame that comes to those ruined by a conviction, and to listen to me in silence,[3] preferably, if possible, with more goodwill toward me than toward him, since it is natural to show greater goodwill to those who are in danger; but if not, with at least an equal measure of goodwill. [2] I happen, gentlemen of the jury, to feel confident about your part in this matter and about my belonging to the city and to have great hopes of doing well in court; but on the other hand, I am fearful of the city's current keen excitement over the disenfranchisement of citizens. Since many men have been rightfully expelled from all the demes, we who are the victims of plotting are tarnished by their disgrace, and each of us is in a trial that touches on those men's guilt and not just our own individual circumstances, with the inevitable result that we are afraid. [3] Although this is the situation, I will tell you first what I regard as just. You see, I think you should be angry at those who are exposed as aliens if they have secretly and

---

[2] The phrase is tantamount to "be citizens." The speaker switches from first-person singular to plural as a way of referring imprecisely to his wider circle, usually his family.

[3] For appeals to the jurors both for silence and to shout, see Bers 1985.

against your will taken part in your sacred communal rites without having asked you or persuaded you to grant them the privilege; but you should help and save those unlucky people who demonstrate that they are citizens. Consider that the most pitiable things would befall the victims of injustice, if because of your anger over this matter, we who should rightfully be in your company exacting the penalty will instead be among those who pay the penalty and would join in being the victims of injustice. [4] Now I think, gentlemen of the jury, that Eubulides and all those who are now bringing accusations in disenfranchisement proceedings should tell precisely what they know and bring no hearsay evidence into such a trial. After all, this practice was long ago so emphatically judged wrong that the laws do not even permit hearsay evidence to be included in testimony, not even in trivial cases. And reasonably so, since when some men are plainly lying when they claim to know something, why should we believe someone who speaks of what he himself has no personal knowledge? [5] Further, when a man is not permitted to harm anyone else by passing on what he says he has heard, even if he takes responsibility for it, how can it be proper for you to believe someone who cannot be held to account? Since Eubulides, knowing the laws rather too well,[4] makes the accusation unjustly and for his own advantage, I am forced to speak first about how I was abused among the members of the deme. [6] I ask, men of Athens, that you not yet regard the expulsion voted by the deme members as evidence that I do not belong to the city. After all, if you believed that the deme members could decide all cases rightly, you would not have allowed appeals to be brought before you. The fact is that because you thought something like this would happen as a result of ambition, envy, personal hatred, and other reasons, you established this recourse to your courts, men of Athens, for those who had been treated unjustly, and by means of applying this procedure honorably, you have rescued all those who have been wronged. [7] So first I will tell you in what way the deme members handled the review of citizens. I take it that this constitutes "speaking to the spe-

---

[4] In Athens, great familiarity with the law could be presented in a negative light. Someone often involved in litigation may be thought to have ulterior motives for prosecuting and possibly resemble a sykophant (Introduction, VE).

*overwhelming defeat → huge fine
cannot charge same
crime again.*

cific point,"[5] to reveal everything that happened to a man unjustly
victimized by political strife, contrary to the decree.

[8] You see, men of Athens, as many of you know, Eubulides, this
man here in court, indicted the sister of Lacedaemonius[6] for impiety
but did not get one-fifth of the votes. I testified honestly at that trial
but in opposition to Eubulides, and because of animosity over that
event, he attacked me. He was serving on the Council, gentlemen of
the jury, and in charge of both the oath and the documents for summoning members of the deme, so what does he do? [9] First, when the
deme members were called together, he wasted the day in making
speeches and introducing decrees. It was not by chance that he did
this; rather, he was plotting to hold the review in my case as late as
possible. And this he managed to do. Seventy-three of us deme members were sworn in, and we did not start on the review until late in the
afternoon; consequently, it happened that when my name was called,
it was already dark. [10] My name was around the sixtieth, and I was
last of all the men called that day. By then the older deme members
had left for the countryside, since, gentlemen of the jury, the deme is
thirty-five stades[8] from the city and most of the members live there, so
the majority had gone off. Those who remained numbered not more
than thirty, and among this group were all those whom Eubulides had
set up. [11] When my name was called, Eubulides leapt to his feet and
immediately began slandering me, over and over, and shouting, as he

---

[5] The speaker repeatedly protests that he is sticking to the point. This may
reflect a requirement, perhaps adopted not long before the date of the speech, that
litigants in private cases (*dikai*) swear to speak to the issue when addressing the
court (*Ath. Pol.* 67.1). In general, speakers in Attic lawcourts very often strayed
without apology into what a modern judge would declare irrelevant material.

[6] Probably the man whose brother's service as an arbitrator is mentioned at
Dem. 59.45. Nothing more is known about the charges against the woman.

[7] That Eubulides was not barred from participating in the prosecution of Euxitheus despite his earlier failure to get one-fifth of the votes shows that Athenian
law sometimes imposed the penalty of only partial *atimia* (loss of citizen rights)
for unsuccessful prosecution: see Hansen 1976: 63–64.

[8] About four miles south of the city. It is not clear why the meeting was not
held in a place more convenient to a majority of the men who attended. See Jones
1999: 87–88.

has been doing just now. He offered no witness to support his charges—no member of the deme or any other citizen—yet called on the deme members to strike me from the rolls. [12] I demanded that the meeting be adjourned to the next day because of the lateness of the hour and because I had no one to help me, and the business had caught me unawares; the purpose of my demand was that he be able to make all the accusations he wanted and to put forward any witnesses he had, and I would be able to make my defense before all the deme members and put forward my own people as witnesses. And I was willing to accept whatever verdict was given in my case. [13] He paid no attention to my proposal but immediately put the vote to those members of the deme who were present; he offered me no chance to defend myself, and he produced no reliable proof. His accomplices jumped up and cast their ballots. It was dark, and each of them took two or three ballots from Eubulides and threw them into the urn. The evidence for this is that though there were not more than thirty men who voted, the ballots numbered more than sixty, which stunned us all. [14] I will provide witnesses that I am telling the truth: that the vote was not submitted to all the deme members, and the tally was larger than the number of men who had voted. Because of the late hour and my failure to ask anyone to stay, it happens that none of my friends or other Athenians were present to serve as witness on these matters; instead, I will have recourse to the very men who have wronged me as my witnesses. I have written down for them things they will not be able to deny. [*To the clerk*] Read this.[9]

[DEPOSITION]

[15] Gentlemen of the jury, if it had happened that the members of Halimus had conducted the vote on all the deme members that day, it would have made sense for the voting to run late, so they could accomplish everything your decree had mandated before leaving. But when more than twenty deme members remained who had to be

---

[9] This refers to the procedure known as *exōmosia*, in which a hostile witness is called on to give testimony or swear that he has no knowledge of the matter. Despite the implications of several speakers, the oath of denial was probably sworn before the trial. See Carey 1995a and Thür 2005: esp. 167–169.

Rigid

voted on the next day, and when in any event it was necessary for the members to reassemble, what did Eubulides find so difficult about postponing the vote to the next day and having the deme members vote on my case first? [16] The reason was, gentlemen of the jury, that Eubulides knew very well that if I were given the floor and all the deme members were on hand and the vote were fairly conducted, his accomplices could do nothing. When I speak about my family, if you want to hear about it,[10] I will tell you what motive these men had for their plot. [17] But now, what do I think is a just claim and what am I prepared to do, gentlemen of the jury? To demonstrate to you that I am an Athenian on both my father's and my mother's side and to present witnesses to this fact whom you will agree are honest. Also, to refute their insults and accusations. If I seem to you, once you have heard these things, to be a citizen victimized by a conspiracy, then save me. If not, do whatever seems to you the pious thing to do.[11] I'll start with this. [18] You see, they slander my father, when they say he spoke like a foreigner.[12] They leave out the fact that he was captured by the enemy during the Decelean War[13] and sold into slavery, then taken to Leucas,[14] where he fell in with Cleandrus the actor, and after a long interval returned safely to his family; so they accused him of speaking with an accent, as though we should be ruined on account of his bad luck. [19] But I think I can demonstrate to you, from these very facts, that I am an Athenian. So, I will provide witnesses first that he was captured and returned safely; then, that on his return he got a share of his uncles' property; and further, that no one ever accused him, not among the deme members, not among his fellow phratry members, not anywhere else, of being an alien on the ground that he spoke with an accent. [*To the clerk*] Please take the depositions.

---

[10] More often than most speakers, Euxitheus defers (or pretends to defer) to the jury's desire to hear certain material.

[11] I.e., in accordance with the jurymen's oath (Introduction, VC).

[12] From what Euxitheus goes on to say in the next sentence, it seems that his father had acquired a West Greek dialect.

[13] The Decelean War (413–404) is one period of the Peloponnesian War.

[14] An island off the coast of Acarnania in the Ionian Sea.

[DEPOSITIONS]

[20] You have heard, then, about my father's capture and how it came about that he was rescued and brought back here. Now, gentlemen of the jury, to prove that he was a fellow-citizen of yours—for this really and truly was the case—I will call my father's living relatives.[15] [*To the clerk*] Please call first Thucritides and Charisiades. You see, their father Charisius was the brother of my grandfather Thucritides and my grandmother Lysarete—my grandfather married his half-sister from a different mother—and Charisius is my father's uncle. [21] Then call Niciades. His father Lysanias was the brother of Thucritides and Lysarete, and the uncle of my father. Next call Nicostratus. His father Niciades was my grandfather's and grandmother's nephew, and my father's cousin. Please call up all these men and stop the water clock.

~ ne brings in family members

[WITNESSES]

[22] You have heard, men of Athens, from my father's relatives, who testify and swear that he was an Athenian and was related to them. None of them, surely, standing alongside men who would know that he is lying, calls down curses on himself.[16] [*To the clerk*] Please take also the deposition of my father's relatives on the female side.[17]

[DEPOSITIONS]

[23] These living relations of my father, on both the male and female side, have testified that he was an Athenian on both sides and rightly had a share in the city. [*To the clerk*] Please call the members of my phratry (brotherhood) and then members of my clan (*genos*).[18]

---

[15] Here begins an unusually detailed presentation of a family tree. See Davies 1971: 93–95.

[16] I.e., calls down ruin for himself if his testimony is false.

[17] The relatives of his father's mother would testify that she too was an Athenian.

[18] The phratries (roughly, "brotherhoods") were social and political units of great antiquity that survived Cleisthenes' reforms (Introduction, IVB). Within a

[WITNESSES]

Take the depositions of the deme members and of my relatives that my fellow phratry members elected me an official of the phratry (*phratriarchos*).

[DEPOSITIONS]

[24] You have heard the testimony of all the appropriate people, members of my phratry, members of my deme, and members of my *genos*. From them you can learn whether a man who had these people to vouch for him was an Athenian (*astos*) or an alien. You see, if we for protection looked to one or two men, we would be subject to some suspicion that these witnesses were set up. But if my father, during his lifetime, and now I, have clearly passed muster with all the affiliated groups, as each of you has—namely, phratry members, relatives, deme members, *genos* members—how could I manage to rig all these pseudo-relatives? [25] Now, if my father was rich and blatantly giving money to these men to talk them into declaring themselves his relatives, the argument that he was not an Athenian might arouse some suspicion. But being poor, if he presented as his relatives the same men as those he listed as giving him a share of their property, then it is surely crystal clear that he is in truth related to them. If he were related to none of them, they certainly wouldn't have given him a share in their *genos* and also given him money. No, he *was* their relative, as the facts have made clear and as has been confirmed by testimony. Furthermore, he was selected for a magistracy by lot, was approved at his scrutiny,[19] and held office. [*To the clerk*] Please take this deposition.

[DEPOSITION]

[26] Does anyone of you suppose that the deme members would have allowed that man to hold office among them if he were an alien

---

phratry were smaller kinship units called *genē* (clans). Among their functions was the maintenance of a registry to which members would add the names of their legitimate sons.

[19] For the scrutiny (*dokimasia*), see the Introduction, IVA. The speaker implies that his father's citizenship could have been challenged at this scrutiny but evidently was not.

and not a citizen and would not have pro— person prosecuted him or accused him of any— were compulsory review procedures, in which the— to swear on sacrificed animals when their deme register— the administration of the *demarch*[20] Antiphilus, father of— and they drove out some of the members. But nobody spoke abo— father or brought any charge against him. [27] Yet every man's ends at his death, and it is right that his children always have to defend themselves against any charge the man incurred while alive. But it is really outrageous if someone comes forward[21] to judge the children on charges no one brought against a man while he was alive. If no account of these matters had ever been tested, we might grant that the matter of his citizenship slipped by unnoticed. But if there was discussion, and they conducted the review, and no one ever accused him, it is certainly right that I would be counted an Athenian on my father's side, since he died before there was any dispute about his ancestry. I call witnesses to these matters also, to show that this is true.

[WITNESSES]

[28] Further, my father had four children from the same mother as mine. When they died, he buried them at his ancestral tombs, which belong to those who share his *genos*. No member of that *genos* ever said he could not, or prevented him from doing so, or sued him. Now, really, who would permit people not in the *genos* to be buried in their ancestral tombs? [*To the clerk*] Take this deposition attesting the truth of my statements.

[DEPOSITION]

[29] That is what I have to say about my father's being an Athenian, and I have provided witnesses who were confirmed as citizens by these self-same men, to testify that he was their cousin. It is clear that for all the time he lived here, my father was never challenged as an alien; no, he found protection with those who were his relatives, and these peo-

---

[20] A man selected by lot to serve for one year to preside at deme meetings and look after the deme's list of members.

[21] The Greek is *ho boulomenos,* "the man who wishes [to bring a prosecution]."

[handwritten: er not citizen & basically becau... it.]

...r property as one of their
...en if he was an Athenian
...as entitled to be a citizen
...onship of Eucleides.[22] Now
...have slandered me in her case,
...say. Still, men of Athens, he
...only in violation of the decree
...and that the man is liable to a
...e or female citizen about his work
...wledge that we sell ribbons and do not
...e. And, Eubulides, if you take this as a
...ans, I will show you the exact opposite, that
an a... ...ed to work in the agora. [*To the clerk*] Please take
and read first th. .aw of Solon. *[handwritten: if she is a metic-need pay taxes]*

[LAW]

[32] [*To the clerk*] Take also the law of Aristophon. You see, men of
Athens, you thought Solon enacted such a just and democratic law
that you voted to restore it. *[handwritten: these are people who lie in courts and bring cases — make money]*

[LAW]

It is fitting for you to help the laws, not by thinking that workers
are aliens but by thinking sykophants are wicked, because, Eubulides,
there is another law, dealing with idleness, one to which you, who
slanders us who work, are liable. [33] But such a great misfortune
envelops us now that he is permitted to defame me in irrelevant matters and do anything whatever to keep me from getting what I deserve.

---

[22] Pericles' citizenship law (Introduction, IVB) was neglected during the
Peloponnesian War but reinstated in 403/2.

[23] There is no other evidence for this curious prohibition of a rather innocuous
form of slander (*kakēgoria*). In Athenian law the truth of the allegations was evidently not a sufficient defense, as it would be in modern laws on libel and slander.
See Todd 1993: 260. In Lys. 10, the only surviving speech from a prosecution
for slander, we hear that accusations of homicide, desertion of one's station in
the hoplite phalanx, and physical abuse of parents counted as defamatory
speech.

Perhaps you will criticize me if I talk about the way he does business as he goes about the city, and rightly so: what need is there to speak of what you all know? But do consider this. You see, for my part, I regard our working in the agora to be a very strong indication that the charges he brings against us are false. [34] You see, many people who knew that woman who is, as he says, a notorious ribbon-seller, could properly give testimony and not only testimony based on hearsay evidence; and if she was an alien, they ought to have examined the duties paid in the agora and should have shown whether she was paying the alien tax and where she was from. If she was a slave, the man who bought her should have come forward to testify against her, and if not he, then the man who sold her; if not he, then some other man should have testified, either that she was a slave or that she had been set free. But in fact, he showed none of these things but only hurled abuse, so it seems to me, of every sort. This is the sykophant's game: to allege everything but prove nothing. [35] He also has said this about my mother, that she was a wet nurse. We do not deny that this happened when the city suffered misfortune and everybody was doing badly. I will tell you clearly how and for what reason she was a wet nurse. None of you, men of Athens, should take this in the wrong way, since even now you will find that many Athenian women (*astai*) are wet nurses; if you wish, I will identify them for you by name. Now, if we were rich, we would not be selling ribbons, nor would we be in such dire straits. But what does this have to do with our ancestry? Nothing, in my opinion. [36] No, gentlemen of the jury, do not dishonor the poor— being poor is trouble enough for them—or those who choose to work and get a living by honest means. Instead, once you have heard us out, if I show that my mother's relatives are the sort of people free men should be, and they deny under oath these slanders cast upon her, and they—people whom you will acknowledge as credible—testify that they know she is an Athenian, cast your vote for justice.

[37] Now, my grandfather, men of Athens, my mother's father, was Damostratus of the deme Melite. He had four children; from his first wife he had a daughter and a son, whose name is Amytheon; with Chaerestrate, his second wife, he had my mother and Timocrates. They had children: Amytheon had a son named for my grandfather Damostratus, as well as Callistratus and Dexitheus. Amytheon, my

mother's brother, was among those who fought and died in Sicily, and he is buried in the public tombs: this too will be attested. [38] His sister married Diodorus of the deme Halae, and they had a son, Ctesibios, who died in Abydus, on campaign with Thrasybulus; of these, still living is Damostratus, Amytheon's son, my mother's nephew. Apollodorus of the deme Plotheia married the sister of my grandmother Chaerestrate. Their son is Olympichus, and they had a son, Apollodorus, who is living. [*To the clerk*] Please call them.

[WITNESSES]

[39] You have heard these men testifying and swearing the oath. Now I will call a man who is related to my mother on both sides, together with his sons. You see, Timocrates, my mother's brother, from the same father and mother, had a son, Euxitheus, and Euxitheus had three sons. All these men are living. [*To the clerk*] Please call those of them who are in Athens.

[handwritten: witnesses from both sides]

[WITNESSES]

[40] [*To the clerk*] Please take the depositions of my fellow phratry and deme members related to my mother, men who have the same ancestral tombs.

[handwritten: another piece of evidence that she is accepted as Athenian]

[DEPOSITIONS]

I have demonstrated that as regards my mother's descent, she was an Athenian on both the male and female side. My mother, gentlemen of the jury, was first given in marriage by Timocrates, her brother from the same father and mother, to Protomachus, and had a daughter; subsequently, with my father, she had me. You should hear how it came about that she married my father. I will give you a clear account of all the charges Eubulides makes concerning Cleinias and my mother working as a wet nurse. [41] Protomachus was a poor man. Because he stood to win the inheritance of a rich heiress (*epiklēros*), Protomachus wanted to marry my mother off, and he persuaded my father Thucritus, an acquaintance of his, to take her.[24] My father married her in a cer-

---

[24] An *epiklēros*—a woman whose father had died without leaving male descendants—was "attached" to an inheritance but not truly an heiress in her

emony in which her brother, Timocrates of the deme Melite, gave her away, and both his uncles and other men witnessed the ceremony. Those men in that group still alive will give you their testimony. [42] Later on, when my mother had two babies, my father went away on campaign with Thrasybulus; because she was without means, she was forced to serve as a wet nurse to Cleinias the son of Cleidicus. Doing that brought no advantage, by Zeus, to me in the danger that would come, since this work as a wet nurse is the source of all the slander about us; but perhaps she did this both under the compulsion of the poverty that beset her and as a way of adapting to it. [43] Now it is plain, men of Athens, that my mother's first husband was not my father, but Protomachus, and that he had children with her and gave their daughter in marriage. Protomachus is dead, but he bears witness by his actions that my mother was an Athenian (*astê*) and a citizen (*politis*). [*To the clerk*] To show that what I say is true, please call first the sons of Protomachus; next, those who were present when my father married my mother and men close to him in his phratry, for whom he gave the marriage feast for my mother; then Eunicus of the deme Cholargus, who from Protomachus received my sister in marriage; and then my sister's son. Call these men.

[WITNESSES]

[44] I would certainly suffer most pitiably of all people if despite all these many relatives here testifying under oath that they are related to me—and no one claims that any of them are not citizens—you vote that I am an alien. [*To the clerk*] Please take the depositions of Cleinias and his relatives. These people certainly know who my mother was when she nursed him. You know, the oaths do not demand that they attest what I'm saying today but what they have known all along about a woman thought to be my mother and Cleinias' wet nurse. [45] You know, if the wet nurse is a humble thing, I do not run away from the truth. We did nothing wrong, after all, if we were poor, but only if we

---

own right, since only males could inherit. By marrying an *epiklēros,* Protomachus would become the trustee of the property, pending the maturity of sons from that marriage, but he was obliged first to find a husband for his current wife, Euxitheus' mother.

were not citizens: and the present trial now is not about our luck or our money but about our descent. Poverty forces free men to do many servile, humble things: and it would be more in keeping with justice if they will be pitied for that, men of Athens, than if they are pushed further into ruin. I have heard that owing to the city's misfortunes at the time, many Athenian women became wet nurses, servants, and grape harvesters, and many Athenian women rose from poverty to riches. But I'll turn to that subject soon. [*To the clerk*] For now, call the witnesses.

[WITNESSES]

[46] That I am an Athenian (*astos*) on both my mother's and father's side you have all learned from the testimony just given and from what was earlier presented concerning my father. It remains for me to speak to you about myself—I think what I have to say is perfectly straight-forward and most in accord with justice—that I, an Athenian on both sides, the heir to both my estate and line of descent, am a citizen. Nevertheless, by providing witnesses I will demonstrate all the perti-nent facts: that I was introduced to my phratry and enrolled in my deme,[25] I was chosen by the deme members themselves to draw lots with men of the best lineage for service as priest of Heracles, and that, after passing the scrutiny, I served in office. Please call them.

[WITNESSES]

[47] Isn't it terrible, gentlemen of the jury? If I had drawn the lot for priest when I was selected to participate in the drawing, I would have been required in my own person to sacrifice on behalf of the deme members, and Eubulides would have been required to sacrifice along with me, but as it is, these same men do not allow me to sacrifice with them? Thus I have been clearly acknowledged, men of Athens, all along, by all my current accusers, as a citizen. [48] After all, Eubulides would not have allowed this alien or metic, as he now says I am, to serve in magistracies or to be selected to draw lots for the priesthood alongside him. He too, you see, was among those selected to draw lots. And as my enemy from long before, he would not have waited until

---

[25] For the phratry, see above, 23n; for deme enrollment, see the Introduction, IVB.

this opportunity now, which no one anticipated, if he had known such a thing about me then. [49] But he did *not* know it, and that is why until now, while he was a member of the deme with me and participating in the lottery for the priesthood, he saw none of these things; but only when the whole city was filled with anger at the men who had outrageously jumped into the demes, did he *then* start to plot against me. On that earlier occasion a man who was certain of the truth of his assertion should have acted. But the present occasion is the time only for a personal enemy or a man who wants to play the sykophant to come forward.

[50] Now please, gentlemen of the jury, by Zeus and the other gods, let no one shout, let no one get angry at what I am about to say. I think of myself as an Athenian, just as each of you does; I thought my mother was, from the start, the woman I have been describing to you, and I was not pretending to be her son while really the son of another woman. And the same thing, men of Athens, goes for my father. [51] So if you rightly take it as a sign of people being aliens that they are exposed as hiding the identity of their true parents and pretending they are someone else's children, then surely the opposite should show that I am a citizen. I would not, after all, claim to have a share in the city, while inscribing myself as the son of an alien woman and man. Instead, if I knew this was the case, I would have searched for people to claim as my parents. But I did not know any such thing, and so, sticking with my real parents, I claim my rightful share in the city. [52] Further, I was left an orphan,[26] and they say that I am well off and that some of my witnesses are paid to testify that they are my relatives. They simultaneously criticize me for the disgrace of poverty and slander me in regards to my descent, *and* they say that with my riches I have bought everything. [53] So which claims should be believed? Certainly it was open to these people who testified on my behalf to inherit all my property if I was in fact illegitimate or an alien. So then, they chose for a small payment to run the risk of a suit for false witness and to perjure themselves—rather than receive everything, risk free and without subjecting themselves to utter destruction?[27] This is impossible. Instead, I think that, being my relatives, they did

---

[26] A Greek *orphanos* had no father; his mother might be alive.

[27] See 57.22 with note.

the right thing in helping one of their own. [54] They are not just doing this because they were persuaded,[28] but right away when I was a baby they introduced me to the phratry,[29] to the shrine of our ancestral Apollo, and to the other sacred places. I certainly could not, when a boy, bribe them to do that! No, my father, while still alive, himself swore the customary oath when he introduced me to the phratry members, that he knew that I was an Athenian (*astos*) born of an Athenian woman (*astē*) betrothed to him, and this has been presented in testimony. [55] So I am an alien? Where did I pay the tax on metics?[30] Who in my family ever did so? Did I go to some other deme, and when I could not persuade them to enroll me, did I inscribe myself here? Where did I do any of the things that men improperly made citizens are seen doing? Nowhere, but quite simply, the deme of my father's grandfather, my grandfather, and my father is the deme in which I too am clearly a member. Now, how could anyone show you more plainly that he has a share in the city? [56] So let each one of you, men of Athens, think how he would show that his relatives were the same from the start using another method than I have: by having them give testimony under oath.

Feeling confidence in myself for these reasons, I have turned to you for refuge. After all, men of Athens, I see that the courts hold greater authority not only than the voters of the deme Halimus who have excluded me but even than the Council and the Assembly—and rightly so, since your decisions are in all matters the most just.[31] [57] You who are members of the large demes, think about this too, that you have deprived no one of the opportunity to accuse or defend—and may you all enjoy many blessings for dealing with this business in a just manner—because when men were asking for postponements, you did not take away the opportunity to prepare. By that policy you have exposed the sykophants and those who lay plots in pursuit of private enmity. [58] You deserve praise, men of Athens, just as those who

---

[28] In Greek rhetoric, "persuaded" often implies "paid" or "bribed."

[29] See 57.23n.

[30] Amounting to twelve drachmas a year, not an onerous sum.

[31] Aristotle, *Politics* 1274a4–5: Some blamed Solon for "making the court all powerful."

wrongly use a good and just procedure deserve blame. You will not find that more terrible acts happened in any other deme than ours. These men struck from the rolls some full brothers but not others, and they excluded men who were old and poor but retained their sons. If you wish, I will provide witnesses to these acts too. [59] But the most awful thing of all that these conspirators did was this—and by Zeus and the gods, let no one be annoyed if I show that those who have wronged me are wicked men, since I think that in revealing their wickedness to you I am speaking precisely on the subject of what happened to me.[32] Now then, these men, men of Athens, divided among themselves some aliens who wanted to become citizens, Anaximenes and Nicostratus, and they took money from them, each of them getting five drachmas. Eubulides and the others of his group would not deny on oath they knew about this business, and they did not now[33] strike them from the rolls. Now, what do you think these men would *not* do in private matters, seeing that they dared to do that in a public matter? [60] Gentlemen of the jury, the men who conspire with Eubulides have ruined and saved many men for money. Even before— I will speak to the issue, men of Athens—when he was serving as *demarch,* Eubulides' father Antiphilus, as I have mentioned, contrived to get money from certain men; he claimed that he lost the public deme register, and thus he persuaded the men of the deme Halimus to conduct a review of their deme; he prosecuted and expelled ten of the deme members, all but one of whom the court restored to membership. All the older men know this. [61] It is very unlikely that they left on the rolls any who were not Athenians, seeing that they expelled true citizens, whom the court restored. And yet, although he was an enemy of my father, Antiphilus did not then make an accusation against him and in fact did not even vote that he was not an Athenian. How do we know this? Because absolutely all the deme members voted that he was. But why should we talk about fathers? This man here, Eubulides himself, when my name was put on the register and all the deme members, under oath, cast their ballots about my case in the proper way, neither made an accusation nor voted against me. You see, on

---

[32] See 57.7n.

[33] I.e., in the review by which Euxitheus was expelled from the deme.

that occasion too they voted unanimously that I was a member of the deme. And if they say I am lying about this, any one of them who wants may give testimony during my allotted time. [62] If, gentlemen of the jury, you think these men have a strong point in arguing that the deme has now voted to expel me, I show that four times before, when they voted in a pious fashion, in the absence of any conspiracy, they voted that I and my father were fellow deme members: first, the time when my father underwent his scrutiny (*dokimasia*); then at my own scrutiny; then in the earlier review, when these men made the register disappear; and finally, when they voted to select me for the lottery for the priesthood of Heracles, along with others from the best families. All this too has been attested.

[63] But if I must mention my service as *demarch,* which caused some to be angry at me, because I quarreled with many of them when I exacted payments, many for sacred lands[34] and for other things they stole from public property, I would like you to hear about it—but perhaps you will regard this as off the point. In this matter too I can produce evidence that they have conspired. You see, they have expunged from the oath the phrase "will vote with my most honest judgment and without favoritism or enmity."[35] [64] This business became notorious, and also that those men whom I made reimburse the Public Treasury conspired against me: they committed the sacrilege of stealing the arms—this *will* be said—that I had dedicated to Athena and erased the decree that the deme members voted in my honor. And they have become so shameless that they have been going around saying that *I* did this to help my defense. Who among you, gentlemen of the jury, would convict me of such extreme insanity that just to have evidence of such significance for my case I would commit acts worthy of execution and do away with the inscription that brought me distinction? [65] And they surely would not say that I contrived the most outrageous act of all. You see, my luck had just turned bad when immediately, as if I were already in exile[36] and a ruined man,

---

[34] Presumably rent payments were at issue.

[35] Presumably the speaker means the oath taken by the deme members before voting in a review, but he also alludes to the jurymen's oath (Introduction, VC).

[36] See the Speech Introduction for the possibility of evading slavery by leaving Attica.

some of them came to my small house in the country at night and tried to carry off what was inside. That is how great a contempt they had for you and the laws. If you want, we will call those who know these facts.   *~ summarizes case ·*

[66] I have many other things to show, things they did and lies they told, that I would gladly tell you, but since you regard them as off the point,[37] I will omit them. But remember those things I have told you and see with what an abundance of just claims I have come before you. Just as you interrogate candidates for *thesmothetēs,* so will I in the same way interrogate myself.[38] [67] "Sir, who was your father?" "My father? Thucritus." "Are there relatives who will testify for him?" "Certainly. To start, four first cousins,[39] then a cousin's son, then the men who married the female cousins, then phratry members, then clan members sharing a cult of Ancestral Apollo and Household Zeus, then those who shared the same tombs, then deme members to attest that he often passed scrutiny (*dokimasia*) and served in magistracies, and who themselves clearly confirmed him as a citizen at the review. How could I more properly or honestly show you the facts about my father? I will call these relatives for you, if you wish. Now hear the facts about my mother. [68] My mother is Nicarete, the daughter of Damostratus of the deme Melite. Which relatives will testify for her? First a nephew, then two sons of another nephew, then a cousin's son, then the sons of Protomachus, who was my mother's first husband, then Eunicus of the deme Cholargus, who married my sister, Protomachus' daughter, then my sister's son. [69] Further, her relatives' fellow phratry members and also their fellow deme members have given the same testimony. What else do you need? After all, there has already been testimony that my father married in accordance with the laws and held a wedding feast for his phratry. Besides, I have demonstrated that I myself participated in everything appropriate to free men. The result is that you would honorably and properly abide by your oaths if you

---

[37] Perhaps the jury and spectators shouted the speaker down at the trial, impelling him to omit some of what he was going to say, and this event motivated a revision when the speech was published.

[38] For the Thesmothetae, see above, Ant. 6.21n. On this passage, see Scafuro 1994.

[39] See 57.21n.

cast your ballot for us. [70] Further, gentlemen of the jury, when you interrogate the nine Archons, you ask whether they treat their parents decently. Well, I was left orphaned by my father, and I beg and beseech you: by this trial give me back the right to bury my mother in our ancestral tombs, and do not prevent me from doing so. Do not make me an outcast from my city, do not deprive me of so many family members, and do not utterly destroy me. Rather than leave them behind if I cannot be saved by them, I would kill myself, so they could at least bury me in my fatherland.

LYSIAS 23. AGAINST PANCLEON

~~~~~~

INTRODUCTION

The connection between Plataea and Athens has been discussed in the Introduction to Lysias 3 (above). In that speech there are incidental problems of interpretation arising from the status of Theodotus, the male prostitute who forms the object of the dispute and who does not appear to be an Athenian citizen, even though he seems unquestionably to be from Plataea.[1] In Lysias 23, on the other hand, the status of the speaker's opponent Pancleon is central, in that he is evidently claiming to be an Athenian citizen by virtue of being a Plataean, a claim that the speaker is contesting.

Despite the manuscript title, Lysias 23 is not in fact a prosecution speech, but a defense against what it describes as an *antigraphē* brought by Pancleon (23.5). This procedure is not otherwise attested, but it appears to be a variant form of *paragraphē* or countersuit, arguing that the case was inadmissible for one of a number of reasons (see Dem. 35, below). These include the plea that the *dikē* had been brought before the wrong court, which is apparently the basis of Pancleon's argument here (23.2). When the speaker initially summoned him before the court of the Polemarch, the Archon who dealt with most cases involving metics (Introduction, IVB), Pancleon asserted that as a Plataean he was an Athenian citizen. Private prosecutions against citizens had to be brought before the tribal judges (Introduction, IVA), and the speaker had therefore demanded to know Pancleon's deme (Introduc-

---

[1] Athenian citizenship was granted to those citizens of Plataea who chose to register for it after the destruction of Plataea by Thebes in 427.

tion, IVB), partly to know how to issue the correct summons but also by implication to be in a position to challenge the veracity of Pancleon's claim.

In an elaborate and fascinating account of his detective endeavors, the speaker recounts how he had questioned first of all the members of the deme Decelea at the barber's shop that they use as an informal meeting place (23.3) and then the citizens of Plataea at what appears to be their monthly plenary meeting (23.6). This account highlights the continuing existence of the Plataeans as an identifiable group at Athens at the date of the speech,[2] with regular meetings serving to maintain this identity despite the dispersal of their members among the various Athenian demes, and the role of oral memory rather than a written membership list in identifying members of the group.

The narrative leads inexorably and with superficial plausibility to the attempted seizure of Pancleon by Nicomedes (23.9–11), who claims that Pancleon is his slave. Nicomedes is introduced with a studied impression of casualness: he has evidently appeared as one of the witnesses in 23.8 but without being named. The inference that we are clearly intended to draw from 23.9–11 is that Nicomedes' claim is justified, and it has indeed been suggested that the speaker is colluding with Nicomedes to this end, or in other words that the speaker is aiming not so much to win his original case as to have the satisfaction of watching Nicomedes seize Pancleon the moment the verdict makes it clear that Pancleon is lying about his status.[3] This hypothesis is not capable of proof, but it would account for one very peculiar feature of the speech: whereas all the other extant speeches from *paragraphē* disputes (Isoc. 18 and Dem. 32–38) deal not only with the technical question of whether the case is admissible but also (and exhaustively) with the dispute itself, in this speech uniquely the speaker displays no interest whatever in the dispute.

One other odd feature of this speech is the persistent reference to

---

[2] Evidently after the introduction of *paragraphē* in or soon after 403, and presumably before the rebuilding of Plataea in 386.

[3] For this interpretation, see Todd 1993: 168–169; contra E. Cohen 1994: esp. 147–148.

the water clock (Introduction, VC), used to regulate the time allotted
to each litigant, when introducing witnesses (23.4, 8, 11, 14, 15). This is
mentioned nowhere else in the corpus of Lysias but occasionally in the
speeches of other orators (e.g., Dem. 54.36). The use of the formula
here is regarded by some scholars as evidence that this speech is not
really by Lysias but by another orator, though it is also possible that
there may be tactical reasons for its use, for instance, to create an
impression that the speaker has no time to waste.[4]

Lysias 23 is discussed as one of the case studies in Todd 1993:
167–170.

LYSIAS 23. AGAINST PANCLEON

[1] I would not be able to speak at length about this case, members
of the jury, and there seems to me no need to do so. But I shall attempt
to show you that I have acted correctly in initiating this *dikē* against
Pancleon here, since he is not a Plataean.

[2] Because for a long time he would not stop doing me wrong, I
went to the fuller's where he worked; and thinking that he was a metic,
I served him with a summons to appear before the court of the Polemarch. On his claiming that he was a Plataean, I asked him his deme,
because one of the bystanders advised me to issue an additional summons before the court of whatever tribe he claimed to belong to.
When he replied that he was from Decelea, I summoned him also
before the judges for the tribe Hippothontis,[5] [3] and I went to the
barber's near the Herms, which is frequented by the members of
Decelea,[6] and asked those of the Deceleans I met there whether they

---

[4] For which cf. the emphasis at 23.1 and 23.11 on not talking at length and the
use of no fewer than five sets of witnesses (who do not use up the speaker's time)
in such a short speech.

[5] Hippothontis is the tribe that includes the deme Decelea. For the (forty)
tribal judges, see the Introduction, IVA.

[6] The Herm was a nonrepresentational image of the god Hermes, consisting of
a tetragonal pillar surmounted by a head and (in the archaic and classical periods)
with an erect phallus projecting from the front. These images stood at the front of
private and public buildings.

knew any deme member from Decelea called Pancleon. None of them claimed to know him—and I discovered that there were also other *dikai* before the Polemarch, in which he was defending himself or had already been forced to pay damages—and so I too initiated proceedings against him.

[4] I shall produce for you as witnesses first those of the Deceleans whom I questioned, and then also any of the others who have initiated proceedings against him before the Polemarch and have won their *dikai* against him, if they happen to be present. Please stop the water for me.[7]

[WITNESSES]

[5] I trusted this information and initiated the *dikē* against him in the court of the Polemarch. However, when Pancleon brought an *antigraphē*,[8] claiming that my *dikē* was not admissible, I was very concerned that nobody should think me eager to behave with arrogance (*hybris*) rather than simply wanting to obtain satisfaction for the wrongs done to me. So I first asked Euthycritus, who I knew was the oldest of the Plataeans and I thought would be the best informed, whether he knew a Plataean called Pancleon the son of Hipparmodorus. [6] He replied that he knew Hipparmodorus but was not aware of any son, either Pancleon or anybody else. So I then asked also those others whom I knew to be Plataeans. None of them knew his name, but they said I would obtain the most accurate information by going to the fresh-cheese market on the last day of the month, because the Plataeans assemble there on a monthly basis. [7] So I went on that day to the cheese market and asked them whether they knew somebody called Pancleon, a fellow-citizen of theirs. The others said they knew nothing, but one man stated that although he was not aware that any of the citizens had this name, nevertheless he said he had a slave called Pancleon, who had run away. He told me the slave's age, which was that of the defendant, and the occupation (*technē*), which was the one that the defendant

---

[7] In private cases the water clock (Introduction, VC) was stopped for the reading of documents, such as witnesses' testimonies.

[8] For the use of this "countersuit," see the Speech Introduction.

practices. [8] As witnesses that this is true, I shall produce Euthycritus, whom I first asked, and the other Plataeans I met, and Nicomedes, the one who claimed to be the defendant's master. Please stop the water for me.

[WITNESSES]

[9] Not many days later, I saw the defendant Pancleon being dragged off by Nicomedes, who has testified to being his master. I went up to them, wishing to know what exactly was happening about him. When they stopped fighting, some of those with the defendant said he had a brother who would vindicate his status as a free man. On this basis they departed after pledging themselves as sureties that they would produce the brother the next day. [10] So next day, in view of this *antigraphē* and the *dikē* itself, I decided I should be present with witnesses, so that I would be aware of the person who was due to vindicate his status, and what he would say when he did. Neither a brother nor anybody else turned up to fulfill the pledges, but a woman came, claiming that he was her slave.[9] She began an argument with Nicomedes and refused to allow him to take Pancleon away. [11] It would be a lengthy account to describe everything that was said there, but the defendant himself and those accompanying him reached such a level of violence that although Nicomedes on the one hand, and the woman on the other, were both willing to let him go if anybody vindicated his status as a free man or arrested him claiming he was his slave, they did none of these things but left, taking him with them. I shall produce witnesses for you that sureties were pledged on these conditions the previous day and that on the day in question they carried him off by force. Please stop the water for me.

[WITNESSES]

[12] It is easy therefore to be sure that not even Pancleon believes in himself—not simply that he is not a Plataean but that he is not even

---

[9] It is interesting that a woman can claim this in her own right, even if only in the informal context of a street dispute rather than the formal context of a lawcourt.

free. If somebody is willing to be forcibly carried off and so render his close friends liable to prosecution for violence, rather than to have his status as a free man vindicated according to the laws and to exact a penalty from those who arrest him, it is not hard for anybody to recognize that such a person knew full well that he was a slave but was afraid to appoint sureties and stand trial on the question of his status.

[13] I imagine you are pretty clear from this that he is far from being a Plataean. Moreover, you will easily discover from his own actions that even the defendant himself, who is in the best position to know his own affairs, did not expect you to regard him as a Plataean. At the pretrial oath[10] in the *dikē* that Aristodicus here initiated against him, when he was claiming that *dikai* involving him should not be brought before the court of the Polemarch, he was the object of a *diamartyria*[11] that stated that he was not a Plataean. [14] He gave a formal undertaking (*episkēpsis*) that he would prosecute the *diamartyria* witness but failed to do so. Instead, he allowed Aristodicus to win the *dikē* against him. When he defaulted on the debt,[12] he paid off the penalty on whatever terms he could persuade Aristodicus to accept. I shall produce witnesses for you that these events are true. Please stop the water for me.

[WITNESSES]

[15] Before coming to this agreement with him, Pancleon moved away and lived as a metic at Thebes, because he was afraid of Aristodicus. I imagine you realize that if he really was a Plataean, it would be more sensible for him to live as a metic anywhere else rather than

---

[10] The *antōmosia,* which was sworn by the rival litigants.

[11] *Diamartyria* is a procedure by which, in the legal preliminaries before a trial, a litigant (in this case, Aristodicus) produces a witness formally to testify to a fact that has procedural consequences that are binding on the court until and unless the opponent succeeds in convicting the witness of giving false testimony. Here, the formal testimony is that Pancleon, as a non-Plataean, is subject to the jurisdiction of the Polemarch's court.

[12] Presumably referring to a debt arising out of a judgment won by Aristodicus.

Thebes[13]—so I shall produce witnesses to show you that he lived a long time there. Please stop the water for me.

[WITNESSES]

[16] I believe that my arguments are sufficient, gentlemen of the jury. If you bear them in mind, I know you will vote for justice and truth, which is precisely what I ask of you.

---

[13]Thebes had been responsible for the destruction of Plataea in 427 and for the massacre of those inhabitants who had surrendered.

DEMOSTHENES 59. AGAINST NEAERA

~~~~~~

INTRODUCTION

The author of this speech is almost certainly Apollodorus, father-in-law (also brother-in-law) of the man who delivers the first sixteen sections. The style of *Against Neaera* is repetitious and sprawling and shows other signs that the speech is not by Demosthenes himself. Yet *Against Neaera* holds exceptional interest for its picture of aspects of Athenian life seldom touched on with such detail in other texts. We see in particular how *hetairai,* deluxe prostitutes, played a part in the erotic and public lives of many Athenians, some of them very prominent.

Prostitution itself was not a crime in Athens, and men were at no risk of prosecution for employing prostitutes. Moreover, just beneath the surface of the speakers' contempt for prostitutes and their righteous denunciations of Neaera's alleged offenses against the city of Athens and her gods, we can see the possibility that some element of genuine affection and concern might have coexisted with the inherent brutality of paid sex with slave women and with manumitted women at risk of losing their freedom. Lysias was eager to bestow on his favorite the benefits of initiation into the Mysteries (21). Phrastor, when an invalid, felt closer to Neaera and her daughter than to his own relatives, despite the trick the women played on him (55–56). Epainetus, once Neaera's lover, though blackmailed and humiliated, was willing to contribute to a dowry for her daughter (69–70). In addition, in the often-quoted passage distinguishing wives from what we might call "kept" women (122), the speaker assigns the latter group the domains of "pleasure" and "tending," leaving wives only the role of mothering legitimate children and serving as "guardians" of the household.

The legal issue, then, is not prostitution and dissolute living but the integrity of Athenian citizenship. The prosecution has brought a *graphē xenias* against Neaera, a public action charging the fraudulent exercise of rights belonging exclusively to Athenian citizens. Athenian citizenship was highly valued by the Athenians for both its practical and symbolic advantages. Pericles' citizenship law (Introduction, IVB) restricted citizenship to those born to an Athenian father and mother. After the Peloponnesian War, when the law was neglected because of a shortage of manpower, the Athenians not only reinstated the Periclean law but went on to introduce further restrictions, as can be seen in the law quoted at 16. The procedures for enfranchising a foreigner, known mostly from this speech, were remarkably complex—"as if the aim is to restrict eligibility at all costs" (Todd 1993: 176)—and the prosecution's appeal to a sense of outrage at the alleged offense against citizen rights was certainly a plausible strategy. But it is quite apparent—in fact, all but explicit in the opening sections—that the prosecution's real motive is revenge against Stephanus, the man with whom Neaera was living.

In 348, some five to eight years before the trial for which this speech was written, Stephanus had successfully charged Apollodorus with proposing an illegal decree (*graphē paranomōn*),[1] though the jury opted for a fine far smaller than Stephanus had proposed (3–8). Later, Stephanus tried, without success, to have him convicted of homicide (9–10). Considering the damage they would have suffered if Stephanus fully succeeded in these court actions, it is hardly surprising that Apollodorus and his family were eager to strike back in the same forum. The prosecution, then, was really aiming at Stephanus, though its legal action was formally lodged against Neaera. If she was convicted, Stephanus would have been fined one thousand drachmas, a large but not crushing sum, and his children's status as Athenians might have been challenged; Neaera would have returned to slavery and lost all her property (16).[2]

---

[1] For the *graphē paranomōn* ("indictment for illegality"), see the Introduction, VA; cf. 59.90–91.

[2] Stephanus retreated from a greater risk to his property when threatened by Phrastor with prosecution for marrying off Neaera's daughter to him as if she were a citizen (52).

There is only one other surviving example of a speech written for a trial in which a woman was the defendant: Antiphon 1 *Against the Stepmother*. A few other such trials are mentioned in the course of Demosthenes' speeches (25.57, 57.8). But if our surviving speeches are at all representative of litigation in general, legal action against women was very rare.[3] Athenian men were hardly chivalrous, and so we may assume that legal and cultural restrictions on women's power and property rights normally made them not worth prosecuting. Neaera, one of those rare female defendants, was almost certainly in the courtroom to hear the charges against her; at least the speech refers to her as present (esp. at 115). Like other women, even those who enjoyed unchallenged Athenian citizenship, Neaera was not permitted to present her own defense but had to rely on men to speak for her.[4]

By dint of Neaera's profession, the speech received relatively scant attention until classical scholars became interested in the lives of ancient women and could publish their research on sexuality in frank English. English-speaking readers can now consult a rich bibliography, including Carey 1992, Kapparis 1999, and Hamel 2003.

DEMOSTHENES 59. AGAINST NEAERA

[1] Gentlemen of the jury,[5] many things have spurred me on to bring this action against Neaera and come before you in court. You see, Stephanus has done us—my brother-in-law, me, my sister, my wife—great harm, and it is because of him that we came into extreme danger. Therefore, I am not taking the initiative in bringing this case but am seeking retribution. In fact, I am acting in self-defense: he was

---

[3] Note, however, that a woman involved in an inheritance dispute could easily be one of the claimants in a *diadikasia* ("adjudication hearing"), in which, properly speaking, there were no prosecutors and defendants; see, for instance, Dem. 43.8, where the speaker mentions serving as his wife's advocate in an earlier *diadikasia*.

[4] Some readers may see Neaera as a sort of Moll Flanders, but Defoe's heroine could at least speak for herself in court.

[5] Theomnestus, the prosecutor, speaks first. Apollodorus, in the role of "cospeaker" (*synēgoros*), takes over at 16 and completes the speech. See Rubinstein 2000: 133–135.

*think speaker married to Andollous daughter
think hcis Andopolous brother.*

the one who started the quarrel, though he had not had any trouble from our side—not in words, not in action. I want to start by telling you what he has done to us and how we have fallen into the great risk of exile and disenfranchisement. That way you will be more sympathetic to me as I present my defense.

[2] Now then, when the Athenian Assembly[6] voted to make Pasion and his descendants Athenian citizens, in gratitude for the good things he had done for the city,[7] my father agreed with the Assembly's gift of citizenship. He gave his daughter, my sister, in marriage to Pasion's son Apollodorus; and Apollodorus had children by her. Apollodorus was good to my sister and the rest of us and thought of us truly as family, as people who should share all that was his; and I took Apollodorus' daughter, my niece, to be my wife.

[3] Time went by, and Apollodorus was assigned by lot to serve on the Council. He passed the preliminary scrutiny (*dokimasia*) and swore the oath required by law. Then[8] the city found itself in a military emergency, which presented two possibilities. One was that you would prevail and be the greatest city of the Greeks: you would, without question, get your own possessions back in your hands and defeat Philip decisively. The other was that you would be too slow with your help and would forsake your allies; in that case, your army, lacking resources, would be disbanded, which would mean ruining those allies and appearing untrustworthy to the other Greeks; and it would mean also running the risk of losing your remaining possessions: Lemnos, Imbros, Scyros, and the Chersonese. [4] When you were on the verge of marching in full force to Euboea and Olynthus, Apollodorus, as a Council member, introduced a bill in the Council, and it passed, an agenda item (*probouleuma*) to be taken to the Assembly, providing for that body to make a choice by its vote whether the leftover funds of the financial administration were to be applied to the military fund or

---

[6] "Assembly" translates the Greek word *dēmos*. Besides this institutional sense, equivalent to *ekklēsia*, the word can also mean "the people" or "the poor people."

[7] Much is known about Pasion's career; see the Introduction to Isocrates 17. Pasion's benefactions recognized by the Assembly's decree included the gift of one thousand shields and voluntary service as a trierarch (Dem. 45.85).

[8] In the spring of 348.

the theoric⁹ fund. The laws required that in wartime the funds go to the military, but he thought that the Assembly should have the right to do whatever it wanted when it came to its own resources. He swore he would offer the people of Athens his best counsel, and all of you¹⁰ were witnesses at that critical time. [5] The vote was held, and *nobody* voted against using the funds for the military. In fact, even now, if the matter ever comes up for discussion, everybody agrees that the man who gave the best advice on that occasion was treated unfairly. It's right to be angry at a man who tricks the jurymen with his words—but not at those who got tricked. What happened was that Stephanus, this man here, indicted this decree as illegal;¹¹ in court he introduced false witnesses to claim that Apollodorus had been in debt to the Public Treasury for twenty-five years and brought up lots of other charges irrelevant to the indictment; and he got the decree declared illegal.

[6] If Stephanus thought he had done well to bring this about, we have no complaint. But when the jurors turned to voting on the penalty,¹² we begged him to compromise; he refused and proposed a fine of fifteen talents, meaning to take citizen rights away from Apollodorus and his children and to put my sister and all of us into the deepest poverty, with absolutely nothing to our names. [7] Apollodorus' total property, from which such a big fine would have to be paid, came to not quite three talents; and if he didn't pay off the fine before the ninth Prytany,¹³ the fine would be doubled, and Apollodorus would be listed as owing the Treasury thirty talents. Then his belongings would be put on the list of public property, and once they were sold off, he and his children and wife and all of us would end up completely ruined. [8] On top of that, he would not be able to marry off his other daughter. After all, who would marry a girl who had no dowry and whose father was in debt to the Treasury and penniless? So Stephanus gave us all such great trouble, though he had not yet been

---

⁹ A fund to help poor Athenians pay for tickets to the theatrical events during the Dionysia and Lenaean festivals.

¹⁰ Athenian orators often speak as if the jurors in a particular case also participated in or observed certain actions by the Assembly or a lawcourt, even if they were not alive at the time.

¹¹ By means of a *graphē paranomōn* (Introduction, VA).

¹² For this procedure (*timēsis*), see the Introduction, VC.

¹³ A Prytany was one-tenth of the Athenian year (Introduction, IVA).

harmed by us. I really do feel grateful to the jurors who decided that case in one point at least, that they did not let him be ruined but instead fined him one talent. That much he could pay off, though it was hard. To Stephanus, though, we have tried—as is only just—to give a dose of the same medicine he was giving to others.

[9] In fact, he not only tried to ruin us but actually tried to run Apollodorus out of his own country. You see, he brought a false charge against him, claiming that once, when he had gone to Aphidna[14] on the trail of a runaway slave of his, he hit a woman, who in the end died of her wounds. Stephanus bribed some slaves and coached them to say they were from Cyrene[15] and then announced that he was bringing a homicide charge against him in the Court of the Palladion.[16] [10] Then Stephanus, the man before you, presented his case. He swore on his own head, on his family, and on his house that Apollodorus killed that woman with his own hands. But that never happened; and he did not see it happen; and he never heard it from anybody else. It was proved that Stephanus perjured himself and brought a false charge, and it was clear that he had been paid off by Ctesiphon and Apollophanes[17] to drive Apollodorus into exile and take away his citizen rights. He got only a few of the five hundred votes,[18] and people thought he had committed perjury and was a scoundrel.

[11] Gentlemen of the jury, please think over in your minds what

---

[14] A town in Attica northeast of Athens.

[15] On the coast of north Africa (modern Libya).

[16] Though this account of the prosecution is far from clear, it seems likely that the woman who died was a slave owned by Stephanus. First, Apollodorus' assault was presumably intentional, and the trial was held not in the Areopagus, the venue when the victim of intentional assault was a citizen, but in the Palladion, the court that heard cases when the victim was a slave, foreigner, or metic (resident alien). Second, the woman is not identified as Stephanus' relative; hence he would be excluded from prosecuting unless she was his slave. Theomnestus' claim that Stephanus was disguising the slaves as Cyreneans suggests that this was a ploy to allow them to testify without being subject to torture.

[17] There are two men named Ctesiphon known from the sources as politicians associated with the sort of action here described, but no candidate has emerged for identification as Apollophanes.

[18] Some manuscripts of the speech have the word "drachmas" after "five hundred." This translation follows those editors who regard the word "drachmas" as a mistaken addition to the original text.

makes sense. How could I face myself, my wife, and my sister if Apollodorus was injured by Stephanus' plots against him in either the first or second trial? Imagine my shame and misfortune! [12] Everybody was coming to me in private and urging me to try to get back at him for what he had done to us. They were scolding me, saying I was no man if I didn't get justice for people who were so close to me—my sister, and brother-in-law, and nieces, and my own wife; and I was no man at all if I didn't bring before you in court the woman who was openly defiling the gods, insulting the city, and scorning your laws, and show you that she is guilty. That way I would put *you* in charge, and you could deal with her as you wanted. [13] Just as Stephanus here tried to ruin my people, violating your laws and decrees, so I have come here to show you that he is living with a foreign woman against the law, has brought other men's children before the phratries and deme[19] assemblies, and has married off the daughters of *hetairai* as if they were his own; also that he has committed impiety against the gods and has robbed the people of their power to decide whom *they* want to make Athenian citizens. After all, who will try to get this gift of citizenship from the people, spending money and going to trouble, if it's possible to get citizenship from Stephanus, at a smaller price?— that is, if the same power to grant citizenship falls into his hands.

[14] I have now told you how Stephanus did me wrong before I brought this suit. Next, I will move on to other things you must understand: that Neaera here is a foreigner, that she lives with Stephanus as married,[20] and that she has committed many illegal offenses against the city. So now I'll ask you, gentlemen of the jury, something that I think proper for someone both young and without experience in public speaking to ask: please let me call Apollodorus up here to help me do the speaking.[21] [15] He is older than I am, more experienced in the law,

---

[19] See Dem. 57 and the note on 57.23.

[20] "Lives with" literally translates the Greek word *synoikein,* which in Athens generally connoted legal wedlock. The words "as married" are not explicit in the Greek. See 59.16n and 122, where Apollodorus tries to insist that *synoikein* suggests the intention to present sons produced by the union as eligible for citizenship and daughters as his own.

[21] As the jury did not need to assent to the calling of a *synēgoros,* Theomnestus' request is probably a ploy to win some sympathy for his inexperience and at the

and has looked into these matters with great care. Stephanus here has done Apollodorus wrong, so you must not be angry with him for taking vengeance for what has happened. And you are obliged, after you have listened to the details in both the prosecution's speech and the defense speech, to cast your vote on the basis of the truth— for the sake of the gods and the laws, justice, and yourselves.

[SPEECH BY APOLLODORUS, THE *SYNĒGOROS*]

[16] Theomnestus has told you, men of Athens, of the wrongs I have suffered at Stephanus' hands that have led me to rise and accuse Neaera, this woman here. I want to show you clearly that Neaera is a foreigner, and that she is living as married with Stephanus in violation of the law. But first the law that is the basis of Theomnestus' present suit and the reason why this case has come before you in court will be read out.[22]

[LAW] *If a foreign male by any manner or means lives as married[23] with an Athenian woman* (astē), *let anyone who is entitled to do so and wishes bring an indictment* (graphē) *before the Thesmothetae of the Athenians.[24] If he is convicted, let him be sold into slavery and his property sold. A third part of the proceeds is to go to the successful prosecutor. And if a foreign female cohabits with an Athenian man* (astos), *the same applies, and the man who cohabited with the foreign woman who has been convicted is to owe [the Treasury] one thousand drachmas.*

[17] You have heard the law, gentlemen, which forbids a foreign woman from living with an Athenian man, and an Athenian woman from living with a foreign man, and absolutely forbids such couples

---

same time anticipate and disarm antagonism to Apollodorus on the part of some of the jurors.

[22] The law that follows is accepted as genuine by all modern scholars, as are most of the other documents in this speech (which has an unusually large number and variety of them).

[23] See 14n. Since this law envisions false claims of citizenship on behalf of children born to couples who live together but are not both Athenian citizens, the connotation comes close to "cohabit."

[24] Any fully enfranchised Athenian citizen who wished could bring a *graphē* (Introduction, VE). For the Thesmothetae, see the Introduction, IVA.

from having children,[25] by any manner or means. But if someone does so, despite the law, it provides that a public action (*graphē*) be brought against them before the Thesmothetae, against both male and female foreigners, and the law orders that they be sold into slavery if convicted. That Neaera here is a foreigner is what I want to lay out for you, from the beginning of the story and in detail.

[18] A woman named Nicarete acquired seven little girls to raise from early childhood.[26] Nicarete was a freed slave of Charisus from Elis; her husband was Hippias, Charisus' cook. She was very shrewd at sizing up the physical attributes little girls would develop, an experienced expert at raising and educating them. That was the craft she had developed, and from it she made her living. [19] She called these girls her "daughters," so as to get the largest possible fees from men who wanted to be intimate with supposedly free women. She milked the profit of each girl's youthful years, then sold them outright, all seven of them: Anteia, Stratola, Aristocleia, Metaneira, Phila, Isthmias—and Neaera, this woman right here. [20] Just how each man acquired each of the women, and how they won their freedom from the men who bought them from Nicarete, I will tell you in the course of my speech—if you want to hear about it and I have enough time.[27]

But I want to go back to when Neaera belonged to Nicarete and worked with her body, getting paid by those who wanted to have sex with her. [21] Now then, Lysias, the sophist,[28] was a lover of Metaneira. Besides the other money he paid out for her, which he thought all went to Nicarete, her owner, he wanted to pay for Metaneira to be

---

[25] This would be understood to mean children who would be falsely presented as the legitimate offspring of two citizen parents and therefore entitled to Athenian citizenship.

[26] These were presumably girls either knowingly handed over to Nicarete by mothers or intermediaries, or exposed and then brought to her for possible adoption.

[27] As at 14, the speaker acts as if he will respond to the jury's wishes but in fact does not return to the subject.

[28] Almost certainly the celebrated orator. The term "sophist" could be applied to people who received payment (or were thought to do so) for a wide range of intellectual activities (cf. Aes. 1.173, where Socrates is so designated).

initiated in the mystery cult at Eleusis.[29] The expenses connected with
that festival and the rites would be for Metaneira's benefit alone, so she
would be grateful to him. He asked Nicarete to come to the ceremony,
bringing Metaneira along, so the girl could be initiated, and he promised that he himself would get her initiated. [22] When the women
arrived, Lysias did not take them to his own house, since he was
embarrassed to do so in front of his wife, Brachyllus' daughter, who
was also his niece, and his elderly mother, who lived there too. Instead,
he put up Metaneira and Nicarete with Philostratus of the deme Colonus, a friend of his, still a young man. This woman Neaera came along
with them, already working as a prostitute though she was not fully
grown. [23] I call Philostratus himself as a witness that I am telling the
truth when I say that Neaera belonged to Nicarete, went along with
her, and worked as a prostitute for any man willing to pay.

[DEPOSITION] *Philostratus son of Dionysius of the deme Colonus, testifies that he knew that Neaera was the property of Nicarete, who also
owned Metaneira, and that since their home was in Corinth, they
stayed with him when they were in Athens for the Mysteries. Lysias son
of Cephalus, his good friend, put them up with him.*

[24] Well then, men of Athens, after this, Simus the Thessalian
came to Athens with Neaera to attend the Great Panathenaea.[30] Nicarete accompanied her, and they stayed with Ctesippus son of Glauconides of the deme Cydantidae; Neaera joined the large company of
men eating and drinking, just as a *hetaira* does.[31] I will call witnesses
to the truth of my statements. [25] Please call up Euphiletus son of
Simon of the deme Aexone, and Aristomachus son of Critodemus of
the deme Alopece.

---

[29] Initiation in the Eleusinian Mysteries was not restricted to Athenian citizens: any Greek speaker, male or female, slave or free, was eligible to participate
in a ritual that evidently held out some hope for a better lot after death. For a
general discussion of mystery religion, see Burkert 1987.

[30] By far the most spectacular festival every four years at Athens. The Pana-
thenaic Procession is depicted in the Parthenon frieze, much of which is in the
British Museum.

[31] Respectable women were normally excluded from this sort of social contact
with men to whom they were not related.

ITNESSES] *Euphiletus son of Simon of the deme Aexone, and Aris-
machus son of Critodemus of the deme Alopece testify that they know
that Simus the Thessalian came to Athens for the Great Panathenaea,
and with him Nicarete and Neaera, the woman now on trial. Also,
that they stayed with Ctesippus son of Glauconides and that Neaera
drank with them, in the manner of a hetaira, and that many other
men were present and participated in the drinking in Ctesippus'
house.*

[26] Afterwards, when she brazenly plied her trade in Corinth and
became a celebrity, Neaera had other lovers, including Xenocleides the
poet and Hipparchus the actor; these men paid to keep her as their
mistress. As far as Xenocleides goes, I cannot provide his testimony
that I am telling the truth, since the laws do not permit him to be a
witness. [27] You see, when at Callistratus' urging you were rescuing
the Spartans, Xenocleides spoke in the Assembly in opposition to giving them assistance. He had bought the two-percent tax on grain in
peacetime[32] and was required to take his payments to the Council
building each Prytany, and so was exempt under the laws from going
out on that military expedition. But Stephanus here indicted him for
not taking part and slandered him in his speech in the lawcourt. Xenocleides was convicted and disfranchised. [28] Now, don't you think
this is scandalous, that this Stephanus has robbed men of their right
to speak in public, men who are citizens by birth and have a legitimate role in the city's affairs, while he thrusts men who are not part of
the city into citizenship—in violation of all the laws? But I will call
Hipparchus himself and force him, in accordance with the law, to
testify or to swear he knows nothing of the business. If he does not
come, I will subpoena him.[33] Please call Hipparchus.

[DEPOSITION] *Hipparchus of the deme Athmonon testifies that in
Corinth he and Xenocleides hired Neaera, the woman now on trial,*

---

[32] Under this tax-farming arrangement, a man or group of men making the
highest bid would be granted the exclusive right to collect the duty on all grain
entering or leaving Attica. How well or poorly the tax-farmer would do would
depend on the amount of grain subject to the duty as well as his efficiency in
making collections.

[33] Presumably Hipparchus has sworn an *exōmosia* (Introduction, VD) and does
not affirm this deposition; cf. Dem. 57.14n.

as a prostitute (hetaira), *one of those who hire themselves out. Neaera would drink with him in Corinth and also with Xenocleides the poet.*

[29] After this, she had two lovers, Timanoridas the Corinthian and Eucrates from Leucas. Since Nicarete was extravagant in her demands—she felt entitled to get all her daily household expenses out of these men—they paid thirty minas[34] to buy Neaera from her, in accordance with the city's laws, and make her, without qualification, their own slave. Then they kept her and used her for as long as they wanted. [30] But when they were about to marry, they told Neaera that since she had been their own mistress, they didn't want to see her working in Corinth or under the thumb of a brothel-keeper.[35] Instead, they would gladly get back less money than they had paid for her and also see her get something good out of it. Accordingly, they told her they would free her from slavery for one thousand drachmas less than the purchase price, five hundred for each man. They told her to find the other twenty minas and pay it to them. When Neaera heard what Eucrates and Timanoridas had to say, she called several of her ex-lovers to Corinth, in particular Phrynion of the deme Paeania the son of Demon and brother of Demochares. Phrynion lived a wild life and was a very big spender, as the older men among you will remember. [31] When Phrynion visited her, she told him what Eucrates and Timanoridas had said. She gave him the money she had collected from her other lovers as a contribution toward winning her freedom, together with whatever money she had put aside for herself; and she asked him to add in the rest needed to make up the twenty minas and pay it on her behalf to Eucrates and Timanoridas so she could be free. [32] Phrynion heard this with pleasure. He took the money contributed by her other lovers, added the remainder himself, then gave the twenty minas to Eucrates and Timanoridas for her freedom, on the condition she not work in Corinth. To attest the truth of what I am saying, I call as a witness a man who was there: please call Philagrus of the deme Melite.

---

[34] An impressive sum, given the prices reported for other slaves, e.g., three, five, and six minas for craftsmen mentioned at Dem. 27.9 (below).

[35] Evidently, the men regarded the arrangement as incompatible with the more settled life into which they were entering.

[DEPOSITION] *Philagrus of the deme Melite testifies that he was present in Corinth when Phrynion, Demochares' brother, paid twenty minas to Timanoridas of Corinth and Eucrates of Leucas for Neaera, the woman now on trial; and that after he paid the money, he took Neaera with him to Athens.*

[33] Next, Phrynion came here to Athens, with Neaera. He carried on with her in an unruly and reckless way. He would take her along everywhere to eat and drink, and he was always partying with her. He would openly take his pleasure with her[36] whenever and wherever he wanted, showing off to onlookers just how loose he was with her. He visited many men for entertainment with the woman, including Chabrias of the deme Aexone, when he threw a party to celebrate his victory in the four-horse chariot race at the Pythian Games in the archon year of Socratides. He had bought the team of horses from the sons of Mitys of Argos, and when he came back from Delphi, he gave a victory dinner in Colias.[37] There she got drunk, and many men were intimate with her while Phrynion slept—even Chabrias' slaves who were present to serve the refreshments. [34] As witnesses to the truth of what I am saying, I will provide men who were there and saw what happened. Please call up Chionides of the deme Xupete and Euthetion of the deme Cydathenaeum.

[DEPOSITION] *Chionides of the deme Xupete and Euthetion of the deme Cydathenaeum testify that Chabrias invited them to dinner when he gave a party celebrating his victory in the chariot race, and they were entertained at Colias. They know that Phrynion was present at that dinner and had with him Neaera, the woman now on trial; that they themselves fell asleep, and also Phrynion and Neaera; and that they noticed, during the night, that men got up and went to Neaera, including some of the attendants, slaves of Chabrias.*

[35] Now, since she was badly mistreated by Phrynion, and not loved as she expected she would be, and since he did not do her bidding, Neaera gathered things from his house and as much clothing

---

[36] The Greek can be understood as suggesting sexual intercourse.

[37] The party took place near, or just possibly in, a famous temple of Aphrodite.

and jewelry as he had given her, and also two slave girls, Thratta and Coccaline, and escaped to Megara. This was in the year when Asteius was Archon, when you were for the second time at war with the Spartans.[38] [36] She spent two years in Megara, the year of Asteius' archonship and the next year, when Alcisthenes was Archon. Her work as a prostitute was not bringing in enough money for her to run her household, since she was a big spender, and the Megarians are cheap and fussy; also, there wasn't much foreign traffic because the Megarians had sided with Sparta, and you had control of the sea. Neaera could not return to Corinth, since the terms of her being set free by Eucrates and Timanoridas prohibited her from working there.

[37] But when peace came, during the archonship of Phrasicleides[39] and the Spartans and the Thebans fought the Battle of Leuctra,[40] Stephanus went to Megara and established relations with Neaera as his mistress (*hetaira*) and had sex with her. She told him everything that had happened, including how Phrynion had mistreated her, and she gave him what she had taken from Phrynion when she left him. She was eager to have her home here in Athens but was afraid because she had wronged Phrynion: he was angry with her, and she knew his violent and disrespectful manner. She made Stephanus her protector (*prostates*).[41] [38] In Megara, Stephanus inflamed her emotions with his braggadocio, saying that Phrynion would be sorry if he touched her, that he would take her himself as his wife, that he would introduce the children she already had to the phratries as his own sons and make them citizens,[42] that nobody would do her wrong. So he brought her from Megara to Athens, along with her three children, Proxenus, Ariston, and a daughter, whom they now call Phano. [39] And Stepha-

---

[38] In 373/2.

[39] 371/0.

[40] In this battle, fought in Boeotian territory, Thebes dealt Sparta a decisive blow from which it never recovered.

[41] The term, which literally means "one standing in front," might here carry a technical sense. If so, Neaera was entering Athens as a freed slave (i.e., a metic) required to have an Athenian citizen acting as her official patron (*prostatēs*). But the term might be used informally to mean merely that Stephanus was looking out for her interests.

[42] See above, Dem. 57.23n.

nus set Neaera and the children up in a small house near the statue of the Whispering Hermes, between the houses of Dorotheus the Eleusinian and Cleinomachus. That's the house that Spintharus just recently bought from him for seven minas. Seven minas, then, was the extent of Stephanus' wealth, and no more. He brought Neaera to Athens for two reasons, to get himself a good-looking mistress for free and to have her provide for daily expenses by her work as a prostitute and keep the house going. You see, he didn't have any other income, except for what he made as a sykophant.

[40] When Phrynion learned that she was at Athens, with Stephanus, he took along some young men, went to Stephanus' house, and tried to take her away. Stephanus took legal action asserting that she was free,[43] and Phrynion made him post bond with the Polemarch. I will bring the man then serving as Polemarch to verify that I am telling the truth. Please call Aeetes of the deme Ceiriadae.

[DEPOSITION] *Aeetes of the deme Ceiriadae testifies that when he was Polemarch, Neaera, the woman now on trial, was required by Phrynion, brother of Demochares, to post bond; and the sureties for her were Stephanus of the deme Eroeadae, Glaucetes of the deme Cephisia, and Aristocrates of the deme Phalerum.*

[41] With Stephanus as her guarantor, Neaera lived with him and continued plying her trade no less than before. But now, exploiting the façade of living with a husband, she demanded higher fees from men who wanted to engage her. And together with Neaera, Stephanus would commit legal blackmail[44] on any rich foreigner he caught having sex with her, claiming that the man was a debaucher (*moichos*)[45] taken in the act. He would lock him in and demand money, lots of it—as you would expect. [42] Neither Stephanus nor Neaera had enough resources with which to meet their daily expenses. And their

---

[43] The action is called *aphairesis eis eleutherian* (lit. "take away to freedom"). Stephanus would have had to take along men prepared to guarantee her appearance in court (see the deposition that follows). For the Polemarch, see the Introduction, IVA.

[44] Lit. "would act as a sykophant" (Introduction, VE).

[45] For *moichos,* usually translated "adulterer," see the Introduction to Lys. 1, n. 1.

lifestyle was lavish, since there were the two of them to support and three young children whom she took along to live with him; also, three servants, two women and one man. The problem was aggravated by her having in the past learned to live luxuriously—at other people's expense. [43] And Stephanus was getting nothing worth mention from his participation in the city's affairs. He wasn't yet a public speaker, only a sykophant, one of those men who stand around the podium shouting, and is paid to indict people and brings *phasis* actions[46] and puts their names on other people's motions. Then he came under the thumb of Callistratus of the deme Aphidna. I will explain how and why[47] when I show you that this woman Neaera is a foreigner, that she has done you great wrongs, and that she has profaned the gods. [44] Then you will know that on his own, Stephanus deserves a punishment no smaller than Neaera but actually far greater: far greater because he boasts that he is an Athenian, and still he has so much contempt for the laws and for you and for the gods that not even shame for his own crimes restrains him, but he maliciously pursues me and others in the courts. Stephanus has thus brought it about that he himself and this woman have been brought by Theomnestus into court on a very serious charge and caused us to probe into just who she is and expose his wickedness.

[45] Then Phrynion brought suit against Stephanus because he had taken Neaera away from him by asserting her freedom and because Stephanus had received property that she had carried off from his house. But some friends brought the two men together and talked them into letting them arbitrate the dispute. Satyrus of the deme Alopece, Lacedaemonius' brother, served as an arbitrator representing Phrynion; representing Stephanus was Saurias of the deme Lamptrae. They chose Diogeiton of the deme Acharnae as the impartial arbitrator. [46] These men gathered in the temple and heard what happened from both men and from the woman herself. Then they gave their opinion. They granted her her freedom and control over her own affairs, but she was to return everything she had taken from Phrynion, except the clothes, jewelry, and serving women, which had been

---

[46] Here *phasis* is used for the formal denunciation of a man for possession of property belonging to the city.

[47] In fact, Apollodorus says no more on the subject (cf. above, 14 and 20n).

bought specifically for her. She was to stay with each man on alternate days, but if the men came to some other agreement with each other, that agreement would be valid. The man who had her on any given day was to provide for her needs, and from then on, the men were to be on friendly terms and not bear any grudge. [47] These, then, are the terms of reconciliation in the matter of Neaera decided on by the arbitrators for Phrynion and Stephanus. The clerk will read the deposition to show that I am telling the truth. Please call up Satyrus of the deme Alopece, Saurias of the deme Lamptrae, and Diogeiton of the deme Acharnae.

> [DEPOSITION] *Satyrus of the deme Alopece, Saurias of the deme Lamptrae, and Diogeiton of the deme Acharnae testify that, serving as arbitrators, they reconciled Stephanus and Phrynion to each other in the matter of Neaera, the woman now on trial. The terms of the reconciliation are as Apollodorus presents them.*

> [TERMS OF RECONCILIATION] *Phrynion and Stephanus have settled their quarrel on these terms. Each is to have and enjoy Neaera an equal number of days each month, unless they mutually agree to some other arrangement.*

[48] The reconciliation accomplished, the friends of the two sides left the scene of the arbitration, and something happened that I suppose is common in such matters, especially when a quarrel involves a *hetaira*. They went to dinner at each man's house when he had his turn with Neaera, and she ate and drank with them, just as a *hetaira* does. Please call those who were present as witnesses to the truth of what I am saying: Eubulus of the deme Probalinthus,[48] Diopeithes of the deme Melite, and Cteson of the deme Cerameis.

> [WITNESSES] *Eubulus of the deme Probalinthus, Diopeithes of the deme Melite, and Cteson of the deme Cerameis testify that when the reconciliation in the matter of Neaera had been arranged for Phrynion and Stephanus, they often ate and drank together, along with Neaera, the woman now on trial; sometimes they were at Stephanus' place, sometimes at Phrynion's.*

---

[48] Eubulus was one of fourth-century Athens' most distinguished politicians. It is startling that he is testifying for Apollodorus, for some five to eight years before, he was involved in litigation against him.

[49] So far, I have shown in my speech and it has been confirmed by witnesses that she was from the start a slave, that she was sold twice, that she used her body working as a *hetaira,* that she escaped from Phrynion and went to Megara, and that when she came here she needed to post bond as a foreigner with the Polemarch. Now I want to show you that even Stephanus himself, this man here, gave testimony against her, saying she was a foreigner. [50] You see, Stephanus gave Neaera's daughter, the one she brought with her to Athens as a little girl, who was then called Strybele but is now called Phano, in marriage to an Athenian, Phrastor of the deme Aegilla, together with a dowry of thirty minas—making her out to be his own daughter. But when the girl went to Phrastor, a conscientious workman, one who had assembled his wealth by living carefully, she didn't know how to fit in with his way of doing things; instead, she tried to follow her mother's character, including her wildness. I guess that was how she was brought up. [51] Anyway, Phrastor saw that she was not a respectable woman and was refusing to obey him. At the same time, he had learned for certain that she was not Stephanus' daughter, but Neaera's. At first when he agreed to marry the girl, he had been tricked into regarding her as Stephanus' daughter, not Neaera's, a daughter whom Stephanus had with an Athenian woman before he lived with Neaera. Phrastor was furious at this. Feeling insulted and duped, he threw the girl out of his house after she had lived with him about a year and was pregnant. He refused to give back her dowry. [52] Stephanus initiated a private suit at the Court at the Odeion[49] against him, demanding that he pay to support the girl (*dikē sitou*).[50] Stephanus took this action in accordance with the law that if a man sends his wife away, he is to return the dowry; otherwise, he must pay interest on it at an annual rate of eighteen percent,[51] and the woman's guardian (*kyrios*) can bring

essay.

---

[49] This passage shows that at the time of the trial, there was a specific venue for some sorts of litigation. The Odeion (lit. "a building for songs") was originally built as a concert hall. Not long after, the system was altered to make the assignment of magistrates (together with the cases over which they presided) to the various sites one of several procedural steps decided by lot the morning of the trial (*Ath. Pol.* 66).

[50] Lit. "a (private) law case pertaining to grain or in a wider sense to food."

[51] Lit. "at nine obols," i.e., nine obols per mina (600 obols) per month, amounting to 1.5% per month or 18% per year. This is a typical interest rate.

suit at the Odeion over the matter of her support. Phrastor initiated a public action (*graphē*)[52] against Stephanus before the Thesmothetae, claiming, in accordance with the following law, that Stephanus had betrothed to him, an Athenian, the daughter of a foreign woman whom he presented as his own but was in fact the daughter of a foreign woman. Please read out the law.

[LAW] *If a man gives a foreign woman in marriage to an Athenian man, claiming that she is his own relative, he is to lose his citizen rights, his property is to be confiscated, and the man who brings a successful prosecution is to receive one-third of the property. The actions* (graphai) *are to be initiated before the Thesmothetae, just like actions claiming usurpation of citizen rights* (graphai xenias).

[53] I have had the law read out under which Phrastor indicted Stephanus before the Thesmothetae. Because he knew that he was in danger of being exposed for marrying off the daughter of a foreign woman and incurring the most extreme penalties, Stephanus came to terms with Phrastor, abandoned the dowry, and dropped his suit for the woman's support. Phrastor in turn dropped his action before the Thesmothetae. I will call Phrastor himself as a witness to the truth of what I'm saying and, as the law provides, compel him to testify.[53] [54] Please call Phrastor of the deme Aegilia.

[DEPOSITION] *Phrastor of the deme Aegilia testifies that when he realized that Stephanus had given him in marriage the daughter of Neaera, as if she were his own daughter, he brought a* graphē *against him before the Thesmothetae in accordance with the law; that he expelled the woman from his house and did not continue to live with her; and that when Stephanus started a* dikē *for support of the woman in the Court at the Odeion, he and Stephanus came to an agreement with one another that provided that the* graphē *before the Thesmothetae be dropped and also the* dikē *for support initiated against me by Stephanus.*[54]

---

[52] Phrastor's move represents an escalation, as a *graphē* was generally more serious than a *dikē*.

[53] This suggests that he swore an *exōmosia* (Introduction, VD) and does not affirm this deposition.

[54] The sudden switch from third to first person is one of several peculiarities in this document that have led scholars to question its authenticity.

why would you give this to the women

[55] Now let me present some other testimony, both from Phrastor and his phratry members and clansmen (*gennetai*),[55] that Neaera here is a foreigner. Not long after Phrastor sent Neaera's daughter away, he got sick. His condition was very poor, and he had simply no way to help himself. He had, long before, quarreled with his relatives, and there was anger and hatred on both sides. Besides that, he had no children. With Phrastor in this condition, Neaera and her daughter worked on his emotions, exploiting his need to be cared for. [56] You see, they had gone to him when he was sick and had nobody to nurse him in his illness, and were taking him the right things and watching over him. I'm sure you all realize how useful a woman is when you're sick, being there when you're doing badly. Anyway, Phrastor was talked into taking back and adopting as his own son the little boy whom Neaera's daughter was carrying when she was expelled from his house, pregnant, because he had found out that she was Neaera's daughter, not Stephanus', and he was angry at being tricked. [57] Phrastor put two and two together, as anybody would, figuring that he was in bad shape and there was not much hope he would survive; and so, to keep his relatives from taking his property and so as not to die childless, he adopted the boy as his son and took him into his house.[56]

essay

He would *not* have done this if he had been in good health, as I will show you with clear and compelling evidence. [58] As soon as Phrastor recovered and had pretty well regained his strength, he married an Athenian woman in accordance with the laws—Diphilus' sister, the legitimate daughter of Satyrus of the deme Melite. This should count as proof for you that Phrastor did not recognize the boy willingly. No, he was forced by illness, by his not having other children, by his need to be taken care of by the women, and by his feud with his relatives, whom he wanted to keep from inheriting his property if something happened to him. And what happened next makes the point even better. [59] When Phrastor was sick, he took that boy, the son of Neaera's daughter, to the phratry and the Brytidae—that was Phrastor's clan—the clan members, I suppose, knew that the woman whom Phrastor had first married was Neaera's daughter, and how he sent her away, and that it was because of his illness that he was persuaded to take the boy back. And so, they voted against the boy and would not enroll him in

---

[55] See Dem. 57.23n.

[56] These were common motives for adoption.

the phratry. [60] When Phrastor brought a suit against them for not enrolling his son, the clan members challenged him to swear, before an arbitrator, over sacrificial offerings that he regarded the son as born to him from an Athenian woman (*astē*), legally married to him. When the clan members made this challenge before the arbitrator, Phrastor refused the oath and did not swear. [61] I will present as witnesses to the truth of my statements members of the clan Brytidae who were in attendance.

[WITNESSES] *Timostratus of the deme Hecale, Xanthippus of the deme Eroeadae, Evalces of the deme Phalerum, Anytus of the deme Laciadae, Euphranor of the deme Aegilia, Nicippus of the deme Cephale testify that they and Phrastor of the deme Aegilia are members of the clan called Brytidae; and that when Phrastor asked that his son be enrolled in the clan, since they knew for themselves that the boy's mother was Neaera's daughter, they prevented his enrolling the boy.*

[62] I will show you, very clearly, that even Neaera's closest friends have testified that she is a foreigner, both Stephanus, who now has her, and Phrastor, who took her daughter in marriage. Stephanus, for his part was unwilling to go to trial in support of his daughter when he was charged by Phrastor before the Thesmothetae with giving him, an Athenian, the daughter of a foreign woman in marriage. Instead, Stephanus relinquished the dowry and would not take it back. [63] Phrastor, for his part, after he married Neaera's daughter, expelled her from his house on learning that she was not Stephanus' daughter and did not return the dowry. Later, when he was persuaded to adopt the boy—owing to his sickness, his childlessness, and his feud with his relatives—he brought him to his *genos,* but the *genos* voted to reject him, and when they challenged him to swear under oath, he refused; instead, he preferred to avoid perjury. Afterward, he married another woman, an Athenian (*astē*), in accordance with the law. These actions were performed in the open, and they give powerful testimony against Neaera and Stephanus that this woman Neaera is a foreigner.

[64] You should also observe Stephanus' shameful, wicked way of turning a profit. That's another way you can know that Neaera here is no Athenian (*astē*). You see, Stephanus plotted against Epainetus, a man from Andros.[57] Epainetus had been Neaera's lover and had spent

---

[57] An island in the Aegean, very near Athens.

a lot of money on her. Whenever he came to Athens he stayed with Neaera and Stephanus, since he was her friend. [65] Stephanus here plotted against Epainetus. He invited him to the country, supposedly for a sacrifice, and then seized Epainetus for illicit sex with Neaera's daughter.[58] This frightened Epainetus into settling with him for thirty minas.[59] Stephanus accepted as sureties Aristomachus, who had served as a Thesmothetes, and Nausiphilus the son of Nausinicus, who had been Archon; then he let Epainetus go on his promise to deliver the money. [66] After Epainetus left and was back in control of his person, he brought a *graphē* against Stephanus for false arrest (*adikōs heirchthēnai*).[60] This was under the law that provides that if a man falsely arrests someone on the claim that he is engaged in fornication, he is to be indicted before the Thesmothetae for illegal restraint; and if the complainant convicts the man for false arrest, and the verdict is that the complainant is the victim of criminal plotting, the complainant is immune, and the sureties are released from their guarantee. But if it is decided that the complainant is a debaucher,[61] the law provides for the sureties to hand him over to the man who arrested him, who can then, in a lawcourt, do to the debaucher whatever he wishes, provided he does not use a weapon.[62]

[67] It was in accord with this law, then, that Epainetus brought a *graphē* against Stephanus. Epainetus admitted having sex with Neaera's daughter but denied that he was a debaucher. He said that she was not Stephanus' daughter, but Neaera's. The mother knew her daughter was intimate with him, and he spent much money on the women, supporting the whole household when he was in town. Besides that, he cited a provision of the law that forbids seizing a man as a debaucher if the woman is set up in a brothel or is openly available as a prostitute. Epainetus said that Stephanus' house was a brothel, and prostitution was the business conducted there, and they profited handsomely from that business. [68] Those are the arguments Epainetus made in sup-

---

[58] This episode shows that the term *moicheia* (see above, 41n) could also be used in cases in which the "protected" woman was not the man's wife.

[59] Cf. the offer to settle at Lys. 1.25.

[60] Lit. "for being unjustly restrained," i.e., for entrapment.

[61] In Greek, "one who commits *moicheia*."

[62] Some sources (admittedly from the comic stage) speak of pushing a radish into the debaucher's anus.

port of his *graphē*. Now, Stephanus knew that he would be exposed as a pimp and sykophant, so he offered to go to arbitration with Epainetus, using those very sureties as arbitrators. The sureties would be released from their commitment, and Epainetus would drop his *graphē*. [69] Epainetus was persuaded to accept these terms, and he abandoned the *graphē* he was pursuing against Stephanus. They had a meeting, with the sureties sitting as arbitrators. Stephanus had no just claim to put forward but said he thought Epainetus should contribute to a dowry for Neaera's daughter. He said she was without means and mentioned the bad luck she had dealing with Phrastor and added that he had lost the dowry and could not provide another one. [70] "You've enjoyed the woman," he said, "so it's right that you do something nice for her." And he added other cajoling arguments, the sort of thing a man says when he's in great trouble. After the arbitrators heard both sides, they brought the two men to an agreement. They persuaded Epainetus to contribute one thousand drachmas for the dowry of Neaera's daughter. I will call as witnesses to the truth of what I have said the sureties, who also served as arbitrators.

[71] [WITNESSES] *Nausiphilus of the deme Cephale and Aristomachus of the deme Cephale testify that they were sureties for Epainetus of Andros when Stephanus declared that he had seized Epainetus in an act of illicit sex. Subsequently, when Epainetus left Stephanus' house and resumed control of his person, he brought a* graphē *against Stephanus before the Thesmothetae, charging him with false arrest. Later, as arbitrators, they reconciled Epainetus and Stephanus. The terms of reconciliation are the ones presented by Apollodorus.*

[TERMS OF RECONCILIATION] *The arbitrators have reconciled Epainetus and Stephanus on the following terms: They are to bear no grudge in the matter of the arrest, and Epainetus is to give one thousand drachmas to Phano for her dowry, since he enjoyed her company many times. Stephanus is to make Phano available to Epainetus whenever he is in town and wishes to be with her.*

[72] This man Stephanus and this woman Neaera were so outrageous and lacking in decency that they had the brass not just to claim that she was an Athenian (*astē*)—this woman who was openly acknowledged to be a foreigner and with whom he had dared to seize a man on the pretext of performing illicit sex. No, they went further: they

saw that Theogenes of the clan of the Coironidae had been appointed
by lot to serve as Basileus.[63] He was well born but poor and inexperienced. Stephanus stood by him when he was undergoing his scrutiny
(*dokimasia*)[64] and helped him meet his expenses when he entered into
his office. Then sneaking into Theogenes' affairs, Stephanus bought
the office of Assessor (*paredros*)[65] from him; finally he married that
woman Phano, Neaera's daughter, to him, making out that she was his
own daughter. That's how contemptuous he was of you and your laws.

[73] This woman performed the secret sacrifices on the city's behalf.
She saw things that were not proper for her, as a foreigner, to see. A
foreigner, she entered where no Athenian—and there are a great many
Athenians—other than the wife of the Basileus has ever entered. She
administered the oath to the elderly priestesses who tend to the sacred
rites. She was given as bride to Dionysus. On the city's behalf she
performed the many, secret ancestral rituals honoring the gods. If no
one is allowed even to hear about these things, it is certainly a profan-
ity if just any woman whatsoever does them, especially a woman like
this, who has committed acts like that.

[74] I want to relate these things one-by-one from the beginning in
greater detail so that you may give more care to the punishment and
so that you realize that you will be voting not only for yourselves and
the laws but also for the sake of piety toward the gods, when you take
vengeance for acts of impiety and punish the wrong-doers.

Now, men of Athens, in olden times there was monarchy in the
city, passed down through the generations and held by those who had
primacy because they were autochthonous.[66] The Basileus performed
all the sacrifices, and his wife performed the most solemn and secret,
which made sense, since she was the Queen (Basilinna). [75] But when
Theseus united the Athenians into a single city[67] and created the

---

[63] One of the nine Archons (Introduction, IVA); the Basileus plays a major
role in Ant. 6.

[64] For the scrutiny, see the Introduction, IVA.

[65] The Archon, Polemarch, and King each had two *paredroi* to assist them.

[66] Athenians often boasted that, unlike others, their ancestors were not immi-
grants (e.g., Thucydides 6.2; Lys. 2.17; Dem. 60.4).

[67] Like the claim of autochthony, Theseus' *synoikismos,* the political unification
of Attica, is a prominent element in the legends of early Athenian history. It is less
usual to credit him with founding the democracy.

where is the son.

democracy, and the city's population grew larger, they continued as before to choose the King by voting, looking for manly excellence (*andragathia*) from a group of preselected candidates. And they made a law that he had to marry an Athenian woman (*astē*) who had not had sex with any other man but was a virgin. The object was that the Queen would perform the secret sacrifices in traditional fashion on the city's behalf and that the customary rites would be performed with due reverence for the gods with nothing left out or altered. [76] They had this law inscribed on a stone pillar, and they set it up alongside the altar in the Temple of Dionysus in the Marshes. The actual pillar is still standing, even now, with its old Attic alphabet, the inscribed letters now faint.[68] With this law the democracy bears witness to its piety toward the god, and for future generations marks a sacred obligation that we should expect a woman to be like this if she is to be married to Dionysus and perform the sacred rites. For this reason, they erected the pillar in the most ancient and august Temple of Dionysus in the Marshes, to keep the general run of people from knowing what is written on it, for only once a year is the temple opened, on the twelfth day of the month Anthesterion.[69]

[77] It is therefore right, men of Athens, that you give serious attention to these holy and sacred rituals, rituals that your ancestors so nobly and generously tended, and right that you punish those who wantonly dishonor your laws, shamelessly committing impiety against the gods. There are two reasons to do so: to make sure that the violators pay the penalty for their crimes and in order that the others take heed and be afraid to wrong the gods and the city.

[78] I want to call the Sacred Herald who attends the wife of the Basileus when she swears in the elderly priestesses in the ceremony at the baskets by the altar before they touch the sacred objects. This is so you may hear the oath and other things that are said—as much as it is legal to hear—and so you appreciate just how august, sacred, and ancient our observances are.

---

[68] During the archonship of Eucleides (403/2) the city adopted a slightly different alphabet for official documents. The faintness of the letters might refer to erosion of the stone's surface or the flaking away of the paint (normally red) applied to the incisions.

[69] Corresponding to late February and early March.

[OATH OF THE ELDERLY PRIESTESSES][70] *I am pure, chaste, and without taint from things that are impure, including intercourse with men. I celebrate the Festival of the Wine God* (theoinia)[71] *and the Bacchic rite* (iobaccheia)[72] *honoring the god in accordance with the ancestral rule and at the appointed times.*

[79] You have heard the oath and our ancestral practices, to the extent that it is permitted to speak of them. And you have heard that the woman Stephanus gave in marriage, as his own daughter, to Theogenes, when he was serving as Basileus, performed these sacred rituals and swore in the elderly priestesses; also, you have heard that it is not allowed, even for the women themselves who observe the rites, to speak of these things to any other person. And now, let me present testimony to you that is illegal to quote, but that I can still put clearly and truly before you by means of the acts themselves. [80] You see, after these rites had been performed, the nine Archons went up to the Areopagus on the appointed days. The Council of the Areopagus, a worthy body especially in matters of state religion,[73] immediately conducted an inquiry into the identity of Theogenes' wife. They revealed her for who she was and took care for the sacred rites. They punished Theogenes to the extent they were empowered to do. The proceedings were confidential and orderly. They do not, after all, have the right to punish just any Athenian at their whim. [81] There was discussion, and the Council of the Areopagus was indignant and punished Theogenes for marrying such a woman and permitting her to perform the secret rituals for the city. But Theogenes, throwing himself at the Council's mercy and begging, asked them to relent. He said he did not

---

[70] Presumably this testimony was given in the standard fashion, i.e., the clerk would read it and the witness (here, the herald) would assent to it.

[71] Our only source for this festival (Harpocration, first or second century CE) describes it as involving sacrifices to Dionysus performed by clans in each deme.

[72] The name apparently derives from the cry, "O Bacchus!" (Euripides, *Bacchae* 528).

[73] The Areopagus (Introduction, VB) supervised certain sacred lands and sacred olive trees (see Lys. 7) and selected certain officials of the cult of the Eumenides. Its precise competence in other religious matters, including the fining of Theogenes, is controversial. For a broad treatment of this court, see Wallace 1989.

know that she was Neaera's daughter but had been tricked by Stephanus into accepting her as his legitimate daughter, as defined by law. It was because of his inexperience and naïveté that he made Stephanus his Assessor,[74] because he thought he would manage that office as a loyal friend, and that was why he became related to him by marriage. [82] "I will show you," he said, "with clear and convincing proof that I am not lying. I will send the woman away, since she is Neaera's daughter, not Stephanus'. If I do that, then you should believe right away what I've told you, that I was tricked. If I do not send her away, then punish me on the spot as an evil man, guilty of impiety to the gods." [83] That was what Theogenes promised when he made his plea. The Council pitied him for his honest ways, and at the same time they thought that he really had been tricked by Stephanus, and so they relented. When Theogenes came down from the Areopagus, he immediately threw the daughter of this woman Neaera out of his house and expelled Stephanus, the man who had fooled him, from his board of Assessors. And that is how it happened that the members of the Areopagus ended their trial and were no longer angry with Theogenes, but instead forgave him because he had been tricked. [84] I now call Theogenes and require him to give testimony that what I say is true.[75] Please call Theogenes of the deme Erchia.

> [DEPOSITION] *Theogenes of the deme Erchia testifies that when he was Basileus he married Phano, thinking she was the daughter of Stephanus; but when he found out that he had been tricked, he dismissed the woman and no longer lived with her. He also expelled Stephanus from his board of assessors and no longer allowed him to serve as his assessor.*

[85] Clerk, please take this law on these matters, and read it, so the jury will know that being the type of woman she was and having done the things she had done, Phano should have kept away not only from seeing these sacred things and performing any of the established, ancestral rites for the city, but also from seeing all other things of this sort in Athens. A woman with whom a debaucher has been found is not permitted to attend any of the city's rites, which the laws allow

---

[74] See above, 72.

[75] Again, Apollodorus' words suggest that Theogenes swore an *exōmosia* (Introduction, VD) and does not affirm this deposition.

even foreign and slave women to attend as observers or suppliants.
[86] The law forbids only those women with whom a debaucher has
been taken from entering the city's rites. If they enter in contravention
of the law, any man who wishes may with impunity do anything to
them, short of killing them. The law grants any man the right to
administer punishment for these offenses. The law provides that the
woman cannot get legal redress for any treatment she suffers except for
death, for this reason: that no pollution or impiety sully the sacred
rituals. The law frightens women enough to keep them chaste and
law-abiding, staying at home behaving properly. The law teaches them
that if they commit this sort of crime, they will be expelled from their
husband's home and from the city's sacred areas. [87] Once you have
heard the law itself read out, you will know that this is so. Clerk, please
take the text.

> [LAW ON DEBAUCHERY] *When a man catches a debaucher with his
> wife, it is not permitted for him to continue to live with her. If he does
> live with her, he is to be disenfranchised. And it is not permitted for
> the woman with whom a debaucher has been taken to appear at the
> city's sacred rituals. If she does so, she may be made to suffer anything
> short of being killed, immunity being granted to the person who pun-
> ishes her.*

[88] Next, men of Athens, I want to provide you testimony of the
seriousness with which the Athenian *dēmos* regards these religious
matters, and how much thoughtful care it has put into these things.
You see, the Athenian *dēmos* holds the greatest authority in the city,
and it may do whatever it wishes. It considered Athenian citizenship
to be so fine and august a gift that it instituted laws for itself that must
be followed if it wants to make someone a citizen. These are the laws
that now lie in the mud, thanks to Stephanus and those who have
married as he has. [89] Still, you will benefit from hearing about them,
and you will know how the noblest and most august gift the city can
bestow on its benefactors has been defiled. First, there is an established
law that prohibits the Assembly (*dēmos*) from making anyone an Athenian citizen who is not worthy of it by virtue of his upright action on
the city's behalf.[76] Second, when the city is persuaded to give this gift,

---

[76] "Upright action" normally took the form of lavish expenditure on public
works or military equipment.

it does not make the decree valid until, at the next meeting of the Assembly, it is approved by a secret vote of more than six thousand citizens.[77] [90] The law requires the Prytaneis[78] to place the ballot urns out for the Assembly before foreigners enter, and the barriers are lifted to make sure that each Assembly member think over entirely by himself whether the man up for citizenship is worthy to receive this gift. Then, the law provides that an indictment for an illegal proposal (*graphē paranomōn*)[79] can be instituted by any Athenian who wishes. He is allowed to go to court to expose a man as not worthy of the gift of citizenship and holding it in violation of the laws. [91] Already in some cases after the Assembly, hoodwinked by the speeches of the petitioners, granted citizenship, a *graphē paranomōn* was instituted: the man who had received the gift was exposed as unworthy, and the court stripped him of citizenship. Now, it would be a major project to go through the many cases from the past, but you all remember that the court canceled the citizenship given to Peitholas of Thessaly and Apollonides of Olynthus. [92] These cases are not too ancient for you to remember them. And although the laws on citizenship regulating how one becomes an Athenian are so excellently and effectively composed, there is another law of the greatest authority that has been enacted in addition to all the others. Such was the care the *dēmos* devoted on its own behalf and on behalf of the gods, to ensure that the sacrifices on the city's behalf are made in piety. The law explicitly forbids those made citizens by an act of the Athenian Assembly from holding any of the nine archonships or participating in any priesthood. The *dēmos* does, however, grant a share in all these privileges to

---

[77] The prosecution might be suspected of exaggerating, but in fact, citizenship was rarely bestowed, and the process was in fact difficult to transact. "The double procedure was introduced in about 370, and between 368 and 322 we have knowledge of fifty grants of citizenship, to sixty-four foreigners; since the sources are fragmentary as usual, it may be conjectured that several hundred people obtained citizenship by naturalization in those forty-seven years, but that is no great number, and most of them were foreign princes and statesmen who had no intention of settling in Athens, so that their citizenship was in practice honorary" (Hansen 1991: 94).

[78] The executive committee of the Council (Introduction, IVA).

[79] See the Introduction, VA.

the second generation, adding the qualification, "if they are born to a woman who is an Athenian (*astē*) and legally married." [93] And I will show that this is true by strong, clear evidence. I want to go back to the beginning in telling you about this law, how it was established and with what sort of people, what upstanding and reliable friends of the *dēmos* it had in mind. From all this you will learn that the *dēmos'* gift, one reserved for the city's benefactors, has been besmirched, and what great benefits are being taken out of your hands by this man Stephanus and those who have married and had children in the same way.

[94] You see, men of Athens, the Plataeans were the only Greeks who came to your aid at Marathon when Datis, general of King Darius, left Eretria after bringing Euboea under his control.[80] He entered Attica with a large force and was laying it waste. To this day, a memorial, a painting in the Stoa Poikilē,[81] memorializes the Plataeans' manly virtue. They are the men in the Boeotian helmets, each one coming to help as fast as he can. [95] And again, when Xerxes marched against Greece and the rest of the Thebans took the Persian side, the Plataeans had the moral strength to remain your friends.[82] Alone among the Boeotians, they fought on the Greek side. Half of them, standing side-by-side with Leonidas and the Spartans, fell in the Battle of Thermopylae. The other half embarked on your triremes, since they did not have their own ships, and fought with you at the battles of Artemisium and Salamis. [96] And at the final battle at Plataea against Mardonius, the Persian King's general, they fought alongside you and the other Greeks in the struggle for Greek liberation and won freedom for the other Greeks. Then Pausanias, the Spartan king, tried to insult you and was not content that the Greeks thought the Spartans alone worthy to be their leader. Although Athens was truly freedom's champion for the Greeks, it did not compete with Sparta from fear that the allies would be jealous. [97] In these circumstances Pausanias, a king of Sparta, puffed up with pride, put the following inscription on the

---

[80] Events of 490. Eretria is in Euboea, the large island just off the east coast of Attica. For the status of Plataeans at Athens, see the Introduction to Lys. 3.

[81] The "Painted Porch" on the north side of the agora in Athens, famous for its fifth-century murals by prominent artists of the time.

[82] Events of 480–479. Plataea was a Boeotian town near the border with Attica.

tripod in Delphi: "erected by the Greeks who fought together at Plataea and won the victory at sea in the Battle of Salamis." The tripod, a memorial of valor from the spoils of war taken from the barbarians, was dedicated to Apollo:

> Commander of the Greeks, when he destroyed the army of the Persians,
> Pausanias dedicated this monument to Phoebus Apollo.

The implication was that the deed and the dedication belonged to him, not to the allies working in common.

[98] The Greeks were angry, and at the Amphictyonic Council[83] the Plataeans, on behalf of the allies, instituted a suit against the Spartans for one thousand talents and forced them to chisel out the letters and inscribe instead the names of the cities that shared in the deed. This was the main reason the Spartans and their royal family began to hate the Plataeans. At the time, they had no way to attack the Plataeans, but fifty years later,[84] in time of peace, Archidamus son of Zeuxidamos, a king of the Spartans, tried to capture their city. [99] He worked from Thebes with the assistance of Eurymachus, the son of Leontiades the Boeotiarch.[85] Naucleides, together with a few others, was bribed to open the gates of the city during the night. When the Plataeans realized that the Thebans had entered during the night and that their city had suddenly been captured in peacetime, they organized and came to their city's defense. At daybreak they saw that the Theban contingent was not large—only the vanguard had entered, as heavy rain during the night had kept the full force from entering. The Asopus river was running high and was not easy to cross, especially at night. [100] Now, when the Plataeans saw the Thebans in the city but realized they did not have their whole army, they attacked and defeated them in battle. They were able to crush them before the other Thebans could come to their assistance. Then they immediately sent a messenger to you to report what had happened, announce their victory in the battle, and ask you to help them if the Thebans ravaged their land. When the Athenians heard this, they quickly sent help to Plataea.

---

[83] A council that administered the affairs of Delphi.

[84] In 431, just before the outbreak of the Peloponnesian War.

[85] A leader of the Boeotian League.

When the Thebans saw the Athenians helping the Plataeans, they returned home.

[101] Since the Theban attempt failed and the Plataeans put to death the prisoners they took in the battle, the Spartans were angry and right away, without offering any excuse, they launched an attack on Plataea. They ordered all the Peloponnesians, with the exception of the Argives, to send two-thirds of their forces from each city to take part in the expedition; to the Boeotians, including the Locrians, Phocians, Malians, Oetaeans, and Aenians, they sent the order to join the campaign with their full forces. [102] Once the Spartans had laid siege to the Plataean wall with this large contingent, they sent messages to the Plataeans, saying that if they were willing to hand over their city, they could retain the land and enjoy the use of their property, but they would have to abandon their alliance with Athens. The Plataeans refused and answered that they would do nothing without the Athenians. So the Spartans encircled the city with a double wall and continued the siege for two years, making many attempts to take the city by various means. [103] When the Plataeans were exhausted, and had no resources left and despaired of rescue, they divided themselves up by lot. One group stayed in the besieged city, but the others waited for a night with rain and strong wind, then escaped from the city, then scaled the enemy's siege walls without being detected, killed the men on watch, and against all expectations made their way safely here— though in a terrible state. Plataea was taken by force, and of those who had remained, all the adult men were slaughtered, and the women and children enslaved. But those who did not stay in the city when they realized the Spartans were attacking escaped to Athens.

[104] Now, consider again how you gave a share in Athenian citizenship to men who so clearly demonstrated their goodwill toward our *dēmos*, giving up all that was theirs, even wives and children. The law will be clear to all from your decrees, and you will know that I am telling the truth. Clerk, please take this decree and read it to the jury.

[DECREE CONCERNING THE PLATAEANS] *Hippocrates made the motion: The Plataeans are to be Athenian citizens from this day forward, with the rights enjoyed by the other Athenians, and they are to have a share of all that the Athenians share, sacred and secular, except for a priesthood or rite belonging to a clan and service as one of the nine*

Archons,[86] *though their descendants may do so. The Plataeans are to be distributed among the demes and tribes.*[87] *Once the distribution takes place, it will not be permitted for any other Plataean to become an Athenian citizen, unless he obtains that right from the Athenian* dēmos.

[105] You see, gentlemen, how fine and just a decree the speaker proposed for the Athenian *dēmos.* He required, first, that the Plataeans take the gift only after undergoing the scrutiny (*dokimasia*), man by man, in court, to see whether each one was a Plataean and a friend of the city. This provision guarded against many getting citizenship by false claim. Second, the names of those who passed the scrutiny were to be inscribed on a stone pillar to be erected on the Acropolis next to the temple of Athena, so that the gift of citizenship would be preserved for the Plataeans' descendants, and it would be possible for any individual to prove his relationship. [106] And the decree does not allow anyone to become an Athenian citizen later who did not become one at this time after scrutiny by the court. The purpose was to prevent a multitude from claiming to be Plataean and thereby concocting citizenship for themselves. Further, in the decree he prescribed the law for the Plataeans, in the interests of both the city and its gods, that effective immediately no Plataean could obtain any of the nine archonships nor any priesthood, though their descendants may, if born to a legally married Athenian woman (*astē*).

[107] Isn't it shocking? On the one hand, when it comes to our neighbors, men acknowledged to be the best of all the Greeks in their dealings with our city, you have legislated with such precise care the conditions under which each individual may enjoy the gift of citizenship; while on the other, you will allow this woman, a whore known to all Greece, to treat our city with disgrace and contempt and get away with profaning the gods, this woman who is not Athenian by her birth and not a citizen by act of the *dēmos.* [108] Is there a place she has *not* sold her body? Is there a place she has *not* gone to earn her daily living? She's been all over the Peloponnese, in Thessaly, and in Magnesia with Simus from Larissa and Eurydamas the son of Medeius; in

---

[86] Cf. above, 16n.

[87] Cf. above, 13 with n.

Chios and in most of Ionia she followed Sotades from Crete around, rented out by Nicarete, who still owned her. What do you suppose a woman will do when under the thumb of different men, traipsing after any man who pays her? Isn't she going to serve up every sort of pleasure to the men who use her? And *then*, will you vote citizenship for a woman of this character, notorious to all for making her living from three holes,[88] street-walking the world?

[109] If someone asks you, just what fine deed will you say you have accomplished? What shame and impiety will not rightfully be blamed on you? Before she was indicted and came to trial and everybody learned her true identity and profane acts, the crimes were her doing, and the city was merely negligent. Some of you did not know. Others, when they looked into it, were furious and said so, but there was nothing they could do to her as long as no one brought her to court and gave you the chance to vote on her. But now that you all have the information and the power and authority to punish her, the impiety is yours, if you fail to punish her. [110] If you acquit this woman, what will each of you say when you return home to your wife or daughter or mother when they ask you, "Where were you?" You answer, "We were judging a case." The next question will be, "Who was on trial?" Of course you'll answer, "Neaera. The charge was that she is a foreigner who lived with an Athenian as married to him, in violation of the law, and that she gave her daughter, a corrupted woman, to Theogenes when he became Basileus; and that she performed the secret, holy sacrifices for the city and was made the wife to Dionysus." And you will go through the rest of the accusations against her, recalling how memorably and carefully each of the charges was presented. [111] When they hear this, they will ask, "Well, what did you do?" And you will say, "We acquitted her." At once, the most upright of the women will be angry with you for having thought it proper that this woman share the city and its religion on an equal basis

---

[88] Hermogenes, a second-century AD writer on rhetoric, reports that the words "making her living from three (drilled) holes" appeared in some texts of this speech. They are not to be found in any surviving manuscript, and most scholars believe that the expression is too crude for Attic oratory. But since the entire passage passes the normal limits of decorum, Apollodorus probably did venture this gibe.

with them. As for the women with less sense, you will plainly be directing them to do whatever they want, since you and the laws have granted them immunity. You will seem to be reckless, lazy, and in sympathy with Neaera's way of life. [112] The result will be that it would be better for this trial not to have taken place at all than for you to acquit her, because in that case there will be complete license for whores to live with whomever they wish and to claim that their children were fathered by just anybody. As far as you are concerned, the laws will lose their force, and the lifestyle of *hetairai* will have the authority to bring about whatever those women want. Give a thought to the interest of our female citizens so that the daughters of poor men will not go unmarried. [113] As it is now, even if a girl is without resources, the law contributes a sufficient dowry if her looks are halfway presentable.[89] If you trample this law in the mud and invalidate it by acquitting Neaera, the business of prostitution will be the lot of the daughters of Athenian citizens who cannot be married off owing to poverty, while the *hetairai* will achieve the dignity of free women if they can with impunity have whatever children they want and share in the city's rituals, religion, and honors.

[114] So each one of you should think of himself as casting his vote in the interests of his wife, or daughter, or mother, or of the city and its laws and its religion. Your purpose is to keep the women in your care from being brought down to the same level of honor as this whore. You must keep women who are brought up in strict chastity and care by their family and given in marriage according to the laws from publicly attaining the same honor as a woman who has spent each day in obscene practices, over and over complying with each customer's desires.

[115] Do not suppose it is I, Apollodorus, who is speaking, nor the citizens who will speak to defend and support her, but imagine that the laws are actually in litigation with Neaera here over the things she has done. When you are hearing the prosecution, listen to the laws themselves, those laws that govern the city and that you have sworn to follow in your judgments. What do those laws require, and how have these people violated them? When you hear the defense, keep in mind

---

[89] It is not known whether Apollodorus is referring accurately to any real law.

the laws' accusations and the speakers' clear proofs. Observe her appearance and consider only this: being Neaera, did she do these things?[90]

[116] It is also worth considering this, men of Athens. You punished Archias, who had been the Hierophant,[91] when he was shown in court to have committed an impiety by sacrificing in violation of our ancestral practices. There were many charges against him, but the main one was that at the Haloa[92] on the altar in the Eleusinian court he sacrificed an animal brought to him by the *hetaira* Sinope, even though it was not legal to sacrifice animals that day, and the sacrifice was not for him to perform, but for the priestess. [117] Would this not be shocking? You punish a man of the Eumolpidae clan,[93] with ancestors of the highest quality, a citizen of Athens, because he appeared to have violated some element of the laws. The pleas of his relatives and his friends did not help, nor did the liturgies[94] that he or his ancestors had performed for the city, nor his ancestry, nor his position as Hierophant. No, you punished him because you decided he had done something wrong. Will you then turn around and *not* punish this woman Neaera, guilty of impiety towards the same god and towards the laws—the woman herself and her daughter?

[118] I, for my part, am wondering what in the world they will say to you in their defense speech. Will they claim Neaera is an Athenian woman (*astē*) and that she lives with Stephanus in conformity with

---

[90] The meaning of this instruction to the jury is obscure: perhaps Neaera, though a woman well into middle age, was still flaunting her beauty in a way the jurors might find shocking. Or perhaps, just because she strove for a look of decorous respectability, Apollodorus was inducing the jury to look past this disguise by remembering the lurid past associated with her name. Merely that her name is mentioned at all, perhaps aggravated by her presence in court (see the Introduction to this speech), may in the etiquette of the Athenian courts have marked her as a prostitute.

[91] The priest who exhibited sacred objects during the rituals of the Eleusinian Mysteries.

[92] A fertility festival that took place in early winter. Men were excluded from at least part of the festival.

[93] One of the two clans that supplied the main priests for the mystery cult at Eleusis.

[94] For these public services, see the Introduction, IVC.

the laws? There has, however, been testimony that she is a *hetaira* and was Nicarete's slave. Will they claim that she is not his wife but is living with him as a concubine (*pallakē*)? But Stephanus presented the boys to the phratry as sons of Neaera and gave her daughter in marriage to an Athenian, clearly demonstrating that he did keep her as his wife. [119] I do not think that either Stephanus himself or anyone speaking for him will show that the charges and testimony are not true and that Neaera is an Athenian (*astē*). I hear that he will present a defense going something like this: he did not keep her as a wife but as a *hetaira,* and the children were not hers but were his by another woman, an Athenian (*astē*), a relative of his, whom he will say he had married earlier.

[120] In response to the shamelessness of his speech, and the trickery of his defense, and of the witnesses he had coached, I issued a specific and just challenge, which would have made it possible for you to know the whole truth: he should hand over for torture[95] Thratta and Coccaline, the slave women who remained in Neaera's service when she came from Megara to Stephanus' house, and also the women she acquired later, when she was with Stephanus, Xennis and Drosis. [121] They have accurate information about Proxenus, who has died, and Ariston, who is still alive, and Antidorides the runner, and Phano—I mean the woman called Strybele, the one who lived with Theogenes when he was Basileus—all these are Neaera's children. And if the interrogation under torture showed that Stephanus married an Athenian woman, and the boys were born to another Athenian woman (*astē*), not to Neaera, I was willing to abandon the trial and not pursue this indictment. [122] "Living with a woman" means, after all, that a man has children with her and introduces his sons to the phratry and deme, and he gives his daughters away to be married, presenting them as his own. We have *hetairai* for the sake of pleasure, concubines (*pallakai*) for meeting our bodily needs day-by-day, but wives for having legitimate children and to be trustworthy guardians of our household.[96] So if he had married an Athenian woman (*astē*) before, and

---

[95] For evidence taken under torture, see Ant. 1.6n.

[96] This often-quoted statement must be taken in context: Apollodorus' intention is to distinguish sharply between wives and other women, and he therefore does not bother to distinguish clearly between the services provided by *hetairai* and *pallakai*.

these sons were born to her, not to Neaera, he could have presented proof coming from the most accurate testimony—by handing over these slave women for torture. [123] To prove that I issued a challenge, the clerk will read out the testimony and the challenge. Please read the testimony and then the challenge.

[DEPOSITION][97] *Hippocrates the son of Hippocrates, of the deme Probalinthus, Demosthenes son of Demosthenes, of the deme Paeania,[98] Diophanes son of Diophanes, of the deme Alopece, Deinomenes son of Archelaus, of the deme Cydathenaeum, Deinias son of Phormos, of the deme Cydantidae, and Lysimachus son of Lysippus, of the deme Aigilia testify that they were present in the agora when Apollodorus challenged Stephanus and demanded that he hand over his slave women for interrogation under torture concerning the charges Apollodorus has brought against Stephanus concerning Neaera. Stephanus refused to hand over the slave women. This is the challenge that Apollodorus made.*

[124] Read the very challenge, the one I presented to this man Stephanus.

[CHALLENGE][99] *Apollodorus challenged Stephanus concerning the indictment he had brought against Neaera,[100] charging that she is a*

---

[97] Probably a trustworthy document, since it contains names of men not mentioned in the text but whose existence is recorded on inscriptions. The presence of such external testimonia, often epigraphic, helps confirm documents found in the manuscripts as genuine, as opposed to those that might have simply been composed from internal references long after the speech was written.

[98] The father's name and deme identification make it certain that this is the very Demosthenes to whom the manuscripts attribute the entire speech (see the Introduction).

[99] The text presents several textual problems and puzzles (for more detailed discussions, see Carey 1992 and Kapparis 1999), but as with the deposition just before, details that cannot be derived from the text strongly suggest an authentic document.

[100] A problematic statement, since Theomnestus makes out that he is the prosecutor and Apollodorus only a *synēgoros* (see 1 and 14). Perhaps Apollodorus is relating an action he initiated and then abandoned; more likely he regards himself as the de facto prosecutor. In the next two sections, Apollodorus again speaks of himself as the principal. There is also a discrepancy between the third person used at the start of the challenge and the first person (except in one manuscript) near the close.

foreign woman living with an Athenian (astos). Apollodorus is prepared to take Neaera's slave women for interrogation under torture, those she brought with her from Megara, Thratta and Coccaline, and those she acquired later when living with Stephanus, Xennis and Drosis. These women have accurate knowledge concerning Neaera's children, that they are not Stephanus'.[101] *They are Proxenus, now deceased; Ariston, who is still living; Antidorides the runner; and Phano. And if the slave women agree that these are Neaera's children, Neaera is to be sold in accordance with the laws, and her children are to be classified as foreign. If, however, they agreed that they are not Neaera's children but from another woman, an Athenian (astē), I was willing to abandon my case against Neaera; and if the women were injured in the torture, I was willing to pay compensation for the injuries.*

[125] This, gentlemen of the jury, was my challenge to Stephanus, which he refused to accept. Doesn't it seem to you that Stephanus himself has already delivered the verdict, finding Neaera guilty of the charges I have brought against her? And that I have told you the truth and have presented truthful testimony? And that everything he tells you will be a lie? And that he will convict himself of saying not one honest word?—all this by refusing to hand over for interrogation under torture the slave women I requested?

[126] Gentlemen of the jury, it was to avenge the gods against whom these people have committed impiety and to avenge myself that I have brought them to trial and subjected them to your vote. With the understanding that the gods, whom they have offended with their crimes, will observe how each of you will cast his ballot, you must vote for what is right and bring vengeance—in the first place for the gods and then for yourselves. If you do this, all will think that you have well and fairly tried this case that I have brought against Neaera, that she is a foreign woman who lives as though married to an Athenian (*astos*).

---

[101] This translation follows Rennie's 1931 Oxford Classical Text, which follows the manuscripts in the order "Neaera's"/"Stephanus'" and adds "not." Other editors, thinking that the children's maternity is the real issue, switch the position of "Neaera's" and "Stephanus'." Others accept the manuscript reading whereby Neaera's children are also Stephanus': this is a stronger claim than is made earlier in the speech.

AESCHINES 1. AGAINST TIMARCHUS

❧❧❧

INTRODUCTION

Context

In 346 an Athenian delegation, led by Philocrates and including Aeschines and Demosthenes, negotiated a peace treaty with Philip of Macedon. Although there was majority support for the peace, there remained elements in the city implacably and explicitly opposed either to the idea of peace with Macedonia or to the terms of the Peace of Philocrates. There were others, like Demosthenes, who saw the peace as a necessary but temporary arrangement. The opponents of the peace began working against it from the moment it was concluded. Aeschines was an early target. All Athenian officials had to submit to an audit on the expiry of their term of office. When Aeschines submitted to this process after the second embassy to Macedonia of 346, he was accused of misconduct by Timarchus, a minor politician of whose background we know no more than Aeschines tells us and on whose precise political affiliations we are badly informed, and by Demosthenes.

On the useful principle that attack is the best form of defense, Aeschines responded by launching a prosecution. He chose Timarchus, the weaker target. Demosthenes was both wealthy and, though not yet forty, a formidable political operator and public speaker. Neither his private life nor (at this stage) his political activity offered a secure base for prosecution. It is clear, however, from the present speech (and from Demosthenes' grudging admission at 19.284) that Timarchus had had a scandalous youth. The speech can be dated to 346/5, though it is difficult to fix the date more precisely.

Despite the factual (though not rhetorical) weakness of the speech, which is ultimately no more than a sustained attempt to throw sand in the eyes of the jurors, Aeschines won the case and Timarchus was disfranchised (Dem. 19.257, 284). Though Demosthenes was later to treat Timarchus as an object of pity, the reader should bear in mind that it was Timarchus who picked the fight. His mistake was to underestimate his intended victim. By demonstrating his ferocity and skill as a political fighter and his credibility with a judicial panel of ordinary Athenians, Aeschines effectively checked his enemies' attempts to bring him to trial, and it was three years before Demosthenes felt able to return to the attack. The defeat stung Demosthenes, who revisits the subject of Timarchus repeatedly in his speech *On the Embassy* (Dem. 19), written for the prosecution of Aeschines in 343; he also in that speech takes a certain grim pleasure in using against Aeschines arguments used by Aeschines against Timarchus.

The Charge

The legal action used by Aeschines against Timarchus was *dokimasia tōn rhētorōn,* literally "scrutiny of public speakers."[1] The term "public speaker" (*rhētōr*) was applied to individuals who regularly addressed the Assembly. Such people were professional politicians in the double sense that they devoted much of their time to politics and they could hope to earn substantial sums from individuals and groups keen to gain access to their political influence, though, unlike modern democratic politicians, they received no income from the state. The purpose of the *dokimasia tōn rhētorōn* was to test the credentials of those who sought to direct public policy in the Assembly and to remove from influence those deemed unworthy. It was open to any Athenian citizen to initiate it by publicly declaring his intention to subject a speaker to the process, which took the form of a trial before a jury. It is a strangely hybrid action. The process of

---

[1] The date of the creation of this process is uncertain; it clearly reflects the distinction, observable in the fifth but increased in the fourth century, between the regular speaker (*rhētōr*) in the Assembly and formally appointed state officials (especially the generals) and probably belongs to the period of the restoration of the democracy in 403.

initiation locates it within the public actions open to any prosecutor (*ho boulomenos*) against alleged infractions of the its title fixes it within the various processes of formal scrutiny (*dokimasia*) automatically imposed on the commencement of certain rights or responsibilities (Introduction, IVA). Accordingly, as Todd (1993) has emphasized, the penalty is merely the confirmation of the formal restrictions automatically attaching (in most cases) to the activities it addresses.

Although Aeschines focuses specifically on one aspect of the *dokimasia*, it is clear from his account of the law in 28–32 that there was a list of acts that rendered a man ineligible to address the Assembly. The list, which may not be exhaustive, included violence toward or failure to support parents, military derelictions, prostitution, and squandering an inheritance. With the exception of the last item, these were all acts for which *atimia*, loss of citizen rights, was the prescribed penalty, and the penalty for an individual convicted on the *dokimasia tōn rhētorōn* was likewise *atimia*. Aeschines charges Timarchus specifically with having prostituted himself as a young man but also throws in for good measure the allegation that he squandered his inheritance (42, 94–101). Aeschines cannot formally accuse Timarchus of mistreating his father, who appears to have died when Timarchus was young, but he does draw on associated values by accusing him of mistreating an aged uncle (104).

Homosexuality and Male Prostitution

Greek homoeroticism is a complex subject that has attracted scholarly interest in recent years. The following summary of the subject is offered merely as a rough guide. Though on occasion we find dissenting and condemnatory voices, many Greek sources from the archaic period onward take it for granted that grown men find males around the age of puberty sexually attractive. Although it was possible to be exclusively homosexual (as with Misgolas in this speech), there is no automatic assumption that homosexual tastes preclude heterosexual. Structurally, the practice of homosexuality differed from modern experience in that there is normally an age difference between the partners. As with sex in most societies, there appear to be elaborate proprieties. The roles of the partners are perceived as distinct, with the older man as pursuer, the younger as pursued, the older as achieving physical gratification, the younger as providing it.

Participation in such relationships was not in itself illegal, and prostitution, homosexual or heterosexual, was a legitimate profession for many noncitizens. But the sale of sexual favors was felt to be incompatible with citizen status and brought an automatic penalty of disfranchisement. No further penalties were imposed unless an individual so barred sought to exercise citizen rights. In addition to the *dokimasia tōn rhētorōn*, available against public speakers believed to have prostituted themselves, there was also a public action (the *graphē hetairēseōs*) that could be brought against any Athenian male who infringed the automatic bar consequent upon male prostitution, the penalty on conviction being death. Though this may look like a straightforward issue, in fact it was riddled with complications. Quite apart from the obvious difficulty of obtaining evidence about an activity carried out by two people in private, the common practice of giving gifts to a lover meant that the question of payment was necessarily a grey area.

The Speech

After an opening that stresses the orator's own moderation, an introductory section (4–6) stresses the importance of the laws. Aeschines then moves into an account of the laws dealing with decent conduct (6–36), arranged chronologically in order of the age of the individuals covered and culminating in those dealing with the morality of politicians and the conduct of the political process. Much of this section is at best only tangentially relevant to the main issue, though it does create a high moral tone and underline the importance of adherence to high standards of decency in public and private life.

After a transitional section (37–38) reasserting the moderate and decent character projected by the speaker, Aeschines proceeds to a narrative of Timarchus' sexual career (39–70) with testimony.

At this point Aeschines interrupts his narrative and turns to anticipation of the defense arguments, boldly tackling head-on the lack of any shred of solid evidence against Timarchus (71–94). The essence of his answer, reiterated in a variety of ways, is that the members of the audience all know the truth and therefore have no need of further evidence. The last section of this refutation (94) acts as a springboard for the next section of narrative, which deals with the rest of Timarchus' career, his squandering of his inheritance (95–105), and his corruption and criminality in public office (106–116).

Aeschines now reverts to anticipation of defense arguments. First, he deals with arguments anticipated from Demosthenes, who (he claims) will stress the absence of evidence from the officials who collect the prostitution tax and the unfairness of conviction on the basis of rumor (117–131). The first objection is met partly by righteous indignation, partly by insisting that the fact that Timarchus has not worked in a known brothel says nothing about the nature of his activities. The second is met by a magisterial appeal to the divine authority of Report, *Phēmē,* a mystical force that promulgates the truth.

The next section of refutation (132–159) responds to an anticipated appeal to the traditions of Greek homosexuality. Aeschines will be presented by his opponents as inconsistent, as a pursuer of young men who attacks a young man who has had pursuers. It will also be claimed that homosexual relationships have long been sanctioned by tradition and have been the inspiration for noble deeds. Aeschines' response is to distinguish (without ever making explicit the basis for the distinction) between chaste homosexual love and the indecent conduct of people like Timarchus.

In 160–165 he returns to the problem of lack of evidence, to demolish the defense's demand that he produce a sexual contract between Timarchus and a client. In 166–169 he dismisses Demosthenes' anticipated attempts to use Macedonia as a means of exciting prejudice against Aeschines. After insisting that the jurors must not accept irrelevant pleas from the defense, he turns to an irrelevant character assassination of Demosthenes (170–176), finishing with a demand that the jurors keep Demosthenes to the point. In 177–187 he returns to the earlier theme of maintaining the laws, using both Sparta and the Athenian ancestors as examples.

At this point the speech accelerates, moving rapidly over an appeal to religion (188), the notoriety of Timarchus' life (189), and the wider implications of such conduct (190–191), before turning to the implications for Athens of the verdict in the present case (192–193) and a warning about the supporters of Timarchus (192–195). There is a brief conclusion (195).

Although it is possible to distinguish different sections within the speech, the boundaries are made fluid by a tendency on Aeschines' part to make use of narrative even in sections devoted to argument. Perhaps the most interesting aspect of the structure is the way narrative and proof (mainly refutation) are each divided and then interleaved. Part of the reason may be a desire for variety. But a more telling reason is the absence of solid proof. To impose on the speech a neat division of the sort recommended by rhetoricians, with separate long sections devoted to narrative and proof, would call attention to the factual weakness. As it is, the emotive power of the narrative is deployed to distract attention from this problem.

Given the difficulty of obtaining evidence, it strikes the modern reader as surprising that the prosecution succeeded. Probably we should conclude that Timarchus had a colorful past and was therefore a person against whom allegations such as these could plausibly be made. Moreover, we cannot tell how far the prosecution's case was helped by the political climate and Aeschines' own enhanced credibility as a result of his role in the negotiation of the peace. But we should also give due credit to the skill with which Aeschines presents the case. The prosecution is conducted throughout with dignity. The speaker projects a personality that is decent, moderate, and restrained, a character that invites trust. This mask enables him to turn the absence of incriminating detail to his advantage by attributing it to the salacious nature of the narrative and his consequent (laudable) reluctance to be explicit. He also undermines the moral authority of his opponents by tainting them, especially Demosthenes, with the crimes for which Timarchus is on trial and ably forces them to the defensive by making their prima facie powerful demand for evidence an evasion that is tantamount to an admission of guilt.

AESCHINES I. AGAINST TIMARCHUS

[1] Never before, men of Athens, have I brought an indictment (*graphē*)[2] against any man or persecuted him at his final audit;[3]

---

[2] For the procedure of *graphē*, see the Introduction, VE.

[3] For the audit (*euthynai*) required of all officials after a term in office, see the Introduction, IVA. Given the role of litigation in Athenian politics, Aeschines' claim is surprising, but given his high profile at the time (which would make it

no, I have in my opinion shown restraint in all such matters. But since I could see that the city was suffering serious damage from this man Timarchus, who addresses the Assembly illegally, and since I am personally the victim of his malicious prosecution (just how, I shall explain later in my speech), [2] I concluded that it would be utterly disgraceful not to intervene in defense of the city as a whole, the laws, you, and myself. And in the knowledge that he is guilty of the charges that you heard the clerk read out just now, I declared this formal scrutiny[5] against him. It seems, men of Athens, that the claims usually made in public cases are not untrue: private enmities very often do put right public wrongs. [3] So you will see that Timarchus can put the blame for this whole prosecution not on the city or the laws or you or me but on himself. The laws warned him not to address the Assembly because of the disreputable life he has led; in my judgment, this was not a difficult command but a very easy one. And in my case he was free not to persecute me, if he had any sense. I hope, then, that my opening words on this matter have been reasonable.

[4] I am well aware, men of Athens, that you will certainly have heard already from others what I am going to say at the outset; but I think it appropriate that I, too, should now make the same statement to you. It is agreed that there are three kinds of constitution in the whole world, dictatorship (*tyrannis*), oligarchy, and democracy,[6] and dictatorships and oligarchies are governed by the temperament of those in power, but democratic cities are governed by the established laws. [5] You are aware, men of Athens, that in a democracy the per-

---

difficult to lie about something so obvious), it may well be true. It could be (Harris 1995: 36) that he was constrained by his background, which left him without the network of influential supporters on which a wealthy Athenian could draw. The penalties for failure to obtain 20% of the votes cast included a fine of 1,000 drachmas, which might deter a man with limited resources. This does not mean that Aeschines had not been involved in any political litigation, since he could have acted as a supporting speaker.

[4] For "malicious prosecution" (*sykophantein*), see the Introduction, VE.

[5] Greek *dokimasia;* see the Speech Introduction.

[6] The (commonplace) tripartite division of constitutions is found as early as Pindar in the 470s (*Pythian* 2.85–86); cf. e.g., Herodotus 3.80–82; Plato *Republic* books 8–9.

sons of citizens and the constitution are protected by the laws, while dictators and oligarchs are protected by distrust and armed guards. Oligarchs and all who run a constitution based on inequality must be on guard against people who attempt to overthrow the constitution by force; but you, and all who have a constitution based on equality and law, must watch out for people whose words and way of life contravene the laws. For your real strength is when you are ruled by law and are not subverted by men who break them. [6] My own belief is that whenever we pass laws, our concern should be how to make laws that are good and advantageous for our constitution, and once we have passed them, we should obey the laws in existence and punish those who disobey, if the city is to flourish.

Consider, men of Athens, how great a concern for decency was shown by that ancient legislator Solon, and Draco, and the other legislators of that period. [7] First, they legislated for the decency of our children, and they laid down explicitly how the freeborn boy should live and how he should be brought up; second, for young men; and third, for the other age groups in succession, not only for private citizens but also for public speakers. They wrote these laws down and entrusted them to your care, making you their guardians.

[8] What I want to do now is to use the same order in my own speech to you as the legislator uses in the law. First of all I shall describe the laws that are laid down for the good conduct of your children; then second, those for the young men; and third, in succession the laws for the other age groups, not only for private citizens but also for public speakers. In this way, I think, my argument will be easiest to grasp. At the same time, men of Athens, I also want first to give you a preliminary account of the city's laws, and then after that to examine Timarchus' character; for you will find that his way of life has been contrary to all the laws.

[9] To start with, in the case of teachers,[7] into whose care of necessity we hand our children, for whom decency means a livelihood and the opposite means poverty, even so the legislator was clearly suspicious, and he lays down explicitly the time of day when a free boy should go to school, then how many other children should go there

---

[7] It is to be borne in mind that there was no state provision for schooling in Athens; the state merely set rules within which such establishments must operate.

with him,[8] and the time he should leave. [10] He forbids the teachers to open the schools and the athletic trainers to open the wrestling schools before the sun is up and instructs them to shut them before sunset. He holds seclusion and darkness in particular suspicion. As to the young pupils, he prescribes who they should be and what ages, and the official who is to be responsible for them, and provides for the oversight of slave attendants[9] and the celebration of the festival of the Muses in the schools and of Hermes in the wrestling schools, and finally for the company kept by the boys at school and the circular dances.[10] [11] For he instructs that the chorus producer,[11] who will be spending his own money for you, should be over forty years of age when he undertakes this task, so that he is already at the age of greatest self-control when he is in the company of your sons.

Now the clerk will read out these laws to you, to show you that the legislator believed that a boy who had been brought up properly would be a useful citizen when he reached manhood. But when the individual's nature at the outset gets a corrupt start in its education, he thought that badly brought up boys would become the sort of citizens that Timarchus here is. Read these laws to them.[12]

[12] [LAWS] *The teachers of the boys are not to open the schools before sunrise and are to close them before sunset. People older than the boys*

---

[8] If Aeschines is presenting the legal situation accurately, presumably the aim is to ensure that numbers (which the teachers have a financial incentive to maximize) are kept to a level at which pupils can be properly supervised.

[9] Any boy whose parents could afford it would be accompanied everywhere by a slave attendant (*paidagōgos*), who would provide physical protection and prevent admirers from becoming a nuisance or compromising the boy's reputation.

[10] The *kyklios choros* or circular dance was the dithyramb in honor of Dionysus.

[11] For the "liturgy" of producing a chorus, see the Introduction, IVC, and Ant. 6.

[12] This is the only speech by Aeschines for which the manuscripts preserve what purport to be the documents cited in the trial. Unfortunately, all are later forgeries; they were probably intended not to deceive but to give an impression of what the original might have looked like. In the present case, instead of "several laws" (1.11), the composer has cobbled together a single law combining provisions from different areas (schools, choral training), relying wherever possible on Aeschines' own words.

are not to enter while the boys are inside, except for the teacher's son or brother or daughter's husband. If anyone enters in defiance of this rule, he is to be punished with death. And the gymnasium masters are not to allow anyone who has reached manhood to participate in the Hermaea with them. If he so permits and does not exclude them from the gymnasium, the gymnasium master is to be liable under the law dealing with the corruption of the freeborn. The chorus producers appointed by the people are to be over forty years of age.

[13] Now after this, men of Athens, he legislates for offenses that, though they are grave, still (I think) occur in the city. For it was the fact that some unseemly acts actually took place that led the men of old to lay down the laws. Anyway, the law states explicitly that if any father or brother or uncle or anyone at all in the position of guardian hires a boy out as a prostitute—it does not allow an indictment (graphē) to be brought against the boy in person but against the man who hired him out and the man who paid for him, the former because he hired him out and the latter, it says, because he hired him. And it has made the penalties the same for each of them, and it adds that any boy who has been hired out for prostitution is not obliged on reaching maturity to keep his father or provide him with a home, though on the father's death he is to bury him and to carry out the other customary rites. [14] Observe how fair this is, men of Athens. In life, the law deprives him of the advantages of parenthood, as he deprived his son of the right of free speech,[13] while after death, when the recipient cannot perceive the benefit conferred on him but it is the law and religion that receive the honor, finally it instructs the son to bury his father and to perform the other customary rites.

What other law did he lay down to protect your children? The law against procuring, to which he attached the most severe penalties, if anyone procures for prostitution a free boy or woman.

[15] What other law? The law of outrage (hybris),[14] which sums up in a single statement all such acts. In this law is written explicitly that if anyone commits outrage against a boy (and anyone who hires him commits outrage, I imagine) or man or woman, whether free or slave, or if he does anything contrary to law to any of these, it has allowed

---

[13] I.e., the right to address the Assembly, the Council, or the courts.

[14] For the law against hybris, see the Introduction to Dem. 54 above.

Based on rumour.

for an ⌐indictment⌐ (*graphē*) for outrage and prescribed assessment[15] of the penalty he is to suffer or pay. Read out the law.[16]

[**16**] [LAW] *If any Athenian commits outrage against a free boy, the boy's guardian is to bring an indictment before the Thesmothetae, on which he is to specify the penalty assessed. Anyone convicted by the court is to be handed over to the Eleven and put to death the same day. If anyone is condemned to pay a fine, he is to pay it within eleven days of the trial, if he is unable to pay it immediately. He is to be imprisoned until he has paid. Those who commit offenses against the persons of slaves are also to be liable to these charges.*

[**17**] It may be that someone at first hearing might wonder why on earth this term, slaves, was added in the law of outrage.[17] But if you consider it, men of Athens, you will find that it is the best provision of all. For the legislator was not concerned about slaves; but because he wanted to accustom you to keep far away from outrage on free persons, he added the prohibition against committing outrage even against slaves. Quite simply, he thought that in a democracy, the man who commits outrage against anyone at all was not fit to share the rights of citizenship. [**18**] Please remember this, too, men of Athens, that at this point the legislator is not yet addressing the boy in person but those connected with the boy—father, brother, guardian, teachers, in sum, those responsible for him. But once he is entered in the deme register[18] and knows the city's laws and is now able to determine right and wrong, the legislator from now on addresses nobody else but at this point the individual himself, ⌐Timarchus.⌐ [**19**] And what does

_____

name also. ✓

[15] For the assessment of penalties (*timēsis*) after a conviction, see the Introduction, VC.

[16] Again, the document is spurious; it contains garbled details (such as the boy's guardian as prosecutor in a public action in which the prosecution should be explicitly open to anyone, the fluctuation in the conception of the penalty) and conflicts with the (more plausible) text of the law offered at Dem. 21.47 (though the authenticity of this, too, is contested).

[17] Demosthenes (21.48–49) also stresses the paradoxical inclusion of slaves under *hybris* law. Since the concept of *hybris* is closely connected with views on status and honor, this provision is surprising. Todd (1993) explains this element as reflecting a degree of residual status for slaves. More probably it is a protection of owners' rights.

[18] Citizens were listed on the deme register at age eighteen; see Dem. 57.

can you witness?

he say? If any Athenian (he says) prostitutes himself, he is not to have
the right to serve as one of the nine Archons (the reason being, I think,
that these officials wear a sacred wreath), nor to undertake any priesthood, since his body is quite unclean; and let him not serve (he says)
as advocate[19] for the state or hold any office ever, whether at home or
abroad, whether selected by lot or elected by a vote;[20] [20] let him not
serve as herald, nor as envoy (nor let him bring to trial people that
have served as envoys, nor let him act as a sykophant[21] for pay), nor let
him voice any opinion in the Council or the Assembly (not even if he
is the cleverest speaker in Athens). If anyone acts against these provisions, he has allowed for indictments (*graphai*) for prostitution and
imposed the most severe penalties. Read this law out to them as well,
to make you aware of the noble and decent character of the established
laws, against which Timarchus has dared to address the Assembly, a
man whose way of life is known to you all.[22]

[**21**] [LAW] *If any Athenian has prostituted himself, he is not to have
the right to become one of the nine Archons or to undertake any priesthood or to serve as advocate for the people or to hold any office whatsoever, whether at home or abroad, whether selected by lot or elected by
vote; nor is he to be sent out as herald, or to voice an opinion, or to enter
the public temples or to wear a garland when the citizens collectively
are wearing garlands, or to enter within the purified area of the agora.[23]
If anyone acts in defiance of these restrictions when convicted of prostitution, he is to be punished with death.*

---

[19] Greek *syndikein*, from *syndikos* (lit. "supporter in a suit"). The term here
refers to individuals elected to present the prosecution in certain political cases.

[20] For offices that were filled by lot, see the Introduction, IVA. In the case of
offices for which specific skills or experience were required, election was by show
of hands (not secret ballot, which was rare in the Assembly).

[21] For the *sykophantēs*, see the Introduction, VE. Aeschines' use of documents
(perhaps influenced by his years as a public clerk reading out documents) is astute.
Here he mixes quotation from the law with (pejorative) addition and interpretation.

[22] The document contains no detail independent of the preceding text (it is
also silent on the important issue of legal procedure) and is probably a forgery.

[23] The Greek says literally "pass within the containers of sprinkling water," i.e.,
the area demarcated by the containers of lustral water for purification purposes
situated (according to the ancient commentators) at the entrance to the agora,
which was the political and religious center of the city.

irrelevant information only setting the tone.

[22] This was the law he passed to deal with young men who commit reckless offenses against their own bodies, while the ones he read to you a little earlier deal with boys; and the ones I am now about to describe deal with the rest of the Athenians. Having finished with the previous laws, the legislator turned his attention[24] to the way in which we should deliberate collectively in the Assembly about matters of the greatest importance. Where, then, does he begin? "The laws on discipline," he says. He began with morality, in the belief that the best governed city will be the one with the most orderly conduct. [23] So how does he instruct the Chairmen (*Proedroi*)[25] to conduct business? When the purifying victim[26] has been carried around and the herald has pronounced the traditional prayers, the legislator instructs the Chairmen to deal first with voting on matters of traditional religion, heralds, embassies, and secular matters, and then the herald puts the question: "Who wishes to speak, of those who are over the age of fifty?" And only when these have all spoken does he invite any other Athenian who wishes, and has the right,[27] to speak. [24] Observe how fair this is, men of Athens. The legislator was not unaware, I think, that older men are at the peak of their powers of reasoning, and their daring has already begun to diminish because of their experience of the world. Because he wanted to make it a habitual and compulsory practice for the men with the best judgment to speak on public business, since he could not address each one of them by name, he includes them under the title of the whole age group and invites them to the

---

[24] Aeschines presents as a single coordinated process a whole range of laws that were probably the products of different periods.

[25] For much of the fourth century, meetings of the Council and the Assembly were chaired by a body of nine *Proedroi* selected on the day of the meeting from within the Council (*Ath. Pol.* 44.2), one from each tribal contingent, except the one serving as the Prytany (Introduction, IVA).

[26] Pollution and purification played a major role in Greek religion. Ritual pollution could be acquired in a whole range of ways, varying from the criminal (such as homicide) to unavoidable contact with contaminating agents (such as the dead or childbirth) that are neither criminal nor immoral in themselves. Pollution was contagious (see the Introduction to Ant. 2); accordingly, public meetings were preceded by a purification involving the sacrifice of a victim and the sprinkling of the periphery with its blood.

[27] This would exclude those who had been deprived of their citizen rights; the term for such a person was *atimos*, literally "without honor(s)."

platform and encourages them to address the people. At the same time, he teaches the younger men to show respect for their elders and to take second place to them in all matters, and to honor the age to which all of us will come, if we are spared. [25] And those public speakers of old, Pericles and Themistocles and Aristides (who bore a title quite unlike that of this man Timarchus—he was known as "the just") were so decent that in their day this habit that we all practice nowadays, of speaking with the hand outside the clothing, was considered something brash, and they avoided doing it. And I think I can offer you convincing and solid evidence of this fact. I am certain that you have all sailed to Salamis and have viewed the statue of Solon,[28] and you yourselves could bear witness that Solon stands in the agora on Salamis with his hand inside his robe. This, men of Athens, is a representation and a reminder of the posture that Solon in person used to adopt when he spoke to the Athenian people.

[26] Now observe, men of Athens, the enormous difference between Solon and those great men whom I mentioned a little earlier in my speech and Timarchus. While they for their part thought it shameful to speak with their hand outside their robe, this man here, not some time ago but just the other day, threw off his robe and cavorted like a pancratiast[29] in the Assembly, stripped, in such a vile and shameful physical condition on account of drunkenness and other abuses that decent men covered their faces out of shame for the city that we take advice from people like this. [27] With this in mind, the legislator explicitly declared who should address the people and who should not speak in the Assembly. He does not expel a man from the platform if his ancestors have not served as generals, nor if he works at some trade to provide for the necessities of life; indeed, he especially welcomes these men, and this is why he repeatedly asks: "Who wishes to speak?"

[28] Which men, then, did he think should not speak? People who have lived a life of shame—these are the ones he does not allow to address the people. And where does he state this? When he says: "The

---

[28] Demosthenes (19.251–252) sneeringly replies that the statue was a modern one and had no bearing on the actual posture of Solon. From Demosthenes' account, it is clear that Aeschines acted out the posture of the statue.

[29] Cf. below, 33n.

scrutiny of public speakers: if anyone who beats his father or mother or does not keep them or provide a home[30] speaks in the Assembly"; this man he does not allow to speak. A fine rule, by Zeus, in my personal opinion. Why? Because if anyone mistreats the ones he should honor on a level with the gods, what sort of treatment, says the legislator, will people unconnected with him, and indeed the city as a whole, receive from him? [29] And who are the next ones he forbids to speak? "Or anyone," he says, "who has not performed all the military service he is ordered to, or has thrown away his shield,"[31] and rightly. Why exactly? Mister, when you do not take up arms for the city or because of cowardice cannot protect it, do not presume to give it advice. Who are the third group he addresses? "Or anyone who has been a prostitute," he says, "or has sold himself."[32] For the man who has willfully sold his own body would, he thought, casually sell out the interests of the city. [30] Who are the fourth group he addresses? "Or anyone who has squandered his paternal estate," he says, "or any other property he has inherited."[33] For he considered that the man who has mismanaged his private household would treat the city's interests in much the same way; and the legislator could not conceive that the same individual

---

[30] Athenian laws gave parents the right to nurture in old age and protection from violence at the hands of their children. The rights were covered by a public action so that anyone could intervene; the penalty for the convicted offspring was loss of citizen rights.

[31] The penalty for failure to serve or desertion in battle was loss of citizen rights. The offense was covered by a public action (*graphē*), and the case was judged by soldiers who had served on the campaign, with the military officers presiding.

[32] The Greek uses two distinct verbs, *porneuesthai*, "to work as a prostitute" (from *pornos/pornē*, "male/female prostitute"), and *hetairein*, literally "be companion (to)." The distinction suggested below (51) between the former as promiscuous sex for pay and the latter as denoting the position of a financially dependent passive homosexual partner is supported by other sources, though the difference appears to have had no juridical significance.

[33] That is, from any other branch of the family. The hostility toward the squandering of inherited property reflects the recognition (attenuated but persisting in the classical period) of the solidarity of the family, that is, the family as a unit that subsumes and transcends its individual members. Thus, there were limits on disposing of property by will and disinheriting legitimate sons. There is evidence that a man had more freedom to dispose of acquired wealth.

could be worthless in private life and useful to the public good, nor did he believe that a public speaker should come to the platform fully prepared in his words and not in his life. [31] He believed that statements from a good and decent man, even when expressed in a clumsy or simple way, would be of advantage to the hearers, while those from an unprincipled man who had treated his own body with contempt and disgracefully squandered his ancestral property would not benefit the hearers even when expressed with great eloquence. [32] These, then, are the men he bars from the platform; these are the ones he forbids to address the people. And if anyone in defiance of these rules does not just speak but plays the sykophant and behaves unscrupulously, and the city can no longer tolerate such a man, ["Let any Athenian who wishes and has the right," he says, "declare a scrutiny,"] and at that point he bids you to decide the case in court. And it is under this law that I have now come before you.

[33] Now, these regulations have long been law. But you added another new law after the splendid pancratium[34] this man staged in the Assembly, in utter shame at the incident: that at each Assembly a tribe should be selected by lot to preside over the platform.[35] And what did the proposer of the law order? He instructs the members of the tribe to sit as protectors of the law and the democratic constitution on the ground that, unless we summon help from some source against men who have lived like this, we shall not be able to debate even the most serious matters. [34] It is useless, men of Athens, to attempt to drive people of this sort from the platform by shouting them down; they are without shame. We must use punishments to change their ways; this is the only way to make them bearable.

Now he will read out to you the laws established to ensure the orderly conduct of public speakers. For the law on the presiding role of the tribes has been indicted as inexpedient[36] by a coalition consist-

---

[34] The pancratium was a particularly brutal mixture of boxing and wrestling. The association of the law with Timarchus' (alleged) conduct is not demonstrated.

[35] That is, the speaker's platform on the Pnyx, where the Assembly met.

[36] By a *graphē nomon mē epitēdeion theinai*, "indictment for having made an inexpedient disadvantageous law"; cf. the *graphē paranomōn* (Introduction, VA). In both procedures, if the action was brought within a year, the target was the

ing of this Timarchus and other speakers of the same sort, to free them
to live and speak just as they choose.

[35] [LAWS] *If any public speaker addresses the Council or the Assembly*
other than on the subject that is under discussion, or does not speak on
each issue separately, or speaks twice on the same subject on the same
day, or speaks abusively or slanders anyone, or heckles, or stands up
when business is being conducted and speaks on a subject that is not
part of the proceedings, or urges on others, or assaults the Chairman,
once the Assembly or Council is adjourned, the Chairmen (Proedroi)
are empowered to register a fine of up to fifty drachmas for each offense
and pass the record to the Collectors. If he deserves a more severe pun-
ishment, they are to impose a fine of up to fifty drachmas and refer the
matter to the Council or the next Assembly. When the summonses are
lodged, the relevant body is to judge the case, and if he is convicted by
secret ballot, the Chairmen are to record his name for the Collectors.[37]

[36] You have heard the laws, men of Athens, and I have no doubt
that you consider them sound. But whether these laws are to be of use
or not depends on you. If you punish the guilty, your laws will be
sound and valid, but if you let them go, the laws will still be sound but
no longer valid.

[37] But as I proposed at the beginning of my speech, now that I
have spoken about the laws, I want to turn to the examination of
Timarchus' way of life, so you will realize how much it differs from
your laws. And I ask you, men of Athens, to pardon me if, when
forced to speak about activities that by their nature are distasteful but
have actually been practiced by this man, I am induced to use any
expression that resembles Timarchus' actions. [38] It would not be fair
for you to criticize me, if in my desire to inform you I were to use
rather plain language, but rather criticize this man, if he has actually
led such a life that anyone describing his behavior is unable to say

---

proposer of the suspect legislation; after that period, the legislation could be
indicted and repealed, but the proposer was no longer personally liable. As we can
see from Aes. 3.4, the law survived this attack.

[37] The content of this law is more plausible than the rest of the documents
inserted in the speech. It may simply be a more felicitous forgery, though it may
conceivably contain details derived from a reliable source.

what he wants to say without using expressions of this sort. But I shall avoid doing so to the very best of my ability.[38]

[39] Observe, men of Athens, how reasonable I shall be in dealing with this man Timarchus. Any abuses he committed against his own body while still a boy I leave out of this account. Let it be void, like events under the Thirty[39] or before Euclides,[40] or any other official time limit of this sort that has been laid down. But the acts he has committed since reaching the age of reason and as a young man and in full knowledge of the laws, these I shall make the subject of my accusations, and I urge you to take them seriously.

[40] Now this man first of all, as soon as he ceased to be a child, settled in Piraeus in the establishment of the doctor Euthydicus, ostensibly to learn the profession but in reality because he had determined to sell himself, as events themselves showed. I pass over voluntarily all the merchants or other foreigners or our fellow-citizens who had the use of his body during that period, so that nobody can say that I am dwelling excessively on every detail. I shall confine my account to the men in whose house he has lived, bringing shame on his own body and the city, earning a living from the very practice that the law forbids a man to engage in, or forfeit the right to address the people.

[41] There is a man named Misgolas son of Naucrates of Collytus, men of Athens, a man who in other respects is decent and above criticism but who has a phenomenal passion for this activity and is always in the habit of having male singers and lyre-players[41] in his company.

---

[38] Aeschines established at the outset a persona based on moderation and decency that operates throughout the speech (cf., e.g., 1.39). Here and elsewhere the speaker both dissociates himself from the salacious material he has (of his own volition) decided to narrate and frees himself from the need to provide detail.

[39] In a brief but brutal oligarchic coup, the Thirty ruled Athens for less than a year (404–403) before they were overthrown and the democracy was restored. The restored democracy declared a general amnesty (with specific exceptions) for acts committed under the oligarchy.

[40] A revised set of laws (Introduction, VA) came into effect in the archonship of Euclides (403/2) and, in the case of new provisions, was not retroactive.

[41] Presumably Aeschines has in mind entertainers who performed at symposia; certainly in the case of females in this category, the borderline between musician and prostitute was fluid.

I say this not to indulge in low gossip but so you will recognize who he is.[42] This man, perceiving the reason for Timarchus' spending his time at the doctor's house, paid a sum of money in advance and moved Timarchus and set him up in his own house, a fine figure of a man, young and unprincipled and ready for the acts that Misgolas was eager to perform, and Timarchus to have done to him. [42] Timarchus had no inhibition but submitted to it, though he did not lack the resources for all reasonable needs. For his father had left him a very large estate, which he had squandered, as I shall show later in my speech. No, he did all this as a slave to the most disgraceful pleasures, gluttony and expensive eating and flute-girls and courtesans[43] and dice and the other activities that should never have control of a decent and freeborn man. But this vile man felt no shame in abandoning his father's house and living with Misgolas, a man who was not a friend of his father nor one of his own age group nor a guardian, no, a man who was unconnected and older than himself, a man without restraint in such activity, when he himself was young and handsome.

[43] Of the many ridiculous acts of Timarchus in that period, there is one that I want to recount to you. It was during the procession for the City Dionysia, and Misgolas, the man who had taken him up, and Phaedrus son of Callias of Sphettus were both taking part in the procession. This man Timarchus had agreed with them that he would join them in the procession, and they were busy with their preparations; but Timarchus had not returned. Angry at this, Misgolas went in search of him with Phaedrus; acting on information received, they found him dining in a lodging house with some foreign guests. Misgolas and Phaedrus threatened the foreigners and ordered them to

---

[42] Less probably "what he's like." The point is disingenuous.

[43] The Greek term *hetaira* is difficult to render. It is used of the common prostitute (for which the more usual term was *pornē*, see above, 29n) but also of the cultivated and expensive females like Neaera (in Dem. 59) whose skills encompassed far more than sex (for which the now outmoded word "courtesan" is the nearest modern equivalent). The objection to spending money on courtesans derives less from disapproval of extramarital sex by males than from hostility toward squandering money and its consequences. The combination of homosexual and heterosexual activity strikes the modern reader as surprising but is not unusual for classical Greece.

come with them at once to the prison for corrupting a free youth; the
foreigners took fright and ran off, leaving everything behind.[44]

[44] The truth of this story is known to everyone who was familiar
with Misgolas and Timarchus at that time. And I find it very gratify-
ing that my dispute is with a man who is not unknown to you, and is
known for precisely the practice on which you will be casting your
vote. For in a case that concerns unknown individuals, it is perhaps
incumbent on the prosecutor to offer explicit proof, but where the
facts are generally agreed, it is no great task in my view to act as prosecutor; for he needs only to remind his hearers. [45] Now, although
the matter is generally agreed, since we are in a lawcourt, what I have
done is draft a deposition for Misgolas,[45] one that is accurate but not
gross, or so I believe. The actual terms for the acts he committed on
this man are not included, nor have I written down anything that
renders a witness admitting the truth subject to punishment under the
laws;[46] what I have written is recognizable to you but without risk to
the witness or disgrace.

[46] Now, if Misgolas is prepared to come forward here and testify
to the truth, he will be doing what is right. But if he would rather
ignore the summons[47] than testify to the truth, then you can see the
whole business plainly. For if the active partner is to feel ashamed and
prefer to pay 1,000 drachmas to the Treasury to avoid showing his face
to you, while the passive partner is to speak in the Assembly, it was a
wise legislator who barred people as vile as this from the platform.[48]
[47] But if he obeys the formal summons but takes the most shameless

---

[44] The allegation is never proved, since Aeschines evidently anticipates that
Misgolas will refuse to testify.

[45] Aeschines presents this deposition (in 50) knowing full well that Misgolas
will not affirm it (see the Introduction, VD, and below, 46n). Thus much of his
discussion leading up to the deposition is intended for rhetorical effect only.

[46] The statement is based on Aeschines' earlier tendentious definition of *hybris*
(1.15).

[47] I.e., refuse to swear the *exōmosia* even after being summoned (Introduction,
VD).

[48] Aeschines astutely compensates for his lack of testimony by making Misgolas' refusal to confirm his account a tacit confirmation. Cf. 1.71–73, which make
clear that the lack of evidence will be seized on by the defense, and where again
Aeschines blusters.

course, which is to deny the truth on oath, with the intention of show-ing his gratitude to Timarchus and at the same time demonstrating to others that he knows how to keep such activities secret, first, he will be harming himself, and second, he will achieve nothing.[49] I have drafted another deposition for the people who know that this man Timarchus abandoned his father's house and lived with Misgolas, though the task I am attempting is, I think, a difficult one. For I must offer as witnesses neither my own friends nor their enemies, nor peo-ple who know neither of us, but their friends.[50] [48] But if it transpires that they dissuade these witnesses from testifying (I don't think they will, not all of them anyway), this at least they will never be able to do, eradicate the truth, nor the general report in the city about Timarchus; I did not create this for him, he did it for himself. For the decent man's life should be so clean that it does not allow even the suspicion of blameworthy conduct.

[49] I want to say something else in advance, in case Misgolas obeys the laws and your authority. There are men who by their nature differ from others in their physical appearance as far as age is con-cerned. There are some men who, though young, appear mature and older, while others, though old when one counts the years, seem posi-tively young. Misgolas is one of these. He is in fact a contemporary of mine and was an ephebe[51] with me; we are both in our forty-fifth year.[52] And I myself have all these grey hairs that you see, but he

---

[49] The passage shows that there was no formal penalty attaching to the (alleged) false oath of disclaimer, unlike false testimony, for which a litigant could sue his opponent's witnesses.

[50] Witnesses tended to be friends of the litigant (it was normal for anyone approaching matters that might involve subsequent litigation to take friends as witnesses) or neutral observers; in extreme cases (as here and Dem. 57.14), a liti-gant might have to rely on hostile witnesses. Witnesses in Athens were often as much supporters as testifiers to fact (some scholars go too far in arguing that they were solely or predominantly supporters).

[51] The *ephēbeia*, consisting of two years' military service from the age of eigh-teen, was probably an old institution. It seems to have been fairly loosely admin-istered until it was reorganized along more rigid lines after the defeat at Chaeronea in 338.

[52] Various calculations show that Misgolas and Timarchus were about the same age (see Harris 1988). Aeschines' account implies that Misgolas was the older

doesn't. Why do I give this advance warning? So that when you suddenly see him you will not be surprised and mentally respond: "Heracles! He is not much older than Timarchus!" For it is a fact both that his appearance is naturally like this and that Timarchus was already a youth when Misgolas had relations with him.

[50] But to delay no longer, first of all call the witnesses who know that this man Timarchus lived in Misgolas' house, then read out the deposition of Phaedrus, and finally take the deposition for Misgolas himself, just in case he agrees to attest the truth out of fear of the gods and shame in front of the people who know the facts, the rest of the citizen body and you the jurors.

[DEPOSITIONS] *Misgolas son of Nicias of Piraeus testifies as follows. Timarchus, who once stayed at the establishment of the doctor Euthydicus, was associated with me, and from my earlier acquaintance with him to the present I have not ceased to hold him in high regard.*[53]

[51] Now, men of Athens, if this man Timarchus had stayed with Misgolas and had not gone to live with anyone else, his conduct would have been more decent, if indeed there is any decency in such behavior, and I would have hesitated to charge him with anything beyond the frank term used by the legislator, that is, only with having been a kept lover. For I think that this is exactly the charge for anyone who engages in this activity with a single partner but does so for pay. [52] But if, ignoring these wild men, Cedonides and Autoclides and Thersander, into whose houses he has been taken to live, I remind you of the facts and demonstrate that he has earned his living with his body not only at the home of Misgolas but also in the house of another and then another, and that he went from this one to yet another, then it will be clear that he has not only been a kept lover but (and by Dionysus!—I don't think I can evade the issue all day) has actually prostituted him-

---

partner in the relationship, but apparently he looks younger, and Aeschines feels the need to address this discrepancy directly.

[53] Forgery is betrayed by the presence of a single deposition where the speech calls for several, by the false demotic and patronymic, and by the garbled format; depositions in Athenian courts were made in the third person ("X attests/XX attest that, etc.").

self. For I think that this is exactly the charge for anyone who engages in this activity casually with many partners for pay. [53] Now, when Misgolas tired of the expense and dismissed Timarchus from his house, Anticles the son of Callias of Euonymon next took him up. Anticles is away in Samos as one of the colonists;[54] but I shall tell you what happened after that. When this Timarchus left Anticles and Misgolas, he did not reflect on his conduct or turn to better ways but spent his days at the gaming house where the gambling board is set up and people engage in cock fighting and dice playing. I imagine that some of you have already seen the place or, if not, have at least heard of it. [54] One of the people who passes his time there is a man called Pittalacus; this person is a public slave of the city.[55] Now Pittalacus, who was financially well-off and had seen Timarchus passing his time there, took him up and kept him at his house. And this vile creature was not bothered even by this, that he was about to shame himself with a person who was a public slave of the city; no, his only concern was to get a backer (*chorēgos*)[56] to finance his vile habits, while to questions of decency or disgrace he gave not a moment's thought. [55] Now the abuses and outrages that I have heard were committed on the person of Timarchus by this individual were such that—in the name of Olympian Zeus!—I could not bring myself to describe them to you. The acts that this man felt no shame to commit in practice are ones that I would rather die than describe clearly in words among you.

---

[54] Athenian colonists ("cleruchs," see the Introduction to Ant. 5) were sent out to Samos after its capture in 365. Anticles' absence is convenient for Aeschines, since it provides an excuse for his lack of evidence for this stage in Timarchus' career.

[55] If Aeschines is telling the truth about Pittalacus' status, this incident is very revealing for the role, economic potential, and status of public slaves. Since they were themselves property, slaves technically had no possessions (though see below, 97n); Pittalacus appears to be wealthy and to associate freely with well-born Athenians. He is also represented as bringing a suit (1.62); slaves lacked legal personality and were unable either to bring a suit or to address a court. It has been suggested plausibly that Aeschines misleads us and that Pittalacus was a freedman (i.e., ex-slave); the fiction would enable the prosecutor to stir up prejudice against a defendant who was allegedly ready to sell himself even to a slave.

[56] For the *chorēgos* (here metaphorical), see the Introduction, IVC and Ant. 6 passim.

tragical.

his income is from the gambaling house.

But about the same time that this man was living with Pittalacus, Hegesander sailed back to Athens from the Hellespont. I am aware that you have been puzzled for some time at my failure to mention him, so notorious are the events I am about to narrate.

[56] This Hegesander, whom you know better than I, arrived. As it happened, he had at that time sailed to the Hellespont as treasurer to Timomachus of Acharnae, who served as general, and he returned to Athens the beneficiary, it is said, of Timomachus' gullibility, in possession of not less than eighty minas of silver;[57] and in a way he was not the least to blame for Timomachus' ruin. [57] Well-off as he was, and as a regular visitor to the house of Pittalacus, who was a gambling partner of his, he saw Timarchus there for the first time. He was impressed, and his passion was aroused, and he wanted to take him into his own house; he thought, I imagine, that Timarchus' nature closely resembled his own. First of all, he spoke to Pittalacus, urging him to let him have Timarchus; and when he could not persuade Pittalacus, he assailed Timarchus here in person. It did not take much argument; he persuaded him instantly. Indeed, when it comes to the actual business, his candor and openness to persuasion[58] are remarkable; for this very reason he should properly be an object of hatred.

[58] After Timarchus had left Pittalacus and been taken in by Hegesander, Pittalacus was, I think, distressed at having spent so much money (as he saw it) to no purpose and jealous of what was going on. And he kept going to the house. And because he was annoying them, observe the great feat of Hegesander and Timarchus! At one point they and some others whose names I prefer not to mention got drunk and [59] burst at night into the house where Pittalacus was living. First of all, they broke his equipment and threw it into the street (throwing dice and dice cups and other gaming items), and they killed the quails and cocks[59] on which the wretched man doted, and finally they tied

---

[57] A substantial sum of money (1⅓ talents in a society where three to four talents made a man liable to the liturgy system, for which see the Introduction, IVC).

[58] "Candor and openness to persuasion": The words are said with contempt and refer to Timarchus' readiness to do business frankly and consider all offers. An alternative in the manuscripts would read "wickedness and infidelity."

[59] The reference is to quails and cocks kept for fighting (with attendant gambling).

damage all the gaming equipment.
→ he is not a citizen so hard to
prove.

Pittalacus himself to a pillar and inflicted on him the worst whipping imaginable for so long that even the neighbors heard the commotion. [60] Next day, Pittalacus, enraged at the treatment, went robeless into the agora and sat as suppliant at the altar of the Mother of the Gods.[60] A crowd assembled, as usually happens, and Hegesander and Timarchus, in panic that their vile behavior might be announced to the whole city (the Assembly was about to meet), ran up to the altar, accompanied by some of their dicing partners. [61] They clustered around Pittalacus and begged him to leave the altar, maintaining that the whole incident had been a drunken prank. Timarchus himself (who was not yet as ugly-looking as nowadays—heavens, no—but still serviceable) touched the fellow's chin in supplication and said he would comply with all his wishes. Eventually they induced the fellow to quit the altar on the understanding that he would receive some sort of justice. But once he left the agora they took no further notice of him. [62] And Pittalacus, angered at the outrageous treatment, brought a suit against each of them.[61]   *→ law suits*

When he was bringing these suits, observe the great feat of Hegesander! This fellow had done him no wrong but, quite the reverse, had been wronged by him; he had no connection with him but was the public slave of the city. Yet Hegesander seized him as a slave, claiming he was his property. In his wretched situation, Pittalacus encountered a real man and a truly good one. There is a man named Glaucon of Cholarge. This man asserted Pittalacus' freedom.[62] [63] Lawsuits now began. After a period of time they[63] entrusted the decision[64] of the

---

[60] The shrine of the Mother of the Gods was on the west side of the agora, and the altar referred to here was in front of the shrine. Many people going to the Pnyx for an Assembly would go through the agora (either because it was on their way or because they wanted to shop en route) and pass the shrine, hence the parenthesis in the next sentence.

[61] For the slave bringing a suit, see above, 54n.

[62] For this action, see Dem. 59.40 with note. If Aeschines is telling the truth about Pittalacus' status in 1.54 (see note), either public slaves enjoyed an ambiguous status or Glaucon used the intervention process to challenge Hegesander's ownership rather than to make an absolute statement about Pittalacus' status.

[63] I.e., the parties to the suits.

[64] For this sort of private arbitration, cf. Dem. 59.45–47. In such cases, the parties usually agreed to abide by the arbitrator's decision, in which case it was final.

An Athenian citizen steps forward. starts building public image

dispute to Diopeithes of Sunium, a member of Hegesander's deme who had already in fact had dealings[65] with him when he was young. On taking over the case, Diopeithes caused delay after delay as a favor to these people. [64] And when Hegesander began to appear as a speaker at your platform, at the time when he was also engaged in a feud with Aristophon of Azenia, before the latter threatened him in the Assembly with exactly the declaration of formal scrutiny[66] that I have made against Timarchus, and when Hegesander's brother Crobylus[67] was a regular speaker in the Assembly and these people had the nerve to advise you on the politics of Greece, at that point Pittalacus lost confidence in himself. He reflected on who he was and who his enemies were and (the truth must be said) reached a sensible decision: he kept quiet and was grateful to receive no fresh abuse. At this point, having won this glorious victory with ease, Hegesander kept Timarchus here in his house. [65] You all know the truth of my account. Which of you has been to the food stalls and not observed the extravagance of these people? Which of you has come upon their carousing and brawls and not felt resentment for the city's sake? Still, since we are in a lawcourt, please call Glaucon of Cholarge, the man who asserted Pittalacus' freedom, and read out the other depositions.[68]

[66] [DEPOSITIONS] _Glaucon son of Timaeus of Cholarge testifies. I asserted the freedom of Pittalacus when he was being seized as a slave_

---

[65] Greek _chrēsthai,_ an ambiguous term that can mean "associate with," etc., socially, but whose primary meaning is "use," which can include sexual use.

[66] That is, the _dokimasia tōn rhētorōn_ (see the Speech Introduction and above, 28–30). The statement is never substantiated.

[67] Given name Hegesippus; Crobylus ("Topknot," an antiquated hairstyle) was a nickname.

[68] That these depositions are forgeries is indicated principally by the use of the first person in these depositions (see 1.50n), also by the discrepancy between the number of depositions called for by Aeschines and the number preserved in the text. One would like to know how much of the narrative was confirmed here. Glaucon will presumably confirm that Hegesander claimed Pittalacus as his slave and that he intervened. He and the other witnesses will confirm that Pittalacus instituted and then dropped proceedings against Hegesander. But the narrative background, including the role of Timarchus, may not have figured in the depositions.

probably actually money

by Hegesander. Subsequently Pittalacus came to me and said that he wanted to send to Hegesander and resolve his dispute with him on the basis of the withdrawal of his suit against Hegesander and Hegesander's action for slavery against him. And they resolved the dispute.

Likewise Amphisthenes testifies. I asserted the freedom of Pittalacus when he was being seized as a slave by Hegesander and so forth.

[67] So then, I shall call Hegesander in person for you. I have drafted for him a deposition more decent than his character but a little more explicit than the one for Misgolas. I am aware that he will swear the disclaimer and lie on oath. Why, then, do I call him to give the testimony? To show you the way this practice affects the characters of men, how contemptuous of the gods they become, how disrespectful of the laws, how indifferent to every source of shame. Please call Hegesander.[69] → him saying he won't agree.

[68] [DEPOSITION] *Hegesander son of Diphilus of Steiria testifies. When I sailed back from the Hellespont, I found Timarchus son of Arizelus living at the house of Pittalacus the gambler, and as a result of that acquaintance I consorted with Timarchus and used him for the same activity as I had used Leodamas previously.*

[69] I was not unaware that he would show no respect for the oath, men of Athens; I warned you in advance. And one thing is certainly clear, that since he now refuses to give evidence, he will shortly appear for the defense. And by Zeus, it is no wonder. He will mount this platform, I expect, with confidence in his way of life, an upright man, enemy of wickedness, who doesn't even know who Leodamas was, Leodamas at whose name you all yelled when the deposition was being read out. [70] Shall I bring myself to speak a little more frankly than is my nature? Tell me, in the name of Zeus and the other gods, men of Athens, when a man has shamed himself with Hegesander, don't you think he has played whore to a whore? What excesses of vile behavior do we suppose they did not practice when drunk and on their own? Don't you think that Hegesander, trying to compensate for

---

[69] That the deposition is forged is indicated by the formal flaws (1.50n) and factual errors (the deposition inverts the relationship between Hegesander and Leodamas, for which see 111 below).

his notorious activities for Leodamas, of which you all know, made arrogant demands in the belief that his own past behavior would seem moderate in comparison with the extremes of Timarchus?

[71] Nonetheless, you will see that Hegesander himself and his brother Crobylus will leap up here shortly and, with considerable deviousness and rhetorical skill, will claim that my case is one of downright stupidity. They will demand that I present witnesses who testify explicitly where he carried out the acts and who saw and what kind of act. This I think is a scandalous demand. [72] I don't consider you so forgetful that you do not recall the laws you heard read out a little earlier, in which it is written that anyone who hires an Athenian for this activity or anyone who hires himself out is liable to the most severe penalties, the same in both cases. What man is so witless that he would agree to give explicit testimony of this sort, by which it is certain, if he attests the truth, that he proves himself liable to the most extreme penalties? [73] So, then, all that is left is for the passive partner to admit the facts himself. But this is why he is on trial, because after engaging in this activity, he addressed the Assembly in defiance of the laws. So do you want us to abandon the whole issue and not investigate? By Poseidon, we shall really manage the city well, if when we know that acts are taking place, we are to ignore them simply because someone does not come forward in court and testify explicitly without shame.

[74] Consider the issue on the basis of parallels; and I suppose the parallels will have to resemble Timarchus' practices. You see these men who sit in the brothels, the ones who on their own admission practice this activity. Yet these men, when they are required to engage in the act, still throw a cloak over their shame and lock the doors. Now if someone were to ask you, the men passing by in the street: "What is this person doing at this moment?" you would immediately give the name of the act, without seeing who had gone in; no, once you know the chosen profession of the individual, you also recognize the act. [75] So you should investigate Timarchus in the same way and ask not whether anyone saw him but if this man has engaged in the practice. For by the gods, what is one to say, Timarchus? What would you yourself say about another person who was being tried on this charge? What is one to say when a young lad leaves his father's house and spends his nights in the homes of others, a lad of unusual beauty, and enjoys lavish dinners without making any contribution, and keeps flute-players and the most expensive courtesans, and plays at dice,

while he pays out nothing himself but another man pays for him? [76] Does one need to be clairvoyant? Isn't it obvious that the man who makes such enormous demands of others must himself inevitably provide certain pleasures in return to the men who pay out the money in advance? By Olympian Zeus, I can find no more decorous way of referring to the grotesque acts that you have practiced.

[77] Consider the matter, if you would, on the basis of parallels from political affairs, too, and especially matters with which you are currently dealing. Ballots[70] have taken place in the demes, and each of you has submitted himself to the vote, to see who is truly Athenian and who is not. And when I personally find myself in the courtroom and listen to the litigants, I see that the same factor is always influential with you. [78] Whenever the accuser says: "Jurors, the demesmen with their vote rejected this man on oath, though nobody in the world accused him or bore witness against him; they voted on the basis of their own knowledge," without hesitation, I think, you make a commotion, convinced that the man on trial has no claim to citizen rights. For your view, I think, is that you need no further discussion or testimony in matters that a man knows himself for certain. [79] Come now, in the name of Zeus, if Timarchus had been compelled to submit to a vote on this way of life of his like that on birth qualifications, to determine whether he is guilty or not, and the issue was being decided in court, and was being brought before you as now, but it was forbidden by some law or decree either for me to make an accusation or for Timarchus to offer a defense; and the herald here standing near me put to you the proclamation in the law: "Of the voting counters, the hollowed one for whoever believes Timarchus has prostituted himself, the solid one for whoever believes he has not,"[71] how would you have voted? I know full well that you would have convicted him. [80] And if any of you were to ask me: "How do you know whether we would have convicted him?" I should reply: "Because you have spoken frankly

---

[70] Greek *diapsēphisis*, lit. "voting among/between." For the review of the citizen lists by the demes in 365/4, see above, Dem. 57.

[71] Each member of the panel of jurors in court was issued two disc-shaped votes: one had a short hollow bar through the center; the other, a short solid bar (Boegehold 1995: 82–90 with plates 15–22). There were two voting urns, one for the vote reflecting the juror's positive verdict, the other for the voided vote. The system guaranteed anonymity.

and told me." When and where each of you did so I shall now remind you: whenever this man steps up in the Assembly, and last year when he was a member of the Council.[72] Whenever he mentioned work on walls or a tower or said that someone had been taken off somewhere, you would yell out at once and laugh and yourselves utter the terms for the acts of his you know about.[73] [81] I shall leave out most of these occasions that occurred some time ago; but I do want to remind you of what happened in the actual Assembly when I made formal declaration of this scrutiny against Timarchus.

The Council of the Areopagus[74] was appearing before the Assembly in accordance with the decree that this man had proposed on the subject of the houses on the Pnyx.[75] The man who was speaking for the Areopagites was Autolycus, a man who has lived an honorable life, by Olympian Zeus and Apollo, with dignity and in a manner worthy of that body. [82] And when in the course of his speech he said that the Areopagus disapproved of Timarchus' proposal, "and on the matter of this deserted locality and the area of the Pnyx, do not be surprised, men of Athens, if Timarchus is more familiar with it than the Council of the Areopagus,"[76] at that point there was uproar, and you said that what Autolycus said was true, that this man was familiar with the place. [83] And Autolycus, not understanding the reason for your uproar, scowled fiercely and, after a pause, said: "Men of Athens, we members of the Areopagus neither accuse nor defend (it is not our traditional practice), but we have some sympathy for Timarchus for

---

[72] Timarchus will no doubt have replied that he had passed a *dokimasia* (preliminary scrutiny) for the Council in which his citizenship qualifications were tested and an opportunity was offered to anyone to query them.

[73] The passage is full of sexual double meanings that are lost on the modern reader. The comic playwrights of the fifth and early fourth centuries indicate that the stock of Greek colloquial sexual metaphor was very rich.

[74] For the Areopagus, see the Introduction, VB. The second half of the fourth century saw a growth in its political influence.

[75] Evidently, Timarchus had proposed a measure for clearing the area around the Pnyx. The Pnyx, adjacent to the Areopagus, was the hill on which the Assembly met.

[76] Autolycus presumably means that as an active politician frequenting the Pnyx, Timarchus would know the area well; his audience takes this as a reference to sexual encounters in deserted places.

the following reason; he perhaps," he said, "thought that while things were so peaceful, the outlay for each of you was small."[77] Once more at the mention of quiet and small outlay he met with still greater commotion and laughter from you. [84] When he mentioned foundations and cisterns, you just couldn't contain yourselves.[78] At this point Pyrrhander came forward to reproach you and asked the Assembly if they were not ashamed to be laughing when the Council of the Areopagus was present. But you shouted him from the platform and replied: "Pyrrhander, we know that we should not be laughing in their presence. But so strong is the truth that it overcomes all human logic." [85] This I take to be the testimony offered to you by the Athenian people, who cannot properly be convicted of false witness. Isn't it bizarre, men of Athens, if without a word from me, you yourselves shout out the name of the acts you know he has committed, but when I state them you forget? Or if he was convicted when the issue did not come to trial, but he is to be acquitted now that it has been proved?

[86] Since I have mentioned the deme ballots and the policies of Demophilus, I want to offer another example in this connection. For this same man made a similar maneuver before. He alleged that there were individuals who were trying to bribe the Assembly and the lawcourts as well, an allegation also made by Nicostratus recently. Some of the trials on these charges took place a while ago, and others are still pending. [87] Well then, by Zeus and the gods, if those involved had resorted to the same defense used now by Timarchus and his supporting speakers, and insisted that either there should be explicit testimony on the charge or the jurors should disbelieve it, then it would certainly be necessary following this logic for the one man to attest that he offered a bribe and the other that he took it, when there is a penalty of death laid down in law for each, just as on the present matter if someone hires out an Athenian for abuse, and again if any Athe-

---

[77] Another unintentional double meaning. Autolycus means presumably that Timarchus feels that at a time of peace the financial burden of the clearance project would be small; his audience takes this as a reference to the low cost of sex with Timarchus in a quiet place.

[78] Again, we have words whose metaphorical meanings carry sexual connotations. Presumably "cistern" would refer to the anus and "foundation" to the buttocks or anus.

copper boy - catch them in the act.
if admit guilt → killed without trial.

nian willingly takes money for the shameful use of his body. [88] Is
there a man alive who would have given evidence, or any accuser who
would have attempted to prove the case on this basis? Certainly not.
So what happened? Were the accused acquitted? No, by Zeus; they
were condemned to death, when they had committed a much less
serious offense—by Zeus and Apollo!—than this person here. In the
case of those unfortunate men, they met with this catastrophe because
they were unable to protect themselves against old age and poverty
together, the worst evils in human life, in Timarchus' case because he
could not restrain his own vile nature.

[89] Now if this trial were taking place in another city that had
been called to adjudicate, I should have expected you to be my witnesses, as the ones who know best that I am telling the truth. But since
the trial is in Athens and you are at the same time judges and witnesses
to my account, my task is to remind you and yours not to doubt me.
For in my opinion, men of Athens, Timarchus here is concerned not
only for himself but also for all the rest who have practiced the same
profession. [90] If this practice is to take place, as is usually the case,
secretly and in isolated spots and private houses, and the man who
possesses the fullest knowledge, but has shamed a citizen, is to be liable
to the most severe penalties if he testifies to the truth; while the man
on trial, against whom his own life and the truth have given evidence,
is to insist on being judged on the basis not of what is known but of
the depositions, the law and the truth are destroyed and a clear route
has been revealed for those guilty of the worst felonies to be acquitted.
[91] For what mugger or thief or seducer or homicide, or anyone else
who commits the gravest offenses but does so in secret,[79] will be punished? For in fact, those of them who are caught with their guilt mani-

---

[79] Muggers and thieves belonged to a class of criminal called *kakourgoi* (see
above, Ant. 2.1.4n). They could be hauled before the officials called the Eleven,
and if they confessed, they were executed without trial; if they denied guilt, they
were tried, and executed if convicted. Homicides, too, could in certain circumstances be subjected to summary arrest, though (despite the next sentence) they
could be executed without trial only if they were previously convicted homicides
returning from exile without permission. Homicide law exempted from punishment someone who killed a seducer (*moichos*; see Lys. 1). Scholars dispute
whether seducers could be classed as *kakourgoi*.

fest are executed at once if they confess, but those who go undetected and deny their guilt are tried in the courts, and the truth is discovered on the basis of likelihood.] - *hypothetical* .

[92] Now take as an example the Council of the Areopagus, the most exact body in the city. I have often at meetings of that Council seen men who spoke well and provided witnesses convicted; and before now I know of some men who spoke very badly and had no witnesses for their case but succeeded. For they vote not just in response to the speech nor to the witnesses but on what they themselves know and have investigated. And so that body continues to enjoy respect in the city. [93] Now, men of Athens, you, too, should judge this case in the same way. First of all, nothing should have greater credence with you than your own knowledge and conviction concerning Timarchus here, and second, you should consider the issue not in relation to the present but in relation to the past. For the statements that were made in the past about Timarchus and his way of life were said because of their truth, but those that will be made on this day will be said because of the trial in order to deceive you. Cast your vote, then, in favor of the longer period, the truth, and your own knowledge.

[94] Yet a speechwriter,[80] the one who has devised his defense, claims that I contradict myself.[81] He says that in his view it is impossible for the same man to have prostituted himself and squandered his inheritance; to have misused one's body is the conduct of a child, while to have squandered one's inheritance is the conduct of a man. Furthermore, he claims that men who shame themselves charge fees

---

[80] I.e., Demosthenes. There is independent testimony that speechwriters were regarded with hostility and distrust, though their services were evidently much in demand.

[81] The anticipation of defense arguments was a standard feature of prosecution speeches. Litigants would have had a very good idea of the opponent's case, from either the arbitration (Introduction, VB) or other sorts of preliminary hearings, because no new evidence could be introduced afterwards. In addition, a litigant would have such information as he could glean from common gossip, direct approaches from the opponent's enemies, and common sense. Since we rarely have both sides of a dispute, it is often difficult to determine whether we are offered solid information, guesswork, or invention.

How to proof:
witness, likelihood + rumor.
↳ neutral → ↑ strength .

[handwritten: implying he cannot have inherited alot: money if he is now charging for sex.]

for the practice. So he is going around the agora expressing surprise and wonderment that the same man has prostituted himself and squandered his inheritance. [95] But if anyone does not realize how the matter stands, I shall attempt to lay it out more clearly in my account. While the estate of the heiress whom Hegesander, Timarchus' husband, had married, and the money that he brought back from his period abroad with Timomachus lasted, they indulged in enormous excess and extravagance. But when it was all gone, wasted on dicing and lavish dinners, and Timarchus had passed his prime, as one would expect, nobody would pay money any more, while his vile and unholy nature still longed for the same pleasures, and in its extreme dissipation made continuing demands on him, and he was drawn back to his daily habits; [96] at that point he turned to eating up his inheritance. And he not only ate it up, but—if one can say this—drank it up as well! And indeed, he sold off each of his possessions, and not even at its true value; he could not wait for a profit or a good price but sold it for what it would realize immediately. So compelling was his haste to enjoy his pleasures.

[97] For his father left him an estate from which another man would actually have performed public services,[82] but this man proved unable even to preserve it for his own use. There was a house behind the Acropolis, a country property at Sphettus, another farm in Alopece, and in addition nine or ten slave craftsmen who made shoes,[83] each of whom paid him a commission[84] of two obols a day, while the foreman of the workshop paid three, and besides, a woman skilled in working linen, who took her work to the market, and a male embroiderer, and debtors owing him money and furniture.

[98] To prove I am telling the truth in this, I shall now, by Zeus, provide you with clear and explicit testimony from the witnesses. For unlike before, there is no danger or disgrace facing anyone attesting the truth. The house in the city he sold to Nausicrates the comic poet, and

---

[82] For liturgies, see the Introduction, IVC.

[83] For manufacturing using slave labor, see, e.g., Dem. 27 or Hyp. 3.

[84] Some slaves lived apart from their masters and carried out a trade independently, paying a commission to the master. They were termed *chōris oikountes* (lit. "living apart").

Cleaenetus the chorus-trainer subsequently bought it from Nausicrates for twenty minas. The country estate was bought from him by Mnesitheus of Myrrinus; it was a substantial property but had been left by Timarchus to run wild to an appalling degree. [99] The farm at Alopece was eleven or twelve stades[85] from the city wall; his mother had begged and pleaded with him, so I am told,[86] to leave this, if nothing else, unsold and to leave this plot at least for her to be buried in. But he did not hesitate; he sold this, too, for 2,000 drachmas. And he left none of the male and female slaves but has sold them all. And to prove I am telling the truth, I for my part will provide witnesses to the fact that his father left them to him; let him, if he claims that he has not sold them, provide the slaves visibly in person. [100] And to prove that his father had also lent out money to some people, which Timarchus spent when it was repaid, I shall present Metagenes of Sphettus, who had owed the father more than thirty minas and repaid to Timarchus here seven minas, the amount outstanding when his father died. Please call Metagenes of Sphettus. But first of all read out the deposition of Nausicrates, the man who bought his house. And take all the other depositions on the points I have made on the same subject.

[DEPOSITIONS]

[101] Now I shall prove to you that his father had no small sum of money, which this man has squandered. For in his fear of liability for public services, he had sold off his properties,[87] apart from the ones already mentioned; these were a farm at Cephisia, another at Amphitrope, and two processing plants[88] in the region of the silver mines, one at Aulon and the other at Thrasymus.

---

[85] The stade was approximately 185 meters, giving a distance of about two kilometers.

[86] Unsubstantiated but effective, adding the force of Athenian attitudes on duties to parents to their hostility to profligacy.

[87] I.e., to conceal the extent of his property in order to assess it below the threshold for liturgies (Introduction, IVC).

[88] The silver mines were the property of the state, but the ore was extracted by private individuals who leased concessions from the state. The plants in question were for processing the silver ore.

[102] How he acquired these I shall tell you. There were three brothers, Eupolemus the trainer, and Arizelus, Timarchus' father, and Arignotus, who is still alive today, though old and without his sight. Eupolemus was the first of them to die, while the estate was still undivided; next was Arizelus, Timarchus' father. While he was alive, he managed the whole property because of Arignotus' frailty and his unfortunate loss of sight, and because Eupolemus was dead, and he gave Arignotus an agreed sum for his support. [103] When Arizelus, the father of Timarchus here, also died, in the early period, while Timarchus was still a boy, Arignotus received all that was reasonably due to him from the guardians of the estate. But when Timarchus here was enrolled in the deme register and gained control of the estate, he pushed aside an old and unfortunate man, his own uncle, and squandered the property; he saw to none of Arignotus' needs; no, after such wealth, he left him to collect the disability dole.[89] [104] Finally, and most outrageous, when the old man had been missed from the list for consideration and had made formal supplication before the Council for the dole,[90] though Timarchus was serving on the Council and was presiding on that day, he did not see fit to speak in his support, but stood by while Arignotus lost the allocation for that Prytany.[91] To prove the truth of this statement, please call Arignotus of Sphettus and read out the deposition.

[DEPOSITION]

[105] It might be suggested that after selling his inherited estate, he acquired other property elsewhere in the city, and that instead of the country estate and the farm at Alopece and the slave craftsmen, he invested in the silver mines like his father before him. But he has noth-

---

[89] For the disability dole, see below, Lys. 24.

[90] Supplication, individual and collective, was a means of formalizing both a request and the commitment made by the individual of whom the request is made. It could involve ritualized gestures (touching the knee or cheek) or postures (such as taking refuge at an altar). Formal supplication of the Assembly (cf. Aes. 2.15) was allowed at one of the regular Assembly meetings each Prytany. The rules for the Council of Five Hundred were similar.

[91] A little over one month's pay. For the ten Prytanies, see the Introduction, IVA.

ing left, no house, no apartment, no farm, no slaves, no money out on loan, none of the other sources of income for men who aren't felons. Instead of his ancestral property, what he has left is vileness, syko-phancy, rashness, self-indulgence, cowardice, unscrupulousness, and an inability to blush at what is shameful, things that produce the most immoral and useless citizen.

[106] Now he has devoured not only his inherited property but in addition all of your public property that he has had in his control. For at the young age that you see, there is no office he has not held, and he acquired none of them by selection by lot or election but bought every one illegally. The majority of them I shall ignore and just men-tion two or three. [107] He became auditor[92] and did enormous dam-age to the city by receiving bribes from people guilty of malpractice in office, though his favorite practice was to persecute[93] innocent men undergoing their final audit. He was magistrate at Andros,[94] an office he bought for thirty minas, money he borrowed at a rate of eighteen percent,[95] using your allies as a means of funding his vile habits. And he displayed appetite on a scale never before seen from anyone in his treatment of the wives of free men. I present none of the men here to testify in public to the personal misfortune that he chose to conceal; I leave it to you to investigate. [108] But what do you expect? When the same man committed outrages (*hybris*) not only on others but also on his own person while here in Athens, under the rule of law, with you watching and his enemies nearby, who could imagine that once he obtained impunity,[96] opportunity, and public office, he would leave undone any act of the most extreme wantonness? Many times before

---

[92] The board of ten auditors (*logistai*) examined the accounts of all outgoing magistrates as the first stage of the process of *euthyna* (Introduction, IVA).

[93] *Sykophantein;* see the Introduction, VE.

[94] Athenian magistrates are attested for Andros and Amorgos.

[95] A high rate of interest for a nonmaritime loan. The normal rate was 12% per annum.

[96] Not literally true. Though he was not immediately visible to the Athenians, the allies could complain to Athens; and he had to face an audit on his return. No evidence is ever adduced to prove the allegation; so presumably no formal charge was ever brought. Aeschines tacitly meets this objection by offering a reason why victims might keep quiet.

now, by Zeus and Apollo, I have reflected on the good luck of our city, not least among many reasons for the fact that in that period no buyer could be found for the city of Andros!

[109] But perhaps one could argue that he was unprincipled when holding office alone but upright when he had colleagues. How could that be? This man, men of Athens, was appointed to the Council in the archonship of Nicophemus.[97] Now to attempt an account of all the crimes he committed in that year is not reasonable in a small portion of a day. But I shall give you a brief account of the ones most relevant to the charge that forms the basis of the present trial. [110] During the same archonship in which Timarchus was a member of the Council, Hegesander the brother of Crobylus was treasurer to the goddess,[98] and in collaboration, like good friends, they stole 1,000 drachmas from the city. A decent man, Pamphilus of Acherdus, who had quarreled with the defendant and was angry with him, observed what had happened, and during an Assembly he stood up and said: "Men of Athens, a man and a woman are between them stealing 1,000 drachmas of your money." [111] When you were puzzled at what he meant by a man and a woman and what he was talking about, he paused for a moment and said: "Don't you understand what I'm saying? The man is Hegesander over there—now, though before he was himself Leodamas' woman; the woman is Timarchus here. How the money is being stolen I shall tell you." Then he gave a fully informed and lucid account of the affair. And after giving this information, he said: "So what do I advise you to do, men of Athens? If the Council convicts Timarchus of the offense, expels him, and hands him over to a lawcourt, give them their reward,[99] and if they don't punish him, withhold it and hold this against them until that day." [112] When the Council next entered the Council chamber, they expelled him in the straw vote but accepted him back in the formal ballot.[100] And because they did not hand him over to a law-

---

[97] 361/0.

[98] That is, one of the board of treasurers of the sacred monies of Athena.

[99] It was customary (though not inevitable) for the outgoing Council to be awarded a gold crown for its service; see Rhodes 1972: 14–16.

[100] The present passage is our most substantial piece of information on the disciplinary powers and procedures of the Council against its own members.

court or eject him from the Council chamber, though it pains me to mention it, still I must tell you that they did not receive their reward. So, men of Athens, do not show your anger against the Council and deprive 500 citizens of their crown for failing to punish this man, and then yourselves acquit him and preserve for the Assembly a public speaker who was useless to the Council.

[113] Yet one might argue that though in offices obtained by lot he behaves like this, in elective offices he is more upright. And who among you does not know that he was notoriously exposed as a thief? He was sent by you as auditor of the mercenaries at Eretria;[101] and he was the only one of the investigators who admitted to receiving money. He did not address his defense to the question of fact but admitted his guilt and without hesitation directed his plea to the penalty. And you fined the ones who denied their guilt a talent each, while you fined Timarchus thirty minas. Yet the laws instruct that for thieves who admit their guilt, the punishment is death; the trial is for those who deny it.[102]

[114] As a result, he developed such contempt for you that right away he took 2,000 drachmas in bribes during the deme ballots.[103] He claimed that Philotades of Cydathenaeum, a member of the citizen body, was a freedman of his and persuaded the deme members to reject him; he presided over the case for the prosecution in the court and, taking the sacrificial victims in his hand, swore that he had taken and would take no money, swearing by the gods who watch over oaths and calling down destruction on himself. [115] But it was proved that he had received twenty minas from Leuconides, Philotades' in-law, by way of Philemon the actor, money that he spent in a short time on the courtesan Philoxene; so he abandoned the case and betrayed his oath. To prove I am telling the truth, please call Philemon, who gave

---

There appears to have been an informal vote ("straw vote," though the Greek verb *ekphyllophorein* suggests the use of leaves), followed by a formal hearing.

[101] A city on the island of Euboea. For the opportunities for peculation by falsifying the numbers for mercenaries, cf. Aes. 3.146. The *exetastes,* "auditor"/"assessor," was a financial official, associated by Aristotle (*Politics* 1322b) with the *logistai* (above, 107n).

[102] See above, 91n.

[103] Under the Demophilus decree; see above, 77n.

Timarchus the money, and Leuconides, the in-law of Philotades, and read out the copy of the agreement under which he sold out the case.

[DEPOSITION, AGREEMENT]

[116] Now his behavior toward citizens and relatives, his shameful squandering of his inheritance, and his casual attitude to the abuse (*hybris*) of his own body are things you knew even before I spoke of them, and my account has given you adequate reminder. But there are two features of my accusation left, and I pray to all the gods and goddesses that I personally shall speak on these matters as I have resolved for the city's sake; and I would wish you for your part to pay attention to what I am about to say and follow it closely.

[117] My first theme is an advance account of the defense that I am told will be offered, in case, if I fail to mention it, the man who advertises that he can teach young men the art of speaking[104] tricks you with false logic and prevents a result to the city's advantage. My second theme is to exhort the citizens to right conduct (*aretē*). I see many of the younger generation present in court, and many of the older men, and no small number from the rest of Greece gathered to listen. [118] Do not imagine that they have come to see me; no, they would much rather know whether you not only know how to pass laws but also can judge between right and wrong, whether you know how to respect good men and whether you are willing to punish people who make their way of life a disgrace to the city. I shall speak to you first of all about the defense argument.[105]

[119] That consummate speaker Demosthenes claims that either you must expunge the laws or else you must pay no attention to my arguments. He says he is amazed if you don't all remember that every year the Council sells off the prostitution tax,[106] and that those who buy the right to exact the tax do not guess but have precise knowledge

----

[104] It is difficult to determine whether Demosthenes actually offered instruction, formal or informal, in rhetoric or whether Aeschines is merely using Demosthenes' career as a professional speechwriter to present him as a teacher of rhetoric, exploiting the hostility to professional rhetoricians from the fifth century onward.

[105] For anticipation of defense arguments, see above, 94n.

[106] For the collection of taxes, see above, Dem. 59.27n.

of the people who engage in this trade. While I have had the audacity to charge that Timarchus has no right to address the people when he has prostituted himself, Demosthenes claims that the practice itself calls not for an allegation from a prosecutor but for a deposition from a taxman who has collected the tax from Timarchus. [120] Men of Athens, see whether you find the reply I make to this simple and frank. I am ashamed for the city's sake if Timarchus, the people's adviser, the man who has the nerve to serve on embassies to the rest of Greece, will not attempt to cleanse his reputation of the whole business but instead will query the locations[107] where he offered himself and ask if the tax collectors have ever collected the prostitution tax from him. [121] He should abandon this line of defense for your sake. I shall offer you another line of defense, an honorable and just one, which you should use, if you have nothing shameful on your conscience. Steel yourself to look the jurors in the face and say what a decent man should about his youth: "Men of Athens, I have been reared among you, from my childhood and adolescence, and my way of life is no secret. I am seen among you in the Assembly. [122] And I think that, if I were addressing any other body on the charge for which I am now on trial, your testimony would enable me to refute the accuser's statements easily. I think the rest of my life not worth living, not only if I have committed any of these acts but if it is your belief that the life I have lived resembles the accusations made by my opponent, and I freely offer the punishment you inflict on me as a means for the city to defend itself in the eyes of Greece. I have not come to plead with you for mercy; no, destroy me, if you think me this sort of man."

This, Timarchus, is the defense that befits a noble and decent man, one who has confidence in his way of life and properly treats every attempt at slander with contempt. [123] In contrast, the argument that Demosthenes is trying to persuade you to use is not the speech of a free man but of a prostitute who is quibbling about locations. But since you take refuge in the names of the lodgings and demand that the case be proved on the basis of the establishment where you plied your trade, once you have heard what I am about to say you will not use this argument if you have any sense. It is not buildings or lodgings

---

[107] This suggests that there was a list of brothels that served as the basis for tax collection.

that give their names to the occupants, but occupants who give the titles of their individual practices to their locations. [124] Where a number of people have rented a single building divided among them, we call it an apartment building. Where one man lives, we call it a house. Surely if a doctor moves into one of the shops by the roadside, it is called a doctor's surgery. If he moves out and a blacksmith moves into the same shop, it is called a smithy. If it is a fuller, it is called a laundry; if it is a carpenter, it is called a carpenter's shop. If a pimp and prostitutes move in, it gets the name brothel from the trade itself. And so you have created a lot of brothels from your skill in the profession. So then, don't ask where you ever engaged in the acts, but defend yourself on the ground that you have not done so.

[125] Another argument, it seems, will be offered, contrived by the same sophist. He maintains that there is nothing more unjust than common report; and he offers examples picked up from the market-place[108] and entirely consistent with his own life. First of all, he points out that the apartment building at Colonus called "Demon's" is falsely named; it isn't Demon's. Then there's the Herm called "Andocides' Herm,"[109] which, he says, isn't Andocides' but a dedication made by the Aegeis tribe. [126] And he offers himself as example by way of a joke, like a good-humored man making jokes about his own way of life. "Unless," he says, "I, too, must respond to the crowd when they call me not Demosthenes but Batalus, because my nurse gave me this nickname."[110] So if Timarchus was beautiful and is the butt of jokes in slanderous distortion of the fact and not because of his own conduct, surely, says Demosthenes, he doesn't deserve to be ruined for this.

[127] Myself, Demosthenes, where dedicatory offerings and houses and possessions, in short all voiceless objects, are concerned, I hear many tales of all sorts and never consistent. For they have no capacity

---

[108] As the administrative hub of the city and the main market, the agora was a place for idlers to pass their time.

[109] For Herms, see above, Lys. 23.3n.

[110] The nickname is acknowledged by Demosthenes at 18.180. So it must have admitted an innocent explanation. Yet here (131) and at 2.99, Aeschines connects it with passive homosexuality. Evidently, we have two distinct derivations producing identical or near-identical words. In its innocent sense, it may have denoted a stammerer; in its indecent sense, "anus."

for noble or base action; it is the man who happens to become associated with them, whoever he may be, who furnishes the common account according to the scale of his own reputation. But where men's lives and actions are concerned, of its own accord a true report spreads through the city announcing an individual's conduct to the public at large, and often predicting future events, too. [128] This statement is so patently true and uncontrived that you will find that both our city and our ancestors established an altar to Report[111] as a goddess of very great power. You will find that Homer often says in the *Iliad* before some event that was about to happen: "Report came to the host,"[112] and that Euripides declares that this goddess is able to reveal the character not only of the living, whatever it may be, but also of the dead, when he says,

Report declares the noble man, even when hidden in the ground.[113]

[129] And Hesiod actually describes her explicitly as a goddess. His words are quite clear for anyone who is willing to understand them. He says,

Report in no wise dies away completely, if many people utter it. She, too, then, is a god.[114]

And you will find that people who have lived decent lives are admirers of these poems. For all men who have public ambitions believe that they will win their reputations from common report. But people whose lives are base do not respect this god. They see in her their

---

[111] Greek *Phēmē*. The tendency to attribute divine status to what we would term abstract qualities is from the first a marked feature of Greek thought and appears both in creative literature and in actual cult. The existence of the altar is confirmed by the later traveler Pausanias (1.17.1). It has been suggested plausibly that *Phēmē* is not mere rumor but a mysterious force that promulgates information; hence the seriousness with which Aeschines can treat "Report" here.

[112] These words are not found in Homer. Either they come from a lost archaic epic or, more probably, Aeschines has invented an epic formula. *Phēmē* does not appear in the *Iliad,* though the similar figure of *Ossa,* "Rumor," calls the Greeks to assembly at *Iliad* 2.93–94.

[113] Euripides, fr. 865 Nauck.

[114] Hesiod, *Works and Days* 763–764.

undying accuser. [130] So recollect, gentlemen, the report you have encountered concerning Timarchus. Isn't it the case that as soon as the name is uttered you ask the question: "Which Timarchus? The whore?" So then, if I were offering witnesses, you would believe me. Yet if I offer the god as witness, will you not believe, when in all piety one cannot charge her with false testimony? [131] As to Demosthenes' nickname, he is rightly called Batalus, by common report and not by his nurse, having earned the name for unmanly and pathic ways. For if someone were to remove these smart robes of yours, and the soft tunics in which you write speeches against your friends, and carry them around and place them in the hands of the jurors, I think that if someone were to do this unannounced, they would be at a loss whether they were holding the clothing of a man or a woman.

[132] And one of the generals will take the stand for the defense, I'm told, head held high and preening himself, with the air of a man who has frequented the wrestling schools and the philosophers' haunts. And he will attempt to discredit the whole basis of the dispute, maintaining that I have initiated not a prosecution but the start of an appalling coarseness. He will cite first of all your benefactors, Harmodius and Aristogiton,[115] and speak of their mutual loyalty and the good their relationship did for the city. [133] He will not shrink, they tell me, even from using the poems of Homer or the names of heroes, but will sing the praises of the friendship of Patroclus and Achilles, based on love, they say, and will now eulogize beauty, as though it had not long since been considered a blessing—if it is combined with self-control. If certain people, by slandering this physical beauty, bring ruin on those who possess it, he claims, your collective vote will be at odds with your individual prayers. [134] For he finds it strange, so he says, if in the case of sons as yet unborn all of you who are about to sire children pray that they may be born noble in appearance and a credit to the city, but in the case of sons already born, who ought to be a source of pride for the city, if they stun people with their out-

---

[115] Harmodius and Aristogiton were lovers who formed a conspiracy to kill the late sixth-century tyrant Hippias. In the event, they killed the tyrant's brother, Hipparchus. Nonetheless, and despite the fact that the tyranny endured several years after the assassination, they passed into legend almost at death and were credited with the overthrow of the tyranny.

standing youthful beauty and become objects of lovers' rivalry, you will evidently disfranchise them under the influence of Aeschines. [135] And then he intends to make a direct attack on me, I'm told. He'll ask if I'm not ashamed to subject the practice to censure and risk, when I make a nuisance of myself in the gymnasia[116] and have been in love with many. And finally, so certain individuals inform me, in an attempt to encourage idle laughter among you, he says he will exhibit all the erotic poems I have written to individuals and claims he will provide testimony to quarrels and blows[117] that the practice has brought me.

[136] Personally, I neither criticize legitimate desire, nor do I allege that boys of outstanding beauty have prostituted themselves; nor do I deny that I myself have felt desire and still do. And I do not deny that the rivalries and fights that the thing provokes have befallen me. As to the poems they ascribe to me, some I admit to, but in the case of the rest I deny that their character is that presented by my opponents, who distort them. [137] According to my definition, desire for those who are noble and decent is characteristic of the generous and discerning spirit, but debauchery based on hiring someone for money I consider characteristic of a wanton and uncultivated man. And to be loved without corruption I count as noble, while to have been induced by money to prostitute oneself is shameful. The distance that separates them, the enormous difference, I shall try to explain to you in what follows. [138] Our fathers, when they were legislating about conduct and activities dictated by nature, prohibited slaves from engaging in activities that they thought should belong to free men. "A slave," says the law, "may not exercise and rub himself down with oil in the wres-

---

[116] Since Greeks usually exercised naked and the gymnasia played a major role in the physical training of (well-to-do) young men, they offered opportunities both for voyeurism and for seduction. The connection between the gymnasia and homoerotic pursuit is vividly depicted in Plato's *Charmides*. For predatory males cruising the gymnasia, see Aristophanes *Peace* 762–763.

[117] Fights over lovers (either young males or courtesans) were not unknown; see Dem. 54.14 and Lys. 3 and 4. However, our sources indicate that such behavior was not respectable; Aeschines indicates that he will be attacked not only as a hypocrite but as falling short of the conduct expected of his age and social station.

tling schools." It did not add further: "But the free man is to rub himself down and exercise." For when the legislators in considering the benefits derived from the gymnasia prohibited slaves from participating, they believed that with the same law in which they prohibited these, they were also encouraging free men to go to the gymnasia. [139] And again the same legislator said: "A slave may not be the lover of a free boy or follow him, or he is to receive fifty blows of the public lash." But he did not forbid the free man from being a boy's lover or associating with and following him, and he envisaged not that this would prove harmful to the boy but that it would be testimony to his chastity. But since the boy is at this stage not responsible, and is unable to distinguish between real and false affection, it is the lover he disciplines, and he postpones talk of love to the age of reason, when the boy is older. And he considered that following and watching over a boy was the most effective way of securing and protecting his chastity. [140] In this way the city's benefactors, Harmodius and Aristogiton, those men of outstanding virtues, were brought up by that decent and lawful feeling—call it love or what you will—to be men of such merit that when their deeds are praised, the panegyrics seem inadequate to their achievements.

[141] But since you speak of Achilles and Patroclus and of Homer and other poets, as though the jurors are men without education, and represent yourselves as impressive figures whose erudition allows you to look down on the people, to show you that we have already acquired a little knowledge and learning,[118] we, too, shall say something on the subject. For since they see fit to talk about wise men and take refuge in tales told in verse, look at the poets, men of Athens, who are acknowledged to be noble and edifying and see how great a distance they perceived between decent men, lovers of their equals, and those whose love is illicit, men who recognize no limits.

[142] I shall start with Homer, whom we count among the oldest and wisest of the poets. For Homer, though he often speaks of Patroclus and Achilles, is silent about love and gives no name to their

---

[118] Aeschines presents his opponents as talking down to the jurors; in contrast, in using the first-person plural, he associates himself with his audience.

friendship;[119] he thinks that the remarkable strength of their affection is obvious to the cultivated among his audience. [143] At one point, when Achilles is lamenting Patroclus' death, he mentions, as one of his most painful memories, that he has betrayed his promise to Patroclus' father Menoetius, that he had declared he would bring the son safe back to Opus, if the father would send him to Troy and entrust him to Achilles' care. And this makes it quite clear that it was for love that he had taken responsibility for his care. [144] The verses in question I shall now recite to you:

> Alas, pointless, then, the words I let fall on that day
> when I assured the hero Menoetius in his halls.
> I said I would restore his glorious son to Opus
> as sacker of Troy with his due share of spoil.
> But Zeus does not fulfill all of men's intents;
> for it is fated that both[120] stain the same earth red.

[145] And it is not only here that he complains bitterly; so powerful was his grief for Patroclus that after his mother told him that if he did not go in pursuit of his enemies but left Patroclus' death unavenged, he would return home and die in old age in his own homeland, while if he avenged it he would soon lose his own life, he preferred keeping faith with the dead man to survival. Such was the noble strength of purpose that drove him to punish his friend's killer that, though everyone urged him to bathe and take food, he vows he will do none of this until he brings Hector's head to Patroclus' tomb. [146] And while he is asleep at the pyre, as the poet tells us, Patroclus' ghost appears to him; and the memories he stirred, and the solemn instructions he gave Achilles, deserve both our tears and our admiration for their virtue and their friendship. He foretold that Achilles himself was not far from the end of his life and instructed him that, if at all possible, he should ensure that, in just the same way that they had grown up and lived together, in death, too, the bones of both should lie in the same

---

[119] The relationship of Achilles and Patroclus is not presented as homoerotic in Homer. They were presented as lovers in Aeschylus' (now lost) *Myrmidons*, and this is taken for granted by speakers in Plato's *Symposium*.

[120] Achilles and Patroclus. These lines are from *Iliad* 18.324–329.

vessel. [147] In his grief he speaks of the pursuits they shared in life, and says: "No more will we, as before, sit together apart from our other friends and deliberate on the most serious matters"; for he holds (I think) that the loss most keenly felt is loyalty and affection. To enable you to hear the poet's sentiments in verse, the clerk will read to you the epic lines in which Homer has described this. [148] To begin with, read the verses about taking vengeance on Hector.

> Yet, dear comrade, since I shall enter the earth after you,
> I shall not carry out your rites until I bring here Hector's
> armor and head, those of your proud-hearted killer.[121]

[149] Now read out what Patroclus says as Achilles sleeps about their burial together and the pursuits they shared in life.

> For no more in life apart from our dear comrades
> shall we sit and take counsel. No, I am swallowed
> by hated doom, which fell to my lot at my birth.
> And for yourself, too, it is fated, godlike Achilles,
> to die beneath the walls of the noble Trojans,
> fighting with the enemy for fine-haired Helen.
> This, too, I shall tell you, and fix it in your heart.
> Place not my bones apart from your own, Achilles,
> but so the same earth may cover yourself, too,
> in the golden casket your lady mother gave you,
> just as we were raised together in your halls,
> when from Opus as a small child still Menoetius
> brought me to your house through grim man-slaying,
> on that day when I slew the son of Amphidamas,
> in childish folly, not intending, in anger over dice.
> There in his halls Peleus the knight welcomed me,
> reared me unstinting, and called me your companion.
> Just so let the same vessel also cover our bones.

[150] Now to show that he could have survived if he had not avenged Patroclus' death, read out what Thetis says:

---

[121] *Iliad* 18.333–335. The next passage (149) is from *Iliad* 23.77–91, though Aeschines' text diverges from that of our manuscripts of Homer.

> *"Swift will be your fate, child, from what you say.*
> *For straight after Hector your doom is waiting."*
> *To her in turn spoke swift-footed godlike Achilles:*
> *"Let me die now, since it seems I was not to save*
> *my comrade from death, he who was far dearest to me."* [122]

[151] And Euripides, as wise as any of the poets, took chaste love to be one of the noblest emotions. He saw love as something worth praying for, and says somewhere:

> *Love that leads to decency and virtue*
> *deserves men's envy. Might such love be mine!* [123]

[152] Again, the same poet in his *Phoenix,* when defending him against the false charge from his father and schooling people to judge not from suspicion and slander but from a man's life, declares:

> *Oft have I been asked to judge disputes*
> *and oft seen claims oppose each other,*
> *both witnessed, about the same event.*
> *And thus do I, and any man who's wise,*
> *reckon the truth, by looking to the nature*
> *of a man and the way he spends his days.*
> *And if any man enjoys bad company,*
> *I've never questioned him—I know full well*
> *he resembles those whose company he enjoys.* [124]

[153] Observe the views expressed by the poet, men of Athens. He says that he has already decided many disputes, just as you now are judges, and he says that he bases his decision not on the testimony of witnesses but on a man's way of life and the company he keeps. He considers how the man on trial lives his daily life and the way he runs his household, on the ground that he will run the city's business in a similar way, [125] and whose company he enjoys. And finally he declared

---

[122] *Iliad* 18.95–99. Aeschines again differs from the Homer manuscripts.

[123] The quote comes from Euripides' lost *Sthenoboea,* fr. 672 Nauck.

[124] From Euripides' lost *Phoenix,* fr. 812 Nauck.

[125] The tactic used here, of inserting an "editorial" comment that has the effect of magnifying the support supposedly derived from the text cited, is identical to that in 1.19–20.

without hesitation that a man resembles those whose company gives him pleasure. So it is proper that you apply Euripides' reasoning to Timarchus. [154] How has he managed his property? He has squandered his inheritance, and, though selling his body and taking bribes in political life, he has wasted it all, and so he has nothing left but the resultant disgrace. Whose company does he enjoy? Hegesander's. And what are Hegesander's habits? The sort for which the laws forbid the practitioner to address the people. As for me, what charge do I make against Timarchus; what exactly figures in my written accusation? That Timarchus addresses the people when he has prostituted himself and squandered his paternal estate. And you, what have you sworn? That you will cast your vote on the charge brought by the prosecution.[126]

[155] But I don't want to talk at excessive length about the poets. Instead, I shall tell you the names of older men who are well known, and young men and boys. Some of these have had many lovers because of their beauty, while others are still in the bloom of youth now; but none of them has ever been exposed to the same accusations as those made against Timarchus. And in contrast I shall give you the names of men who have practiced shameful and blatant prostitution; remembering these will help you to put Timarchus in the proper category. [156] I shall start with the names of people who have lived in the honorable manner that befits free men. Men of Athens, you know that Crito the son of Astyochus and Periclides of Perithoidae and Polemagenes and Pantaleon the son of Cleagoras and Timesitheus the runner were in their day the most beautiful not only of the Athenian citizens but in all Greece, and that they attracted the largest number of lovers, and the most decent. Yet nobody has ever found fault with them. [157] Again, among those who are young men or still children even now, there is Iphicrates' nephew, the son of Tisias of Rhamnus,[127] who bears the same name as the defendant Timarchus. Though he is good-looking, he is so foreign to shameful conduct that the other day, at the Rural Dionysia during the performance of the comic plays at Collytus, when the comic actor Parmeno spoke an anapestic line to

---

[126] For the jurors' oath, see the Introduction, VC.

[127] The father and son of this Timarchus (both called Tisias) are known from fourth-century inscriptions; Timarchus himself is known only from this passage.

the chorus in which mention was made of certain "big Timarchian prostitutes," nobody suspected a reference to the young man; everyone saw a reference to you. So firm is your claim to the practice. And again there is Anticles the sprinter and Phidias the brother of Melesias. Though I could mention still more, I shall stop there, to avoid seeming to flatter any of them with my praise.

[158] Turning to those who share Timarchus' habits, I shall avoid making enemies and speak of those who least concern me. Who among you does not know of Diophantus, known as "the orphan," who arrested the foreigner and brought him before the Archon for whom Aristophon of Azenia was serving as assistant? He alleged that he had been cheated of four drachmas owed for this service and cited the laws that instruct the Archon to take care of orphans,[128] when he himself had broken those which cover chastity. What citizen was not offended by Cephisodorus, known as the son of Molon, who had defiled his most beautiful appearance with the most infamous acts? Or Mnesitheus, known as the cook's son, and many others whose names I purposely forget. [159] I don't want to pursue each of them by name spitefully. In fact, in my love of my city I would dearly wish to have a shortage of such cases to cite. But now that we have mentioned some examples of each type, dealing separately with the objects of chaste love and those who abused their own persons, I want you now to answer this question from me: to which category do you assign Timarchus, to the people who have lovers or to the prostitutes?[129] So then, Timarchus, do not try to desert the society you have chosen and defect to the way of life of free men.

[160] If they try to argue that a man has not prostituted himself if he did not make a contract to hire himself out, and demand that I provide documentation and witnesses to this effect, first, remember the laws concerning prostitution; nowhere does the legislator mention contracts. He did not ask whether anyone had disgraced himself under a written contract, but, however the activity takes place, he absolutely bars the man who has engaged in it from the public affairs of the city. And rightly so. If any man in his youth abandoned noble ambitions for the sake of shameful pleasure, he believed that this man should not

---

[128] For the duties of the eponymous Archon, see the Introduction, IVA.
[129] Presumably Aeschines pauses here for the audience to shout out.

in later years enjoy political rights. [161] Furthermore, one can easily detect the idiocy of this argument. We would all agree that we make contracts out of lack of trust for each other, so that the party who has not broken the written terms can obtain satisfaction in court from the one who has. Well, then, if the matter calls for litigation, the protection of the laws is still available for people who have prostituted themselves under a contract and are wronged, according to the defense arguments. And what case would each party make? Imagine that you're not hearing it from me but seeing the thing taking place. [162] Let's suppose that the one who hired is honest in the business and the person hired is dishonest and unreliable, or alternatively the opposite, that the person hired is reasonable and conforms to the agreement while the one who has hired him and had the pleasure of his youth has cheated him. Imagine that you yourselves are sitting in judgment. So then, the older man, when given his allocation of water to make his case, will present his accusation with gravity, looking straight at you, of course, and say: [163] "Men of Athens, I hired Timarchus to be my prostitute on the basis of the contract in the keeping of Demosthenes" (there's no reason why this shouldn't be what's said),[130] "and he is not doing what he agreed for me." And obviously he'll go on to tell the jurors of this agreement and explain what a person like this is required to do. And then won't he be stoned, this man who hires an Athenian in contravention of the laws?[131] Won't he leave the court not only liable for compensation[132] but also convicted of serious outrage (*hybris*)?

[164] Or say that it is not this party but the one who was hired who brings the action. Now let clever Batalus[133] come forward to speak for him, so we'll know what on earth he will say. "Jurors, somebody or other" (it makes no difference) "hired me to be his prostitute for

---

[130] Contracts were often lodged with third parties, commonly bankers. Here the effect is to drag Demosthenes into the fiction of debauchery, making him almost a pimp for Timarchus, just as in 131 he is made a fellow pervert.

[131] Based on Aeschines' interpretation of the law (above, 15).

[132] Greek *epōbelia*, a penalty of one-sixth of the sum in dispute paid to the winning party by the losers in certain private cases. We do not know the full range of cases to which it applied nor whether it applied only to failure to win or to failure to obtain a certain minimum proportion of the votes cast.

[133] For Demosthenes' nickname, see above, 126.

money. And while I have done everything, and still do now, that a prostitute should according to the written contract, the defendant is in breach of the agreement." And then won't he be met with loud shouting from the jurors? Won't they all say: "Despite this do you invade the marketplace, wear the crown of office, do any of the things we do?" So then, the contract is no use.

[165] How, then, has it become an established practice to maintain that before now people have prostituted themselves by contract? This I shall now tell you. It is said that a certain citizen (I shall omit the name in a desire to avoid enmity),[134] who failed to anticipate any of the problems I described to you just now, prostituted himself under a contract that was deposited with Anticles. Since he was not a private citizen but entered public life and was subjected to insults, the result was that the city became accustomed to the expression, and this is why some people ask if the activity has taken place under a contract. But the legislator did not concern himself with the way the activity has taken place; no, the legislator condemned a man to disgrace if he hires himself out in any way whatsoever.

[166] Yet though these issues have been defined so clearly, Demosthenes will discover many diversionary arguments. The wickedness of his statements on the main issue might not arouse so much resentment. But the irrelevant arguments he will drag in to the detriment of the city's system of justice deserve your anger. Philip will be there in plenty; and the name of his son Alexander will be thrown in, too. For in addition to his other faults, this man is a crude and insensitive individual. [167] His offensive remarks against Philip in his speech are uncivil and inappropriate, but less serious than the wrong I am about to mention; for his abuse will be directed incontrovertibly against a man, for all that he himself is not a man. But when with the use of labored ambiguous language he drags in shameful insinuations against the boy, he makes a laughingstock of the city. [168] In an attempt to spoil the audit[135] I am about to undergo for my service on the embassy, he alleges that when he was giving the Council an account of Alexan-

---

[134] The lack of detail, while given a veneer of plausibility by the parenthesis, suggests that the story is an invention by Aeschines.

[135] For the *euthynai*, see above, 1n. The reference is to the second embassy in Macedonia in 346.

der the other day—how he played the lyre to us while we were drinking and recited speeches and debated with another boy—and was
telling the Council all he knew about the matter, I grew angry at the
jokes against the boy as if I were not one of the envoys but a relative.[136]
[169] In fact, I have not spoken with Alexander, naturally, because of
his youth.[137] But Philip I praise right now for his auspicious statements. If his conduct toward us matches his present promises, he will
make it a safe and easy task to praise him. I criticized Demosthenes in
the Council chamber not out of a desire to curry favor with the boy
but because I felt that if you listened to such things, the city would
appear to share the speaker's lack of decency.

[170] But in general, men of Athens, you should not admit lines of
defense irrelevant to the main issue, first of all because of the oaths you
have sworn,[138] and second, to avoid being misled by a fellow who is a
master of the art of speaking. I shall take my story back a little to give
you the information. When Demosthenes had squandered his
inheritance,[139] he went around the city hunting for rich young
orphans[140] whose fathers were dead and whose mothers were in charge
of the property. I shall omit many of them and mention one of the
victims of appalling treatment. [171] He noticed a household that was
rich but badly run. The head of the house was a proud but unintelli-
gent woman, but the property was handled by a half-mad orphaned
youth, Aristarchus the son of Moschus. He pretended to be in love
with this young man, drew him into this intimate relationship, and
filled him full of false hopes that he would very soon be a leading

---

[136] The allegation appears to be that Aeschines is sexually attracted to Alexander, who would have been about ten at this time, an accusation that combines
suggestions of treason with hypocrisy and possibly bad taste (since the ideal age
for the object of homoerotic pursuit was the mid-teens). The mockery of Alexander may amount to laughing at the Macedonian "barbarians" for aping Greek
culture, or it could be mockery of alleged ineptitude by Alexander.

[137] As a young male, Alexander is a potential sexual target for older men;
Aeschines shows discretion in avoiding contact that might compromise the boy.

[138] For the jurors' oath, see the Introduction, VC.

[139] Aeschines gives a distorted version of Demosthenes' early career (for which
see 1.94n), presenting him as a kindred spirit of Timarchus in financial as in sexual
activity.

[140] A Greek *orphanos* had no father; see the Introduction, VE.

public speaker; and he showed him a list of names.[141] [172] And he encouraged and taught him to commit acts of a sort that the young man is now in exile from his fatherland, while this man, having got hold of the money that was to support Aristarchus in his exile, has robbed him of three talents; and Nicodemus of Aphidna has been violently murdered by Aristarchus, with both his eyes gouged out, poor wretch, and the tongue cut out with which he exercised free speech in confidence in the laws and in your authority.

[173] So then, men of Athens, you put Socrates the sophist to death, because it was found that he had taught Critias, one of the Thirty who overthrew the democracy;[142] yet is Demosthenes to get his comrades[143] off in your court, this man who has exacted such terrible revenge from ordinary men loyal to the democracy for their free speaking? At his invitation, some of his pupils have come to listen. For I'm told he declares to them, drumming up business at your expense, that without your noticing he will shift the ground of debate and your attention; [174] that he will bring confidence to the defendant the moment he appears in court and reduce the accuser to panic and fear for himself; that he will summon such loud and hostile heckling from the jurors by dragging in my political speeches and criticizing the peace that was brought about through me and Philocrates that I will not even turn up in court to defend myself, when I submit to audit for my service as envoy; I'll be content if I receive a moderate punishment and am not condemned to death! [175] Under no circumstances must you allow this sophist to laugh and amuse himself at your expense. No, you must imagine you are seeing him back home from the court,

---

[141] That is, the names of former pupils of Demosthenes, now successful politicians.

[142] Socrates was tried and executed in 399 on a charge of disbelieving in the city's gods and corrupting the youth. Aeschines distorts in narrowing the focus to Critias and in ignoring the religious dimension; he does, however, accurately pick up on one strand of the popular prejudice that led to Socrates' death.

[143] The Greek term is *hetairos*, which need be no more than "close associate/ friend," but since Demosthenes is presented in 1.172–173 as setting himself above the laws and curtailing the democratic rights of citizens, Aeschines probably also intends the sense of the word that became established late in the fifth century, referring to members of the oligarchic clubs that plotted the overthrow of the democracy.

preening himself in the company of his young men and telling them how successfully he stole the case from the jurors: "You see, I led them away from the charges against Timarchus; I guided them toward the accuser, Philip, and the Phocians[144] and fixed their attention there, and I dangled fears before the eyes of my listeners; the result was that the defendant became prosecutor and the prosecutor found himself on trial, while the jurors forgot the case they were trying and listened instead to a case they were not trying." [176] Your duty is to resist these attempts firmly, to follow everything assiduously, and at no point to allow him to deviate or to press arguments irrelevant to the case. Just like in chariot races, you must keep to the actual track of the subject at issue. And if you do this, you will not be treated with contempt, and you will display the same attitude as legislators and jurors. Otherwise, you will give the impression of feeling anger in anticipation of crimes about to happen but losing interest in crimes actually committed.

[177] To put the matter briefly: if you punish wrongdoers, your laws will be noble and valid, whereas if you acquit them, the laws will still be noble but no longer valid. My reason for saying this I shall not hesitate to tell you frankly. And my account will serve as an example. Why do you think, men of Athens, that the laws are fine but the city's decrees are inferior and the judgments reached in court sometimes excite amazement? I shall explain the reasons for this. [178] It is because in making the laws you take account of all the principles of justice. You do not act for dishonest profit or favor or enmity, but consider only justice and the public good. And being naturally more intelligent, I think, than other men, as one would expect, you make the best laws. But in the Assembly and the courts you often lose sight of the arguments relating to the main issue; you are misled by deceit and posturing and admit the most unjust practice into your trials. You allow the defendants to bring counteraccusations against their accusers. [179] When you are distracted from the case for the defense and your minds are on other matters, you become forgetful of the prosecution case, and you leave the courts without getting satisfaction from

---

[144] That is, Demosthenes reverses the roles of prosecutor and defendant. The presentation of Demosthenes' boasts achieves plausibility by vividness but remains no more than unsubstantiated character assassination.

either side. Neither from the accuser (for his fate is not put to the vote) nor from the defendant (for by using his accusations against others to brush off the actual charges against him, he has evaded the court). And the laws are overturned, and the democracy is corrupted, and the practice becomes still more widespread. On occasion you are too ready to admit an argument that is not supported by an upright life.

[180] Not so the Spartans—and it is laudable to imitate the virtues of foreigners as well.[145] Once when someone was addressing the Spartan assembly, a man whose life had been disgraceful but who was a superlatively able speaker, and the Spartans, so they say, were about to vote as he advised, one of the Old Men came forward. These are the ones they revere and fear; they regard the office named after this age group as the most important, and they form it from men whose lives have been decent from childhood to old age.[146] One of these, it is said, came forward and vigorously berated the Spartans and even abused them along the following lines, that they would not long inhabit a Sparta unravaged by war if they listened to advisers like this in their assemblies. [181] At the same time he called upon another Spartan, not a gifted speaker but a man who had won glory in war and was outstanding in justice and self-discipline, and instructed him to utter as best he could the views expressed by the previous speaker. "So that," he said, "the Spartans may vote on the words of a good man, and close their ears entirely to the voices of men who are confirmed cowards and villains." This was the advice given to his fellow-citizens by an old man who had lived a decent life since childhood. He would have been keen to allow Timarchus or the pervert[147] Demosthenes to take part in public life!

[182] But I don't want to give the impression of flattering the Spartans. So I shall speak also of our own ancestors. They were so severe in

---

[145] The justification for the digression anticipates possible resentment from the jurors at the comparison between Athens and Sparta in which Sparta emerges as superior. The incident narrated could be a piece of contemporary "folklore," but the resemblance to the alleged situation of Timarchus is so convenient that one suspects invention by Aeschines.

[146] A reference to the Gerusia, the council of elders at Sparta.

[147] The Greek term used, *kinaidos*, is more precise, in that it refers to the male recipient of homosexual penetration. See further 185n.

their attitude toward shameful behavior and took so extremely seriously the chastity of their children that one citizen who found that his daughter had been corrupted and had not preserved her maidenhood honorably until marriage sealed her up in an empty house with a horse, knowing that she would be killed by it if they were shut in together. To this day the foundations of this house are still standing in your city, and the spot is called "the place of the horse and girl." [183] And Solon, the most illustrious of legislators, has drafted ancient and solemn laws on the orderly conduct of women. If a woman is caught with a seducer,[148] he does not allow her to wear finery or to enter the public temples, to prevent her from corrupting innocent women with her company. And if she enters them or wears finery, he allows anyone who encounters her to tear her clothing, remove her jewelry, and beat her, though he is not permitted to kill or maim her; Solon thus deprives such a woman of honor and makes her life intolerable. [184] And he allows for indictment (*graphē*) of procurers, male and female; and if they are convicted, he makes death the punishment. The reason is that when people who wish to sin hesitate through shame to come together, the procurers offer their own lack of shame for pay and advance the affair to the point of discussion and action.

[185] So then, this was the view of your fathers on the issues of shame and honor. Will *you* acquit Timarchus, a man guilty of the most shameful practices? A man, with a male body, who has committed the offenses of a woman?[149] Which of you, then, if he catches his wife in

---

[148] The Greek term is *moichos*, for which see above, Dem. 59.41 with n. The penalties for the *moichos* could be severe, including the right for the aggrieved male to kill a *moichos* caught in the act (see Lys. 1, above). Those for the woman were scarcely less severe, since the ban on entry to public temples barred her from the one area in which Greek women played a significant public role. The embargo is confirmed by Dem. 59.87. The present passage is our sole source for the ban on wearing jewelry and fine clothes.

[149] The passage simultaneously appeals to Greek stereotypes of male and female character (it was widely accepted that women were less able than men to resist temptations) and hints at the different sexual roles, suggesting that Timarchus allows his body to be penetrated by other males. Although there is no evidence that this in itself laid a male citizen open to prosecution, there was evidently a prejudice against it, and it may in the Athenian mind have been associated with male prostitution. The evidence of homoerotic scenes on vase paintings indicates

misconduct, will punish her? Who will not seem stupid if he shows anger at a woman who does wrong according to her nature but uses as his adviser[150] a man who has abused himself against nature. [186] What will be the state of mind of each of you when he goes home from court? The man on trial is not obscure; he is well known. And the law on the scrutiny of public speakers is not a poor one but quite excellent. It is to be expected that boys and young men will ask their relatives how the case has been judged.[151] [187] So what will you say, you who now have the power to vote, when your sons ask you if you convicted or acquitted? The moment you admit to acquitting him, won't you overturn the whole educational system? What's the use in keeping slave chaperones or appointing gymnastic trainers and teachers for our children, when the men who have been given responsibility for the laws are deflected from their duty when faced with disgraceful acts?

[188] I also find it surprising, men of Athens, if you, who hate brothel-keepers,[152] intend to let go people who have voluntarily prostituted themselves. Evidently this same man, who will not be allowed to obtain the priesthood of any of the gods, since under the laws his body is unclean, will draft in the text of decrees prayers to the Solemn Goddesses[153] for the good of the city. Then why be amazed at the failure of public policy, when speakers like this man attach their names to decisions of the people? Shall we send abroad as envoy a man whose life at home has been disgraceful and entrust to him our most important interests? What would a man not sell when he has sold off the abuse (*hybris*) of his person? Who would this man pity when he has shown no pity for himself?

[189] Which of you is unfamiliar with the disgusting conduct of

---

that (face-to-face) intercrural rather than anal coitus was the "proper" position for homosexual acts between social equals, and Athenian comedy of the fifth century directs its mockery at males who succumb to penetration, not at males who play an active homosexual role.

[150] I.e., a speaker in the Assembly.

[151] For a similar attempt to shame the jurors with reference to their relatives, cf. Dem. 59.110–111.

[152] Pimps in ancient texts are stereotyped as avaricious and unscrupulous.

[153] The *Semnai,* identified at Athens at least from the mid-fifth century with the *Erinyes* (Furies); they had a shrine below the Areopagus.

Timarchus? In the case of people who exercise, even if we don't attend the gymnasia, we can recognize them from a glance at their fit condition. In the same way, we recognize men who have worked as prostitutes from their shameless and impudent manner and from their general behavior even if we're not present at their activities. For if a man has shown contempt for the laws and for morality on the most important issues, he has a certain attitude of mind that is visible from his disorderly manner.

[190] You will find that it is men such as this more than all others who have destroyed cities and have themselves encountered the worst disasters. Don't imagine, men of Athens, that wrongdoing has its origin in the gods and not in the willfulness of men, or that Furies pursue men guilty of impiety, as in the tragedies,[154] and punish them with burning brands. [191] No, unrestrained physical pleasures and a feeling that nothing is ever enough, these are what recruit to gangs of robbers, what fill the pirate ships, these are each man's Fury; these are what drive him to slaughter his fellow-citizens, serve tyrants, conspire to overthrow democracy. They take no account of the shame or the consequences for themselves; it is the pleasure success will bring that mesmerizes them. So eradicate natures such as this, men of Athens, and turn the ambitions of young men toward virtue.

[192] Of this you may be sure, and please be particularly mindful of what I'm about to say: if Timarchus is punished for his practices, you will be making a new start for discipline in the city; if he is acquitted, it would have been better if the trial had not taken place. For before Timarchus was put on trial, the law and the name of the courts inspired some fear. But if the leading and most notorious exponent of vice comes to court and gets away safely, he will inspire many more to wrongdoing, and in the end what rouses you to anger will not be words but a crisis. [193] So don't wait to vent your wrath on a crowd, but do it on one man. And watch out for their cunning tricks and their supporting speakers. I won't mention any of them by name, so that they won't use this point to begin their speech by saying that they would not have come forward if they had not been mentioned by name. This is what I'll do. I'll remove the names and describe the

---

[154] Especially Aeschylus' *Eumenides*, in which the chorus of Furies visibly pursues Orestes.

practices and enable you to recognize their physical features. Each of them will have only himself to blame, if he mounts this stand and shows no shame. [194] Timarchus has three kinds of supporting speaker to help him: those who have squandered their inheritance with their daily expenditures; those who have misspent their youth and abused their bodies and are afraid not for Timarchus but for themselves and their way of life, in case they are brought to trial at some point; and others who are people without any restraint who have made unrestricted use of men like him and whose motive is that trust in the aid they offer[155] will make people more ready to do wrong. [195] Before you listen to their speeches in support of Timarchus, remember their way of life. Tell the ones who have done wrong to their own bodies not to pester you but to stop addressing the people; for the law does not examine the conduct of private citizens but of public men. Tell the ones who have squandered their inheritances to work and make their living in some other way. And tell the hunters of the young men who are easily caught to turn their attentions to foreigners and resident aliens; then they won't be deprived of their chosen passion and your interests will not be damaged.

[196] You have had from me all you could justly demand. I have informed you of the laws, I've examined the defendant's way of life. So now it is for you to judge my words; shortly I shall observe your acts. The final decision depends on your judgment. If it is your wish, if you vote justly and in your own best interests, we shall be more zealous in exposing lawbreakers.

---

[155] I.e., to anyone accused of such a crime.

PART III FAMILY AND PROPERTY

The Athenian household (*oikos*) was headed by the husband and father and typically included his wife, one or more children, perhaps one or more slaves, and sometimes other older or more distant relatives. Girls were typically married in their mid or late teens, boys in their late twenties. Marriages, sometimes to a fairly close relative (uncle or cousin), were normally arranged by the father. There were no marriage certificates, but in most cases a formal betrothal, usually accompanied by the promise of a dowry, took place in front of witnesses. Either spouse could initiate a divorce, but the dowry would have to be repaid (unless the wife was guilty of adultery), which offered some protection to the woman. A man who had no natural son could adopt one, either while alive (*inter vivos*) or through a will (testamentary); if he had a daughter, he would sometimes direct that she marry the adopted son. If he had only a daughter, she would have to marry a relative to keep the estate in the family. In the absence of direct heirs, a man could write a will; he normally revealed its contents before witnesses.

When a man died, a natural son or one adopted *inter vivos* could take over the property directly (by *embateusis*). Otherwise, if more than one claimant appeared, a judicial hearing (*diadikasia*) was held to adjudicate the claims. Wills were often challenged in inheritance disputes, with claimants arguing that the deceased preferred them and would never have left his property to the person named in the (fraudulent) will or that the will was void because the testator was not in his right mind or acted under the influence of a woman. Isaeus 1, 7, and 8 illustrate various sorts of issues that are commonly raised in inheritance disputes, which often last for several generations and become very complex. A will could also provide for the guardianship of a man's minor children and of their property until they came of age, as we see in Lysias 32 and Demosthenes 27.

ISAEUS 1. ON THE ESTATE OF CLEONYMUS

INTRODUCTION

Cleonymus[1] son of Polyarchus died childless, leaving his estate in a will to some relatives whose precise number and relationship to him cannot be determined.[2] The validity of the will was challenged in a rival claim (*diadikasia*) made by Cleonymus' nephews, one of whom delivered the present speech. It is a possible, but by no means necessary, inference from remarks made by the speaker that the opponents were twice as many in number, since he claims that their friends and relatives thought the two parties deserved an equal share in the estate (1.2, 35; cf. 28), and that the nephews deserved a one-third share (1.16). One of the legatees was called Pherenicus (1.31, 45); another was probably Poseidippus (1.22–23, cf. 14–15); and a third, Diocles (1.14, 23). Poseidippus and Diocles may have been the brothers referred to in 1.45, but the Greek does not make it clear how many brothers there were or even if they were the brothers of Pherenicus, though this is perhaps the natural interpretation. What is clear is that the other names mentioned in the speech, Cephisander (1.16, 28) and Simon (1.31–32), were not among the heirs.

As for their relationship to Cleonymus, the heirs must have been further removed than the nephews, who challenge the validity of the will on the ground of closer affinity to Cleonymus (1.20; cf. 17, 36).

---

[1] In the family tree (below), M denotes an unnamed male, F denotes an unnamed female, X denotes unnamed parents, and = denotes marriage.

[2] We might have expected him to adopt one of them, but there is no mention of this, and the will may not have been concerned with testamentary adoption. See Rubinstein 1993: 118.

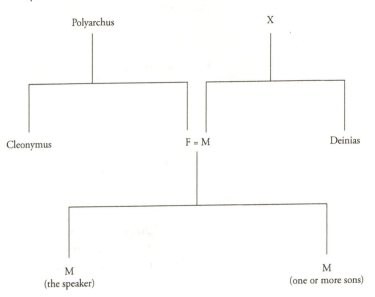

Details of the nephews are equally obscure. The speaker is unnamed, and the number of brothers he has is not stated. They were probably the sons of Cleonymus' sister, since it was their uncle Deinias rather than Cleonymus who became their guardian on the death of their father, and Deinias and Cleonymus clearly were not brothers (cf. 1.9, "their previous friendship"). It is likely, therefore, that Deinias was their paternal uncle, though it is possible that Deinias was nominated guardian of his sister's children in their father's will because the father, like Deinias, was at odds with his brother Cleonymus. This in turn would have been a reason for the speaker not to mention his father's circumstances, since it was a further motive for Cleonymus not to leave his estate to his nephews.

On the face of it, Isaeus' client does not have a strong case. In the absence of direct or adopted descendants of Cleonymus, his will should have been decisive: it had evidently been drawn up a number of years before Cleonymus' death and had been deposited with the City Magistrates, so there was no question of arguing that Cleonymus was of unsound mind or under other duress when he wrote it or that the will was a forgery. However, Cleonymus' behavior on his deathbed

(1.14) opened up an avenue of attack. The heirs claimed that in sending for the magistrate, Cleonymus wished merely to make corrections to the will (1.18), and indeed there had been plenty of opportunity for him previously to change it in favor of his nephews. It may also be inferred that the heirs either were living with Cleonymus at the time of his death or were in close contact with him; otherwise, why did he not send one of his nephews to the magistrate if he intended to alter the will in their favor? But the speaker seizes the opportunity to put a different interpretation on this action, that Cleonymus wished to revoke the will, which therefore did not represent his last wishes.

To support this, he adduces two arguments. The first is that the nephews were the next of kin. The speaker's evasiveness on the exact relationship of the heirs to Cleonymus (cf. 1.36) serves to emphasize his claim to the succession through closer affinity, and there is no doubt that many of the jurors will have sympathized with him—the bias of Athenian juries in favor of kinship over wills was notorious (cf. Aristotle *Problems* 29.3), and the speaker plays on this in particular at 1.41–43 (cf. 1.17).[3] His second argument is the subjective claim, reiterated throughout the speech, that Cleonymus was closer in affection to his nephews than the heirs—he brought them up and looked after their affairs, and the quarrel that led to the will being made in the heirs' favor was not with themselves but with Deinias. Moreover, the speaker alleges that Cleonymus had fallen out with some of the heirs just before his death, though in fact he cleverly generalizes from a dispute between Cleonymus and Pherenicus (1.30–34). This pervasive theme of Cleonymus' greater affection for his nephews than his heirs, when added to the kinship argument, will doubtless have had a significant effect on the minds of the jurors.

Furthermore, Isaeus makes the most of the case rhetorically. In the proem (1.1–8) he sets out the main points of his clients' case and goes on the attack right from the start, assuming in the very first section of the speech what he is trying to prove,[4] that Cleonymus bequeathed his

---

[3] He also claims in passing, and with little conviction, that the wishes of his grandfather Polyarchus were that, if anything happened to Cleonymus, he was to leave the property to his nephews (1.4).

[4] The figure *petitio principii;* cf. Is. 3.1, 8.1.

property to his nephews. He begins the characterization of the nephews as innocent victims, and in contrast repeatedly emphasizes the shamelessness of their opponents in seeking to deprive them of their inheritance (1.2, 5, 8; cf. 26). The opposing attitudes of the parties are further highlighted by the commonplace argument that litigation between kin was undesirable (1.6). In the narrative (1.9–16) the speaker carefully contrasts Cleonymus' enmity against Deinias with his kind treatment of his nephews, from which he argues Cleonymus' real intentions could be inferred. He immediately bolsters this with the story of Cleonymus' attempt at the last to change his will. In the proofs section, which forms the core of the speech (1.17–47), the speaker begins by summarizing the theme of his main refutatory argument: kinship is the most important factor in inheritance cases (1.17). Arguments from probability (*eikos*) demonstrate that a sane Cleonymus must have wanted to change the will in the nephews' favor (1.18–21), while the opponents' behavior, if they really believed Cleonymus was going to alter the will in their favor, was absurd (1.22–23); and his intended alteration of the will must mean that he was dissatisfied with it (1.24–26).

An attack on the opponents' shamelessness follows (1.26–29), which lays the foundation for the charge that Cleonymus had quarreled with them (1.30–35). On the assumption now that Cleonymus was on bad terms with the heirs and wanted to annul the will, the speaker argues that the nephews' closer ties of kinship and friendship should be decisive (1.36–38); then it is argued that obligations to care for next of kin should in turn mean that the closest relatives are entitled to inherit (1.39–40). The speaker next returns to the argument that jurors should decide on the basis of kinship, not a will (1.41–43). The proofs section culminates in an argument from reciprocity: that Cleonymus would, if still alive, have been entitled to inherit the nephews' estate because they were childless, but he would not have been entitled to inherit the estate of the other relatives whose children would have inherited; hence, in the reverse situation, the nephews, not the other relatives, should inherit Cleonymus' estate (1.44–47). In the brief epilogue (1.48–51) the speaker pleads once again that his opponents' arguments, if true, merely demonstrate that Cleonymus was insane, whereas his own contentions show that Cleonymus wanted to revoke the will. He thereby attempts to place the jurors in a dilemma which he first raised in 1.21,[5] and the speech comes to an end with a paradox.[6]

We do not know if the jurors were persuaded by Isaeus' forceful rhetoric, and there are no indications in the speech of the date of the trial.

ISAEUS I. ON THE ESTATE OF CLEONYMUS

[1] The change in my circumstances occasioned by Cleonymus' death, gentlemen, has been great indeed. In life he left his property to us; in death he has caused us to risk losing it. In those days he brought us up with such modesty that we never even went into a lawcourt as listeners; today we have come to fight for everything we possess, since they are claiming not just Cleonymus' property but our patrimony as well, and are alleging besides that we owe his estate money. [2] Their own friends and relatives think we should have an equal share with them even of the undisputed property Cleonymus left, but our opponents have become so shameless that they are seeking to deprive us of our patrimony as well, not through ignorance of what is just, gentlemen, but because they have observed our extreme destitution. [3] Consider the basis of the claims each side is making as we come before you. Our opponents are relying on a will he made in anger at one of our relatives, not because he had any complaint against us, and which he annulled before his death by sending Poseidippus to the magistrate. [4] But we were his next of kin and were closer to him than anybody, while the laws have granted us the right of succession on the ground of kinship and so did Cleonymus himself because of the friendship existing between us. Moreover, Polyarchus, Cleonymus' father and our grandfather, prescribed that if Cleonymus died childless, he was to leave his property to us. [5] Despite such strong claims

---

[5] If Cleonymus did not wish to annul the will, he was insane and it should therefore be declared void by the jurors; if he did, the speaker must win his case.

[6] Specifically, a pathetic paradox (Usher 1999: 367). The opponents had admitted the nephews were entitled to a share of the estate, but a verdict in their favor would entitle them to all of it, so giving them more than they themselves felt was due to them and depriving the nephews even of what their opponents had conceded.

on our side, our opponents, who are our relatives and have nothing just to say, are not ashamed to bring us to trial on matters it would be shameful even for nonrelatives to dispute. [6] But I don't believe, gentlemen, that we feel the same way towards one another. For I think that the greatest of my present troubles is not that I am unjustly in danger but that I am fighting a case against relatives, against whom it is not good even to defend oneself. As they are relatives, I would think it no less a misfortune to injure them in defending myself than to have been injured by them in the first place. [7] Our opponents do not share this opinion, but have attacked us. They have called on their friends to help, procured orators,[7] and done everything in their power as if, gentlemen, they intended to punish enemies rather than harm kinsmen and relatives. [8] You'll understand their shamelessness and greed even better when you have heard everything. I'll begin my account at the point where I think you will most readily understand what our dispute is about.

[9] Deinias, our father's brother, became our guardian, as he was our uncle and we were orphans.[8] Now, he happened to have a dispute with Cleonymus, gentlemen. Which of the two was to blame for the quarrel it is perhaps not my business to decide, except that I might justly blame them both for turning their previous friendship so casually into mutual hostility for no real reason after an exchange of words. [10] Anyway, at that point because of this anger Cleonymus made this will, not because he had any complaint against us, as he later said, but because he saw we were the wards of Deinias and he was afraid in case he should die himself while we were still minors, and that Deinias would gain control of his property if it were ours—he thought it terrible to leave his bitterest enemy as guardian of his relatives and in charge of his property and to have a man he was in dispute with while alive perform the customary rites over him until we grew up.[9] [11] It

---

[7] For supporting speakers (*synēgoroi*), see the Introduction, VC; cf. Apollodorus' role in Dem. 59 above.

[8] A Greek *orphanos* had no father (Introduction, VE).

[9] Performance of rites by the guardian is not attested elsewhere. The guardian's primary role was to manage the property, and on reaching his majority, the ward might accuse him of mismanagement and corruption, as happened most famously in the case of Demosthenes' guardians (see below, Dem. 27; also Lys. 32).

was with these thoughts in mind that, rightly or not, he made this will. Deinias then immediately asked him if he had some complaint against us or our father, and he replied in the presence of every citizen[10] that he had nothing bad to complain of, thereby giving evidence that he made this will out of anger against Deinias and not from good judgment. For if he had been of sound mind, gentlemen, how could he have wanted to harm us, when we had done no harm to him? [12] What he did afterwards furnishes the strongest proof of our contention that he had no wish to harm us even by this action. When Deinias died and we were having a bad time of things, he didn't allow us to want for anything but took us into his own house and brought us up, saved our property from creditors who were plotting to take it away, and took care of our affairs as if they were his own. [13] Now, we should judge his intentions from these actions rather than from the will, and use as evidence not what he did in anger, which naturally leads all of us astray, but what he did later, which made his intentions clear. For towards the end he showed still more how he felt about us. [14] When he was already weak from the illness that killed him, he wanted to revoke this will and instructed Poseidippus to fetch the magistrate, but he not only failed to do so but even dismissed one of the magistrates who came to the door. Cleonymus was angry at him and again gave instructions, to Diocles this time, to summon the magistrates for the next day, even though he was in no fit state due to his illness. But although there was still plenty of hope for his recovery, he died suddenly that night.

[15] I will now present witnesses, first, that he made the will not because he had a complaint against us but because of his fight with Deinias; then that after Deinias died he took care of all our affairs, received us into his own house, and brought us up; and furthermore that he sent Poseidippus for the City Magistrate (*astynomos*),[11] but this

---

[10] Implying that Cleonymus and Deinias quarreled in the Assembly or (allowing for rhetorical exaggeration) at some other public gathering. The speaker may be trying to gloss over the lack of witnesses to support this part of his story.

[11] There were ten *astynomoi*, five in the city and five in Piraeus, whose duties included the hire of entertainers and keeping the streets clean and safe (cf. *Ath. Pol.* 50.2). They had no specific connection with the administration of testamentary law.

man not only failed to summon him but even dismissed him when he came to the door. [16] To prove I'm telling the truth, please call the witnesses.

[WITNESSES]

Next, please also call witnesses that our opponents' friends, including Cephisander, thought we should share the property and have a third of all Cleonymus' possessions.

[WITNESSES]

[17] I think then, gentlemen, that when anyone laying claim to an estate can prove, as we can, that they are nearer the deceased both in kinship and in friendship, it is superfluous to advance other arguments. But since our opponents, with neither of these grounds, have the audacity to claim what doesn't belong to them and are fabricating false arguments, I would like to respond briefly to these points too. [18] They rely on the will and say that Cleonymus sent for the magistrate not because he wanted to revoke it but to revise it and confirm his bequest to them. But consider whether it is more likely that when he became friendly towards us, Cleonymus wanted to revoke the will he had made in anger or that he was seeking even more firmly to deprive us of his property. [19] Other men repent afterwards of wrongs done to their relatives in anger; but our opponents argue instead that, when he was on most intimate terms with us, he wanted to confirm the will he made in anger. If we admitted this and you yourselves believed it, understand that our opponents are accusing him of sheer insanity. [20] For what could be greater madness than that during his dispute with Deinias, he should harm us and make a will by which he didn't punish him but wronged his closest relatives, but now, when he was close to us and valued us above all, he wanted, as our opponents claim, to leave only his nephews without a share of his property? Who in his right mind, gentlemen, would manage his property in this way? [21] So by these arguments they have made a decision on their case easy for you. If he sent for the magistrate because he wanted to revoke the will, as we contend, they have no possible argument; but if he was so insane that he never had the least consideration for us, his closest kin and most intimate friends, you would surely be justified in declaring such a will invalid.

[22] Next, remember that they allege that Cleonymus called for the magistrate to confirm their bequest, yet when ordered, they didn't dare to bring him in but even sent away the magistrate who came to the door. Faced with a choice either to have their bequest confirmed or to offend Cleonymus by not doing as he asked, they chose his enmity in preference to this bequest. How could anything be less credible than this? [23] Those who stood to gain so much by doing this avoided rendering the service as if they were going to be penalized for it, while Cleonymus showed such zeal for their advantage that he was angry with Poseidippus for his negligence and the next day asked the same thing again of Diocles!

[24] Gentlemen, if, as they say, Cleonymus bequeathed the property to them in the will as presently written, I can't help wondering what revision he thought would make it more valid; for everybody else, gentlemen, this is the ultimate form of bequest. [25] Furthermore, if he wanted to add something to it, why didn't he leave this written down in another document when he couldn't get the original document from the magistrates? Gentlemen, he could not revoke any document other than the one deposited with the magistrate, but he could write anything he liked in another one and leave no chance of dispute between us. [26] So if we concede that Cleonymus wanted to revise the will, it is doubtless obvious to all of you that he didn't think it was right. Here again consider their shamelessness: they claim this will is valid, when they admit the testator himself did not think it was right, and then try to persuade you to reach a verdict contrary to the laws, justice, and the intentions of the deceased. [27] And the most shameless of all their statements is when they have the audacity to say that Cleonymus didn't want us to have any of his property. Who else could he have wanted to have it, gentlemen, if not those relatives to whom he gave the most help out of his property when alive? [28] The most amazing thing of all would be if even though Cephisander, their relative, thought it fair for each of us to have a share of the property, Cleonymus, our closest relative, the one who took us into his own house, brought us up and took care of our affairs as if they were his own, was the only one who did not want us to share in his property. [29] Could any of you believe that our opponents are kinder and fairer towards us than our closest relatives? Or that he, who was obliged to treat us well and would be shamed if he neglected us, should leave us

none of his property, but these men, who have no obligation and for whom neglect brings no shame, should share what they say doesn't belong to us? All of this, gentlemen, is utterly incredible.[12]

[30] Now, if Cleonymus still felt the same about both sides at his death as he felt when he made this will, some of you might reasonably believe my opponents' version; but as it is you will find the exact opposite is true. At the time he made the will, he was in dispute with our guardian Deinias, was not yet close to us, and was on friendly terms with all these people; but at the time of his death he was quarreling with some of these people but was closer to us than to anybody else. [31] There is no point in talking about the reasons for his dispute with my opponents, but I'll give you some strong proofs of it and shall also produce witnesses. Firstly, when he was sacrificing to Dionysus he asked all his relatives and many other citizens to come, but he did not invite Pherenicus.[13] Then, shortly before his death, while traveling to Panormus with Simon, he met Pherenicus and could not bring himself to speak to him. [32] Further, when Simon inquired about the dispute, he told him all about their mutual hostility and threatened that one day he'd show Pherenicus exactly how he felt about him. And to prove I'm telling the truth, call witnesses.

[WITNESSES]

[33] Do you think, gentlemen, that a man who was so disposed towards each side acted towards us, with whom he was on the closest terms, in a way that did not leave us so much as an argument, but considered how to confirm that they would receive his whole property, even though he was quarreling with some of them? And that despite this hostility he thought more of them and tried rather to harm us, despite the growth of such intimacy and friendship? [34] As I see it, if they wanted to attack the will or the deceased, I don't know what else they could have said to you. They represent the will as being neither right nor approved of by the testator, and accuse him of sheer madness

---

[12] As Wyse observes (1904: 207–208), the opponents will have argued that the changes to the will did not involve the nephews but that their proposed compromise showed them as being conciliatory towards the nephews, who for their part were rapacious.

[13] For Pherenicus and Simon, see the Speech Introduction.

when they claim he thought more of those who were quarreling with him than of those who were friends, left his property to those with whom he was not even on speaking terms when alive, and didn't think the ones he was closest to should have even the smallest share. [35] So could any of you vote for the validity of this will, which the testator rejected as being not right, which our opponents are in fact annulling in their willingness for us to have an equal share of the property, and which in addition we can prove to you is contrary to the law, to justice, and to the wishes of the deceased?

[36] But I think you can most clearly learn the justice of our case from our opponents. If they were asked on what grounds they think they should be Cleonymus' heirs, they might reply that they are in some way related to him and for some time he was friendly towards them. Wouldn't they thus be speaking in our favor rather than theirs? [37] For if the right of succession depends on the degree of kinship, we are more closely related; if on existing friendship, everyone knows that he was on closer terms with us. So you must learn the justice of the case not from us but from them. [38] It would be very strange indeed if you voted in other cases for those who prove themselves to be either nearer in kinship to or on friendlier terms with the deceased, but in our case should decide that we, who all admit are both of these, should alone have no share in his property.

[39] If Polyarchus, Cleonymus' father and our grandfather, were alive and lacked life's necessities, or Cleonymus had died leaving daughters in need, we would have been obliged by our kinship to look after our grandfather in his old age, and either to marry Cleonymus' daughters ourselves or to provide dowries and marry them to others.[14] Kinship, the laws, and the shame we would feel before you would have obliged us to do this or else encounter the severest penalties and extreme disgrace. [40] But since property has been left, will you think it just for others to inherit it rather than us? You will not vote justly, then, or in your own interests or in accordance with the laws if you force the next of kin to share in misfortunes but give everyone a greater right than them to the money that has been left.

[41] You should vote, gentlemen, as you do, on grounds of kinship

---

[14] On the obligations of relatives towards unmarried girls, cf. And. 1.117–120; Dem. 43.54.

and the true facts of the case in favor of those whose claims are based on kinship rather than a will. You all know the connection of kinship, and it's impossible to lie about this to you, but many before now have produced false wills, some of them complete forgeries, some made by people who were misguided. [42] In this case, you all know the kinship and relationship on which we base our claim, but none of you knows that the will is valid on which our opponents rely in falsely accusing us.[15] Moreover, you will find that our kinship is admitted even by our opponents, but the will is contested by us, since they prevented its annulment when he wanted this. [43] So, gentlemen, it's far more fitting for you to vote according to the kinship admitted by both sides than according to the will that was not drawn up rightly. Also remember that Cleonymus annulled it when of sound mind, but made it when angry and misguided, so it would be really extraordinary if you allowed his anger to prevail over his wishes.

[44] I think you consider it your right to inherit, and to feel aggrieved if you don't, from those who stand to inherit from you. Supposing, then, that Cleonymus were still alive, and our family or our opponents' family had been left without heirs, consider from which of us he would inherit. For it's only fair that those from whom he had the right to inherit should have his property. [45] Now if Pherenicus or one of the brothers[16] had died, their children and not Cleonymus were going to become entitled to the property left behind. But if we had met such a fate, Cleonymus was going to become heir to everything, because we had no children or other relatives, but he was our next of kin and the one with the closest personal ties to us. [46] For these reasons, the laws have granted him the right of succession, and we would not have thought anyone else should have this bequest. Surely, we would not have put our property in his hands during our lifetime, thus making his wishes stronger than our own as regards our possessions,[17] and then when we died have wanted there to be heirs

---

[15] Greek *sykophantein* (see the Introduction, VE). Since this case was a *diadikasia*, the speaker's opponents were not his prosecutors, against whom the term was regularly used.

[16] See the Speech Introduction.

[17] As Wyse notes (1904: 228), the nephews did not put their property in Cleonymus' hands, because when he took them on after Deinias' death, they were minors with no say in the matter.

other than our closest kin. [47] Therefore, gentlemen, you'll find us bound to him in both bequest and inheritance, but you'll find my opponents acting shamelessly and talking about intimacy and kinship, because they expect to gain something. But in making a bequest, they would have put many relatives and friends before him as being closer. [48] To sum up what I've said—and you should all pay close attention. As long as my opponents are using these arguments to show and try to persuade you that Cleonymus made this will and never afterwards regretted it, but still wanted us to receive none of his property and to confirm his bequest to them—[49] but while emphasizing all these points they are not showing either that they are closer kin of Cleonymus or that they were on closer terms with him than we were—understand that they are accusing him but are not showing you that their case is just. [50] So if you believe what they say, you should still not make them his heirs but pronounce Cleonymus insane; while if you believe us, you should consider that he was well advised in wanting to annul the will, and that we are not behaving as sykophants[18] but are claiming this estate justly. [51] Finally, gentlemen, you should realize that it's impossible for you to decide the case on the basis of their arguments. It would be really extraordinary if you vote that our opponents should have the whole estate when they recognize our right to receive a part of it, and think they should receive more than they considered themselves entitled to, but don't think that we deserve even what our opponents concede to us.

---

[18] See 42n. The word is more appropriate here, since the speaker is making a claim against the will and would therefore be more open to the charge of sykophancy.

ISAEUS 7. ON THE ESTATE
OF APOLLODORUS

〰〰

INTRODUCTION

The brothers Eupolis, Mneson, and Thrasyllus I jointly inherited a large estate from their father, who was probably named Apollodorus, since both Eupolis and Thrasyllus so named their sons. Mneson died childless, and Thrasyllus died on the Sicilian expedition of 415–413, leaving a son, Apollodorus II, who was a minor and therefore came under the guardianship of his uncle, Eupolis. According to the speaker, Eupolis misappropriated the whole of Mneson's estate, half of which belonged by law to Apollodorus, and embezzled his nephew's property. Meanwhile, Apollodorus' mother had remarried, and her second husband, Archedamus, brought him up in his own house. When Apollodorus reached the age of majority, Archedamus helped him win two lawsuits against Eupolis, securing his share of Mneson's estate and the restoration of three talents. In return, Apollodorus aided Archedamus after the latter had been taken prisoner of war; later, when he was himself about to serve in the Corinthian War (395–386), Apollodorus made a will leaving his estate to his half-sister, Archedamus' daughter, and arranging her marriage.

This will did not come into effect, because Apollodorus survived the war and in due course had a son of his own. However, the son died the year before this trial, and since Apollodorus was by now at least 60, he determined to adopt a son. The obvious choice, given his enmity towards Eupolis' family, was his half-sister's son, Thrasyllus II (the speaker). Apollodorus presented Thrasyllus to his *genos* (descent group) and phratry at the Thargelia festival of 355,[1] but he died before

---

[1] On this procedure, see Andrewes 1961: 5–6.

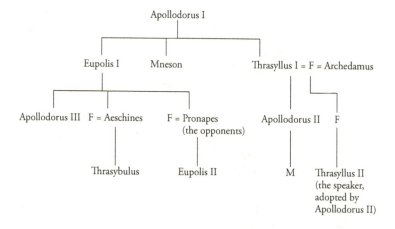

Thrasyllus had been registered in his deme, though the demesmen subsequently admitted him to the list, against the protests of Apollodorus' first cousin, the daughter of Eupolis who was married to Pronapes. Through her husband she challenged the validity of the adoption and claimed Apollodorus' estate by *diadikasia*. Another potential claimant was Thrasybulus, the son of Eupolis' other daughter (who was also now dead); but he did not make a claim, because (according to Thrasyllus) he was satisfied that the adoption was legal (7.21) or because (according to the opponents) he had lost his rights through being adopted into another family (7.23).

The cousin's claim seems, on the face of it, to be a piece of opportunism, an attempt through a technicality to get her hands on the sizeable fortune of a man who had long been at odds with her side of the family. It is hard to imagine that Pronapes will have disputed in court that Apollodorus had fully intended to go through with the adoption; he may have argued that the old man had come under the influence of a woman and so the adoption was invalid, though Thrasyllus makes no direct mention of this (he perhaps hints at it at 7.36). But it is clear that the proper formalities of adoption had not been completed when Apollodorus died, and Pronapes may well have entered a claim immediately. Thrasyllus was left in an awkward position: he could not enter a *diamartyria*[2] that the estate was not adjudi-

---

[2] For *diamartyria*, see Lys. 23.13n.

cable because there was a legitimate son; and he had not been adopted by a will, nor was he the next of kin (since in Athenian law, kin on the father's side took precedence over kin on the mother's side, and Thrasyllus was in any case only Apollodorus' half-nephew, being the son of his half-sister). He therefore emphasizes the affection between the families of Apollodorus and Archedamus and the hostility between Apollodorus and Eupolis; and he describes at length the measures that Apollodorus took to adopt him before his death. He also highlights how his opponents had allowed the family of Apollodorus III, the son of Eupolis and brother of Pronapes' wife, to become extinct, a danger he claims was now threatening the house of Apollodorus II as well. It seems, then, that the law favored the wife of Pronapes, but equity favored Thrasyllus: we do not know how the jurors decided.

Isaeus' main rhetorical strategy in this speech is to give the strong impression that Thrasyllus was Apollodorus' regularly adopted son, papering over the fact that the formalities of the adoption had not actually been completed. In the proem (7.1–4) he immediately contrasts adoption *inter vivos* with testamentary adoption, noting that disputes normally arose only in the latter, and he flatters the jurors by pretending that he could have entered a *diamartyria* but has decided instead to put the full facts to them. Before the *topoi* of asking for the jurors' goodwill and promising to be brief, he inserts a *prothesis:* that he will prove that there was enmity between the two sides of the family and that Apollodorus had adopted him. This twin approach forms the basis of his subsequent main narrative. In the earlier phase of the story the wickedness of Eupolis is contrasted with the kindness of Archedamus, for which he is in turn repaid by the kindness of Apollodorus; and this part of the narrative ends by returning to Eupolis, who gave neither of his daughters in marriage to Apollodorus, thus demonstrating their enmity (7.5–12).

The continuing enmity then forms a link with the second phase of the narrative, as Thrasyllus describes his adoption by Apollodorus in great detail (7.13–17). The importance of registration in the *genos* and phratry is magnified, and Thrasyllus stops short of saying that he was not introduced into the deme before Apollodorus died, but instead he emphasizes that his name was entered in the public register as "Thrasyllus son of Apollodorus." Before broaching the tricky subject of his deme registration, Thrasyllus inserts a long (and dubious) comparative argument (7.18–26): Thrasybulus has a stronger entitlement to the

estate than Pronapes' wife, but he has not claimed it; she should therefore accept the validity of Thrasyllus' adoption.

The complex discussion of the law demonstrates not only Isaeus'
command of its intricacies but also, almost certainly, how to interpret
them misleadingly.[3] It is only now, while the jurors are wrestling with
these legalities, that Thrasyllus tells the crucial part of the story in a
brief third narrative (7.27–28), how his registration in Apollodorus'
deme took place while he was away at the Pythaid festival at Delphi.
This time there is less detail, so as not to highlight the fact that the
formalities were not completed, but Thrasyllus nevertheless boldly
brings forward witnesses from the deme. He naturally does not dwell
on this potentially fatal flaw in his case but moves swiftly on to argue
that even without the hostility that existed, Apollodorus would not
have left his estate to Pronapes' wife (7.29–32): the sisters of Apollodorus III had done nothing to preserve his estate and would act no differently with respect to Apollodorus II's estate. Thrasyllus' own good
character was, however, well known to Apollodorus, who furthermore
was of sound mind (7.33–36); and this proof by character naturally
leads into the conventional praise of the public spiritedness of Apollodorus himself (in contrast to Pronapes) and his father, before Thrasyllus recaps his own services and promises that the right verdict will
ensure further benefits for the city (7.37–42). In the epilogue (7.43–45)
Thrasyllus reminds the jurors of his arguments, contrasting the claims
of both parties and reaffirming that he had a better legal and moral
right to the estate.

The case will have been heard after 357/6, the earliest year in which
joint trierarchies (cf. 7.38) are known. The most likely date is the
spring of 354 (see Parke 1939: 80–83).

ISAEUS 7. ON THE ESTATE OF APOLLODORUS

[1] I thought, gentlemen, that there could not be any dispute over
adoptions of the kind made by a man personally, in his lifetime and
when of sound mind, when he has taken the adopted son to the temples, presented him to his relatives, and entered him in the public

---

[3] See Wyse 1904: 560–563; Harrison 1968: 147–148 note 2. Thrasybulus' adoption by Hippolochides (7.23) may explain why he did not put in a claim for
Apollodorus' estate.

registers, carrying out all the proper formalities himself, though there might be when a man who is about to die has disposed of his property to another, in case anything should happen to him, and has sealed his wishes up in a document and deposited it with others. [2] By the former method the adopter makes his wishes clear, ratifying the whole business as the laws allow him; but by sealing his wishes in a will, the adopter keeps them secret, and consequently many decide to enter a claim against the adopted sons, alleging the will is a forgery. But it seems that in this case it doesn't matter, since even though I was openly adopted, nevertheless my opponents have come on behalf of the daughter of Eupolis and entered a claim against me for Apollodorus' property. [3] If I saw that you preferred a declaration (*diamartyria*) to a direct action (*euthydikia*),[4] I would have produced witnesses that the estate is not adjudicable, since Apollodorus adopted me as his son in accordance with the laws. But since I realize that you would not understand the rights of the matter in that way, I have come forward myself to tell you the facts, so they cannot possibly accuse us of not wanting to put the matter to trial. [4] I will prove not only that Apollodorus did not leave his estate to his next of kin because of the many terrible wrongs they did him, but also that he legally adopted me, his nephew, after receiving great kindnesses from my family. I beg you, gentlemen, all equally to show your goodwill towards me, and if I prove that my opponents are going after the estate shamelessly, to help me obtain my rights. I'll make my speech as brief as I possibly can, showing you the facts from the beginning.

[5] Eupolis, gentlemen, Thrasyllus and Mneson were brothers with the same mother and father. Their father left them a large fortune, which allowed each of them, in your view, to perform public services for you. The three divided this fortune among themselves. Two of them died at about the same time, Mneson here, unmarried and childless, Thrasyllus in Sicily where he served as a trierarch, leaving behind a son, Apollodorus, who has now adopted me. [6] Eupolis, the sole survivor of the three, decided he should enjoy not just a small part of the fortune, but he appropriated the whole of Mneson's estate, half of which belonged to Apollodorus, alleging that his brother had given it

---

[4] I.e., a direct action to claim the estate, rather than a declaration with witnesses that a rival's claim was invalid.

to him. Moreover, as guardian he managed Apollodorus' property so badly that he was condemned to pay him three talents. [7] This was because my grandfather Archedamus, after marrying Apollodorus' mother, my grandmother, saw him being deprived of all his money and brought him up as his own child. And when Apollodorus became an adult, he helped him go to law and secured the half-share of the estate Mneson left him and whatever Eupolis had embezzled as guardian, winning two lawsuits, and so enabled him to recover his whole fortune. [8] Consequently, Eupolis and Apollodorus have always been hostile towards one another, while my grandfather and Apollodorus naturally were close friends. But Apollodorus' actions would be the best evidence that he was treated in a way he thought he should reciprocate to his benefactors. When my grandfather met with disaster and was captured by the enemy,[5] Apollodorus was willing to contribute money for his ransom and act as hostage for him until he could raise the money.[6] [9] With Archedamus reduced from affluence to poverty, Apollodorus helped him look after his affairs and shared what he had with him. And when he was about to leave for Corinth on military service, in case anything should happen to him, he disposed of his property in a will, leaving it to Archedamus' daughter, my mother and his own sister, and giving her in marriage to Lacratides,[7] who has now become Hierophant.[8] This, then, is how he treated us, because we saved him to begin with. [10] To prove what I'm saying is true, that he won two lawsuits against Eupolis, one over his guardianship, the other over the half-share of the estate, that my grandfather helped him go to law and spoke for him in court, and that he recovered his money

_____

[5] Presumably during the Peloponnesian War.

[6] I.e., even swap places with him.

[7] This implies that Apollodorus, by the testamentary adoption of his uterine half-sister, assumed the further right of a father to arrange for the marriage of his daughter, to prevent her being claimed as an "heiress" (see Dem. 57.41) by Eupolis' family. Two other female adoptees appear at Is. 11.8 and 41; it is unclear how common a practice such adoption was or how common was the nomination of a husband for an heiress without adopting him. See on the latter Rubinstein 1993: 97. Of course, the will, and so the marriage, never came into effect.

[8] An official at the Eleusinian Mysteries who displayed the sacred symbols and figures.

through our help and reciprocated these favors, I wish first to provide witnesses on these points. Please call them here.

[WITNESSES]

[11] These, then, are the many important benefits he received from us; but towards Eupolis his hostility concerned such large sums of money that it's impossible to pretend they resolved their differences and became friends. Strong evidence of their hostility is that Eupolis had two daughters, but he gave neither of them to Apollodorus in marriage, even though he and Apollodorus were born of the same family and he could see Apollodorus had money. [12] And yet inter-marriages are thought to reconcile serious disputes not only between relatives but also between ordinary acquaintances, when they entrust one another with what they value most. So whether Eupolis was at fault for not wishing to give his daughter or Apollodorus for being unwilling to receive her, this fact makes clear that their hostility persisted.

[13] I think I've said enough already about their dispute: I know that the older men among you remember that they were opponents, because the importance of the lawsuits and the fact that Archedamus won heavy damages against Eupolis caused a sensation. So now please pay close attention, gentlemen, to these points: that Apollodorus himself adopted me as his son during his lifetime, put me in control of his property, and registered me among the members of his *genos* and phra-try. [14] Apollodorus had a son he educated and cared for, as was only fitting. While this boy was alive, he hoped to make him heir to his property, but when he fell ill and died in Maemacterion last year,[9] Apollodorus, depressed by all his troubles and complaining about his advanced age, did not forget those he had been well treated by origi-nally, but came to my mother, his own sister whom he valued above all others, and said he thought he should adopt me; he asked her per-mission and received it. [15] He was determined to do this as quickly as possible, and so he immediately took me home with him and entrusted me with the management of all his affairs, saying that he could no longer do any of this himself, but I would be able to do all

---

[9] Roughly November.

If you have no hier archon selects who inn normally select someone from acme.

of it. And when the Thargelia[10] came, he took me to the altars bef the members of his *genos* and phratry. [16] They share the same rule, that when a man introduces his son, whether natural or adopted, he swears an oath with his hand on the sacrificial victims that he is intro-ducing the child of an Athenian mother (*astē*) and born in wedlock, whether it's his natural son or an adopted one; and even after he has introduced him in this way, the others still have to vote, and if they agree, then they enter him in the public register, and not till then. Such is the precision with which their procedures are carried out. [17] This being their rule, then, since the members of his phratry and *genos* had full confidence in Apollodorus and knew that I was his sis-ter's son, they voted unanimously and entered me in the public regis-ter, after Apollodorus had sworn the oath with his hand on the vic-tims. And so I was adopted by a living man and entered in the public register as Thrasyllus son of Apollodorus, after he'd adopted me in this way, as the laws have entitled him to do. To prove I'm telling the truth, please take the depositions.

[DEPOSITIONS]

[18] Now, I imagine, gentlemen, that you would be more likely to believe these witnesses if some who are just as closely related as my opponent have clearly testified by their actions that Apollodorus did these things correctly and in accordance with the laws. Now, Eupolis left two daughters, this one who is the present claimant and is married to Pronapes, and another who was the wife of Aeschines of Lusia. She has died, but left a son, Thrasybulus, who is now an adult. [19] There is a law that provides that, if a brother by the same father dies childless and intestate, his property is to be divided in equal shares between his sister and any nephew born of another sister. My opponents them-selves are well aware of this, as they have made clear by their conduct: when Eupolis' son Apollodorus died childless, Thrasybulus received half his property, which easily amounted to five talents. [20] The law, then, grants the sister's son and the sister an equal share of their father's or brother's estate, but for the estate of a cousin or more distant rela-

---

[10] A festival celebrated in the month of Thargelion, at the beginning of June.

If you don't have sons your daughters sons will inherit.

If cannot find any male then female relatives on mother side it goes to dad side

tive, the share is not equal, but the law gives the right of succession to the male relatives in preference to the female. It says, "The males and the descendants of males who have the same origin shall have preference, even if they are more distantly related."[11] This woman, therefore, was not entitled to claim any share of the estate, but Thrasybulus was entitled to all of it, if he thought my adoption was not valid.[12] [21] But neither has he claimed against me from the start nor has he now brought a suit over the estate, but he has agreed that everything is fine; whereas my opponents have dared to claim the whole estate on this woman's behalf, such is their shamelessness. Take the clauses of the law that they have broken and read them to the court.

[LAW][13]

[22] Here sister and nephew have equal shares under the law. Now take this one and read it to them.

[LAW]

If there are no first cousins or children of first cousins, or any relatives on the father's side, then the law gave the right of inheritance to relatives on the mother's side, specifying the order of succession. Now take this law and read it to them.

[LAW]

[23] This is what the laws prescribe, yet Thrasybulus, a male relative, has not even claimed a part of the estate, whereas my opponents have claimed all of it on behalf of this woman; so they don't consider

---

[11] "Same origin" here means same common ancestor; "more distantly related" means more generations removed. Thus, a man's nephew (brother's son) would have a stronger claim to his estate than the man's sister.

[12] Isaeus' argument is that although Thrasybulus and his aunt divided the estate of Apollodorus III (her brother and his uncle), if Apollodorus II, a more distant relative, had no direct heir, Thrasybulus would be entitled to claim his entire estate. Isaeus very probably misrepresents the law here (cf. Is. 11.1–2): the principles of succession applied both to the direct line and to collateral relatives. See Wyse 1904: 560–563.

[13] The law is quoted at Dem. 43.51. Isaeus has it read out in three parts.

shamelessness a stigma. And to prove they should be awarded the whole estate, they will even dare to use arguments like this: that Thrasybulus has been adopted out of his family into that of Hippolochides. This is a true statement with a false conclusion.[14] [24] Why was he any the less entitled to this right of kinship? It was not through his father but through his mother that not only did he receive his share of the estate of Apollodorus the son of Eupolis, but if he thought my adoption was not valid, he was also entitled to claim this estate by this right of kinship, his claim being prior to this woman's. But he is not so shameless. [25] Nobody is removed from his mother's family by adoption, but the fact remains that he has the same mother whether he remains in his father's house or is adopted out of it. Therefore, he was not deprived of his share of Apollodorus' fortune but has received half of it, sharing it with this woman. And to prove I'm telling the truth, please call the witnesses to this.

[WITNESSES]

[26] So not only have the members of the *genos* and phratry been witnesses to my adoption, but also Thrasybulus himself, by not entering a claim, has shown by his conduct that he considers the act of Apollodorus valid and in accordance with the laws; otherwise, he would never have failed to claim such a large amount of money.

But there have been other witnesses to these facts as well. [27] Before I returned from the Pythaid festival,[15] Apollodorus told his demesmen that he had adopted me as his son, had registered me among the members of his *genos* and phratry, and had entrusted his property to me; and he urged them, if anything should happen to him before I returned, to enter me in the deme register as Thrasyllus son of Apollodorus and not to fail in this. [28] The demesmen listened to this and, even though our opponents complained at the deme elections that he had not adopted me as his son, based on what they heard and what they knew, they swore the oath with hands on the victims and

---

[14] We do not know what relationship (if any) existed between Thrasybulus and Hippolochides or whether Isaeus' argument on this point is valid.

[15] Held at Delphi in the summer; it would have taken place after the Thargelia (7.15).

registered me, just as he had asked them to, so well known among them was my adoption. To prove I'm telling the truth, please call the witnesses to this.

[WITNESSES]

[29] My adoption took place, gentlemen, before all these witnesses, when there was a longstanding hostility between Apollodorus and my opponents, but he felt a close friendship and kinship existed with us. But I think it will also be easy to prove to you that even if he felt neither of these things—neither hostility towards my opponents nor friendship towards us—Apollodorus would never have left this estate to them. [30] All men who are soon to die take precautions not to leave their families without heirs and to ensure that there will be somebody to offer sacrifices and perform all the customary rites over them. And so even if they die childless, they at least adopt children and leave them behind. And not only do they decide to do this for themselves, but the city too has publicly so decided, since by law it enjoins on the Archon the duty of ensuring that families are not left without heirs. [31] Now it was quite clear to Apollodorus that if he left his estate in the control of these people, he would render his family extinct. For what did he see before him? That these sisters of Apollodorus inherited their brother's estate but did not give him a son for adoption, even though they had children, that their husbands sold the land he left and his possessions for five talents and split the money, and that his house was thus left shamefully and disgracefully without heirs. [32] Since Apollodorus knew their brother had been treated in this way, how could he himself have expected, even if he was on friendly terms, to receive the customary rites from them, when he was only their cousin, not their brother? Surely there was no hope of this. And now please call the witnesses to the fact that they disregarded their brother's childlessness, possessed his fortune, and allowed a family to die out that could clearly support a trierarchy.

[WITNESSES]

[33] If this was how they were naturally disposed towards one another, then, and if they felt such great hostility towards Apollodorus who adopted me, what better course of action could he have taken than he did? He could have chosen a child to adopt from the family

of one of his friends and given him his property. But because of its age, even the child's parents would not have known whether he would turn out an excellent man or a worthless one. [34] But he knew me from experience and had tested me enough. He knew exactly how I behaved towards my father and mother, that I was attentive to my relatives and knew how to look after my own affairs; and he was well aware that in my position as Thesmothetes[16] I was neither unjust nor greedy. So it was not in ignorance but with full knowledge that he was putting me in control of his property. [35] Further, I was no stranger but his nephew, and had done him services that were not small but great; nor again did I lack public spirit, nor was I going to sell his possessions as my opponents have done with the property of that estate[17] but would be keen to serve as trierarch, in the army and as choregus, and perform all the duties you prescribed, as he himself had done. [36] And so, if I was his relative, friend and benefactor, a public-spirited man who had been put to the test, who could claim that this adoption was made by a man who was not of sound mind? Indeed, I have already performed one of the services approved of by him, as I have acted as gymna-siarch[18] at the festival of Prometheus this year with a public spirit recognized by all the members of my tribe. To prove I'm telling the truth, please call the witnesses to this.

[WITNESSES]

[37] These are the just grounds on which we claim we can properly keep the estate, gentlemen; and we beg you to help us for the sake of both Apollodorus and his father. You will find that they were not use-less citizens but as devoted as possible to your interests. [38] His father performed all the other public services and also acted as trierarch the whole time, not in a group as they do now[19] but at his own cost, not jointly with another but by himself alone; nor did he take a break for

---

[16] One of the six junior Archons; see the Introduction, IVA.

[17] By converting real estate into cash, one would have less "visible" property (see Is. 8.35n) and could more easily avoid these public services, for which see the Introduction, IVC.

[18] Providing a team for the torch race at the festival in October 355 (Davies 1971: 45).

[19] See the Speech Introduction.

two years,[20] but he served continuously and did not discharge his duties perfunctorily but provided the best possible equipment. In return you remembered his actions and honored him, and saved his son when he was being deprived of his fortune, compelling the men who were in possession of his property to give it back to him. [39] Further, Apollodorus himself did not act like Pronapes, who assessed his property at a low valuation, but since he paid taxes as a knight, thought he should hold the appropriate offices, and who seized other people's property by force but thought you should not benefit at all. Instead, he openly declared the value of his property to you and performed all the services you enjoined on him. He did no wrong to anybody but tried to live with public spirit on his own fortune, thinking he ought to be moderate in his personal expenditure and save the rest for the city, so it could cover its costs. [40] As a result of this attitude, what public service did he not completely discharge? What war tax was he not among the first to pay? What duty has he ever neglected? He was victorious when acting as choregus to a boys' chorus, and the well-known tripod stands as a memorial to his public spiritedness. So what is the duty of a respectable citizen? Is it not, while others are using force to take what doesn't belong to them, to do no such thing, but try to save what is one's own? Is it not, when the state needs money, to be among the first to contribute and not to conceal any part of one's fortune? [41] Such a man, then, was Apollodorus. In return, you would justly repay him for this service by approving his wishes concerning his own property. And as for myself, as far as my age allows, you will not find me a bad or useless citizen. I have served the city on its campaigns and I perform my duties: this is what men of my age should do. [42] Thus, for their sake[21] and ours you would reasonably take care, especially since our opponents have allowed a family worth five talents that supported the trierarchy to die out, have sold the estate, and made it extinct, whereas we have already performed public services and will do so in the future, if you approve Apollodorus' wishes by restoring this estate to us.

[43] So that you don't think I am wasting time by speaking on these

---

[20] As the law permitted.

[21] I.e., that of Apollodorus and Eupolis.

matters, before I step down I wish to remind you briefly of the issues on which each side bases its claim. My claim is that my mother was Apollodorus' sister and a close affection existed between them, and no hostility ever arose; that I am his nephew and was adopted by him as his son when he was alive and of sound mind, and was registered among the members of his *genos* and phratry; that I possess the estate he gave me; and that my opponents should not be able to render his family extinct, But what does Pronapes claim on behalf of the claimant? [44] That he should possess a half-share of the estate of his wife's brother, valued at two and a half talents, and also receive this estate, even though there are others more closely related to Apollodorus than his wife, even though he did not give him a son for adoption but has left the house without heirs, nor would he give Apollodorus a son for adoption, and he would similarly leave this family too without heirs. And he makes the claim even though great hostility existed between them and no reconciliation ever took place afterwards. [45] You must consider these facts, gentlemen, and also remember that I am the deceased's nephew, but she is only his cousin; that she is asking to possess two estates, but I claim only this one into which I was taken by adoption; that she was not on good terms with the man who left the estate, but I and my grandfather have been his benefactors. Consider all these points and weigh them in your own minds, and then pass your verdict for what is just.

I don't know that I need say any more: I think you are fully aware of what's been said.

ISAEUS 8. ON THE ESTATE OF CIRON

INTRODUCTION

Ciron I died at an advanced age (8.37), leaving a daughter but no son. The daughter (according to the speaker) was the child of his first marriage to his first cousin, the daughter of his mother's sister. This wife died after four years (7); their daughter was married first and without issue to Nausimenes of Cholargus and then, after his death, to an unnamed husband (also deceased) by whom she had two sons, the elder of whom is the speaker (8, 31, 36). Ciron's second marriage was to the half-sister of Diocles of Phlya, who survived him, but their two sons had both died (36). As soon as Ciron died, the speaker sought to establish his claim to the estate by performing the funeral rites (21–27), but he was opposed by a second claimant, the son of Ciron's brother (31, 38); and their bitter rivalry spilled over into a dispute at the funeral (27). At the subsequent *diadikasia* hearing, the nephew argued that the speaker's mother was not Ciron's legitimate daughter, since Ciron never had a daughter (1), and the speaker's mother was not even Athenian (43). The Argument attached to the speech, which was composed many centuries later, states (on what grounds is unclear)[1] that the nephew also argued that, even if the speaker's mother were legitimate, a brother's son had a stronger legal claim to an estate than a daughter's son, under the law that the descendants of males took precedence over those of females. This law is probably not applicable here, and the speaker ignores it, concentrating on the argument that descendants have a stronger claim than collaterals (30–34).

---

[1]Forster (1927: 283) thinks it is "clear from the speech"; contra Wyse 1904: 585–586, 609.

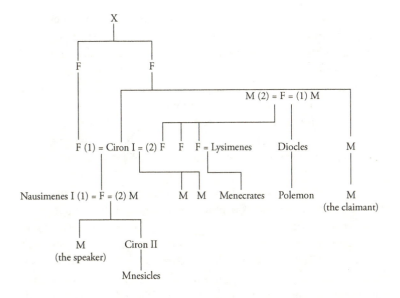

The main issue, as Isaeus saw it, was to establish the legitimacy of the speaker's mother. An immediate problem for the speaker then is that the alleged marriage between Ciron and his grandmother will have taken place some forty years earlier, and so he could not find any witnesses to it but had to rely on hearsay evidence (14, 29). Similarly, he could not prove that Ciron's daughter was regularly introduced to his phratry. He has therefore to base his arguments on her treatment by Ciron (he formally betrothed her to both her husbands, 8–9)[2] and by her husband (he gave a wedding breakfast and wedding feast to the phratry, 18), as well as that afforded her by the wives of the demesmen (19). Further, her children were enrolled in their father's phratry without objection (19). Other circumstantial evidence is adduced, of Ciron's conduct towards the boys (15–17) and that of Diocles (21–27); and the opponents' refusal to allow the examination under torture of Ciron's slaves is taken as further evidence for his case (9–14).

The arguments are weighty but fall short of proving the speaker's legitimacy: he distracts attention from this by a classic attack on the character not of his opponent but of Diocles, Ciron's second wife's

[2] A procedure that is not accepted as proof of Phile's legitimacy in Is. 3.

half-brother who was the subject of two other Isaean speeches (now lost). The attack on Diocles has some justification, since it appears that he is in control of the estate (37) and therefore is to all intents and purposes the opponent. It begins early (3) but reaches a climax towards the end of the speech in 40–44. Diocles is violent (cf. the nickname "Orestes" at 3, repeated at 44) and a murderer (41), he is dishonest (40, 42) and an adulterer (44, 46). The speaker will be taking further legal action against him (44): since his influence lies behind his opponent's claim (3), the jurors could only vote one way. We do not know, however, if they agreed (but see below).

Whatever the outcome, this speech is recognized as one of Isaeus' finest pieces of rhetoric. The proem (1–5) is one of the longest in the corpus, responding to the opponent's case by the adoption of an indignant tone, accompanied by emotive vocabulary: "dare," "do away with rights," "insult" (1); "greed," "force," "dare" again (2). Added to this is the *petitio principii*[3] that the speaker and his brother were "the sons of [Ciron's] legitimate daughter" (1); and given that Ciron was the grandfather, their opponent has been "enlisted" by the violent Diocles (3). The prothesis follows (6), in which the speaker sets out the two main points he will demonstrate: that his mother was Ciron's legitimate daughter and that he and his brother had a better legal claim to the estate than their opponents.

The first of these topics is dealt with in 7–29, with a short narrative of the history of the speaker's side of the family (7–8), followed by a series of proofs. The first concerns the speaker's mother and how her treatment by Ciron, which demonstrates that she was legitimate, could have been confirmed by the evidence of the household slaves (9–14). But slave evidence could be heard in court only if both sides agreed, and, as usual in the orators, the opponents had refused the demand to torture them.[4] This leads in turn to commonplace arguments over the implications of the refusal and the trustworthiness of torture evidence. The witnesses that the speaker does have are then produced, and a series of rhetorical questions builds a probability argument over the reliability of the witnesses on both sides. The speaker juxtaposes to this the circumstantial evidence that Ciron's

---

[3] See the Introduction to Is. 1, at n. 4 (p. 249).
[4] See above, Ant. 1.6n.

behavior towards his grandchildren was further proof of their mother's status (15–17); again, the testimony of the free witnesses produced serves to highlight how important the slaves' testimony would have been. The conduct of the boys' father and of the wives of his demesmen is an additional indication of their mother's legitimacy (18–20); and the grandsons' legitimacy is also demonstrated by their involvement in Ciron's funeral rites and the contrasting behavior of their opponents (21–27). This permits the reintroduction of Diocles, with a narrative of his actions concerning the funeral (21–24). Diocles' dishonesty in monetary matters is emphasized, so too his tacit acceptance of the speaker's position, which is highlighted by imaginary direct speech (24). Finally, the arguments supporting the speaker's first contention are recapitulated (28–29).

The speaker's second main contention, that of the precedence of descendants over collateral relatives, is the subject of 30–34. Scholars have mostly accepted the speaker's claims here, though he does not cite a specific law (if indeed one existed) and instead puts forward two clever arguments. The first (32) is that direct descendants are responsible for the maintenance of their parents and grandparents—how, then, is it right that, if the parents are indigent, their children are liable to be prosecuted for neglect, but if they are wealthy, others might inherit the estate? This law, which concerned the care of aged relatives but not inheritance, is read out (34). The second is a comparative argument (33): if Ciron's daughter is more closely related to him than his brother, and her children are nearer kin than the brother, then *a fortiori* her children are more closely related to Ciron than the brother's children.

Having addressed his two main points, the speaker returns in the remainder of the speech to the attack on Diocles. A third narrative details the estate's wealth and the intrigues whereby Diocles had secured it (which he now denied existed). His patience during Ciron's lifetime, preparing a bogus rival claimant, contrasts with his immediate actions on his death, as he tried to prevent the speaker from involvement in Ciron's funeral rites (35–39). A fourth narrative describes Diocles' corruption and murderous intentions with regard to his half-sisters' inheritance (40–42) and is followed by a pathos-inducing argument over the consequences that a victory for the opponents would have on the status of the grandsons (43–44), rounded off with a final attack on Diocles' character. The speaker moves swiftly into his epilogue (44–46), with a last appeal to the jurors and commonplace reminder of their duty to judge according to their dicastic oath, capped by the masterstroke of ending the speech with a deposition testifying to Diocles' adultery.

The date of the speech is ca. 365. The mention in an inscription dated ca. 330 (*IG* II² 2385.101) of a certain Ciron, who is apparently well off and who may be the speaker's son or nephew, might be an indication that the speaker won his case (Davies 1971: 315–316).

ISAEUS 8. ON THE ESTATE OF CIRON

[1] One cannot but feel indignant, gentlemen, against the kind of people who not only dare to claim the property of others but even hope by their arguments to do away with rights conferred by the laws. This is exactly what our opponents are trying to do now. Although our grandfather Ciron did not die childless but has left us behind him, the sons of his legitimate daughter, our opponents are claiming the estate as next of kin, and insult us by alleging that we are not the children of his daughter and that he never even had a daughter at all. [2] The reason for their acting like this is their greed and the value of the property that Ciron has left, and that they hold by force and are controlling; and they dare both to say that he has left nothing, and at the same time to lay claim to the estate. [3] But you must not imagine that this case today is directed against the man who has brought the suit over the estate; no, it is against Diocles of Phlya, nicknamed Orestes.[5] It is he who has enlisted our opponent to cause us trouble by embezzling the fortune our grandfather Ciron left us when he died and forcing us to risk this trial, so that he will not have to give any of it back if you are deceived into believing this man's words. [4] Since this is what they are plotting, you must learn all the facts, so that you may cast your vote with full awareness and clear knowledge of what's happened. If, then, you have ever paid close and careful attention to any other case, I beg you to pay similar attention to this one, as indeed is only just. Although many lawsuits are heard in the city, it will be clear that nobody has claimed the property of others more shamelessly or bra-

---

[5] Presumably after the mugger Orestes who appears in Aristophanes' plays.

zenly than these people. [5] It's a difficult task, gentlemen, to conduct a case on such important matters against fabrications and perjurious witnesses when one has absolutely no experience of the lawcourts. Still, I have great hopes that I shall obtain my rights from you and speak well enough at least on the matter of justice, unless something should happen to me such as I now happen to expect.[6] I therefore beg you, gentlemen, both to listen to me with goodwill and, if I appear to have been wronged, to help me secure my rights.

[6] First, then, I will prove to you that my mother was Ciron's legitimate daughter. For events of long ago I will rely on reported statements and witness testimony, but for events within living memory, on witnesses who know the facts as well as proofs, which are stronger than testimony. When I've made this clear, I will then prove that it's more appropriate for us to inherit Ciron's property than our opponents. I too will start at the point where they began their narrative of events and will try to show you what happened.

[7] My grandfather Ciron, gentlemen, married my grandmother, his first cousin, who was herself the daughter of his own mother's sister. She was not married for long, but bore him my mother and died after four years. Being left with only a daughter, my grandfather married his second wife, the sister of Diocles, who bore him two sons. He brought his daughter up in the house with his wife and her children, [8] and while they were still alive gave her in marriage, when she was of the right age, to Nausimenes of Cholargus, with her clothes and jewelry and a dowry of twenty-five minas.[7] Three or four years after this, Nausimenes fell ill and died, before my mother bore him any children. My grandfather received her back into his house without recovering the dowry he'd given, because of Nausimenes' poor financial condition, and married her a second time to my father with a dowry of one thousand drachmas.[8] [9] Now then, how could one prove clearly that all these events took place in the face of the charges our opponents are now making? When I looked, I discovered how. Whether my mother was Ciron's daughter or not, whether she lived in

---

[6] An obscure allusion, apparently reflecting the speaker's fears about his opponents' behavior during the rest of the trial.

[7] This dowry was just below an average sum; see Davies 1971: 314.

[8] I.e., ten minas this time.

his house or not, whether he gave two wedding breakfasts on her behalf or not, and what dowry each of her husbands received with her, all these things must be known to the male and female slaves who belonged to him. [10] Therefore, I wished to obtain proof from them by torture[9] in addition to the witnesses I had, so that you would have more faith in these witnesses because they would not be tested in the future, but would have already been tested in the matter of their testimony.[10] And so I asked our opponents to surrender the female and male slaves for torture on these and all the other points they might know about. [11] But our opponent, who is now going to ask you to believe his witnesses, declined the torture examination. And yet if he clearly was unwilling to do this, what else can you think of his witnesses than that they are now giving false testimony, since he has declined such an important test? I don't think there is any other conclusion. But to prove I'm telling the truth, please first take this deposition and read it.

[DEPOSITION]

[12] You consider that in both private and public matters torture examination is the most conclusive test; and whenever slaves and free men are present and some disputed point needs to be clarified, you do not use the testimony of the free men but seek to discover the truth about what happened by torturing the slaves. And reasonably so, gentlemen, since you are well aware that some witnesses before now have been thought to testify untruthfully, but nobody examined under torture has ever been convicted of not telling the truth as a result of the torture.[11] [13] Will our opponent, the most shameless of all men, ask you to believe his fabricated tales and lying witnesses, when he declines such conclusive tests? This is not our approach: we asked to resort to torture to confirm the testimony that was going to be given, but our

---

[9] For the evidence of slaves extracted under torture, see Ant. 1.6n.

[10] I.e., if the slaves' evidence corroborated that of the witnesses, there would be a presumption that the witnesses were telling the truth before their evidence was heard.

[11] A commonplace argument that is repeated almost verbatim at Dem. 30.37, but a counterargument could sometimes be employed (as at Ant. 5.32).

opponent refuses, and so we think that you should believe our witnesses. Take these depositions, then, and read them to the jurors.

[DEPOSITIONS]

[14] Who are likely to know the events of long ago? Clearly those who were close to my grandfather. They, then, have testified as to what they heard. Who must know the facts about giving my mother in marriage? Those who betrothed her and those who were present when they betrothed her. The relatives, then, of both Nausimenes and my father have testified. Who are the ones who know that she was brought up in Ciron's house and was his legitimate daughter? The present claimants clearly testify this is true by the fact that they declined the torture examination. Therefore, without a doubt you have no reason to disbelieve our witnesses but every reason to disbelieve theirs.

[15] Now we have other proofs beside these to put forward to prove that we are the children of Ciron's daughter. As was natural since we were the sons of his own daughter, he never made any sacrifice without us, but whether he was performing a small or large sacrifice, we were always there joining in it with him. And not only were we invited to these ceremonies, but he always took us into the country for the Dionysia;[12] [16] we attended public spectacles with him and sat next to him, and we went to his house for all the festivals. When he sacrificed to Zeus Ctesius,[13] a sacrifice that he took especially seriously and to which he did not admit slaves or free men from outside the family, but performed all the ceremonies personally, we shared in this, laid our hands on the victims with his, placed our offerings with his and assisted him in the other rites; and he prayed that Zeus grant us health and wealth, as was natural for him being our grandfather. [17] Yet if he didn't consider us his daughter's children and didn't see us as the only remaining descendants left to him, he would never have done any of these things, but would have invited our opponent to his side, who now claims to be his nephew. And that all this is true is best known to my grandfather's attendants, whom our opponent refused to hand over for

---

[12] The Rural (not City) Dionysia, which was held in Poseideon (roughly December).

[13] For "Zeus, god of property," see Ant. 1.16n.

torture; but some of his close friends also know it very well, and I will produce them as witnesses. Please take the depositions and read them.

[DEPOSITIONS]

[18] Now it's clear not only from these proofs that our mother was Ciron's legitimate daughter, but also from the actions of our father and from the attitude of the wives of his demesmen towards her. When our father married her, he gave a wedding breakfast and invited three of his friends as well as his relatives, and he gave a wedding feast to the members of his phratry in accordance with their rules. [19] The wives of his demesmen afterwards selected her, together with the wife of Diocles of Pithus, to preside at the Thesmophoria[14] and perform the customary rites with her. Our father also introduced us at birth to the members of his phratry, swearing on oath in accordance with the established laws that he was introducing the children of an Athenian mother (*astē*) and lawfully wedded wife. None of the phratry members objected or claimed this was not true, even though a large number were present and they consider such matters carefully. [20] And you cannot think that if our mother had been the kind of woman our opponents allege, our father would have given a wedding breakfast and wedding feast, rather than hushing all this up; or that the wives of the other demesmen would have chosen her to be the joint overseer of the festival with the wife of Diocles and put her in charge of the sacred objects, rather than entrusting this office to some other woman; or that the members of the phratry would have admitted us, rather than complaining and justifying their objection, if it had not been universally agreed that our mother was Ciron's legitimate daughter. As it was, because the facts were evident and many knew them, no such dispute arose in any quarter. And to prove I'm telling the truth in this, call the witnesses to the facts.

[WITNESSES]

[21] Next, gentlemen, it's easy to recognize from the way Diocles acted when our grandfather died that we were acknowledged to be

---

[14]A three-day women's festival in honor of Demeter, celebrated in the autumn, from which men were excluded.

Ciron's grandchildren. I came with one of my relatives, my father's cousin, to remove his body for burial from my own house. I did not find Diocles at the house, so I entered, accompanied by bearers, and was ready to remove it. [22] But when my grandfather's widow asked me to bury him from that house, and with supplications and tears said that she herself would like to help us lay out and adorn his body, I consented, gentlemen. I went to our opponent and told him in front of witnesses that I would conduct the funeral from there, because Diocles' sister had begged me to do so. [23] When Diocles heard this, he didn't object at all but claimed he had purchased some of the things needed for the funeral and had paid a deposit himself for the rest, and asked that I pay for these. We agreed that I would reimburse him for the cost of the things he'd bought and he would produce the men who received the deposit that he claimed he'd given. And right then he casually remarked that Ciron had left nothing at all, although I'd never said a single word about his money. [24] And yet if I'd not been Ciron's grandson, he would never have made these arrangements but would have said, "Who are you? What gives you the right to bury him? I don't know you; you're not going to set foot in the house." This is what he should have said and what he has now induced others to say. As it was, he said no such thing but told me to bring the money the next morning. And to prove I'm telling the truth, please call the witnesses to this.

[WITNESSES]

[25] And Diocles was not alone, but the present claimant of the estate also said no such thing, but now he is claiming the estate after being suborned by this man. And although he refused to accept the money I brought and alleged the next day that he'd been paid by our opponent, I was not prevented from joining in the burial but assisted in all the rites; and not only were the funeral expenses not paid by him or Diocles, they came out of what Ciron left. [26] And yet if Ciron was not my grandfather, our opponent should have banned me and thrown me out and prevented me from joining in the burial. For I was not related to him: I allowed him to assist in all these rites as being my grandfather's nephew, but he should not have allowed me to do so, if what they now have the audacity to say were true. [27] But he was so struck by the truth of the matter that at the tomb, when I spoke and

accused Diocles of embezzling the money and inducing this man to claim the estate, he didn't dare mutter a sound or say any word of what he now dares to say. And to prove I'm telling the truth in this, please call the witnesses to these events.

[WITNESSES]

[28] Why should you believe what I have said? Shouldn't you because of the testimony? I certainly think so. Why should you believe the witnesses? Shouldn't you because of the torture? It's certainly reasonable. Why should you disbelieve the words of our opponents? Shouldn't you because they declined the tests? That's an absolute necessity. How then could anybody prove more clearly that my mother is Ciron's legitimate daughter than by doing so in this way? [29] I provided witnesses who testified to what they heard of the events of long ago, and where witnesses are still alive I presented those who knew all the details—who knew well that she was brought up in his house, was considered his daughter, was twice betrothed and twice married—and further I showed that on all these points our opponents have declined the torture evidence from the slaves who knew them all. By the Olympian gods, I could not produce stronger proofs than these, but I think the ones that have been given are ample.

[30] Moving on, I will now show you that I have a better right to Ciron's fortune than our opponent. And I imagine that it's a simple fact that's completely clear to you that those who are born of the same stock as Ciron are not nearer in their rights of kinship than those who are descended from him—how could they be, since the former are called collaterals, the latter, descendants of the deceased? But even though this is the case, since they still have the audacity to claim the estate, we will show this still more conclusively from the laws themselves. [31] If my mother, Ciron's daughter, were alive, and if he had died intestate, and if our opponent were his brother, not his nephew, he would be entitled to marry his daughter but not to claim his fortune, which would go to their children when they came of age:[15] this is what the laws prescribe. If, then, not he but the chil-

---

[15] Lit. "two years after puberty," which was commonly thought to happen at the age of fourteen, but in the legal context at sixteen.

dren would have gained control of the daughter's property were she still alive, it's clear that since she is dead and has left us her children behind, it is not our opponents but we who are entitled to inherit the estate.

[32] Again, this is clear not only from this law but also from the one concerning neglect of parents. If my grandfather were alive and lacking life's necessities, we, not our opponent, would be liable to prosecution for neglect. The law prescribes that we look after our parents, parents meaning our mother, father, grandfather and grandmother, and their mother and father if they are still alive, because they are the origin of the family, and their property is passed down to their descendants. For this reason, their descendants are bound to look after them, even if they leave them nothing. So how can it be right that, if they have nothing to leave, we are liable to prosecution for neglect if we don't look after them, but if they have left something, our opponent is the heir and not us? Surely it's not right at all.

[33] I shall now compare the first of the collaterals with the descendants and ask you about the degree of relationship of each, since in this way you would most easily understand the matter. Is Ciron's daughter or brother the nearer of kin? Clearly his daughter, as she is born of him whereas he is merely of the same stock. Are the daughter's children nearer or his brother? The children, surely, as they are direct descendants and not merely collaterals. If, then, we have a stronger claim than a brother, surely we are very far ahead of our opponent, who is only a nephew. [34] But I'm afraid you may think me boring if I repeat things that are universally agreed. You all inherit the property of your fathers, grandfathers, and those still further back, taking up the succession by direct descent without having to go to law, and I don't know that such a case as this has ever been brought against anybody before. So I'll read the law on neglect of parents, and then try to show you why all this is happening.

[LAW]

[35] Ciron possessed a property, gentlemen, that included an estate at Phlya, easily worth a talent, and two houses in the city, one near the shrine of Dionysus in the Marshes that brought in rent and was worth a thousand drachmas, the other in which he himself lived worth thir-

teen minas. Besides this, he had male slaves who were hired out,[16] two female slaves and a slave girl, and the furnishings of the house he lived in, all worth, with the slaves, about thirteen minas. Altogether his visible property[17] was worth more than ninety minas, and apart from this, he had large sums on loan on which he received interest.[18] [36] Diocles began plotting with his sister for this property a long time ago, as soon as Ciron's sons died. He did not try to find her another husband, even though she was still capable of bearing children to one, in case, if she were separated from Ciron, he should plan to dispose of his property in the proper way; but he kept urging her to stay with him by claiming she thought she was pregnant by him, and then pretending she'd accidentally miscarried, so that he was continually hoping he would have children and would not adopt either of us as his son. And Diocles continually slandered my father, alleging that he was plotting against Ciron's property. [37] So he gradually persuaded Ciron to let him manage all the debts that were owed to him and the interest on them, as well as his visible property, seducing the old man by his attentions and blandishments until he took over all his property. He knew that I would seek to gain control of all this property by right when my grandfather died, but he did not try to prevent me from visiting him, taking care of him, or spending time with him, because he was afraid that I would become exasperated and angry with him. Instead, he was preparing someone to claim the property against me, promising him a very small share if he were successful but planning to take the whole property for himself; and he did not even admit to this man that my grandfather was leaving any money, but pretended there was nothing.

[38] As soon as Ciron died, he began making preparations for the funeral, demanding that I pay for it, as you have heard the witnesses testify, but pretending that he'd received the money from our opponent, and he refused any longer to receive it from me, craftily pushing me aside so it might appear that our opponent was burying my grand-

---

[16] The number of these slaves has probably been lost from the text.

[17] Property consisted of "visible" (*phanera*) or real property (land and buildings) and "invisible" (*aphanēs*) property (mostly loans and deposits).

[18] A "modest enough" estate (Davies 1971: 314); cf. above, 8.8n.

father, not I. And when our opponent claimed this house and everything else Ciron left, although he said that he'd left nothing, I didn't think I ought to use force and remove my grandfather's body in such difficult circumstances, and my friends agreed with me about this, but I assisted in the rites and joined in the burial, the expenses being paid out of what my grandfather left. [39] So I acted in this way under compulsion. But to prevent them from gaining any advantage over me by alleging to you that I did not pay any of the funeral expenses, I consulted the exegete[19] and on his advice presented and paid at my own expense for the ninth-day offerings, preparing them in the finest way possible, in order to thwart this sacrilege of theirs, and to remove the impression that they paid for everything and I nothing, but to make clear that I paid my share.

[40] This is pretty much what happened, gentlemen, and why we are involved in this business. If you knew Diocles' shamelessness and how he behaves on other occasions, you would not disbelieve a word of what I've said. The property he possesses, which now makes him so grand, is someone else's because when his three half-sisters by his mother were left as heiresses, he made himself the adopted son of their father, even though the deceased had made no will to this effect.[20] [41] When the husbands of two of the sisters tried to secure their fortune, he shut up the husband of the older one in his house and by plotting disfranchised him,[21] and though he was indicted for hybris,[22] he has not yet been punished for this; and he killed the husband of the younger one using a slave, whom he then smuggled out of the country, and turned the charge against his sister; [42] and by terrifying her with his disgusting behavior, he deprived her son, his ward, of his property—he occupies the farmland, but has given him the stony ground. And to prove I'm telling the truth in this, although his victims

---

[19] An interpreter of sacred law and customs: here, those connected with burial.

[20] The half-sisters' father would have been Diocles' stepfather.

[21] The speaker presumably alleges that Diocles imprisoned the man in his house and then brought a charge against him that he failed to answer, thus losing his civic rights.

[22] By a graphē hybreōs, for which see the Introduction to Dem. 54 above.

are afraid of him, they may yet perhaps be willing to testify for me; if not, I'll produce as witnesses those who know what happened.[23] Please call them here first.

[WITNESSES]

[43] Such, then, is the brutality and violence of Diocles: he has deprived his sisters of their property and, not content with having that, since he has not been punished in any way for it, he has come to deprive us too of our grandfather's fortune. He has given our opponent only two minas (so we hear) but is putting us in danger of losing not only our property but our country as well. For if you are misled into believing that our mother was not a citizen woman, then neither are we citizens, since we were born after the archonship of Eucleides.[24] So is the suit he has fabricated against us really only a trifling matter? While our grandfather and father were alive, we faced no charge, but we lived the whole time free from challenge; [44] but now that they are dead, even if we win today, we will bear a stigma because our rights have been challenged, thanks to this damned Orestes,[25] who was caught in adultery and suffered the appropriate treatment for men who do such things,[26] but even so has not given up the practice, as those who know about it can testify.

You are now hearing, then, what kind of man he is, and you'll learn in even greater detail when we begin our suit against him.[27] [45] But I beg and supplicate you, do not allow me to be insulted and deprived of this estate which my grandfather left, but help me as far as each of you is able. You have sufficient proof from depositions, torture evidence, and the laws themselves that we are the children of Ciron's legitimate daughter and that we have a greater right to inherit his estate than our opponents, being our grandfather's direct descendants. [46] Remember, therefore, the oaths you swore before sitting as jurors,

---

[23] The speaker's uncertainty is purely rhetorical, since he already either has the witnesses' depositions or does not.

[24] In 403/2; see the Introduction, IVB.

[25] See above, 8.3n.

[26] See Dem. 59.66n.

[27] Presumably the one for *hybris* mentioned in 8.41.

the arguments we have put forward and the laws, and pass your verdict for what is just.

I don't know what more I need say: I think you are fully aware of what's been said. But take the remaining deposition, that Diocles was caught in adultery, and read it to the jurors.

[DEPOSITIONS]

LYSIAS 32. AGAINST DIOGEITON

INTRODUCTION

Lysias 32 is not found in the mediaeval manuscripts of Lysias, but it is quoted (with two other speeches) by the rhetorical theorist Dionysius of Halicarnassus in his essay *On Lysias* as an example of Lysias' style.[1] As cited by Dionysius, the text consists of the introduction, the narrative, and part of the proof section. At issue is a private lawsuit dealing with guardianship, which has been brought before a dicastic court by an orphan[2] who has recently become an adult: his brother-in-law (speaking on the young man's behalf because of the latter's inexperience) alleges that the estate has been corruptly mismanaged by its former guardian. Relationships within this family are complicated because the original owner of the property, a man named Diodotus, had married the daughter of his brother Diogeiton.[3] Such uncle-niece marriages were common at Athens and served to keep property within the family. Diodotus had died in battle in 410/09 BC, after leaving his children and his allegedly substantial property in Diogeiton's care, but there had been virtually nothing left when the elder son came of age in the ninth year afterwards.[4]

---

[1] See Usher 1974: 16–99. Dionysius includes a hypothesis (summary) of the speech, for which see Todd 2000: 322.

[2] A Greek *orphanos* had no father (Introduction, IVE) but might have a mother.

[3] Her name is not given, because it was regarded as improper to name a respectable woman during her lifetime in the public context of a lawcourt; see Schaps 1977.

[4] In 401/0. The date of the speech may be a year or two after this.

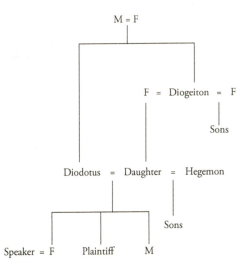

One reason for suspecting that Diodotus may have miscalculated the extent to which his brother could be trusted as guardian (particularly as guardian in charge of liquid assets, which were easier to hide from the heirs than was land) is that both Diogeiton and his daughter appear to have remarried, with both marriages producing sons. Diodotus' own children had therefore become marginal to both households, and the only relative they can find to take the initiative on their behalf is their sister's husband, who is hardly a central figure within the family. Given the dates, however, there may have been good reason for the disappearance of Diodotus' property, because most of it appears to have been invested in ways that were extremely risky (e.g., maritime trade), and the period between his death and his son's majority saw the collapse of the Athenian maritime empire and all that went with it. It is striking that the speaker makes no attempt to counter this point: he may have done so in the lost portions of the speech, or he may have hoped to leave to his opponent the opprobrium of raising an unpopular subject.

After a brief introduction, the speech begins with a lucid statement of the background (4–10), followed by a memorable quoted diatribe against the defendant placed in the mouth of his own daughter (12–17). As a woman, she could not appear in court as a witness, and so this was the only picture the jury would have of her, and it is used effectively

The Value of Diodotus' Estate

	Reference	Athenian Currency	Foreign Currency
Diodotus' Assets			
Silver on deposit (*parakatathēkē*)	5, 13	5 talents (30,000 dr.)	
Maritime loans (*nautika*)	6, 14	7 talents, 40 minas (46,000 dr.)	
Loans on land (*engeios tokos*)	15	100 minas (10,000 dr.)	
Owing from Chersonese	6, 15*	2,000 dr.	
Left with wife	6	20 minas (2,000 dr.)	30 staters**
TOTAL		15 talents (90,000 dr.)	30 staters
Liabilities and Expenditures			
Dowry promised to wife	6	1 talent (6,000 dr.)***	
Dowry promised to daughter	6	1 talent (6,000 dr.)	
Expenditure on children as claimed by Diogeiton	20	7 talents, 7,000 dr. (49,000 dr.)	
Totals			
Size of estate initially admitted by Diogeiton	9, 15	20 minas (2,000 dr.)	30 staters
Size of estate eventually admitted by Diogeiton	28	7 talents, 40 minas (46,000 dr.)	

*It is possible that 32.6 and 32.15 refer to separate investments (the Chersonese is not mentioned at 15). If so, then 2,000 drachmas must be added to Diodotus' total assets.
**From the city of Cyzicus on the Propontis (Sea of Marmara). The value of the Cyzicene stater was 28 drachmas in the mid fourth century but may have fluctuated over time.
***The dowry that Diogeiton eventually paid was only 5,000 drachmas (8).

to create the impression that Diogeiton's behavior has alienated his family and friends. Our text breaks off after a set of arguments about individual expenditures (19–29).

Although calculations based on account books rarely have the capacity to enthrall an audience, these arguments are particularly effective. Small items are used to create pathos (as in the case of the lamb: 21); larger ones are used to create a sense of systematic fraud (as with the maintenance claims in 28). Selected points are supported with evidence to create the impression that other allegations are justified: so, for instance, the argument about the trierarchy in 26–27 is assumed to demonstrate that Diogeiton has been playing the same trick with the tomb and the lamb in 21. We do not of course know the result of the case, or the truth of the speaker's allegations, but artistically this is one of Lysias' most persuasive speeches.

The centrality of the household in this speech, and the role played by Diogeiton's daughter, are discussed in Todd 1993: 202–206.

LYSIAS 32. AGAINST DIOGEITON

[1] If the differences between the parties in this dispute were not so great, gentlemen of the jury, I would not have allowed the plaintiffs to appear before you. In my opinion, it is highly shameful to disagree with family members, and I know that you have a low opinion not only of those who have done wrong but also of those who cannot tolerate ill-treatment at the hands of their relatives. But the plaintiffs have been defrauded of a large amount of money, gentlemen of the jury, and have suffered many terrible things at the hands of those from whom this was least to be expected, and have come to me for help, because I am related to them by marriage. In view of all this, I had no choice but to speak on their behalf. [2] I am married to the plaintiffs' sister, the granddaughter of Diogeiton. After repeatedly entreating both sides, I initially persuaded them to refer the matter to their friends for arbitration, because I thought it important that no outsider should know about their affairs. But Diogeiton could not bring himself to take the advice of any of his own friends about things that were clearly proved to be in his possession. Instead, he preferred to defend himself against lawsuits, to bring counterproceedings alleging that there was no case to answer, and to risk the severest

penalties,[5] rather than to do the right thing and reach a compromise with the indictment (*enklēma*) brought by the plaintiffs. [3] If therefore I can demonstrate that they have been treated more shamefully by their grandfather during his guardianship than anybody in this city has ever been treated even by those who are not relatives, then I ask you to bring justice to their assistance. If I cannot, then you may trust my opponent in every respect and treat us in the future as criminals. I shall try to tell you their story from the beginning.

[4] Diodotus and Diogeiton, gentlemen of the jury, were full brothers by the same father and mother. They divided their invisible property between them, but they held the visible property in common.[6] Diodotus made a lot of money from import trading (*emporia*), so Diogeiton persuaded him to marry his daughter, who was his only child, and they had two boys and a girl. [5] Some time later, Diodotus was called up to serve as a hoplite.[7] He summoned his wife (who was his niece) and her father (who was his father-in-law and his brother and was also grandfather and uncle to the children); he thought that because of these relationships there was nobody who was more likely to behave justly towards his children. He gave him his will and five talents of silver on deposit for safekeeping. [6] He drew attention to seven talents, forty minas that had been lent out on maritime loans,[8] and two thousand drachmas that were owed to him in the Chersonese.[9] He instructed Diogeiton that if anything should happen to him, he was to provide a one-talent dowry for his widow, and give her the contents of the bedroom, and a one-talent dowry for his daughter. He also left behind with his wife twenty minas and thirty Cyzicene

---

[5] A considerable exaggeration; this expression normally designates the death penalty.

[6] For visible and invisible property, see Is. 8.35. The division presumably occurred after their father's death.

[7] Hoplites were heavy-armed infantry.

[8] The total value of these various holdings is very considerable. For the amounts mentioned, and their drachma equivalents, see the Speech Introduction. One further investment is mentioned at 32.15 (one hundred minas invested in loans on land); mention of this may have dropped out of the text here.

[9] Either the Thracian Chersonese (the Gallipoli peninsula) or the Tauric Chersonese (the Crimea).

staters. [7] After completing these transactions and leaving a duplicate copy at home, he went off with Thrasyllus to fight. After his death at Ephesus, Diogeiton for a while concealed her husband's death from his daughter and took possession of the sealed documents he had left behind, saying that he needed them to recover the maritime loans. [8] In due course, he told them about the death, and they performed the customary rites. They continued to live in Piraeus for the first year, because all their supplies had been stored there. When these began to give out, he sent the children to the town (*asty*) and gave their mother in marriage with a dowry of five thousand drachmas, which was one thousand less than her husband had provided for her. [9] In the eighth year after this, the elder of the two young men came of age. Diogeiton summoned him and told him that their father had left them twenty minas of silver and thirty staters. "As a result," he continued, "I have had to spend a lot of my own money on your upkeep. As long as I had enough, I did not mind, but now I too am hard up. Given that you have passed your *dokimasia* and become a man, from now on you must find the means of living for yourself." [10] They were devastated to hear this and went weeping to their mother. Then they brought her to see me. They had been shamefully dispossessed and were reduced to a pitiable state by their sufferings. They wept and pleaded with me not to allow them to be deprived of their inheritance nor to be reduced to destitution by the outrageous treatment (*hybris*) they had received from those who were least expected to behave in this way, but to help them, both for their own and their sister's sake. [11] It would be a long story to recount all the lamentation that took place in my house at that time. In the end, their mother begged and pleaded with me to gather together her father and his friends. She said that even if she had not previously been accustomed to speak in front of men, nevertheless the scale of the disaster would compel her to tell us the whole story of their sufferings. [12] So I went and expressed my feelings to Hegemon, the husband of my opponent's daughter, and talked with the rest of his friends, and persuaded him to undergo an investigation into the money. (Diogeiton at first resisted but was eventually forced into it by his friends.) When the meeting took place, the woman asked him how he had had the heart to treat the children in this way, "given that you are their father's brother, and my own father, and their uncle and grandfather. [13] Even if you were not ashamed of any man, you

ought," she said, "to have feared the gods. But you are the one who
received five talents on deposit from the dead man when he sailed.[10] I
am willing to swear an oath about this in whatever location this man
may name, surrounding myself with the children and swearing
destruction both on them and on those I have borne subsequently.
And yet I am not so wretched, nor do I value money so highly, that I
would depart this life after committing perjury in the name of my own
children or would unjustly take away my father's property." [14] She
then demonstrated that he had received seven talents and four thousand drachmas in maritime loans, and she produced documentation
of this: during the process of dividing up the household, when he
moved from Collytus to the house of Phaedrus,[11] the boys came across
an account book that had been thrown away and brought it to her.
[15] She showed that he had received one hundred minas lent out at
interest on land,[12] and a further two thousand drachmas, and household furniture of considerable value. Moreover, they were receiving
grain every year from the Chersonese. "And did you dare," she said,
"when you had so much money, to say that the father of these boys left
merely two thousand drachmas and thirty staters—the amount that
was left with me and that I handed over to you after his death?
[16] You thought it right to throw out of their own house those who
were your daughter's sons, wearing only threadbare garments, without
shoes, without attendants, without bedding, without clothing, without the household furniture their father left them, and without the
sums on deposit that he placed in your hands. [17] You are at this
moment bringing up my stepmother's children in prosperity, with
plenty of money, and as far as that goes I do not blame you. But you
are wronging my children, by throwing them out of the house in dishonor and by daring to display them in public as beggars rather than
rich men. Such behavior shows that you do not fear the gods, that you

---

[10] Most of the items listed in 13–15 have already been mentioned at 5–6. See
the table in the Speech Introduction.

[11] Phaedrus may be Phaedrus of Myrrhinus (the interlocutor of Socrates in
Plato's *Phaedrus*, for whom see also Lys. 19.15).

[12] I.e., in the form of a mortgage, with land as the security for the debt. (The
contrast is with maritime loans, for which the security is the ship, its cargo, or
both, as at 32.6.)

are not ashamed of my knowing your guilt, and that you do not respect the memory of your brother. Instead, you rate us all as less important than money." [18] By now, gentlemen of the jury, she had recounted terrible things, and all of us who were present had been reduced to such a state by this man's behavior and by the woman's speech—we saw the sufferings the boys had endured, we remembered the dead man and how he had left an unworthy guardian of his property, and we considered how hard it was to find somebody to trust with one's private affairs—we had been reduced to such a state, gentlemen of the jury, that none of those present was able to say anything. Instead, weeping just as much as the victims, we went away in silence.

First of all, then, let my witnesses of this come forward.

[WITNESSES]

[19] I ask you, gentlemen of the jury, to pay close attention to the statement of accounts, so that you may pity the young men because of the scale of what they have suffered, and may realize that my opponent deserves the anger of every citizen. For Diogeiton has reduced all mankind to such a level of mutual distrust that neither alive nor dead can they rely on their closest friends any more than on their bitterest enemies. [20] After denying receipt of part of the money, and eventually acknowledging the rest of it, he has dared to claim that he received and spent seven talents of silver and seven thousand drachmas for two boys and their sister during a period of eight years. He has become so shameless that when he ran out of expenses to claim, he recorded the sum of five obols per day for food for two little boys and their sister. For shoes and laundry and haircuts, instead of a monthly or yearly figure, he recorded as a lump sum over the whole period more than a talent of silver.

[21] On the memorial of their father, he spent no more than twenty-five minas out of the five thousand drachmas he claimed, but he charged half this sum to himself and the rest to their account. And I think you deserve to hear another story as well. He claims, gentlemen of the jury, to have spent sixteen drachmas buying a lamb for the feast of the Dionysia, and of this sum he charged eight drachmas to the boys' account. We were particularly angry about this: it is in this way, gentlemen, that the small things in great crimes sometimes hurt the victims more than the large ones, because they make the wickedness

of the perpetrators so terribly clear. [22] As for the other festivals and sacrifices, he charged to the boys an expenditure of more than four thousand drachmas, and there were all sorts of other things he reckoned up together as a lump sum. It was as if he had been left as guardian for the boys so that he could show them paper instead of money, so that he could make them paupers instead of rich men, and so that they could forget about the enemies (if any) that they had inherited, and should instead fight with their guardian for depriving them of their inheritance. [23] And yet if he had been prepared to behave honestly towards the boys, he could have followed the laws about orphans, which apply to guardians who are incapable of fulfilling their responsibility as well as to those who are capable. He could have rented out the property, thereby ridding himself of many responsibilities, or he could have purchased land and used the income to bring up the children. In either case, they would have been as rich as any Athenian. As it is, it seems to me that he never intended to convert the estate into visible property.[13] Instead, he wanted to keep their property for himself, because he believed that his own wickedness should inherit the dead man's wealth.

[24] The most shocking story of all, gentlemen of the jury, concerns his service as joint trierarch[14] with Alexis the son of Aristodicus. He claimed to have contributed forty-eight minas, but he then charged half of this sum to these boys—even though they were orphans, and the city has not only made them exempt throughout their childhood but has freed them from all liturgies for a year after they come of age. But this man, who is their grandfather, broke the law by charging half the cost of his own trierarchy to his daughter's children. [25] He also sent to the Adriatic[15] a merchant ship with cargo valued at two talents. When it was leaving, he told their mother that the risk was the boys' responsibility, but when it arrived safely and doubled in value, he claimed that the cargo was his own. But if he is going to claim that the losses are theirs, while keeping for himself that part of the property that arrives safely, then he will have no difficulty filling in the accounts

---

[13] See 32.4n.

[14] The trierarchy was a form of liturgy or compulsory public service; see the Introduction, IVC.

[15] Notoriously dangerous for sailing.

to show what the money has been spent on. On the contrary, he will find it all too easy to enrich himself at other people's expense.

[26] It would be a tedious task, gentlemen of the jury, to go through the accounts for you item by item. After I had eventually extracted the documents from him, I took witnesses with me, and since Alexis was dead, I asked his brother Aristodicus whether he had the accounts of the trierarchy. He said that he did, and we went to his house and found that Diogeiton had contributed twenty-four minas to Alexis for the trierarchy. [27] This man claimed, however, to have spent forty-eight minas, so in fact he has charged to the boys precisely the total amount that he spent. But what do you think he has been doing in contexts where nobody else knew his guilty secrets and he had complete control?—given that this is a man who dared to deceive his own grandchildren and charge them forty-eight minas, in dealings that were conducted through other people and that were not difficult to trace.

Let my witnesses of this come forward.

[WITNESSES]

[28] You have heard the witnesses, gentlemen of the jury. However, I will base my calculations on the figure of seven talents, forty minas, which he eventually admitted having received. I will claim nothing in interest payments but will deduct all expenditures from the capital sum. I will allow one thousand drachmas per year (a sum that nobody in the city has ever claimed) for two boys and their sister and their *paidagōgos*[16] and their female slave. That is slightly less than three drachmas per day, [29] and over eight years it comes to eight thousand drachmas. Even so, there remains a balance of six talents and twenty minas out of the original seven talents and forty minas.[17] He cannot show that he has been damaged by pirates, or has suffered losses, or has been paying off creditors. . . .

---

[16] A *paidagōgos* was a male slave who performed the full-time functions of babysitter or nanny for school-aged boys.

[17] The text is uncertain here, and this is one of a number of possible restorations.

DEMOSTHENES 27. AGAINST APHOBUS I

INTRODUCTION

Like Lysias 32, this case involves a suit against guardians for mismanagement of an estate. Demosthenes' father (also named Demosthenes) died in 376, leaving a large estate for his only son, then age seven. He appointed three guardians to manage the estate: Aphobus, Demophon, and Therippides. He also directed his wife, Cleobule, to marry Aphobus and his daughter to marry Demophon when she was old enough, and he provided a substantial dowry for each. When the younger Demosthenes came of age, however, he received only a small fraction of the estate's original value, although (he claims) it should have increased during this period. Demosthenes therefore brought suits against the three guardians for ten talents each, but after winning these, he had to bring additional suits to collect what was owed him (Dem. 27–31). This first speech opens his prosecution of one of the guardians and contains the principal statement of his case against them. It was delivered in 364/3, when he was twenty years old.

He begins by professing his inexperience and his reluctance to go to law—a common type of excuse at the beginning of prosecution speeches, but in this case justified. He then gives an outline of his family situation and of the dispositions made by his dying father, including the appointment of the three guardians. He claims that when he came of age, they handed over to him only about 70 minas' worth of property, although they had themselves registered the estate as being of a much higher value for the purpose of paying the tax called eisphora.

The next part of the speech is the most important: the listing of all the elements of Demosthenes senior's estate, including the value of

The Value of Demosthenes' Father's Estate (*in drachmas*)

Income-producing assets	
Slaves making knives	19,000
Slaves making beds	4,000
Money on loan	6,000
Nonincome-producing assets	
Ivory, iron, wood	8,000
Dye, copper	7,000
House	3,000
Contents of house	10,000
Cash	8,000
Loan to Xuthus	7,000
Deposit at Pasion's bank	2,400
Deposit at Pylades' bank	600
Loan to Demomeles	1,600
Other loans	6,000
Total assets	82,600
Annual income from those assets	
Manufacture of knives	3,000
Manufacture of beds	1,200
Interest on loans	720
Total annual income	4,920

each item and the amounts of income produced. For us, this makes a significant contribution to our understanding of Athenian society and economics. Demosthenes' estimates of the value of the various items are given in the table.[1] (To facilitate calculation all the sums are converted to drachmas.)

Demosthenes claims that by the time he came of age, the estate, including ten years' accumulated income, ought to have been worth about 30 talents, but it is difficult for us to check this claim. He calls for the testimony of witnesses to be read out to confirm many of his figures, but, as often in Athenian speeches, those statements have not been preserved, and we cannot be sure how conclusive their confirma-

[1] The figures are discussed by Davies 1971: 126–131.

tion was.[2] He does seem to press some of his points rather hard, especially where the income is concerned; for example, he assumes that the manufacture of knives and of beds produced the same amount of profit every year and makes no allowance for difficulties in production or changes in market conditions from time to time. Thus, his case may be overstated to some extent; nevertheless, it does appear to be a strong one.

The later part of the speech deals with some subsidiary points, including the guardians' failure to produce Demosthenes senior's written will; their failure to let the estate on lease, which would have absolved them from responsibility for its administration; and the absurd story that Demosthenes senior left the large sum of 4 talents hidden away in the keeping of his wife. Demosthenes concludes with a passage of pathos, pointing out that he, with his mother and sister, will be left in poverty if he loses the case. The speech as a whole is a remarkably accomplished debut by the young orator.

DEMOSTHENES 27. AGAINST APHOBUS I

[1] If Aphobus had been willing to do the right thing, men of the jury, or to refer the disputed questions to our relatives, there would have been no need of trials or proceedings; it would have been enough to abide by their verdict, and I would have had no dispute with him. But since he would not let any decision about our affairs be made by those who are well acquainted with them,[3] and has resorted to you who have no accurate knowledge of them, I am forced to try to obtain justice from him in your court. [2] Now, I know, men of the jury, that it's not an easy matter to contend for the whole of my property against men who are competent speakers and also have powers of manipulation,[4]

---

[2] For Demosthenes' use of evidence in this speech, see Mirhady 2000a: 186–190.

[3] At first Demosthenes and Aphobus agreed to submit their dispute to arbitration by three friends. But when those three gave Aphobus the hint that, if they delivered a verdict under oath (as was normal in private arbitrations), it would be a verdict against him, he promptly withdrew from the arrangement. Cf. Dem. 29.58, 30.2.

[4] This phrase hints at bribery of witnesses.

when because of my youth I'm completely without experience of legal business. Nevertheless, although I'm at a great disadvantage, I have high hopes that I shall obtain justice in your court, and also that, at least to the extent of narrating the events, my own speech will be adequate, so that you won't be left in ignorance of any detail of the facts, and you'll understand the issues on which you will have to vote. [3] I request you, men of the jury, to give me a favorable hearing and, if you decide that I've been treated wrongfully, to give me the support I deserve. I shall make my speech as brief as I can; so I'll try to explain it all to you beginning from the point which will make it easiest for you to understand it.

[4] Demosthenes, my father, men of the jury, left property worth about 14 talents, together with myself, who was aged seven, my sister, who was five, and also our mother, who had brought 50 minas into the house.[5] When he was close to death, he took thought for us and entrusted everything to this man Aphobus and to Demophon son of Demon, both of whom were his nephews, one being the son of his brother and the other of his sister, and also to Therippides of Paeania,[6] who was not a relative but had been his friend since childhood. [5] To the latter he gave the use of 70 minas of my property for the period until I was passed[7] as an adult, so that he might not be induced by desire for money to mismanage any of my affairs; to Demophon he gave my sister and 2 talents for immediate possession;[8] and to Aphobus himself he gave my mother with a dowry of 80 minas, the house for his residence, and the use of my furniture. He believed that, if he made these men even more closely related to me, their guardianship of me would be none the worse for the addition of this relationship. [6] But after receiving those sums of money for themselves at the beginning, and after managing all the other property and being my

---

[5] This means that 50 minas was the amount of her dowry when she was married.

[6] Paeania was also Demosthenes' own deme.

[7] This refers to the scrutiny (*dokimasia*) of a young man for citizenship at the age of eighteen (Introduction, IVA). In effect, Therippides was given an interest-free loan of 70 minas for ten years.

[8] Demophon was to receive the dowry immediately, although the marriage would not take place until the girl was old enough; cf. Dem. 29.43.

guardians for ten years, they have misappropriated all the rest and handed over only the house, fourteen slaves, and 30 minas in cash, amounting to about 70 minas in all.[9]

[7] That's a summary of their offenses, stated as concisely as possible, men of the jury. That this was the total amount of the property which he left, they themselves are my best witnesses; for they arranged on my behalf to make to the symmory contributions of 500 drachmas in each 25 minas,[10] as much as Timotheus son of Conon and men with the highest assessments contributed. But you must hear the details of the items which were producing income and those which were not, and how much each was worth. When you know those exactly, you'll realize that there have never been any guardians who have plundered more shamelessly or more openly than these men have plundered my property.

[8] So first I'll provide witnesses of the fact that they agreed on my behalf to the assessment of this contribution of *eisphora* to the symmory, and next that my father did not leave me poor or possessing property worth 70 minas, but such a large estate that even those men themselves couldn't conceal it from the city because of its extent. [*To the clerk*] Please take and read this testimony.

[DEPOSITION]

[9] So from that too the size of the estate is clear. Out of 15 talents, the assessment was 3 talents; that's the *eisphora* which they thought it right to contribute.[11]

---

[9] Demosthenes later (9–10) gives the original value of the house as 30 minas, and of the slaves as between 6 and 3 minas each. It is not clear how he reaches the total of 70 minas: possibly the house and the slaves had sharply deteriorated in value, or the total does not include the house (and he reckons the slaves at only 3 minas each), or else there is something wrong with the text.

[10] The richer citizens and metics were required from time to time to pay a tax on property (*eisphora*, see the Introduction, IVC). For this purpose, they were divided into groups called symmories. Demosthenes seems to mean here that his guardians registered his estate as being of such a high value that, for each sum of 25 minas payable by the symmory as a whole, he had to pay 500 drachmas (= 5 minas), one-fifth of the total, which was the maximum ever required from one individual.

[11] Because the testimony is not preserved, the meaning of this sentence is obscure to us and has been much disputed. The value of the estate could have been

You'll understand even more exactly when you hear what the estate actually was. My father, men of the jury, left two workshops, each engaged in a not unimportant craft: one with thirty-two or thirty-three knife-makers, worth 5 or 6 minas each, or in some cases at least 3 minas, from whom he was getting a net income of 30 minas a year; the other with twenty bed-makers, who were security for a loan of 40 minas and who brought him a net income of 12 minas; also about a talent of silver, lent at a drachma,[12] on which the interest amounted to more than 7 minas every year. [10] Those were the income-producing assets he left, as these men themselves will agree. Their total capital value amounted to 4 talents 5,000 drachmas, and the income from them to 50 minas a year. Besides those, he left ivory and iron used in the manufacturing and wood for beds worth about 80 minas, and dye and copper purchased for 70 minas; also a house worth 3,000 drachmas,[13] and furniture, cups,[14] gold jewelry, and clothes, my mother's trousseau, all those together worth about 10,000 drachmas, and 80 minas in silver in the house. [11] He left all that at home. In maritime assets[15] he left 70 minas on loan to Xuthus, 2,400 drachmas at Pasion's bank, 600 at Pylades', 1,600 with Demomeles son of Demon,[16] and various loans of 200 or 300 amounting to about a talent. The total sum of this money comes to more than 8 talents 50 minas. You'll find if you check it that the grand total is about 14 talents.[17]

[12] That's the amount of property he left, men of the jury. How much of it has been stolen, and how much each of them has taken

---

estimated at 15 talents, for Demosthenes says that it was actually about 14 talents; cf. 27.11. But 3 talents can hardly be the total amount of *eisphora* paid out of it, which is said later in the speech (37) to have been 18 minas or at any rate not more than 30 minas.

[12] This phrase refers to a standard rate of interest on loans: a drachma per mina per month, equivalent to 12 percent per annum.

[13] The workshops in which knives and beds were made are not listed as separate buildings and must have been in rooms which formed part of the house.

[14] The cups were evidently valuable items, probably silver.

[15] These are loans to merchants of the kind we see in Dem. 35 below.

[16] Pasion, a former slave, was freed and eventually made a citizen (see Isoc. 17 below). Demomeles was a nephew of Demosthenes senior. Xuthus is mentioned in Dem. 29.36 but is otherwise unknown, as too is Pylades.

[17] The figures given actually amount to 13 talents 46 minas.

individually, and how much they are all misappropriating jointly, cannot all be stated in the same allocation of water;[18] it's necessary to take each of them separately. So it will be sufficient to explain what parts of my property Demophon and Therippides have kept at the time when I deliver my prosecutions against them, but I shall speak to you now about what they reveal Aphobus has and what I know he has taken. First, I'll show you that he has kept the dowry of 80 minas, and afterwards the other matters, as briefly as I can.

[13] Immediately after my father's death, Aphobus entered the house and took up residence in accordance with his will, and he took my mother's gold jewelry and the cups which had been left. He kept possession of those, to the value of about 50 minas, and he also received from Therippides and Demophon the proceeds of sale of the slaves[19] to make up the amount of the dowry, 80 minas. [14] Once he had those things, when he was about to sail away to Corcyra as a trierarch,[20] he gave Therippides a written statement that he had them and acknowledged that he had received the dowry. In the first place, Demophon and Therippides, his fellow-guardians, are witnesses of that; besides, Demochares of Leuconoeum, my aunt's husband, and many others have attested that he acknowledged that he had them. [15] For, since he didn't provide my mother with maintenance, although he kept her dowry,[21] and since he refused to lease the estate but thought fit to manage it with the other guardians,[22] Demochares spoke to him about these matters. Aphobus listened to him, and didn't deny that he had the dowry or express indignation at not having received it, but acknowledged it and said that he still had a little disagreement with my mother about some small items of jewelry; when he had got that straightened

---

[18] In one speech timed by the water clock.

[19] Half of the slaves making knives were purchased from the estate by Therippides and Demophon; cf. 27.18, 61.

[20] See the Introduction, IVC.

[21] Whoever held a woman's dowry was legally required to pay for her keep. Demochares' complaint probably means that Cleobule was now living in his house, having moved in with her sister. (The view of Cox 1998: 147, that Cleobule resided with Aphobus without being married to him, is unlikely to be correct; if that had been so, Aphobus would hardly have been accused of failing to maintain her.)

[22] A guardian who did not want to manage his ward's estate himself had the option of letting it to a lessee, so that the rent would be the ward's income.

out, he would deal with her maintenance and the other matters in such a way that everything would be satisfactory for me. [16] But if it becomes clear that he made these acknowledgments to Demochares and the other men who were present, and that he received from Demophon and Therippides the proceeds from the slaves to make up the dowry, and that he himself gave a written statement to his fellow-guardians that he had the dowry, and that he took up residence in the house as soon as my father died, surely it will be obvious, since the matter is agreed by everyone, that he obtained the dowry of 80 minas and that his denial that he received it is quite shameless. [17] [*To the clerk*] To prove that I am telling the truth, take the testimonies and read them.

[DEPOSITIONS]

So in this way he received the dowry and has kept it. But if he didn't marry my mother, the law requires him to owe interest on the dowry, at the rate of 9 obols; but I'll reckon it at only a drachma.[23] If you add together the principal and the income for ten years, it comes to about 3 talents. [18] That sum I can thus prove to you he received and has kept, because he acknowledged it in the presence of all those witnesses. In addition, he has kept 30 minas, which he received as the income from the workshop[24] and has attempted to misappropriate in the most shameless possible way. My father left me an income of 30 minas from the slaves; after these men sold half of them, I should have got 15 minas, proportionately. [19] Therippides, who had charge of the slaves for seven years, reported 11 minas a year, 4 minas less each year than he should have done in proportion. Aphobus, who had charge of them for the first two years, reports nothing at all, but sometimes he says that the workshop was not operating, and sometimes that he wasn't in charge of them himself but the man in charge, Milyas, our freedman, managed them and I should get an account from him. If he tells any of those stories again today, it will be easy to prove that he's lying. [20] If he says it wasn't operating: he himself has rendered accounts of expenditure, not on food for the men but on work, ivory for the workmanship and knife-handles and other supplies; this presumes that the craftsmen were working. He also calculates that he paid Therippides a

---

[23] I.e., 12 percent (see above, 9n); interest at 9 obols would be 18 percent. At a drachma, the total of principal and interest for ten years comes to 2 talents 56 minas.

[24] The next sentences show that this means the slaves making knives.

fee for three slaves he had in my workshop. Yet, if no work was done, Therippides should not have received a fee, and I should not have had this expenditure in the accounts. [21] If on the other hand he says that work was done but there was no sale for the products, surely he ought at least to show that he handed over the products to me and to provide as witnesses the men in whose presence he handed them over. If he hasn't done any of this, he must have kept two years' income from the workshop, 30 minas, since it's so clear that the work was done. [22] If on the other hand he doesn't say any of this but asserts that Milyas managed it all, how can he be believed when he says that he himself paid out the expenditures, more than 500 drachmas, while any profit was kept by Milyas? It seems to me that the opposite would have happened if Milyas had in fact managed it: Milyas would have paid out the expenditures, and Aphobus would have taken the profits, to judge by the rest of his behavior and his impudence. [*To the clerk*] Take these testimonies and read them to them.

[DEPOSITIONS]

[23] So he has kept those 30 minas from the workshop, and eight years' interest on them, which you'll find, if you reckon it at a drachma,[25] is another 30 minas. He, alone and individually, has taken that, and if you add it to the dowry, it makes about 4 talents, including the principal. Now I'll explain to you, one by one, the amounts which he's plundered jointly with the other guardians, and some which he has claimed were not left by my father at all.

[24] First about the bed-makers, whom my father left and these men are making away with: they were security for a loan of 40 minas, and they were twenty in number. I will prove to you that these men are robbing me of them quite shamelessly and openly. They all agree that those slaves were left in our house, and they say that they brought in 12 minas every year for my father; but they themselves report that no profit, not the least bit, came in for me from them in ten years, while Aphobus calculates that the total expenditure on them was nearly 1,000 drachmas; that's how shameless he is. [25] At no point have they handed over to me the men themselves, on whom he says this money was spent. Instead, they tell the emptiest of stories: that

---

[25] See above, 17n.

the man who gave my father the slaves as security is the biggest scoundrel in the world, and that he has defaulted on a large number of friendly loans[26] and defaulted on debts; and they have called a considerable number of witnesses to testify to these facts against him. But who it is who has got the slaves, or how they left the house, or who took them away, or against whom they lost a case about them, they cannot say. [26] Yet, if their story were sound, they would not be producing witnesses of that man's wickedness, which I should not be concerned with at all; instead, they'd be getting hold of the slaves and pointing out the abductors and not letting any of them go. But as it is, in the most highhanded manner possible, although they acknowledge that the slaves were left and they took possession of them and enjoyed the profits from them for ten years, they are now utterly making away with the whole workshop. [*To the clerk*] To prove that what I say is true, please take the testimonies and read them.

[DEPOSITIONS]

[27] Now, Moeriades was not without resources, nor was it a foolish mistake of my father's to make that agreement secured on the slaves, as a very strong proof will show you. After Aphobus took possession of this workshop, as you heard yourselves from the witnesses, he, being a guardian, ought to have prevented anyone else who wished to make an agreement secured on them; but in fact he himself made Moeriades a loan of 500 drachmas secured on those slaves—a loan which he has acknowledged he rightly and properly recovered from him. [28] Yet surely it's a terrible thing if I, whose agreement was made earlier, besides getting no profit from them, have lost the security as well, while the man who made a loan secured on my property and recovered it so much later has obtained both interest and principal out of my property and has suffered no loss. [*To the clerk*] But to prove that I'm telling the truth, take the testimony and read it.

[DEPOSITION]

[29] So just think how much money these men are stealing in the matter of the bed-makers: 40 minas is the actual principal, and ten years' produce from them is 2 talents, for they were getting 12 minas

---

[26] The Greek word (*eranos*) refers to interest-free loans among friends.

every year in income from them. Is that a small sum, from an obscure source and easy to miscalculate? Isn't it quite obvious that it's nearly 3 talents that they've plundered? Since they've purloined it jointly, I think I should recover one-third of it from Aphobus.

[30] And in fact, men of the jury, what they've done in connection with the ivory and iron which were left is similar to that; they don't report those either. Yet, since my father owned so many bed-makers and also owned knife-makers, he can't have failed to leave iron and ivory. Those must have existed; if they hadn't existed, what work would have been done? [31] A man who owned more than fifty slaves and supervised two trades, in one of which easily 2 minas' worth of ivory a month was used for beds, while the knife-factory used at least as much again together with iron—they say he left none of those materials! That's how impudent they've become. [32] Their story is incredible, as it's easy to see from what they themselves say. The quantity[27] left by my father was so large that it was sufficient not only for his own workers' use but also for anyone else who wished to buy it, as is clear from the fact that he himself used to sell it during his lifetime, and after his death Demophon and Aphobus sold it to customers from my house. [33] Yet what amount must be assumed to have been left, when it was evidently sufficient for such large numbers of workers and besides was being sold by my guardians? A small amount? Or much more than is included in the charge? [*To the clerk*] Take these testimonies and read them to them.

[DEPOSITIONS]

That ivory amounts to more than a talent, but they haven't made available to me either the ivory itself or the proceeds; they've completely made away with that too.

[34] In addition, men of the jury, in accordance with the accounts they have rendered, I shall prove to you from their own acknowledgments of what they received that the three of them have kept more than 8 talents of my money, and that of this Aphobus individually has taken 3 talents 1,000 drachmas. I shall reckon their expenditures separately, at a higher rate than they do, and I shall deduct what they have

---

[27] The following sentences show that this refers only to ivory, not iron.

paid me from these amounts, to show you that their actions display no small degree of impudence. [35] The amounts of my money which they acknowledge receiving are: Aphobus, 108 minas apart from what I shall now prove he has kept; Therippides, 2 talents; Demophon, 87 minas. That makes 5 talents 15 minas. Of this, the amount which was not received all at once—the income from the slaves[28]—is nearly 77 minas, and the amount they received immediately is a little less than 4 talents. If you add to that the ten years' interest at a rate of only a drachma, you'll find that with the principal it comes to 8 talents 1,000 drachmas.[29] [36] The cost of maintenance[30] is to be reckoned against the 77 minas coming from the workshop. Therippides paid 7 minas each year for this purpose, and I acknowledge receiving it. So, since they expended 70 minas on my maintenance in ten years, I am giving them additional credit for the extra 700 drachmas, reckoning the expenditure at a higher rate than they do. What they handed over to me when I was passed[31] as an adult and the sum they contributed as *eisphora* to the city[32] has to be deducted from the amount of more than 8 talents. [37] The sum paid me by Aphobus and Therippides was 31 minas, and they calculate that the contributions of *eisphora* were 18 minas. I'll overestimate this at 30 minas, to leave them no room to dispute it. If you deduct this talent from the 8 talents, 7 talents are left, and, from their own acknowledgments of what they received, that's what they must have kept. So, even if they misappropriate everything else and deny having it, they should have repaid that amount, since they acknowledge getting those sums from my property. [38] But, in

---

[28] The profits made in the course of ten years from the manufacture of knives.

[29] On the figures given, the principal (without the income from the slaves) and ten years' interest on it amount to at least 8 talents 4,000 drachmas, so it seems likely that Demosthenes committed an error in his calculation (in 37 he takes the amount as 8 talents).

[30] Food, clothing, and other expenses such as schooling for Demosthenes during his boyhood. Maintenance for his mother and sister should have been paid for by their prospective husbands, Aphobus and Demophon, using the dowries which had been left for them.

[31] See above, 5n.

[32] See above, 7n.

fact, what do they do? They report no interest from the money and say they have spent the whole of the principal too, along with the 77 minas; and Demophon has recorded that I owe him money in addition! Isn't that huge and blatant effrontery? Isn't it the extreme of terrible avarice? What in the world does count as terrible, if such extreme behavior is not considered so? [39] Aphobus for his own part acknowledges receiving 108 minas, and he has kept both that amount and ten years' income from it, about 3 talents 1,000 drachmas. [*To the clerk*] To prove that what I say is true, and in the accounts of the guardianship each of them acknowledges receiving that sum and calculates that it was all spent, take the testimonies and read them.

[DEPOSITIONS]

[40] On this matter, men of the jury, I think you understand well enough the extent of the thefts and crimes of each of these men. You would have still more exact knowledge if they'd been willing to hand over to me the will which my father left. It records, my mother tells me, all that my father left, and the property from which these men were to receive what was given to them,[33] and instructions to lease the estate.[34] [41] When I ask for it, however, they acknowledge that a will was left, but they don't produce it. They do that because they don't want to reveal the size of the property which was left, and which they've plundered, and to conceal their possession of the legacies—as if they weren't going to be easily shown up by the facts themselves. [*To the clerk*] Take for the jury the testimonies of the men in whose presence they gave their answers, and read them.

[DEPOSITIONS]

[42] He[35] says that there was a will, and he testifies that the 2 talents were given to Demophon and the 80 minas to Aphobus; but he does not say that the will also included the 70 minas which Therippides

---

[33] The sums listed in 5.

[34] See above, 15n.

[35] Therippides. Presumably the testimonies just read reported the answers which had been given by Demophon and Therippides to questions posed perhaps at the public arbitrations of their respective cases; cf. 49n.

got, nor the size of the property which was left, nor the instructions to lease the estate, for it's not to his advantage to acknowledge those things too. [*To the clerk*] Now take this man's answer.

[DEPOSITION]

[43] He[36] too says that there was a will and that the cash raised from the copper and the dye was paid to Therippides—which the latter doesn't mention—and the 2 talents to Demophon; but as for what was given to himself, he says it was specified[37] but that he himself didn't assent to it—so that people won't think he received it. He also does not report that the size of the property as a whole was specified, nor the leasing of the estate; to acknowledge those too is not to his advantage either. [44] So, although they omit the property from the will, nonetheless their respective statements about how much money was given to the others make it plain what amount was left. If my father spent 4 talents 3,000 drachmas on giving two of them 3 talents 2,000 drachmas as dowries and the other the use of 70 minas, it's obvious to everyone, I suppose, that the property he was leaving to me, from which he took those sums, was not a small one but more than double that amount. [45] I don't suppose he wanted to leave me, his son, poor, while desiring to make these men, who were rich, still richer; rather, it was because of the large amount that was being left to me that he gave Therippides so much money and Demophon the 2 talents to use, although he wasn't going to marry my sister yet, so as to ensure one of two things: either he would encourage them to perform their duties as guardians better because of the gifts or, if they turned out to be bad guardians, you would show them no mercy when, after being given so much, they wronged me in this way. [46] And then Aphobus himself, besides the dowry, got some female slaves[38] and was residing in the house, and when he should have given an account of these, he says it's his own business; and he's become so avaricious that he has even deprived my teachers of their fees and has failed to make some of

---

[36] Aphobus, whose answer must have been reported in this testimony.

[37] In the will.

[38] Along with Demosthenes' house, Aphobus evidently took over the domestic servants in it.

the payments of *eisphora*—though he charges them to me. [*To the clerk*] Take and read these testimonies to the jury too.

[DEPOSITIONS]

[47] How, then, could one prove more clearly that he has plundered everything, not keeping his hands off even small items, than by proving in this manner, with so many witnesses and arguments, that he acknowledged that he received the dowry and gave the guardians a written statement that he had it; that he had the use of the workshop and didn't report the income; [48] that some of the other property he sold and didn't hand over the proceeds, while some he kept for himself and concealed it; besides, that he committed so many thefts which were proved in accordance with the accounts he himself rendered; and in addition, that he concealed the will, sold the slaves, and managed everything else in a manner that not even my worst enemies would have done? I don't know how one could prove it more clearly.

[49] Before the arbitrator[39] he had the audacity to say that he used the money on my behalf to pay a large number of debts to his fellow guardians Demophon and Therippides[40] and that they took much of my property; but he could not prove either of those statements. He did not show in the written accounts that my father left me in debt, and did not produce as witnesses the men to whom he said the money had been paid; nor was the amount of money he ascribed to his fellow guardians equal to the sum he himself had evidently received, but a great deal less. [50] When he was questioned by the arbitrator about this in detail, and was asked whether he managed his own property from the profits or by spending the capital, and whether, if he had been a ward, he would have accepted this account from his guardians

---

[39] For arbitration, see the Introduction, VB. In the present case, the arbitrator's verdict was in favor of Demosthenes, and Aphobus has insisted on having a trial by jury.

[40] The sentence is ambiguous, but probably Aphobus' claim was that he handed over to Demophon and Therippides funds with which they paid off debts owed by Demosthenes senior to other men, rather than that Demophon and Therippides themselves were the creditors.

or would have wanted to get back the capital with the accrued income, he gave no answer to that, but he made an offer: he said that he was ready to show that the value of my property was 10 talents, and that if there was any shortfall he would make up the difference himself. [51] But when I told him to show that to the arbitrator, he didn't do so. Nor did he show that his fellow-guardians had handed the property over—if he had, the arbitrator would not have decided against him—but he submitted a testimony to that effect, which he'll try to explain to you.[41] So if today too he says that I have the property, ask him who handed it over, and demand that he produce witnesses for each item.[42] [52] And if he says that I have it in the sense that he calculates what is in the hands of each of the other two guardians, it will be clear that he's giving a figure too low by double[43] and still not showing that I actually have it. For, just as I proved that he has kept that large amount, I shall also show that each of the others has kept no less than that. So that's not what he must say; he must argue that either he himself or his fellow-guardians have handed it over. If he doesn't show that, how does this offer of his deserve your notice? He still doesn't show that I have my property.

[53] Not knowing what to say about all this before the arbitrator, and being refuted point by point, just as he is now before you, he had the audacity to tell an absolutely terrible lie, that my father left me 4 talents buried away and put my mother in charge of it. His aim in saying this was that if I expected him to say the same thing now, I should spend time refuting it when I ought to be presenting other charges against him to you, whereas if I were to pass over it on the assumption that it wouldn't be mentioned, he would assert it now, to make me seem rich and less deserving of your sympathy. [54] He didn't submit any testimony of this when he dared to say it; he just made a bare statement and assumed he would be believed without

---

[41] Evidently this testimony just stated in general terms that Demosthenes had already received all his property, without giving details.

[42] This is merely a rhetorical flourish. After an arbitration it was not legally permitted to introduce new testimony at the trial.

[43] He will still be speaking of 10 talents, instead of the 30 talents which Demosthenes claims.

difficulty. When one asks him what he spent so much of my money on, he says he paid off debts on my behalf and tries at this point to make me a poor man; but when he likes, he makes me a rich man, it seems, if my father left me so much money at home. But it's not possible that he's telling the truth, and none of this can have happened, as it's easy to tell for many reasons. [55] If my father had distrusted these men, obviously he would not have entrusted the rest of his property to them, and if he'd left this money in hiding, he wouldn't have told them. It would be strange insanity to tell them about what was hidden if he was not going to make them guardians of his known property; but if he did trust them, he surely wouldn't have put most of his money in their hands and not given them charge of the rest. Nor would he have given this money to my mother to look after while giving her in marriage herself to Aphobus, who was one of the guardians; it doesn't make sense to try to protect the money by means of my mother while putting one of the men he distrusted in charge of both her and the money. [56] Besides, if any of this were true, do you think Aphobus would not have married her, when she was given to him by my father? He already had her dowry of 80 minas as her future husband, but then he married the daughter of Philonides of Melite.[44] If there had been 4 talents in the house in my mother's possession, as he alleges, don't you think he would have rushed to get control of it along with her? [57] He and his fellow-guardians seized so disgracefully the visible property which most of you too were aware my father had left: would he have refrained from taking, when he could, money of which you were not likely to have any knowledge? Who could believe that? It can't be so, men of the jury, it can't be. My father handed over to these men all the money he left, and Aphobus is going to tell this story to diminish your sympathy for me.

[58] I have many other accusations which I could make against him, but by mentioning one, which sums them all up, I'll dispose of all his lines of defense. He could have avoided all this trouble if he'd leased the estate in accordance with these laws. [*To the clerk*] Take the laws and read them.

---

[44] On this marriage, see Dem. 30. For the deme Melite, see above, Dem. 54.7n.

[LAWS]

It was in accordance with those laws that, from an estate of 3 talents 3,000 drachmas, Antidorus in six years was paid 6 talents and more as a result of its being leased, as some of you saw; for Theogenes of Probalinthus, the lessee of the estate, counted out that sum in the agora. [59] In my case, from an estate of 14 talents in ten years, in proportion to the length of time and the lease of Antidorus' estate, more than triple the sum could reasonably be expected to have accrued; so ask him why he didn't do that. If he says it was better for the estate not to be leased, let him show not that I have received double or triple but merely that the original sum has all been paid to me. But if, out of 14 talents, they've passed over to me less than 70 minas, while one of them[45] has put down that I owe him money in addition, how can it be right to accept anything that these men say? Surely it can't be.

[60] Although such substantial property was left to me as you heard at the beginning, producing 50 minas as the income of one-third of it, and these men with their insatiable desire for money, even if they didn't want to lease the estate, could from that income, while leaving the assets just as they were, have paid both for my maintenance and for the city's taxation and have saved up the surplus from that in addition, [61] and by investing the rest of the property, which was double that amount, could have taken moderate amounts from it for themselves, if they had a desire for money, and at the same time, besides preserving my capital, could have increased my estate from the income, yet they did none of those things. Instead, by selling to one another the most valuable of the slaves[46] and making away with others[47] entirely, they deprived me of even the existing income and procured no small income for themselves out of my property. [62] After getting hold of all the rest in that disgraceful manner, they all in unison assert that over half of the money was never left to me at all, and assuming the property to have been only 5 talents, they have rendered their accounts on the basis of an estate of that size; and it's not that

---

[45] Demophon; cf. 38.

[46] Half of the slaves making knives; cf. 13, 18.

[47] The slaves making beds; cf. 24–29.

they fail to declare income from it and produce only the principal, but they quite impudently allege that the capital itself has been spent. And they are not at all ashamed of this audacity.

[63] What would have become of me under their guardianship if I'd been their ward for a longer time? They wouldn't be able to say. When, after a period of ten years, I've recovered such a small amount from two of them and am put down as owing money besides to the other, surely indignation is justified. It's absolutely clear: if I'd been left fatherless at the age of a year and had been their ward for six years longer, I wouldn't have received even this small amount back from them. If the sums they mention have been properly spent, what has now been handed over wouldn't have lasted for six years; either they'd have been paying for my maintenance themselves or they'd have let me die of starvation. [64] When other estates worth 1 or 2 talents have doubled or tripled in value as a result of being leased, so as to be found suitable for liturgies,[48] surely it's a terrible thing if my estate, which was accustomed to performing trierarchies and making large contributions of *eisphora*,[49] will be unable to make even small ones because of these men's shameless activities. What transgressions can one mention which they have not committed? They have concealed the will, expecting that that would not be noticed; they have employed the profits to administer their own property and used my money to make their capital much greater than it was before; and they have completely demolished the principal of my property, as if we[50] had done them the greatest harm! [65] Even when you convict any public offenders, you don't deprive them of all their possessions, but you take pity on their wives and children and leave something for them; but these men are so different from you that even after receiving gifts from us to encourage them to perform their duties as guardians rightly, they have treated us in this insolent way. They didn't even show respect, much

---

[48] There was no fixed property qualification for liability to the liturgies (Introduction, IVC), but possession of property worth about 4 talents was considered enough to make a man likely to be called on to perform those services.

[49] See above, 7n.

[50] "We" may here be taken to mean Demosthenes senior and Demosthenes himself.

less pity, for my sister, who was granted 2 talents[51] by my father but will now get none of what is due to her. They are like bitter enemies, not friends and relatives left behind by him, and they care nothing for family ties.

[66] I am the unhappiest of men, being left with no resources either to dower her for marriage or to manage the rest of my life. Besides, the city is pressing me for *eisphora*, quite justly, for my father left me sufficient property for that purpose, but these men have taken all the money which was left. [67] And now that I'm attempting to recover my property, I'm put at a very serious risk. If Aphobus gets off—as I trust he won't—I shall have to pay *epōbelia* of 100 minas.[52] If you convict him, his penalty is to be assessed, and he'll make the payment not from his own money but from mine; but that penalty for me is a fixed one, so that I shall not only lose my patrimony but be disfranchised as well, if you don't take pity on me today.

[68] So I request you, men of the jury, and beg and entreat you, bearing in mind both the laws and the oaths you swore on becoming jurors, to give me the support I deserve and not to attach more importance to this man's pleas than to mine. It's right for you to sympathize not with people who commit crimes but with those who are unfortunate beyond expectation; not with those who deprive others of their property in this ruthless way but with me, who has long been deprived of what my father left me, and am insulted by these men besides, and now am in danger of disfranchisement. [69] I think my father would be deeply grieved if he could see that the dowries and gifts he gave these men have put me, his son, at risk of *epōbelia,* and that, while some other citizens before now have dowered from their own money daughters of poor men who were relatives or even just friends, Aphobus refuses even to repay the dowry he received, though it's now the tenth year.

---

[51] Her dowry.

[52] In certain cases, a prosecutor who lost had to pay to his successful opponent a penalty of one-sixth of the sum he had claimed, called *epōbelia* (an obol per drachma). If he failed to pay it, he suffered disfranchisement (*atimia*), meaning loss of public rights. Demosthenes was claiming 10 talents from each of the three guardians.

PART IV COMMERCE AND THE ECONOMY

〰〰〰〰〰〰〰〰〰〰〰〰〰〰〰〰〰〰〰〰〰〰〰〰〰〰〰〰〰〰〰〰〰〰〰〰

The classical Greek economy was predominantly agricultural, and much of the countryside was filled with family farms, such as the one in Demosthenes 55. Small-scale commercial enterprises flourished throughout the city. As we see in Demosthenes 27 (above), workshops employing anywhere from one or two to several dozen slaves made furniture, weapons, and many other goods; Hyperides 3 (*Against Athenogenes*) illustrates the sale of one of these. Other merchants, like the speaker of Lysias 24, sold goods and services from small stalls set up in the agora and elsewhere in the city. To the southeast of Athens were rich silver mines, which the city leased to individuals who mined and refined the ore.

In addition, Athens' port, Piraeus, was home to a large market of goods moving to and from ports all over the Mediterranean. In the fifth century, with its control of the sea, Athens established itself as a major center of trade and commerce. Most important, the city became dependent on foreign imports for most of the grain needed to feed its people. In return, it exported produce, especially olive oil, and finished goods, such as pottery. The commercial success of Athens was made possible in part by the availability of loans through private parties and banks that financed commercial operations of various types. They lent money to merchants to buy goods at home for sale abroad and to buy other goods (primarily grain) for import, contracting for repayment when a ship returned to Athens (Isoc. 17). Athenian lending practices were remarkably modern in some respects, such as the use of variable interest rates and the use of collateral as security. Special courts with slightly different rules heard cases involving these maritime contracts (one of which is cited at some length in Dem. 35).

DEMOSTHENES 55. AGAINST CALLICLES

〰〰〰

INTRODUCTION

We cannot date this speech, and we know nothing about the people involved in this dispute beyond what is in the text, not even the name of the speaker. Nevertheless, the speech is interesting for its portrayal of a quarrel that flared between neighboring families over difficulties faced by Attic farmers working steep slopes subject to occasional torrential rainstorms. We have evidence in this speech both for the private exchanges of the neighbors, first cordial, then rancorous, and for their turn to litigation to settle, or perhaps to protract, the dispute.

The speaker assumes that the jury is familiar with the sort of terrain he describes and the precise meaning of various terms for gullies, ditches, roads, and walls. As we are not so well informed, there is some uncertainty about what he claims has happened. A recent account reconstructs the events as follows (Foxhall 1996: 47–48).

The dispute in this speech centers on damage caused by runoff water,[1] allegedly because the defendant (the speaker) had built a wall impinging on the main outlet for the water, a . . . seasonal watercourse. Careful reading of the text (especially 55.10–11) suggests that the disputants had plots on either side of a large gully, which for most of its course coincided with a road. The speaker claims that in the past the field had been neglected. The implication of his description of this neglect in . . . §11 is that during this

---

[1] All we know about the alleged damage is what the speaker says in 24. Callicles undoubtedly described damages more grave than the wetting of a small quantity of grain.

time the [seasonal watercourse] . . . had begun to change its course and the speaker's father had built a field boundary wall, which also served to encourage the seasonal river to go back into its old bed. Both vines and figs were planted on the plot belonging to the speaker (. . . §13). Though the speaker tries to imply they are old, they may have been planted by his father. There were old grave memorials on the land as well. The speaker's trees may have been planted along the road, like those he alleges his opponent to have; that is, planted along the road and then walled in when the trees were quite large.

The speaker is defending himself in a *dikē blabēs,* a private action for recovery of damages. This was a popular category of legal action, employed in a broad variety of circumstances. Some scholars have argued that the speech displays some special variants of the simple *dikē blabēs:* the allegation that the speaker's father had violated a specific law against obstruction of a natural watercourse that could cause damage to another's property, and a penalty that required the defendant, if he could not pay a fine of one thousand drachmas, to surrender to the plaintiff either the section of land where the obstruction was created or the entire plot. That fixed fine that the speaker mentions at 28 is very puzzling, for the case at hand would seem to be an *agōn timētos* (Introduction, VC) with no fixed penalty: see 1, 2, 28, 34, and 35 (with notes). For discussion of this point, see Wolff 1943; MacDowell 1978: 136–137; Todd 1993: 134 and 280–281.

Two recent books discuss the speech as evidence for the litigation culture of fourth-century Athens: Christ 1998, 174–176, and Johnstone 1999, 46–47.

DEMOSTHENES 55. AGAINST CALLICLES

[1] Men of Athens, it turns out that there is nothing harder than having a wicked, greedy neighbor; and that is just what has now happened to me. You see, in his desire to get his hands on my property,[2] Callicles has abused me with malicious litigation (*sykophantōn*).[3] First,

---

[2] The word here translated "property" (*choria*) sometimes carries the more specific meaning "field" or "farm."

[3] See the Introduction, VE.

he got his cousin to dispute the ownership of my property. [2] But after Callicles was plainly shown to be in the wrong, and I survived their plotting, he then got from arbitrators two judgments by default:[4] one was in his own name for one thousand drachmas, the other he got by talking his brother, Callicrates here, into bringing a suit. So I ask all of you to listen and pay attention, not because I am myself good at speaking but so that you may learn from the facts themselves that I am plainly the victim of malicious litigation. [3] I have one answer, men of Athens, to everything they say, and it is a just answer: my father enclosed this field shortly before I was born, and while his neighbor Callipides, the father of these men, was still alive and of course had more accurate knowledge than these men do; Callicles was already a grown man at this time and living in Athens. [4] During all these years, no one ever came forward with a complaint or blamed my father, though clearly in those days too there were many rainstorms.[5] And there was nothing to keep someone from complaining right from the start if my father harmed anyone by enclosing our property. But no one asked him not to do it or made a formal protest for the more than fifteen years that my father lived after that—and their father Callipides lived just as long. [5] Really, Callicles, back then, when you saw the ditch[6] being walled off, you certainly could have complained right away, going to my father and saying, "Tisias, why are you doing this? You're walling off the ditch? But then the rain will flood *our* property." That way, if my father had agreed to stop, there would have been no dispute between us; but if he shrugged off the complaint and later a problem like this arose, you would have the men present at that conversation to serve as witnesses.

---

[4] "Judgments by default" (*dikai erēmoi,* lit. "deserted cases") could be awarded by arbitrators, magistrates, or juries against parties who did not appear for the relevant proceeding. It is curious that the speaker does not explain his absence, especially if the case at hand was an appeal from the first arbitrator's award or the one thousand drachmas was specifically a penalty for nonappearance (see Harrison 1968: 250–251).

[5] Rain in Greece is infrequent but often torrential when it does come.

[6] The Greek word, *charadra,* is translated "ditch" to suggest that it was created, or at least modified, by human agency. It may also be translated "seasonal watercourse" or "gully." It would be dry most of the year but could become the bed of a fast-flowing river in times of heavy winter rains.

[6] Then, by Zeus, you should have proven to everybody that there *was* a ditch,[7] so you could have shown—not just by making speeches but in fact—that my father was doing wrong. Well, not one of them thought it worthwhile to do any of that, because in that case you would not have got the judgment by default against me that you did get, [7] and you wouldn't have profited by malicious litigation. Instead, from his own exact knowledge, my father would have shown what the circumstances were and would have easily refuted these conniving witnesses. I suppose you all look down on me as young and inexperienced. Still, men of Athens, I present their own deeds as the strongest witnesses against all these men. Why, after all, did no one get depositions or bring a complaint or protest even once, but they were content to overlook the wrongs done to them?

[8] I think, then, that I have said enough in answer to their shamelessness. But, men of Athens, I will try to explain to you still more clearly so that you will know that my father did nothing wrong in walling off his property or in anything else and that everything these men have said against me is a lie. [9] In fact, they themselves acknowledge that the property belongs to us, and once this fact is admitted, if you saw the property you would know for sure that I am the victim of malicious litigation. For this reason, it was I who wanted to turn the matter over to knowledgeable, impartial arbitrators, not these men, as they are now trying to claim. This point too will soon be clear to everyone. Please, gentlemen, by Zeus and the gods, do pay attention. [10] You see, there is a road between my property and theirs, and there is a hill that surrounds our properties. As it happens, when rainwater runs off the hill, it is sometimes carried into the road, sometimes into the fields; and the part of the water that flows into the road continues down the road if there's no obstruction, but where there's some blockage, then it is forced to overflow into the fields. [11] And indeed, gentlemen of the jury, after a heavy rain it happened that the water flowed into this field. The field was neglected at that time: it was not yet owned by my father but by a man who was altogether disgruntled with the place and more an urban type. Two or three times the water came in and damaged the fields and cut more and more of a path in

---

[7] Clearly the exact boundary of the ditch is at question, not the existence of *any* watercourse in the area. See below, 10.

the ground. It was in fact because my father saw this happening—so I hear from people who know about it—and because the neighbors were grazing animals on the field and passing through it, that he built this dry wall.[8] [12] And I will provide you, men of Athens, knowledgeable witnesses of the truth of what I say and also proofs much more powerful than witnesses. Now, Callicles says that by walling off the ditch, I do him an injury. But I will show that this is my farm, not a ditch.[9] [13] If it is not agreed that the land is our private property, then we would perhaps be guilty of building something on public land; but the fact is that they do not dispute our ownership, and there are trees, vines, and figs planted on the land. Really, who would think it a good idea to set these plants to grow in a ditch? Nobody, of course. Who would bury his ancestors there? I don't suppose anybody would do that either. [14] But both of these things, gentlemen of the jury, were done. In fact not only were the trees planted before my father enclosed the farm with the dry wall but the ancient monuments were there before we acquired the land. Really, what argument could be more compelling than these facts, men of Athens? The facts give clear proof. [*To the clerk*] Now, please take all the depositions and read them out.

[DEPOSITIONS]

[15] You have heard the depositions, men of Athens. Don't you think they attest explicitly that the property is full of trees and that there are some memorials on it and other things that you find on most other properties; and also that the farm was enclosed while these men's father was still alive; and that neither they nor any other neighbors opposed it? [16] It is also worth hearing, gentlemen of the jury, about the other things Callicles has said. First, consider whether any of you has ever seen or heard of a ditch running along a road. I don't think there is a single such ditch in the whole country.[10] Why would anyone dig a ditch that would carry water coming down the public road into

---

[8] I.e., a wall made of stones fitted together but not held in place by mortar. For a general description of the sort of trouble neighboring farmers could make for each other, see Plato, *Laws* 843–846.

[9] I.e., not a strip, serving when dry as a public road, between two properties.

[10] This passage shows that paths and drainage channels normally coincided in the Attic countryside.

his private property? [17] Second, who among you, whether you live in the countryside or in town, by Zeus, would put up with water flowing down the road getting onto his property or house? Just the opposite: don't we all normally block it up and divert it with a wall if it comes in under pressure? So this man, then, thinks I should let the water from the road on to my property and then, once it has passed his property, should direct the flow back onto the road. But then the neighbor farming the next piece of land will complain. In fact, *everybody* will be able to make the same complaint as these men make. [18] And this too: if I hesitate to direct the water onto the road, I guess I would have to be downright intrepid to let the water out on the adjoining property. Considering that I am being sued for a fixed amount because water running off the *road* came down on this man's property, what will happen to me, by Zeus, at the hands of those who suffer damages from water flowing from *my land* onto their land? If I won't be allowed to discharge water that comes onto my land into either the road or other properties, gentlemen of the jury, by the gods, what is there left for me to do? Surely Callicles won't make me drink it up, will he? [19] Having had this treatment from these men, and many other terrible things besides, I would be happy simply not to owe any additional penalties[11]—never mind getting legal satisfaction. If there *were* a ditch to take water up again past my property, perhaps I would be in the wrong if I didn't let the water come onto my land—there are, to be sure, recognized drainage ditches on some other properties. The farmers highest up take the water in these ditches, as they take the water draining from the houses,[12] and likewise other farmers take the water from them. But no one gives me water in this way, and no one takes any from me. So how could this be a ditch? [20] I suppose water flooding in has, in the past, damaged the property of many men who didn't take precautions against it, and now it has damaged

---

[11] A reference to the thousand drachmas he has been assessed by the arbitrator (2).

[12] The Greek here normally refers to heavy winter rain, but the speaker is most probably not referring to rainwater but to the drainage of excess water from the house. Many houses of the period have drains leading from the inner court to streets or alleys.

this man's property. What's most outrageous of all is this: Callicles puts up a huge stone wall because water flows onto his property, then sues me on the grounds that my father, when this happened to *his* property, did wrong by building an enclosing wall. But if all who suffer damages from flooding in that area prosecute me, my fortune would not be enough, even if multiplied several times over. [21] Now, these men are different from the others to this extent: even though they have suffered no damages, as I will soon show you clearly, while the others have endured many substantial losses, these men alone have the nerve to bring a suit against me. And yet anyone else would have *more* right than they to do this. If my opponents have suffered any damages at all, they have done it to themselves, and they are just engaging in malicious litigation. The others, if nothing else, at least are not guilty of that. But to keep me from getting everything confused as I talk, [*to the clerk*] please take my neighbors' depositions.

[DEPOSITIONS]

[22] Isn't it terrible, gentlemen of the jury, that these men, who have endured damages so great, bring no complaint against me—neither do any of the others who have had bad luck, but instead they put up with their fortune, while this man here engages in sykophancy? You will soon learn more clearly from the depositions that Callicles himself did wrong, first in making the road narrower by extending his wall so as to bring the trees on the road into his own property, then by throwing rubble out into the road, which made it higher and narrower. [23] I will now try to explain to you that he has brought such a serious charge against me, though he suffered no significant loss or injury. Now then, my mother was a friend of these men's mother before they started to bring malicious prosecutions against me. They would visit each other, as you would expect women living as neighbors in the countryside to do and whose husbands, while alive, were friends. [24] My mother went over to their mother's place, and their mother wailed over what had happened and showed her the damage. This is how we learned everything about it, gentlemen of the jury. I am telling you what I heard from my mother. If I tell the truth, may everything turn out well for me, but if I'm lying—the opposite. She said—I swear it—that she saw and heard from their mother that the barley had got

wet; and my mother herself saw it being dried out, and it did not amount to three *medimnoi*; and the wheat came to about half a *medimnos*.[13] And my mother said that a jar of olive oil had fallen over but wasn't damaged.

[25] Gentlemen of the jury, this is the extent of what happened to them; for *this* I am a defendant in a suit for one thousand drachmas. Say my opponent had repaired an old wall; this too would not be something to be charged to my account—a wall that did not fall down or suffer any damage. The upshot is that if I agreed with them that I am responsible for everything that happened to them, well, *that* is what got wet. [26] Why do I need to say anything more, when, from the start, my father did no wrong in enclosing his property, and my opponents never complained over such a long stretch of time, and our other neighbors never made a complaint against me, even though they had often sustained dreadful losses, and you are all accustomed to direct water from your houses and properties onto the road and not, by Zeus, let water from the road flow into your property? It is clear from these facts that I am, plainly, the victim of sykophancy and am guilty of nothing, and they did not sustain the damages they complain about. [27] But so that you know that they threw rubble on the road, and that they narrowed the road by bringing their wall forward, and further that I offered an oath to their mother and summoned my own mother to swear to the same oath, please [*to the clerk*] take the depositions and the summons.

[DEPOSITIONS, CHALLENGE]

[28] Then, could there be men more shameless than these men or more blatant in their sykophancy? After they brought forward their wall and covered up the road with rubble, they sue other people for damages and, on top of that, bring a suit with a fixed penalty for one thousand drachmas, these men who did not lose altogether even fifty drachmas? And consider, gentlemen of the jury, how many people have happened to sustain losses to their farms from floods, whether in Eleusis[14] or elsewhere. And still, Earth and Gods, these people will not think it right to recover their losses from their neighbors! [29] For my

---

[13] A *medimnos* is about 52 liters.

[14] A town west of Athens, subject to flooding by the Cephisus river.

part, though I am the man most entitled to be angry when the road got narrower and higher, I keep my peace. But these men are so superior, so it seems, that they maliciously prosecute the men they have wronged. But, Callicles, if you may enclose your own property, certainly we had the right to enclose ours. If my father did you wrong by enclosing his land, then you are likewise wronging me by now enclosing yours. [30] It's obvious, after all, that with your wall being built of large stones, the water blocked by those stones will come back on my property, whenever by chance and unexpectedly it knocks down my wall. But I will still not complain against them for that reason but will put up with my luck and try to protect my interests. I think, you see, that a man who protects his interests is being sensible, but in litigating against me, he is both very wicked and unbalanced by some disease.[15]

[31] Don't be surprised, jurors, by his fervor, not even if he has dared to bring false accusations against me, considering that before this, he persuaded his nephew to dispute ownership of my property, and he brought in nonexistent contracts, and just now he himself got another such arbitrator's judgment against me by default by indicting Callarus, one of my slaves. You see, on top of their other foul acts, they have hit on this tricky maneuver: they are suing Callarus in an identical action.[16] [32] But really, what slave would enclose his master's property if his master hadn't ordered him to do it? But since they have no other complaint against Callarus, they sue him over my father's building a wall fifteen years before he died. If, on the one hand, I abandon my fields and sell them to these men, or if I exchange the fields with them for other properties, Callarus is in no way guilty; on the other hand, if I don't wish to give up my property to them, then they are suffering the most grievous losses at Callarus' hands, and they look for an arbitrator who will award the properties to them and a settlement through which they will get the property. [33] Well, gentlemen of the jury, if those who plot and bring malicious litigation are bound to win the advantage, there's no use talking. But if you hate

---

[15] The suggestion that one's opponent is suffering from a mental disorder, and not just moral depravity, is very unusual in Attic lawcourt speeches.

[16] Harrison (1968: 174) interprets the passage to mean that a slave could be sued in his own person, but see Todd 1993: 187 n. 35.

men like this, and you vote for what is just, seeing that Callicles lost nothing and was not wronged in the slightest either by Callarus or by my father—then I don't know what more I must say. [34] But so that you know that prior to this, with designs on my property, he set up his nephew and that now in his own name he has won a judgment against Callarus in this other suit—with malevolence towards me, since I value this man—and Callicrates has again initiated another suit against Callarus, testimony on all these matters will be read out to you.

[DEPOSITIONS]

[35] By Zeus and the gods, gentlemen of the jury, do not abandon me, an innocent man, to my opponents. It is not the penalty that matters so much to me, though it would be hard for all men of small means; no, it's that they will expel me, completely, from the neighborhood by their sykophancy. To prove that we did nothing wrong, we were prepared to turn the matter over to knowledgeable, fair, impartial arbitrators; we are prepared to swear the customary oath, for we think that in this way we would be offering you, who are bound by an oath as well, the most powerful argument. [*To the clerk*] Please take my challenge and the remaining depositions.

[CHALLENGE, DEPOSITIONS]

HYPERIDES 3. AGAINST ATHENOGENES

〰〰〰〰〰〰〰〰〰〰〰〰〰〰〰〰〰〰〰〰〰〰〰〰〰〰〰〰〰〰〰〰〰〰〰〰〰

INTRODUCTION

Like all of Hyperides' surviving speeches, this speech was not preserved in manuscripts, as were all the other speeches in this volume,
but in fragments of an ancient papyrus discovered in Egypt in the late
nineteenth century. The text thus has quite a few gaps, and some of
the restored words represent only the gist of the original speech.
The speech was noted by ancient critics particularly for its artistic
merits, and what remains of it certainly does not disappoint. It shows
that gift of characterization, wit, and charm that made Hyperides
famous.

This was the plaintiff's first speech at the trial. As in many private suits,
he later delivered a second speech (Introduction, VC); this may also
have been written by Hyperides, but only a few words of it are known.

Everything we know about the case comes from the speech, according to which the plaintiff, Epicrates (named in 3.24), was a young
farmer who had brought a private suit for damages against Athenogenes, a metic of Egyptian origin. Athenogenes carried on his family's
trade in perfumes and owned three shops, one of which was managed
by his slave Midas and his two sons. Epicrates took a liking to one of
the boys and approached Athenogenes with an offer to set him free.
According to Epicrates, Athenogenes first had the boy refuse Epicrates'
offer unless he also agreed to buy and set free his brother and father;
then Athenogenes enlisted the services of his former mistress Antigone, a famous *hetaira*,[1] who used her charms to persuade Epicrates to
accept the boy's request that he buy the whole family.

---

[1] A high-class prostitute, normally a free noncitizen (see further above, Aes.
1.42n).

According to Epicrates, the whole thing was an elaborate and cleverly staged plot: Athenogenes at first refused any form of compromise,
and then Antigone convinced Epicrates that she was on his side and
would try to persuade Athenogenes to allow him to purchase the freedom of all three. Epicrates was completely duped; he quickly got
together forty minas from friends, and Athenogenes, as a favor to
Antigone (so he claimed), agreed to sell the three slaves to Epicrates,
who could have unrestricted use of the boy and at a later date choose
to set them free. But because he was buying the slaves, Epicrates also
assumed responsibility for any debts that they had accumulated. To
sweeten the offer, therefore, Athenogenes threw in the perfume business, which he claimed would easily cover any debts. Anxious to conclude the deal, Epicrates signed a sales contract without reading it.
Soon after, he discovered that Midas owed five talents in loans to
creditors and friends. Realizing the seriousness of his predicament,
Epicrates gathered his friends and relatives; they examined the document and discovered that many of the debts had not been recorded in
the agreement. They approached Athenogenes in the agora. A heated
exchange followed, but Athenogenes refused to make any concessions
and stuck by the contract. Epicrates was forced to sue Athenogenes for
damages to cover the debts.

In Athens a sales agreement could be, but did not have to be,
included with the sale.[2] In the present case, Athenogenes included a
written agreement to ensure that Epicrates assumed responsibility for
any debts previously accumulated by the slaves who ran the perfume
shop. Laws existed to protect the buyer against fraud and misrepresen-
tation by the seller: according to Epicrates, the seller was forbidden
from making false statements in the agora about his merchandise
(3.14), and in the case of the sale of a slave, the owner was required by
law to inform the buyer of any physical defects the slave might have.
If he failed to do so, the buyer could return the slave and demand his
money back (3.15). Both laws are mentioned by Epicrates in support
of his case, but they do not directly apply to him; he had willingly
agreed to accept any debts incurred by the slaves and had signed an
agreement to that effect. The basis of Athenogenes' defense was a law
that stated that any agreement made by two parties was binding

---

[2] For laws regulating sales, see Millet 1991.

(3.13n), but Epicrates argues that only just agreements are binding and that this agreement was unjust.

The trial took place several years after the battle of Chaeronea in 338, when Athenogenes left Athens for Troezen, where he took up permanent residency—most likely sometime after 330 but before 324. We do not know the verdict. Epicrates' case may not have been the strongest, and in the end, his best strategy was probably to play on the prejudices of the jury, who believed that foreigners like Athenogenes, who prospered in Athens but left the city at a time of crisis, only took advantage of its citizens.

HYPERIDES 3. AGAINST ATHENOGENES

[1] . . .[3] When I told her what had happened, how Athenogenes was hostile to me and was not willing to make any compromise, she said that he was always like this and told me not to worry; she would help me out in everything. [2] She seemed quite earnest when she said this, and she swore the most solemn oath, that she had my best interests at heart and was speaking the whole truth. The result was, to tell you the truth, gentlemen of the jury, that I believed her words. This is how passion, so it seems, unbalances a man's nature, when it enlists a woman's trickery. At any rate, by this deception, she wheedled out of me an additional three hundred drachmas for her kindness, allegedly to buy a girl.[4]

[3] Perhaps, gentlemen of the jury, it comes as no surprise that I was toyed with in this way by Antigone. The woman, they say, was the most treacherous *hetaira* of her day and now remains in the business as a brothel keeper. . . . She has destroyed the house of . . . of Chollidae, which was as wealthy as any. And yet, if she acted like this on her own, what do you think she has in mind now, in enlisting Athenogenes as her ally, a man who is a speechwriter and marketplace type[5] and worst of all, an Egyptian? [4] Finally, to make a long story short,

---

[3] The proem and some of the narrative are lost (how much is uncertain).

[4] The girl would presumably work in Antigone's brothel.

[5] The Greek term, which was obviously pejorative, refers to someone who frequents the agora: one who traffics there could be said to be streetwise or business smart.

she sent for me again later and told me that after considerable pleading with Athenogenes, she just barely managed to persuade him to release Midas and his two sons to me for forty minas, and she instructed me to get the money as quickly as possible, before Athenogenes changed his mind. After I gathered it from every source, pestering my friends and depositing the forty minas with the bank, I came to Antigone's house.[6]

[5] She brought Athenogenes and me together, reconciled us, and urged us from this point onward to treat each other well. I agreed to do this, and Athenogenes here replied that I should thank Antigone for what happened. "And now," he said, "for her sake, I will show you right away how well I'll treat you. You are going to put money down for the freedom of Midas and his sons. But I will sell them to you outright,[7] so that no one can bother you or seduce the boy away from you, and so that the slaves don't cause you any trouble, for fear of what may happen to them. [6] Most importantly, as it now stands, they would think that their freedom was the result of my efforts, but if you buy them outright and later, at your own convenience, set them free, they would be doubly grateful to you. However," he said, "you will assume whatever debts they owe—payment for some perfume to Pancalus and Procles[8] and any other amount occasionally lent to the perfume shop by a customer. But these are quite small, and far more valuable than these are the wares in the workshop, the perfume, the alabaster and myrrh"—and he mentioned some other names—"which will easily cover all these debts."[9]

[7] Gentlemen of the jury, here was the point of the plot and the elaborate deception. If I paid for their freedom, I would lose only what I gave him and would suffer no serious consequences. But if I bought them outright, and agreed to assume their debts, which I assumed

---

[6] Epicrates deposited the purchase money with the bank where the transaction would take place. For a similar situation, see Dem. 47.51, 57, 64.

[7] Lit. "I will give them for buying and selling," the regular expression for a sales contract.

[8] The name given below (10) is Polycles.

[9] As a metic, Athenogenes could not own land; the business that he was selling consisted only of slaves, a stall, and ingredients used to make perfume. The value in the business was in the slaves who had the skills to carry out the operations.

were insignificant, since I had no prior knowledge of them, he intended later to set his creditors and contributors on me,[10] trapping me by the terms of the agreement. And that's precisely what happened. [8] When I agreed to his proposal, he immediately took from his lap a document and began to read the contents of it; it was the agreement with me. Although I listened to what was being read, I was more anxious to complete the business I had come for. He sealed the agreement immediately in the same house, so that none of those who look out for my interests would know the contents, and he added to my name that of Nicon of Cephisia.[11] [9] We went to the perfume shop and deposited the document with Lysicles of Leuconoe.[12] I paid the forty minas and concluded the purchase. Once the transaction was complete, I had a visit from the creditors to whom Midas owed money and from his contributors, and we had a talk. Within three months, all the debts had been disclosed; the result was that I owed, as I said a moment ago,[13] nearly five talents, including loans from contributors.

[10] When I realized my predicament, I gathered my friends and relatives together, and we read my copy of the agreement, in which the names of Pancalus and Polycles[14] were expressly mentioned together with the amounts owed them for perfume. These amounts were small, and they could claim that the perfume in the shop covered the money owed. But most of the debts, including the largest ones, were not written in under any names, but, as something insignificant, in a footnote that read, "And whatever Midas owes to anyone else." [11] For one of the loans from contributors it was noted that three payments were outstanding. This was written under the name of Dicaeocrates, but the other loans from contributors that were made recently and enabled Midas to acquire everything, these Athenogenes had not written in the

---

[10] Two terms are used here to describe those who had lent Midas money: creditors who had furnished commercial loans and charged interest, and "contributors of *eranoi*," or interest-free loans from friends (Dem. 27.25n).

[11] Nicon must have been a friend of Epicrates, who acted as his surety or security for the purchase. See below, 20.

[12] Lysicles may have been the banker with whom Epicrates had already deposited the forty minas (3.5).

[13] This presumably refers to the lost beginning of the speech.

[14] Cf. 3.6n.

agreement but had kept concealed. After some deliberation, we decided to go to him and discuss the matter. We found him near the perfume shops, and we asked him whether he was not ashamed of lying and setting a trap in the agreement by not declaring the debts. He replied that he did not know what debts we meant, and he had no time for us. He had in his possession a document concerning this business of mine. [12] Many men gathered around to listen in on the matter, since our discussion took place in the agora. Although they really cut into him and insisted that we arrest him as a kidnapper,[15] we didn't think we should do this but instead summoned him before you according to the law. First of all, the clerk will read out to you the agreement; for you will learn of this man's plot from the text itself. Read the agreement.

[AGREEMENT]

[13] Gentlemen of the jury, you have heard all the facts in detail. But Athenogenes will at once tell you that the law declares that any agreements made by two parties are binding. Yes, agreements that are just, my good fellow. But for unjust agreements, the law says the direct opposite; they are not binding.[16] I will make this point clearer from the laws themselves. You have made me so fearful of being brought to ruin by you and your cunning that I have been forced to study and examine the laws night and day to the neglect of all else.[17]

[14] The one law stipulates that no one can make false statements

---

[15] Kidnappers could be arrested as *kakourgoi* (see Ant. 2.1.4n), but it is stretching things to want to apply this procedure to Athenogenes.

[16] There was a law that any agreement freely made before witnesses was binding (Dem. 42.12, 47.77, 56.2). Only here are we told that an agreement must be just, but if there were such a law, Epicrates would surely cite it. Moreover, a case could be brought in court (e.g., Dem. 48) claiming violation of an agreement to commit a crime (see Todd 1993: 59). Thus, to prove he was defrauded, Epicrates is forced to cite other laws about making false statements in the agora and disclosing the physical defects of a slave.

[17] Every litigant was expected to represent himself in court, and part of his task involved locating and examining laws that were applicable to his case. But Epicrates has hired Hyperides to write his speech, and he would probably have done much of that work. Epicrates' comments, then, are purely rhetorical, emphasizing his inexperience in court and his nonlitigious nature. Cf. Dem. 54.17–18.

in the agora, a provision that seems to me to be the finest of all.[18] But
you, Athenogenes, lied in the middle of the agora when you made
an agreement against my interests. If you show that you told me
about the loans from contributors and the debts or wrote in the
contract all the creditors' names that later I learned, then I have no
argument with you, but I admit to owing money. [15] Next, there is
a second law covering those who have made contracts by mutual
agreement. It states that when someone sells a slave, he must fully
disclose any physical defects the slave may have; and if he does not,
the slave can be returned. And yet if it is possible to return a slave,
when a seller has failed to reveal the defects caused by chance, how
can you not accept responsibility for crimes that you planned yourself? Moreover, the epileptic slave does not cause further loss to the
buyer, whereas Midas, whom you sold me, has cost even my friends
money.

[16] Consider, Athenogenes, the law's position not only on slaves
but also on free persons. Surely, you and everyone else know that only
children born of lawfully married women are legitimate.[19] But clearly
the simple act of betrothal by the woman's father or brother did not
satisfy the lawgiver, but he expressly wrote in the law, "Whomever a
man lawfully gives in betrothal, children born of her are legitimate,"
and not, "whenever someone betroths another woman, falsely alleging
that she is his daughter." Rather, he stipulates that lawful betrothals are
valid and unlawful ones, invalid.

[17] The law on wills is much like this. For it stipulates that a man
can bequeath his property as he sees fit, except when he is adversely
affected by old age, sickness, or insanity, or under the influence of a
woman, or held in prison or under constraint.[20] But if wills that con-

---

[18] This law was enforced by ten market officials (*agoranomoi*), five appointed
for Piraeus and five for the city, who oversaw the sale of all goods in the agora
and ensured that they were in good condition and their quality not misrepre-
sented (*Ath. Pol.* 51.1).

[19] For a marriage to be lawful, the woman had to be Athenian, and her guardian
had to give her out in marriage by *enguē*, a form of contract; see Dem. 46.18. The word
translated here "betrothal" means just that, "to give or promise in marriage by *enguē*."

[20] For the text of this law, see Dem. 46.14; cf. also Plutarch, *Solon* 21.3. The law
also includes being under the influence of drugs as grounds for contesting a will.

cern our own personal property are invalid when drawn up illegally, how can terms such as these be valid, when Athenogenes made an agreement that harms my property?[21] [18] If a will is invalid, so it seems, even when a man draws it up under the influence of his own wife, must I suffer more, when I was forced by them into making this agreement under the influence of Athenogenes' *hetaira* and when I have the greatest protection afforded by the law? And then, do you insist on sticking to the agreement that you and your *hetaira* tricked me into signing, for which the laws declare you guilty of conspiracy, and do you also expect to profit by it? You were not satisfied with receiving forty minas <for the perfume stall>,[22] but you also <robbed> me <of an additional five> talents, as if I were caught <in a snare by a hunter.>

[19] <Perhaps Athenogenes will say> that he did not know Midas <had so many debts, for the loans were made without his knowledge.> I, who never showed any interest in the business of the agora, within the space of three months came to know exactly what all the debts and loans from contributors were; but this fellow, who is a third generation perfume seller, who sits in the agora every day, who owns three perfume stalls, and who receives accounts every month, he did not know about his debts? In other regards, he is no amateur, but with regard to his own slave, he was a complete simpleton? He knew about some debts, it seems, but he claims ignorance about any others that he doesn't want to know about. [20] Such an argument on his part, gentlemen of the jury, is not a defense but an admission[23] that I should not have to pay off these debts. For if he says that he didn't know about all the money that was owed, then he surely cannot claim that he fully disclosed his debts. Any debts that I was not informed of by the seller

---

[21] Athenian laws were written in rather general terms, which allowed considerable scope for interpretation of the law by a litigant, who would try to persuade the jurors that the lawgiver's intention was this or the law meant that. Litigants often, as here, argue by analogy; see Todd 1993: 60–62.

[22] There are gaps in the text here, and the sense of the missing text is not certain.

[23] There is a play on words here: his *logos* ("argument") is not an *apologēma* ("defense") but a *homologēma* ("admission").

I am not legally bound to pay. I think it is clear to everyone, Athenogenes, that you knew Midas owed this money, particularly because you summoned Nicon as my security. For if <you did not know that the debts were large, my signature on the document would have been sufficient.>

[21] That certainly was not the case. But I want to take issue with your argument, that <you were ignorant and did not know who invested or exactly how much.> Let's examine it in this way. If through ignorance you failed to disclose fully to me all the debts and I made the agreement thinking the only debts were those you informed me of, who is legally bound to pay them? The subsequent buyer or the former owner of the property, when the money was borrowed? I think it's you. But if we disagree on this point, let the law be our arbitrator, which was made not by lovers or by those plotting to get other people's property but by the greatest democrat of all, Solon.[24] [22] Knowing that many sales are made in the city, he passed a law that all agree is just and fair. It states, "Damages and losses caused by slaves are to be paid by the master who owned the slaves at the time they caused them." This is reasonable. For if the slave achieves some success or establishes a business, the benefit goes to the owner. But you ignore the law and speak about contracts being broken. Solon believed that even a decree that was legally proposed should not override the law;[25] but you expect even unjust contracts to override all the laws.

[23] And besides this, gentlemen of the jury, he told my father and my other relatives that he was willing <to give me one of the boys> as a gift and to settle everything satisfactorily and that he had urged me to let him keep Midas instead of buying him, but I was unwilling and wanted to buy them all. I hear that he intends to tell you this, just to appear moderate, as if he were speaking to a bunch of fools who were unaware of his shameless behavior. [24] But you must hear what hap-

---

[24] By the fourth century, Solon was regarded as the founder of Athenian democracy, and orators assigned most laws to him, even if he was not their actual author.

[25] In 403/2, after the restoration of the Athenian democracy, a clear distinction was established between laws and decrees; after that date, no decree could override a law.

pened; for it will clearly fit in with the rest of their plot. He sent me the boy I just mentioned, who said that he would not live with me unless I had his father and brother freed. Then, when I had agreed to pay the money for the three of them, Athenogenes approached some of my friends and said, "Why does Epicrates want to go to this trouble, when he can take the boy and use him as he wants?" [25]²⁶ <I did not suspect> the trickery he was up to, and his words <gave the impression that he was free> of wrongdoing; yet <none of you should> believe that if <he was pleased to give me> the boy <as a gift and to keep the others,> I would have refused, <but I had become so demented that I wanted to spend> forty minas and <now risk to lose a further> five talents . . . [26] . . . I am not a perfume seller and do not practice any other trade, but I farm this small piece of land that my father gave me. And then I was rushed into this purchase by these people. Which is more likely, Athenogenes, that I desired your <trade> in which I had no experience or that <you and> your *hetaira* had designs on my property? Personally, I think all signs point to you.

For this reason, gentlemen of the jury, you can with good reason forgive me for being deceived by Antigone and for being so unlucky to fall in with a man like this, and <you should be angry> with Athenogenes . . .

[27] . . . <Now do you think it's right for me to have all the misfortunes that have come my way because of my simplicity> but for him to have the profits of his fraud? Or for me to be left with the headache of Midas, his daring accomplice, whom he said he was reluctant to set free, and for him to have received money for the boy, much more money than he is worth, although he originally said he was giving him to me as a gift, so even in the end he is not my own but will be set free by your vote?²⁷ Yet I myself do not think it's right that <besides all these other troubles> I should also be disenfranchised by Atheno-

---

²⁶ The text in 3.25 is extremely fragmentary, and the restorations are largely guesses.

²⁷ Epicrates is tendentiously describing the consequences that would follow if he lost his case. Midas and his debt of five talents would in a sense be the price he had paid for the boy, whom Athenogenes said he wanted to give as a gift; but the boy would be free, since it was never Epicrates' intention to buy the boy as a slave.

genes.[28] [28][29] The result would be devastating for me, gentlemen of the jury, if <this fellow should get the best of me. For my part,> I went wrong <because of my naïveté, but for his part he has clearly> done me wrong. <Is it not enough for me to be victimized> by his crimes? <Must I also be assessed the additional> penalty <of disenfranchisement? And to think I am a> citizen, <and should be the victim of a metic like this. Don't get me wrong; I do not want to slander a class that has done you tremendous service, but only this villain, Athenogenes.>

[29] <In the past he was never willing> to risk his life <in our time of need, as most loyal> metics <did.> In the war with Philip, he left the city just before the battle and did not serve with you at Chaeronea but moved to Troezen, contrary to the law that stipulates that a person who emigrates in time of war is subject to denunciation (*endeixis*)[30] and immediate arrest (*apagōgē*), if he returns.[31] Now he did this, it seems, because he suspected Troezen would survive, but our city he sentenced to death. Moreover, he raised his daughters in prosperity that you provided, but <when misfortune fell> he married them off

---

[28] Two possibilities have been suggested for Epicrates' potential disenfranchisement (*atimia*). If he loses the case, his creditors could bring a *dikē exoulēs*, to collect the five talents he owed them or eject Epicrates from the property, and if he was convicted, in addition to what he owed them, an equal amount would also have to be paid to the state; he would thus be a state debtor and lose his civic rights. The other possibility is that in a damage suit, as in some other private suits, in the event of losing the case, the plaintiff had to pay the defendant the *epōbelia* (see above, Aes. 1.164n; Dem. 27.67n), and if Epicrates failed to pay, he could similarly be liable to a *dikē exoulēs* and *atimia* as a state debtor.

[29] The next three sections (28–30) of the text are very fragmentary, and some of the restorations are mere guesses.

[30] *Endeixis* and *apagōgē* were two stages of the process of summary arrest, which could be used against individuals who had broken court-imposed bans. For *apagōgē*, the citizen would make the arrest himself; in *endeixis*, he would submit the name of the offender to the appropriate magistrate. See further Hansen 1976.

[31] The law appears to apply only to metics who emigrate in time of war and not to Athenian citizens, since Lycurgus (1.53, 144) makes no mention of such a law when prosecuting Leocrates for just that crime.

<elsewhere>, [30] intending all along to come back here and take up his business again when peace was restored. Good <metics have never> done this to you; in times of peace <they have shared in your prosperity and> in times of danger <have fought beside you, as they did> at Plataea,[32] uniting <their own interests with those of Athens>. Athenogenes <has never thought of anything but his own personal interests. . . . Although he benefited from our city, he has deserted it in the face of danger.> . . . after violating the social contract with the city, he insists on his private contract with me, as if anyone would believe that the man who holds his obligations to you in utter contempt would care anything for his obligations to me.

[31] This fellow is so perverse and so utterly true to form that after he arrived in Troezen and was made a citizen, he offered himself to Mnesias the Argive, who secured his appointment as magistrate and once in office expelled the citizens from the city, something these men can testify to, since they are here in exile. You yourselves, gentlemen of the jury, welcomed them in when they were exiled, made them citizens, and shared with them all your privileges. You remembered, after more than one hundred and fifty years, the kindness that they showed you when facing the barbarian,[33] and you believe that you should rescue from misfortune those who have rendered you service in times of danger. [32] But this polluted creature, who abandoned you and was registered as a citizen at Troezen, did nothing that was worthy of the constitution or the character of that city but treated those who had welcomed him so cruelly that <he was accused soon after> in their own assembly . . . and fearing <dreadful retribution from the Troezenians>, he fled back here again. [33] To prove that I am telling the truth, the clerk will read you first the law that forbids metics from emigrating in time of war, then the testimony of the Troezenians, and besides that the decree passed by the Troezenians to honor your city, which has prompted you in return to welcome them in and to make them citizens. Read them.

---

[32] In 479; nowhere else do we hear of metics fighting there.

[33] In 480, when the Persian king Xerxes invaded Attica and destroyed Athens, the Athenians evacuated their women and children to Troezen and faced the enemy in their fleet at Salamis.

[LAW, DEPOSITION, DECREE]

[34] Please take the testimony of his father-in-law;[34] <he confirms that Athenogenes received two> inheritances, the estate left <by his father>, and what he got from his brother; and <as soon as he received them, he squandered them> completely, one right after the other <on his *hetaira*> Antigone. <This is sufficient> evidence <to prove his prodigal behavior; he has shamelessly squandered his patrimony, which should have been preserved for his family. There is not one of you who does not find such behavior reprehensible. Now you can better appreciate his present conduct towards me.>

[35] <I think you have heard enough about> what he has done, how Athenogenes has plotted against me, and how he has treated you. He is evil in his private life; he has given up hope for the safety of our city; he has abandoned you; he has expelled those with whom he took up residency. You have this man in your grasp; will you not punish him? [36] As for me, gentlemen of the jury, I beg <and implore you to take pity> on me; understand that in this trial all of you should pity <the plaintiff>, not the <defendant.> In fact, this fellow, if he is convicted, will get nothing he does not <deserve but will suffer> what he should have suffered long ago. As for me, if he is acquitted of the charge I brought, I will be ruined, since I cannot <pay off> even the smallest <portion of these debts>. . . .[35]

---

[34] Much of 3.34 is mere guesswork.

[35] The last few lines of the speech are missing.

LYSIAS 24. FOR THE DISABLED MAN

⟨⟨⟩

INTRODUCTION

This case is probably a scrutiny (*dokimasia*).[1] The use of *dokimasia* to examine the qualifications of those who have been appointed to public office is common in the speeches of Lysias,[2] but in this instance the issue is not an office but a privilege, specifically, a disability pension. Neither the speaker (who is defending his right to continuance of his pension) nor his opponent is named, and there are no indications of date except for a reference back to the speaker's actions at the time of the Thirty in 404/3, which would fit a date for the speech at any time within the career of Lysias (403–380).

The rules governing the payment of disability pensions are outlined in *Ath. Pol.* 49.4, written in the 330s or 320s: those who possess capital of less than three minas, and who are so badly maimed that they cannot do any work, receive a daily payment of two obols, subject to a *dokimasia* conducted by the Council. One clear discrepancy between this system and the situation presupposed in Lysias 24 is that the speaker refers throughout (13, 26) to a payment of one obol rather than two; presumably the level of payment has been raised in the half-century or so between the speech and the *Ath. Pol.* More difficult to avoid are the speaker's implied admission that he is able to do some work, though he claims it is not enough to support him (6), and his failure adequately to discuss the capital value of his property, though he claims not to have inherited wealth (6). It is possible that the regulations for eligibility have been tightened during the intervening

---

[1] See the Introduction, IVA. The manuscript title describes the speech as an *eisangelia* (impeachment), but that is probably an erroneous guess by a copyist.

[2] See Lys. 16, 25, 26, 31, and Fr. 9 (*Eryximachus*).

period, but perhaps it is easier to infer that the speaker is doing his best to conceal the weaknesses of his case.

Overall, the speech is both evasive and irreverent. An example of the former is the response to the allegation about horse riding (10–12), which was presumably intended by his opponent to prove that he was fitter than he admits, but which the speaker manipulates into an allegation about his wealth. Throughout the speech there is an undertone of parody: for example, the speech, like Lysias 16, begins by thanking the opponent for creating the opportunity for the speaker to talk about himself, a claim that is appropriate for a proud and ambitious aristocrat like Mantitheus at his *dokimasia* but is faintly ridiculous in the present context.

The tone of Lysias 24 is one reason why several scholars have argued that it must be a rhetorical exercise rather than a genuine speech; another reason is that if the speaker is really poor, it is difficult to see how he could have afforded to commission Lysias as his speechwriter, or indeed whether this would have been worth his while for the amount at issue. But it is equally possible that a speechwriter like Lysias may have decided to adopt unusual tactics to deal with a patently weak case, by attempting to win the Council's support for his client's personality and encouraging them to laugh the case out of court.[3] As for the speechwriter's fees, not only may the speaker be better off than he admits but people will also sometimes spend more than is justifiable in strictly economic terms to avoid the shame of losing something they have previously held. But perhaps a more likely explanation would be that the orator (whether Lysias or somebody else) might be prepared to reduce or waive his fees in the light of a personal connection with the speaker. This is pure speculation, the more so given that we know nothing about the normal charges for a speechwriter's services, but clearly the speaker had a craft or trade that brought him into contact with many rich people (5), even though he nowhere admits what it is, and it is conceivable that Lysias or one of his friends was among them.[4]

---

[3] It is worth bearing in mind the possibilities of visual theater in this case. A lot could be done to exaggerate the speaker's disability by the way he walked to the podium with the use of two sticks (cf. 24.13), if he trained himself to use them for the day.

[4] The other possibility, of course, is that the speaker's rich friends or clients are paying Lysias on his behalf.

There is a useful commentary on the speech by Usher in Edwards and Usher 1985; see also Carey 1990.

LYSIAS 24. FOR THE DISABLED MAN

[1] I am almost grateful to my accuser, members of the Council, for having devised these proceedings against me. In the past, I had no reason to give an account of my life, but now, because of him, I have one. In my speech, I shall attempt to show that he is a liar and that up to this very day I have been living a life worthy of praise rather than envy—because it seems to me that envy is the only explanation for his having devised this danger for me. [2] And yet, if somebody envies those whom others pity, what wickedness do you think such a man would shrink from? Could he possibly be bringing charges against me for money as a sykophant?[5] If on the other hand he claims that he is seeking vengeance on me as his enemy, then he is lying: I have never had anything to do with him either as friend or as enemy, because of his criminal nature. [3] So then, it is clear, members of the Council, that he is envious of me for being a better citizen than he is, even though I am afflicted with such misfortune. In my view, members of the Council, one should remedy physical weakness with mental qualities. If in the future I can maintain an attitude and lead a life that matches my misfortune, how will I be inferior to this man?

[4] I have said enough on these matters, so I shall speak as briefly as I can about the points I need to discuss. The accuser claims that it is not right for me to receive the money from the city. He alleges that I am physically healthy, not disabled, and that I have a *technē*[6] such that I could live even without this gift. [5] As evidence of my physical strength, he cites my riding of horses; as evidence of my prosperity in my *technē*, my consorting with those who have money to spend. I believe you all know about the alleged prosperity from my *technē*, and my livelihood[7] in general, but all the same I too will discuss them

---

[5] Malicious prosecutor (Introduction, VE).

[6] *Technē* (pl. *technai*) denotes a "skill" or "craft" or "trade." The speaker does not say what his occupation is (cf. 24.5); he is equally cagey about the precise nature of his disability.

[7] Or "life," "lifestyle," Gk. *bios*.

briefly. [6] My father left me nothing, I only ceased to be responsible for my late mother two years ago, and I do not yet have any children who will support me. I have acquired a *technē* that is able to help a little, but already I can perform it only with difficulty, and I have not yet been able to obtain the services of somebody to take it over.[8] I have no other income apart from this, and if you take it away from me, I would be in danger of facing a very difficult situation. [7] Do not unjustly destroy me, members of the Council, when it is in your power to rescue me justly. Now that I am older and weaker, do not take away from me what you gave me when I was younger and stronger. In the past, you were seen to be full of pity, even for those who had suffered no harm. Do not now for my opponent's sake treat savagely those who are objects of pity even to their enemies. Do not have the hardheartedness to wrong me, and so cause others in my position to despair. [8] It would be extraordinary, members of the Council, if I were shown to have been receiving this money when I had a single misfortune, but should be deprived of it now, when I am afflicted by age and illness and the sufferings that accompany them. [9] It seems to me that my accuser could demonstrate the scale of my poverty more clearly than anybody else. If I were to be appointed choregus for tragedy, and were to challenge him to an *antidosis*,[9] he would prefer to serve ten times as choregus rather than to complete the *antidosis* once. Surely it is disgraceful for him to allege that because of my great prosperity I can consort on equal terms with the very rich—whereas if any of the things I am describing were to happen to him, he would recognize that my condition is like that, or even worse.[10]

[10] My opponent has dared to draw to your attention my horse riding, because he does not respect fortune and feels no shame towards you. In this matter, my account can be brief. I am sure, members of the Council, that all those who experience misfortune take as their aim and object of study how to cope with their existing condition with

---

[8] Presumably a slave. The reference to children is vague enough to leave it unclear whether he is married, so it is not necessarily significant that nothing is made of the labor power of a hypothetical wife.

[9] For the *chorēgia* and *antidosis,* see the Introduction, IVC, and Lys. 3.20n.

[10] The text is corrupt, and this translation is merely a guess at the original meaning.

the minimum of discomfort. I am one of those, and because I have encountered such misfortune, I discovered this means of comfort for myself on the longer journeys I have to undertake. [11] The most important evidence, members of the Council, that I do this because of my misfortune, and not—as he claims—because of arrogance (*hybris*), is that I ride horses; if I possessed property, I would travel on a mule with a padded saddle rather than riding other people's horses. As it is, I cannot afford to possess anything of the sort, so I am forced to make frequent use of other people's horses. [12] Surely it is extraordinary, members of the Council, that this man would remain silent if he saw me traveling on a saddled mule—what would he be able to say?—but because I ride borrowed horses, he seeks to persuade you that I am capable.[11] Surely it is extraordinary that he uses my horse riding as evidence that I am able-bodied, but does not also accuse me of being able-bodied in that I use two sticks, whereas others use one. But it is for the same reason that I use both.

[13] To such an extent does he surpass the whole human race in shamelessness that he is attempting by himself to persuade you who are so many that I am not one of the disabled. But if he succeeds in persuading some of you, members of the Council, what would prevent me from drawing lots to be one of the nine Archons?[12] What is there to prevent you all from taking away my obol on the pretext that I am in good heath, and voting it to him out of pity on the pretext that he is disabled? Surely the same man cannot have his grant taken away by you on the grounds that he is able-bodied, and be prevented by the Thesmothetae from drawing lots on the grounds that he is disabled. [14] However, you do not share his opinions, and he is not in his right mind. He has come here to argue about my misfortune, as if for an heiress,[13] and he is seeking to persuade you that I am not the sort of

---

[11] "Capable" is used here to translate *dynatos* (used with its derivatives frequently in this speech), which has connotations of "powerful" or "able-bodied."

[12] The implication is that those classified as disabled were not eligible for this office (which like most others at Athens was selected by lot).

[13] For "heiress" (*epiklēros*), see Dem. 57.41; several claimants might compete (in court) for the hand of an *epiklēros* from a rich family.

person that you can all see. You, on the other hand, as befits those in their right mind, should believe in your own eyes rather than in my opponent's words.

[15] My opponent claims that I am full of *hybris,* violent, and totally dissolute—as though he would be telling the truth if he used frightening words but not if he used gentler language and refrained from lying. But I think, members of the Council, that you should distinguish clearly between those people for whom to commit *hybris* is natural and those for whom it is not appropriate. [16] It is not the poor or the genuinely needy who are likely to commit *hybris* but those who possess far more than the necessities of life; not the disabled but those who are overconfident in their own strength; not those who have already progressed in age but those who are still young and who think the thoughts of young men. [17] The rich buy off danger with their money, but the poor are compelled by their immediate needs to behave responsibly. Young men believe they will be forgiven by their elders, but both young and old alike criticize those older men who commit offenses. [18] Those who are strong can generally commit *hybris* against anybody they wish, without suffering anything themselves; but the weak cannot ward off aggressors when they suffer *hybris,* nor can they overcome those they are trying to hurt if they themselves wish to commit *hybris.* So it seems to me that the accuser is not speaking seriously about my *hybris* but is joking. He does not wish to persuade you that I am that sort of person, but seeks to caricature me, as if he is doing something clever.

[19] He also claims that many people who are criminals meet together on my premises—people who have wasted their own property and are plotting against those who want to keep what is their own. You should all bear in mind that by saying this, he is not accusing me any more than all those others who have *technai,*[14] nor is he accusing those who come to my premises any more than those who visit the premises of other tradesmen. [20] Each of you is accustomed to visit tradesmen: the perfume seller, the hairdresser, the leather cutter, and wherever you might happen to go. Most of you visit the tradesmen who have set up shop nearest to the agora, and very few visit those that

[14] See above, 4n.

are furthest away from it. So if any of you is going to condemn the criminal tendencies of those who come to my premises, you will clearly be condemning also those who spend time with the other tradesmen; and if them, then all Athenians, because you are all accustomed to visit one place or other and spend time there.

[21] I do not see what need there is for me to waste more of your time defending myself in excessive detail against everything that has been said. If I have already spoken about the most important points, what need is there to treat seriously the minor ones, as he has done? I ask you all, members of the Council, to have the same attitude towards me as in the past. [22] Do not, for the sake of my opponent, deprive me of the only thing in my fatherland of which fortune has given me a share. Do not let this one man persuade you to take away what you all collectively gave me in the past. It is because god has deprived us of the best things, members of the Council, that the city has voted to grant us this money, in the belief that both good and ill fortune are common to all. [23] I would surely be the most wretched of men, if because of my misfortune I should have been deprived of what is greatest and best, and if because of my accuser I were to be stripped of what the city has given out of consideration towards those in my condition. Do not cast your votes in this way, members of the Council. Why should I find you so disposed? [24] Is it because anybody has ever been put on trial because of me and has lost his property? But not even one person would be able to show this. Or because I am a busybody, or aggressive, or fond of feuds? I do not happen to enjoy such means of livelihood. [25] Or is it because I indulge in excessive *hybris* or violence? But not even my opponent would say so, unless he wanted to lie about this too, just as he lies about other things. Or is it because I was in power under the Thirty and harmed many of the citizens? But I went into exile at Chalcis[15] with your democracy, and although I could safely have shared in the *politeia*[16] with them, I preferred to share in the danger with all of you. [26] Do not treat me in the same way as those who have committed many offenses, members of the Council,

---

[15] A city in Euboea (the large island immediately north of Attica).

[16] *Politeia* may here denote either "citizenship" (a fairly outrageous claim, given that the Thirty restricted citizen rights to three thousand of the wealthiest Athenians) or possibly "the activity of government" (an even more outrageous claim).

for I have committed none. Instead, cast the same vote for me as your predecessors have done. Remember that I am not giving an account after administering public funds, and I have not held any public office for which I am now undergoing the audit of my accounts (*euthynai*); but instead, I am making this speech simply for a single obol. [27] With this in mind, you will all decide justly; I shall accept your decision and give you thanks. My opponent will learn for the future not to plot against those who are weaker than himself but to overcome those who are like him.

ISOCRATES 17. TRAPEZITICUS

The defendant in this case, Pasion, is the most famous banker (*trapezitēs*) of classical Athens. A former slave, he was also the father of Apollodorus, the author of several speeches later included with those of Demosthenes, including Demosthenes 59 (see Trevett 1992). The acrimony into which this case must have brought Pasion apparently did no serious or long-term damage to his professional reputation. In time, he would even be granted citizenship for service to Athens. He died in 370/69. The prosecutor is a young man from the Bosporus (now the Crimea in southern Ukraine), whose father, Sopaeus, was very close to the region's ruler, Satyrus. The Bosporus was an important area for Athens, the source of much of its imported grain.

The speaker tells us that he came to Athens to see the sights and conduct some trade, and Pythodorus, a Phoenician, introduced him to Pasion. When Sopaeus temporarily fell out of favor with Satyrus, the son took steps to hide his money from Satyrus' agents in Athens. These steps included a feigned denial that he had money on deposit with Pasion and even a (false) admission that he was in debt to the banker. When he decided to leave Athens, he asked Pasion for the money back and was refused (8–9). The obvious person to consult was Cittus, who kept the books at Pasion's bank, but Cittus temporarily disappeared, and then his status was disputed, whether he was a free man or a slave, which confused whether the information he had could be gained from him through torture or not (11–17). For a time it appeared that a resolution would be reached, according to which both men would go to Satyrus and settle the matter before him (18–20). But accusations that Pasion had made against Menexenus, one of the speaker's confidants, that Menexenus had kidnapped Cittus, led to Menexenus bringing charges of his own against Pasion for slander (21–22). This complication nullified the arrangement between Pasion and the speaker, and Pasion then arranged, so the speaker claims, to have a slave alter the document that set out the conditions under which Pasion and the speaker would appear before Satyrus (21–23). The speaker begins his proofs with that document, arguing that Pasion's version of the circumstances of its composition makes no sense of the motives of the two parties (24–34). He then anticipates that Pasion will argue that the speaker was in debt to Stratocles and had had a friend, Hippolaïdas, borrow from Pasion (rather than lending him money himself), and so he explains these circumstances (35–44).

He also takes up the issue of motive again, pointing out that his original charge was made when he was in a straitened situation, when he is unlikely to have engaged in sykophancy (45–48; cf. 21.11–13). He then resumes his narrative with the report that in the end, Pasion finally sent Cittus to go with the speaker to Satyrus, but the two gave conflicting accounts to the king of why they had come to him, with the result that Satyrus sent a letter to the Athenians asking them to resolve the matter (51–52). The speaker then concludes his proof by recalling the torture that he proposed to perform on Cittus (53–55) and pointing out the services of his father and Satyrus to Athens in the past (57–58).

The speech can be dated after 394, when Athens broke Sparta's naval dominance (36). It offers insights into Athenian banking and Athens' relations with the kingdom of Bosporus (see Trevett 1992; E. Cohen 1992). There are also many glimpses of aspects of Athenian judicial procedure, such as private arbitration and the torture of slaves.

ISOCRATES 17. TRAPEZITICUS

[1] Judges, this trial is important to me. I am risking not only a lot of money but also the appearance of unjustly coveting another's possessions. That is what concerns me most. I will still have sufficient property even if I lose, but if I appeared to be making a charge over so much money with no right to it, I would be reviled for my whole life.

[2] The most difficult thing of all, men of the court, is the sort of opponents I am facing. Dealings with people at banks occur without witnesses,[1] and those who have suffered injustice at their hands must run a risk against people who have many friends, who handle lots of money, and who appear credible because of their trade. Nevertheless, despite these circumstances, I believe that I shall make it clear to all that I am being robbed of the money by Pasion.

[3] I shall relate to you as well as I can what happened from the beginning. My father, men of the court, is Sopaeus. All who sail to the Black Sea know that he is so closely connected to Satyrus that he both rules a large area himself and has responsibility over Satyrus' entire empire. [4] But when I learned about this city and the rest of Greece, I desired to go abroad, so my father loaded two ships with grain, gave me money, and sent me off for trade and touring. When Pythodorus the Phoenician introduced me to Pasion, I began to use his bank. [5] Later, when a rumor reached Satyrus that my father was plotting against his rule and I was associating with exiles, he arrested my father and wrote to those visiting here from the Black Sea to seize my money and order me to sail back. If I did none of these things, they were to demand it from you. [6] In these difficulties, men of the court, I told Pasion my troubles. He behaved so agreeably toward me that I would have trusted him completely, not only about money but about everything else. I thought that if I surrendered all my money, I would run the risk, if something happened to my father, of losing everything, since I would be deprived of my money both here and there. But if I admitted having the money and did not surrender it after Satyrus' order, I would put myself and my father under the greatest suspicion in the eyes of Satyrus. [7] We discussed it and decided to surrender the

---

[1] This statement has occasioned much discussion (see E. Cohen 1992: 205–206). It represents a surprising exception to the regular presence of witnesses at all significant transactions. Cohen believes it indicates the banks' involvement in a secretive economy that sought to avoid taxation. But it must be recalled that the bankers' primary role was as currency traders. If the speaker is referring to an Athenian law or custom that dealings with people at banks are to occur without witnesses, this may simply refer to currency transactions, not to deposits, whose acceptance was a secondary function for bankers.

money that was visible[2] and not only to disclaim the money on deposit with Pasion but to appear to be in debt to him and to others on interest, that is, to do everything possible to persuade those men that I had no money.

[8] At the time, men of the court, I thought Pasion was giving me all this advice out of goodwill for me, but when I had dealt with the representatives from Satyrus, I realized he had designs on my money. When I wanted to collect my money and sail to Byzantium, Pasion thought a very fine opportunity had come his way. A lot of money was on deposit with him—certainly enough to be worth some shamelessness on his part—and I had denied having anything before many onlookers. When asked, in plain view of everyone, I also admitted that I was in debt to others.[3] [9] In addition, men of the court, he thought that if I attempted to remain here, the city would hand me over to Satyrus; if I went somewhere else, my words would be of no concern to him; and if I sailed back to the Black Sea, I would be put to death along with my father. Calculating these factors, he decided to steal my money. He pretended to me that he was short of funds at the time and could not pay me back. But when I wanted to understand the matter clearly and sent Philomelus and Menexenus to him to demand it back, he told them he had nothing of mine. [10] Beset with so many troubles from all sides, what thought do you think I had? If I was silent, this man would steal my money. If I spoke up, I would still get nothing and would expose myself and my father to very serious allegations before Satyrus. So I thought it best to keep quiet.

[11] After this, men of the court, messengers came and told me that my father had been released and that Satyrus so regretted what he had done that he had given him the greatest assurances, had made his rule even larger than before, and had chosen to marry my sister to his own son. On learning this, Pasion knew that I would now act openly concerning my money, and he hid his slave Cittus, who had thorough knowledge about the money. [12] Thinking that he would provide the

---

[2] For visible and invisible property, see Is. 8.35n. As a foreigner, the speaker cannot have owned land; he must be referring to the cash and personal possessions he would have had on his person or in his lodgings.

[3] He mentions Stratocles in 35–36, below.

clearest test (*elenchos*) of what I was charging, I went and demanded the man, but Pasion made the most terrible claim: that Menexenus and I had corrupted and bribed him when he was seated at the bank[4] and had received six talents of silver from him. In order that there might be no test or torture[5] about the money, he claimed that we had hidden the slave and had then countercharged him and demanded this slave, whom we ourselves had made disappear. As he said this with cries of anger and tears, he dragged me to the Polemarch,[6] demanded sureties,[7] and did not release me until I supplied him sureties for six talents. Please call witnesses of these events.

[WITNESSES]

[13] You have heard the witnesses, judges. Since I had already lost some money and faced shameful accusations about the rest, I left for the Peloponnesus to investigate,[8] but Menexenus found the slave here. He seized him and demanded that he be tortured both about the deposit and about the charges this man was making about us. [14] Pasion then became so bold that he had the slave released on the grounds that he was free.[9] He had no shame or fear. Although he claimed the man had been kidnapped by us and that we had received so much money from him, he had him released into freedom and so prevented his torture. And what is most terrible of all is that when Menexenus had him give a surety for the slave before the Polemarch, Pasion supplied a surety for him for six talents. Have the witnesses of these things step up.

---

[4]A *trapeza* (lit. "four-footed") was a table where the banker did business; the word thus comes to mean "bank."

[5]Slaves could not appear in court as witnesses, but with the assent of both sides, they could be questioned under torture (*basanos*); see Ant. 1.6n.

[6]For the Polemarch, see the Introduction, IVA. The charge was kidnapping, a serious offense.

[7]Ant. 5.17, with note.

[8]It is unclear what he meant to investigate and why he went to the Peloponnesus.

[9]For the procedure, see the similar scenario in Dem. 59.40, with note. If Cittus were free, he could not be tortured.

[WITNESSES]

[15] Now, after he had acted this way, men of the court, Pasion thought that his past actions had clearly been wrong and believed that he could make things right in the future. So he came to us claiming that he was ready to surrender the slave for torture, and we chose torturers and met at the Hephaesteion. I demanded that they whip the surrendered individual and rack him until he appeared to them to speak the truth. But Pasion here claimed that they had not been chosen executioners, and he told them, if they wanted anything, to find it out verbally from the slave. [16] Since we disagreed, the torturers themselves refused to perform the torture and decided that Pasion should hand the slave over to me.[10] Pasion was so averse to the torture that he refused to obey them and hand him over, but he was ready to return the money if they convicted him.[11] Please call the witnesses of these events.

[WITNESSES]

[17] Now, men of the court, as a result of the meetings, everyone condemned his conduct as unjust and scandalous: first, after hiding the slave—who I claimed knew about the money—he charged that we had hidden him; then, when we seized the slave, he prevented his torture on the grounds that he was free; and later, when he surrendered him as a slave and chose torturers, he called for a verbal interrogation and did not allow an actual torture. Because of this he thought that he would find no safety if he came before you, and he sent a mes-

---

[10] I.e., to be tortured. Pasion was claiming that Cittus was not a slave. If he was free, the torturers might have got into serious trouble if they assaulted him.

[11] This entire episode is an important source for the evidentiary torture of slaves in Athens. But it is also atypical: usually the proposal is for the opponent of the slave's owner to perform the torture, but in this case Pasion seems to have seen the torturers somewhat in the role of arbitrators, who might simply have verbally questioned the slave. He seems to have given them the right to decide the dispute, but by forbidding the torture, he seems to have avoided conceding that Cittus was a slave.

sage and asked me to come and meet him at a sanctuary. [18] When we came to the Acropolis, he had covered his head and was crying. He said that he was compelled by lack of funds to deny what had happened and that he would try to return the money in a short time. He begged me to forgive him and to help cover up his misfortune so that it would not be publicly known that someone who took deposits had done such wrongs. Thinking that he regretted what he had done, I agreed and called on him to find a way, whichever he wished, so that it would turn out well for him and I would get my money. [19] Two days later we met and exchanged a pledge to keep silent about what had been done—a pledge that he broke, as you will realize as the story proceeds—and he agreed to sail with me to the Black Sea and there to return the gold to me so that he might discharge his obligation as far from this city as possible and that no one from here would know the manner of our settlement: when he sailed home he could say whatever he wanted. But if he failed to do these things, he would refer an arbitration to Satyrus on terms[12] that Satyrus would condemn him to pay one-and-a-half times the money. [20] After we wrote these things down and brought to the Acropolis Pyron, a man of Pherae who regularly sailed to the Black Sea, we gave him the agreement for safekeeping and ordered him to burn the document if we reached a settlement, and if not, to give it to Satyrus.

[21] Our affairs, men of the court, had been resolved in this way. But Menexenus was angry about the accusation that Pasion had made against him[13] and brought suit demanding the surrender of Cittus. He claimed Pasion should pay the same penalty for lying that Menexenus would have paid if he had been shown to have done any of these things. And Pasion asked me, men of the court, to settle things with Menexenus, saying there would be no advantage for him if, after sailing to the Black Sea and returning the money according to our agreement, he would still be made a laughingstock here. The slave, if he were tortured, would tell the truth about everything. [22] I thought that I should do whatever he wanted with regard to Menexenus but that he should do what we had agreed to do for me. At that time he

---

[12] In an "arbitration on terms," the arbitrator simply confirms terms already agreed upon by the disputants.

[13] See above, 14.

was weak, unable to deal with his difficulties. He was afraid not only about the torture and the suit that had been brought but also that Menexenus might get hold of the document. [23] Since he was at a loss to discover an escape, he persuaded[14] the slaves of his guest-friend (*xenos*)[15] to alter the document that Satyrus was supposed to receive if we did not reach a settlement. He had hardly accomplished this when he became the boldest of all people. He said he would not sail with me to the Black Sea and that he had no obligation to me. He called on me to open the document before witnesses. Why should I tell you the details, men of the court? We found written in the document that I had released him from all my charges.

[24] I have told you everything that happened as accurately as I can. I think that Pasion, men of the court, will base his defense on the altered document and rely especially on this. So give me your attention. I think that I shall make his depravity clear to you from the very same arguments.

[25] First, reflect on this: when we gave Pyron the agreement, according to which Pasion is claiming that he was released from the charges but I say that I was supposed to recover the gold, we called on him to burn the document if we achieved a settlement between ourselves, but if not, to give it to Satyrus. We both agree that these were the terms. [26] So what encouraged us, men of the court, to direct that the document be given to Satyrus if we did not settle, if in fact Pasion had already been released from the charges and our affair had been concluded? Clearly we wrote this agreement with the thought that there were still outstanding matters between us that Pasion had to resolve with me according to the document. [27] Next, I can tell you, men of the court, the reasons why he agreed to return the gold. For when we were cleared of the allegations made to Satyrus and he could not conceal Cittus, who had thorough knowledge of the deposit, he thought that if he surrendered the slave to torture, his wickedness would become apparent, [28] but if he did not, he would lose the case, and thus he wanted to reach a settlement with me. Ask him to show you what profit I gained or what danger I feared by releasing him from

---

[14] I.e., bribed.

[15] I.e., Pyron. A *xenos* is someone from another city with whom ties of hospitality and assistance have been established.

the charges. If he cannot show you any of these motives, isn't it more just to trust me rather than him about the document? [29] Indeed, men of the court, it is easy for everyone to recognize that since I was making the charges, if I feared testing them,[16] I could have waived the affair good-bye without making any agreement; but because of the torture and the trials that would come before you, Pasion could not be free of danger whenever he wanted unless he persuaded me, since I was making the charges. Therefore, I did not have to make the agreement about his release; he had to make one about returning the money. [30] It would be extraordinary if I had had so little faith in my case before composing the document that I not only released Pasion from the charges but also made an agreement about them and that I would want to come before you after I had composed such a test against myself. Really, who would plan his affairs this way?

[31] The greatest evidence of all that Pasion was not released in the written agreement but agreed to pay back the gold is that when Menexenus brought suit against him[17]—before the document was altered—he sent Agyrrhius, a friend of both of ours, and asked me either to call off Menexenus or else cancel the written agreement I had made with him. [32] And yet, men of the court, do you think he would want to cancel this agreement, which he would use to expose us as liars? He did not use these arguments after he had changed the text; he sought refuge in it about everything and called on us to open the document. I will provide Agyrrhius himself as witness that at first he sought to cancel the agreement. Please come up.

[DEPOSITION]

[33] I think I have shown sufficiently that we made the agreement not as Pasion will try to tell you but as I have reported. It is not surprising, men of the court, that they altered the document. Not only have such things happened often before, but some of Pasion's associates have done much worse things. Who of you does not know that

---

[16] I.e., by the torture of the slave and/or a trial, both of which would test his charges.

[17] See above, 21.

Pythodorus, the shopkeeper, who says and does anything for Pasion, last year opened the water jars and plucked out the names of the judges[18] that had been submitted by the Council? [34] Really, if he dared physical danger for the sake of small gains by opening these jars in secret, these jars that have been stamped by the Prytanies, sealed by the producers of the choruses,[19] guarded by the treasurers, and kept on the Acropolis, why the need for surprise, when they stood to make so much profit, if they changed the text of a little document that was being kept by a guest-friend, either by persuading his slaves or by devising some other trick? I do not know what more needs to be said about these things.

[35] Already Pasion has tried to persuade some people that I had no money at all here, claiming that I had borrowed thirty staters[20] from Stratocles. I think you should hear about this also, so that you may know what sorts of evidence inspired him to steal my money. When Stratocles was about to sail to the Black Sea, men of the court, and I wanted to get as much of my money as possible from there, I asked Stratocles to leave me his gold here and to recover it from my father in the Black Sea. [36] I thought it would be a great advantage if the money were not risked at sea, especially since the Spartans ruled the sea at that time. I do not think that this is an indication favoring his argument that I had no money here. Rather, my dealings with Stratocles are the greatest evidence favoring my argument that I had gold on deposit with Pasion. [37] When Stratocles asked who would pay him back the money if my father did not follow my instructions and he did not reach me here after sailing back, I introduced Pasion to him, and Pasion agreed to pay him back both the capital and the accrued interest. But if no money of mine were on deposit with him, do you think that he would so easily have become my surety for so much money? Witnesses, please come up.

---

[18] I.e., the names of the candidates to be judges for the Festival of Dionysus, where Athens' major dramatic competitions took place. Cf. Lys. 4.3.

[19] For the Prytanies, see the Introduction, IVA. A chorus producer is the speaker in Ant. 6.

[20] Presumably staters from Cyzicus, worth about 28 drachmas each; see below, Dem 35.36n.

[WITNESSES]

[38] Perhaps, men of the court, he will present witnesses to you that before Satyrus' representatives I denied having anything except what I turned over to them, that he himself tried to claim my money since I admitted that I owed him three hundred drachmas, and that I allowed Hippolaïdas, a guest-friend and associate of mine, to borrow from him.[21] [39] Since I was put into the misfortunes that I have related to you, men of the court, having lost all my money at home and being forced to hand over what I had here to those who came, with nothing left unless I could secretly save the gold I had on deposit with Pasion, I admit I did acknowledge owing him three hundred drachmas, and I acted and spoke about other things in such a way that they might be persuaded that I had no money. [40] You will easily realize that this was not because I lacked resources but so that they might believe me. First, then, I shall present witnesses to you who know that I received a lot of money from the Black Sea and then those who saw me using this man's bank and finally those from whom at the time I had bought more than a thousand staters of gold. [41] In addition to this, when a special levy was imposed on us, of the foreigners I contributed the most when others did the registration, and when I was chosen registrar, I registered myself for the largest contribution, but I pleaded with my fellow registrars on behalf of Pasion, saying that he was using my money.[22] Witnesses, please come up.

[WITNESSES]

[42] In addition, I shall present Pasion's activity as support for this testimony. Someone denounced a trading ship,[23] for which I had lent a lot of money, on the grounds that it belonged to a Delian man. When I disputed this and demanded that the ship launch, those who wished to prosecute maliciously swayed the Council in such a way that at first

---

[21] If the speaker had been solvent, he would have provided the loan himself.

[22] The *eisphora* was an extraordinary levy (Introduction, IVC), which metics and foreigners were also compelled to pay.

[23] By a *phasis,* a denunciation of someone holding property that belonged to the state.

I was almost put to death without a trial,[24] but finally they were persuaded to receive sureties from me. [43] I asked Philip, a guest-friend of my father, and he appeared, but he feared a serious risk and left. Pasion, however, provided Archestratus[25] from the bank as surety of the seven talents for me. And yet, if he were losing only a small amount and knew that I had nothing here, he would surely not have become my surety for so much money. [44] It is clear that he called in the three hundred drachmas as a favor to me[26] and that he became my surety for seven talents with the thought that he had sufficient collateral in the gold that was on deposit with him. From the actions of Pasion, therefore, I have shown you, and you have heard from others who know, that I had a lot of money here and that it was on deposit at his bank.

[45] It seems to me, men of the court, that you will make the best decision about what we are disputing if you recall the time and the circumstances when I sent Menexenus and Philomelus to demand the deposit back and Pasion first dared to deny it. You will discover that my father had been arrested and his entire property confiscated. Because of my circumstances, it was impossible for me either to remain here or to return to the Black Sea. [46] Now, is it more likely that in such difficulties I would make an unjust charge or that Pasion would be encouraged by the seriousness of our misfortunes and the amount of money to cheat me? Who has ever been such a sykophant that he would plot against another's wealth while facing physical danger himself? With what hope or purpose would I have unjustly prosecuted this man? Did I think he was immediately going to give me money out of fear of my power? Neither of us was in this situation. [47] Did I think that by coming to trial, even contrary to justice, I would have an advantage before you over Pasion? I was not even prepared to remain here since I was afraid Satyrus would demand me back from you. Would I make myself hateful to the one man in the city with whom I had been especially close in order to achieve nothing? Who of you thinks I should be condemned for such madness and stupidity?

---

[24]Only a lawcourt had the power to sentence a man to death (*Ath. Pol.* 45.1), but this power had been usurped by the Council under the Thirty.

[25]Archestratus was Pasion's former master. Pasion had worked in his bank.

[26]I.e., to help deceive Satyrus' representatives.

[48] It is worth considering, men of the court, the strangeness and unbelievability of Pasion's arguments at each point. When I was in such a situation that I could not have brought suit against him even if he had conceded that he was stealing my money, at that point he accused me of attempting to charge him unjustly. But when I was released from the allegations before Satyrus, and everyone thought he would lose the suit, at that time, he says, he released me from all the charges. What could be more illogical than this?

[49] Perhaps it is only on these points and not on the others that he is clearly saying and doing contradictory things. But he claimed that his slave, whom he himself had hidden, had been kidnapped by us. He registered this same slave in his property assessment as a slave along with his other servants, but when Menexenus demanded him for torture, he had him released, claiming he was free. [50] In addition, while stealing my deposit, he dared to charge us on the grounds that we had six talents from his bank. Whoever tries to lie about such conspicuous matters, why should you believe him about matters he conducted one-to-one?

[51] In the end, men of the court, after he agreed to sail to Satyrus and do whatever he decided, he played a trick in this also. He refused to sail himself, although I invited him to do so many times, but he sent Cittus instead. When Cittus got there he claimed he was a free man, a Silesian by birth, and that Pasion had sent him to inform Satyrus about the money. [52] On hearing both of us, Satyrus decided not to give judgment on dealings that arose here, especially since Pasion was not there and was not about to follow Satyrus' judgment. But Satyrus thought that I had been done such an injustice that he called together the shippers[27] and asked them to help me and not to allow me to be wronged. He also composed a letter to the city and gave it to Centimes the son of Carbines to carry. Please read it to them.

[LETTER]

[53] Although I have so many claims on justice, men of the court, I think the greatest evidence that Pasion is stealing my money is that he was not willing to surrender for torture the slave who knew thor-

---

[27] Merchants residing in Bosporus.

oughly about the deposit. What test would be stronger than this about dealings with those at banks? We certainly do not use witnesses for them. [54] I see that in both private and public matters you acknowledge nothing more credible or true than torture. You recognize that witnesses can be suborned even about what has not transpired, but tortures clearly indicate which side is telling the truth.[28] Knowing this, Pasion wanted you to infer from probabilities about this case rather than to have clear knowledge. Surely he could not say that he would be at a disadvantage in the torture and that for this reason it was unreasonable for him to hand over the slave. [55] You all know that if the slave had denounced him, he would have been abused by this man in the worst way humanly possible for the rest of his life; but if he had held firm, he would have been set free and had a share of what this man stole from me. But although Pasion would have had such a great advantage, he knew what he had done, and so he put up with standing trial and facing other charges[29] just so there would be no torture concerning this case.

[56] Therefore, I ask you to recall these things and vote against Pasion, not to condemn me of such depravity that although my home is by the Black Sea and I have so much property that I can help others, I would come here to prosecute Pasion maliciously by accusing him of lying about his deposits.

[57] It is also worth considering Satyrus and my father, who all this time have regarded you above all Greeks and have often allowed you to import grain although they were sending the ships of other merchants away empty because of the scarcity of grain. In private dealings also, in which they have served as judges, you have come away not only with an equal share but with more. [58] Therefore, it would not be reasonable for you to make light of their letters. I ask you therefore to vote according to justice both about me and about them and not to think that the false words of Pasion are more credible than mine.

---

[28] An argument almost exactly the same as this one is found in Is. 8.12.

[29] I.e., those of Menexenus.

DEMOSTHENES 35. AGAINST LACRITUS

〰〰〰〰〰〰〰〰〰〰〰〰〰〰〰〰〰〰〰〰〰〰〰〰〰〰〰〰〰〰〰〰〰〰〰〰〰〰〰

INTRODUCTION

Lacritus originally came from Phaselis in Asia Minor, but at the time of this speech he was living in Athens, where he must have been registered as a metic (resident alien). He was a rhetorician; he had been a pupil of Isocrates and taught rhetoric himself (15, 41). Little else is known about him. His opponent, the speaker, was an Athenian named Androcles son of Xeinis of Sphettus. He is known from two inscriptions, and his brother Xenocles from a larger number, to have performed liturgies and other financial business; both brothers were probably affluent and prominent figures.[1]

The date of the speech is probably close to 351. It cannot be earlier than 355, which is the earliest possible date of the enactment of the mercantile laws. On the other hand, trade from Athens to Mende and Scione (10) is unlikely to have continued after the Macedonians took control of neighboring Olynthus in 348. In any case, the date cannot be later than 338, because Isocrates, who is mentioned as living (40), died in that year. Many scholars think that the speech is not written in the style of Demosthenes, but there is otherwise no evidence that he is not the author.

One interesting feature of this oration is that all the various documents preserved within the text appear to be genuine, not composed in a later age to fill the gaps. A few of the men named in them as witnesses are also named in fourth-century Athenian inscriptions, which confirms that they have not been invented. Besides, many of the details in the documents are not drawn from the speech itself but deal with complications which would have been unlikely to occur to a

---

[1] For details, see Lambert 2001: 57–58.

reader in later times. That is true especially of the agreement given in 10–13. This contract is of particular importance for the study of Athenian mercantile practice because, although maritime contracts are mentioned in several other speeches, this is the only one of which we have the complete text.

Androcles says that he and a friend of his from Carystus in Euboea lent the sum of 3,000 drachmas to Artemon and Apollodorus, two young brothers who were merchants from Phaselis. Much of the negotiation was carried on by Lacritus, who was the elder brother of the two Phaselites. According to the agreement, which Lacritus drew up for them, the money was to be used to buy cargo for a voyage from Athens, via Mende or Scione in northern Greece, to Bosporus on the north side of the Pontus (the Black Sea) and back to Athens. The security was to be 3,000 jars of Mendaean wine, which evidently were to be taken on board at Mende or Scione and sold in Bosporus in order to buy a return cargo to Athens, probably grain; this (the wine or the grain) would be forfeited to the lenders if the borrowers failed to repay the loan.

But when in due course the two brothers returned to Athens, they neither repaid the loan nor unloaded any grain, wine, or other cargo which Androcles and his friend could take over in lieu of repayment. Lacritus asserted that the cargo had been lost in a shipwreck, and the remaining money had been lent to another Phaselite and was probably lost as well. Artemon and Apollodorus then left Athens again for Chios. Subsequently, Artemon died (we are not told how). Androcles therefore prosecuted Lacritus, as Artemon's heir, along with Apollodorus for recovery of his money by the procedure for mercantile cases, for which there were special requirements: the ground of prosecution had to be that a written agreement[2] existed between the disputants which, the prosecutor alleged, the defendant had failed to fulfill. The agreement must either have been made in the Athenian port (at Piraeus) or concern a voyage to or from the Athenian port.[3]

---

[2] The Greek words are not always clearly defined or distinguished from one another, but I use "contract" to translate *symbolaion*, "written agreement" to translate *syngraphē*, and "terms" to translate *synthēkai*.

[3] I use "port" to translate *emporion*, the area at Piraeus where ships were loaded and unloaded and wholesale transactions took place. I use "market" to translate *agora*, the area for retail buying and selling in the center of Athens.

A common type of transaction was for a lender, who had money available for investment, to lend a sum to a merchant; the merchant used the money to buy goods in Athens, transported them to another city, sold them there at a profit, used the proceeds to buy other goods there, which he transported back to Athens and sold at a further profit, and finally repaid the loan with interest to the original lender while still having some profit for himself. The merchant might share the expenses and profits with the skipper of the ship which he used; the goods, and sometimes the ship itself, served as security for the lender in case the loan was not repaid. The written agreement, which could be quite detailed (see 10–13), usually contained a clause stating that, if the ship was wrecked and the goods lost on the voyage, the loan need not be repaid.

In this case, Lacritus has brought a counter-indictment (*paragraphē*), objecting that he should not be prosecuted by that procedure. *Paragraphē* was a procedure for objecting that a prosecution was inadmissible—not because the accusation was untrue but because the prosecution itself was in some way contrary to law. It initiated a separate trial in which the original prosecutor was himself prosecuted for bringing a prosecution that was not allowed. The original case was postponed until the *paragraphē* case had been decided. The result of the *paragraphē* trial did not settle the original case but only the question whether it should proceed to a straight trial (*euthydikia*). Nevertheless, speakers often confuse these two questions by talking about both of them together in a *paragraphē* speech.[4]

The surviving oration is Androcles' reply to the counter-indictment, arguing that his prosecution should go forward. It is directed against Lacritus only; Apollodorus, although he too is being prosecuted by Androcles (as 34 shows), is not involved in the counter-indictment. Lacritus disclaimed responsibility for the debt on the ground that he was not Artemon's heir, but Androcles brushes this argument aside, perhaps too readily, pointing out that Lacritus has in fact been administering Artemon's estate.[5] However, the question whether Lacritus

---

[4] The view that the *paragraphē* speech and the original accusation were both judged at the same trial is now generally rejected; but see Carawan 2001: 29–31.

[5] No details of Phaselite law are known, but it was probably normal in Phaselis, as in Athens, for the property of a man who died childless to pass to his

ought to pay Artemon's debts was one for a straight trial, not for a counter-indictment, which should be about the legal procedure. The ground for the counter-indictment must therefore have been that there was no written agreement between Androcles and Lacritus; a mercantile case had to be based on a written agreement. That is why Androcles actually has the agreement between him and Artemon read out twice in the course of his speech (in 10–13 and again in 37), to emphasize that a written agreement existed. But whether an agreement with a deceased person counted for this purpose as an agreement with the heir of the deceased was a question which may never have arisen before the present case (since the mercantile laws were a recent innovation). Lacritus was not a merchant, and may well have argued that an action against him should not be tried by the mercantile procedure. We do not know what the jury decided.

Androcles probably sensed that the jury's answer to this legal question was uncertain. So he devotes much of his speech to saying that Lacritus, as the elder brother of the two young men, was really responsible for what they did, or failed to do, in carrying out the terms of the agreement, and that the terms were in fact not carried out properly. They pledged the same goods as security for a second loan; they failed to purchase a return cargo in Bosporus; they lent some of the money to another Phaselite; they failed to bring the ship back into the port at Piraeus; and so on. Some of these allegations are confirmed by the testimony of witnesses. Some are not, and we cannot be sure that they are all true; but there does seem to be sufficient truth in the account to justify the conclusion that the terms of the agreement had not been fulfilled. In any case, the details of the story give us a vivid picture of the conditions of overseas trade in Demosthenes' time.

Another lively feature of this speech is the characterization of Lacritus and Androcles. At the beginning of the negotiations Lacritus presented himself as "a big shot, a pupil of Isocrates," who was ready to arrange everything (15–16). Androcles several times calls him a sophist and his tricks sophistries (2, 22, 39–40, 56). The implication is that he knows how to make false statements appear true, and the jury therefore should not believe anything he says. Androcles by contrast

---

brother, if he had one. However, Lacritus may have said that Apollodorus was Artemon's heir.

is a plain, blunt man, as he declares with an unusually strong oath: "As far as I'm concerned—by Zeus the Lord and all the gods!—I've never made any objection or criticism, men of the jury, if anyone wants to be a sophist and pay cash to Isocrates; I'd be crazy to bother about that" (40). Thus he hopes to convince the jury that he is not a liar. He uses some unusually strong language to attack the Phaselites in general at the start of the speech, and Lacritus and his brothers throughout. If this is skillful presentation of Androcles' bluff character, perhaps we should be cautious about following those scholars who say that the speech is not good enough to have been written by Demosthenes.

DEMOSTHENES 35. AGAINST LACRITUS

[1] It's nothing new that the Phaselites[6] are doing, men of the jury; it's what they usually do. They are the most terrible men for borrowing money in the port, and then, after they get it and draw up a maritime agreement, they immediately forget about written agreements and laws and the need to repay what they received. [2] They think that, if they pay it, it's like losing some of their own personal money, and to avoid paying they devise sophistries and counter-indictments and excuses. They're the most dishonest scoundrels in the world. Here's proof of it: although many men come to your port, both Greeks and foreigners, the Phaselites by themselves always have more lawsuits than all the rest put together.

[3] That's the sort of men they are. I, men of the jury, lent money to Artemon, the brother of this man Lacritus, in accordance with the mercantile laws for a voyage to the Pontus[7] and back to Athens. He died without having repaid my money, and so I've brought this case against Lacritus in accordance with those same laws under which I made the contract, [4] because he is Artemon's brother and has possession of all his property, both what he left at Athens and what he had at Phaselis, and is heir to the whole of his estate. He cannot point to a law which gives him the right to hold his brother's property and to have administered it as he thought fit, and yet not to repay other men's

---

[6] Phaselis was a city on the east coast of Lycia in southern Asia Minor.
[7] The Black Sea.

loans but to say now that he's not the heir and disclaim it. [5] That's the nature of this man Lacritus' offense. Now I ask you, men of the jury, to listen favorably to what I say about this business, and, if I demonstrate that he has done wrong both to us, the lenders, and equally to you, give us the support we deserve.

[6] I had no knowledge at all of these men myself, men of the jury, but Thrasymedes son of Diophantus—the well-known man of Sphettus[8]—and his brother Melanopus are friends of mine, and we get together as often as we can. They came to me with this man Lacritus, having become acquainted with him somehow or other (I don't know how), [7] and asked me to lend money to Artemon, this man's brother, and Apollodorus[9] for a voyage to the Pontus, to set them up in business. Thrasymedes was equally unaware of their dishonesty, men of the jury; he thought they were respectable people, as they claimed and asserted they were, and he believed they would carry out all that this man Lacritus promised and undertook that they would. [8] So he was utterly deceived and quite failed to realize what beasts these men were with whom he was dealing. As for me, because I was convinced by Thrasymedes and his brother, and this man Lacritus undertook that his brothers would deal honestly with me, I lent 30 silver minas jointly with a friend of ours from Carystus.[10] [9] Now, men of the jury, I want you first to hear the written agreement, under which we lent the money, and the witnesses who were present when the loan was made. Then I shall tell you the rest of what happened, to show you what robbers they were concerning the loan. [*To the clerk*] Read out the written agreement, and then the testimonies.

[10] [WRITTEN AGREEMENT] *Androcles of Sphettus and Nausicrates of Carystus lent to Artemon and Apollodorus of Phaselis 3,000 drachmas of silver for a voyage from Athens to Mende or Scione, and from there to Bosporus,[11] and, if they wish, on the left-hand side as far as the*

---

[8] Sphettus was the deme to which Androcles himself also belonged.

[9] Apollodorus was another brother of Lacritus and Artemon, probably the youngest of the three.

[10] A city in the south of Euboea. The friend is named as Nausicrates in the agreement.

[11] Bosporus was the name of a kingdom in the Crimea (not to be confused with the Thracian Bosporus, joining the Black Sea and the Sea of Marmara).

Borysthenes,[12] *and back to Athens, at 225 a thousand*[13]*—and if they sail after Arcturus*[14] *out of the Pontus towards Hierum,*[15] *at 300 a thousand—on security of 3,000 Mendaean jars of wine, which will be shipped from Mende or Scione in the twenty-oared ship skippered by Hyblesius.* [11] *They*[16] *pledge these, not owing any money to anyone else on this security, nor will they obtain any further loan on it. They will convey back to Athens in the same boat all the goods from the Pontus purchased with proceeds from the outward cargo.*

If the goods reach Athens safely, in accordance with the agreement within twenty days of their arrival at Athens the borrowers will pay the accruing money to the lenders in full—apart from any jettison which the fellow-voyagers vote to make jointly and any enemy exaction from them,[17] *but otherwise in full. They will place the security intact under the control of the lenders until they pay the accruing money in accordance with the agreement.*

[12] *If they do not pay within the agreed time, the lenders shall be permitted to pledge the pledged goods*[18] *and to sell them at the prevailing price; and if the proceeds fall short of the amount which ought to accrue to the lenders according to the agreement, the lenders, both singly and together, shall be permitted to exact it from Artemon and Apollodorus and from all their property, both on land and at sea, wherever it may be, in the same way as if judgment had been given against them and they had defaulted in payment.*

[13] *If they do not enter the Pontus, after waiting in the Hellespont*[19]

---

[12] The river Borysthenes (modern Dnieper, in Ukraine).

[13] At interest of 22.5 percent.

[14] The rising of the star Arcturus (in September) marked the end of the usual sailing season. After that, the weather deteriorated, and the voyage would be more risky (hence, the higher interest rate).

[15] Hierum was a promontory on the Asiatic side of the Thracian Bosporus, where it joins the Black Sea. It was a regular meeting place for ships.

[16] Artemon and Apollodorus.

[17] To save a ship in a storm it might be necessary to lighten it by throwing part of the cargo overboard. This would be done after a vote of the merchants on the ship, who would share the loss in proportion to the amount of goods they had on board. Similarly, they would share the loss if enemies or pirates seized part of the cargo.

[18] To use the goods as security for another loan.

[19] "The Hellespont" here means the whole stretch of water between the Aegean and the Black Sea.

for ten days after the Dog-star,[20] *they shall unload in any place where Athenians are not liable to seizure of goods,*[21] *and after sailing back from there to Athens, they shall pay the amount of interest written in the agreement in the previous year.*[22] *If any ship in which the goods are being conveyed suffers irreparable loss but the pledged goods are saved, the lenders shall share what is preserved.*[23] *On these matters nothing else is to prevail over the written agreement.*

Witnesses: Phormion of Piraeus, Cephisodotus of Boeotia, *and Heliodorus of Pithus.*

[14] Read out the testimonies also.

[DEPOSITION] *Archenomides son of Archedamas of Anagyrus testifies that written terms were deposited with him by Androcles of Sphettus, Nausicrates of Carystus, and Artemon and Apollodorus of Phaselis, and the agreement is in his keeping still.*

Read out also the testimony of those who were present.

[DEPOSITION] *Theodotus an equal-tax man,*[24] *Charinus son of Epichares of Leuconoeum, Phormion son of Ctesiphon of Piraeus, Cephisodotus of Boeotia, and Heliodorus of Pithus testify that they were present when Androcles lent 3,000 drachmas of silver to Apollodorus and*

---

[20] The Dog-star (Sirius) rises in late July. If bad weather or other circumstances delayed the ship's arrival in the Black Sea beyond early August, not enough time would remain before the end of the sailing season for a worthwhile trading visit to Bosporus.

[21] This implies that in some cities, unfriendly to Athens, individuals who had suffered loss or damage by Athenian action could seize in compensation any Athenian goods which were landed there.

[22] These words appear to refer to a previous agreement, though it is strange that the amount of interest payable is stated by reference to another document. Some scholars think that, although a new year will have begun (at midsummer), the amount of interest payable when the goods have been merely unloaded and not sold is still to be the same as is specified in *this* document, but this would be an odd way to express this point.

[23] The pledged goods (3,000 jars of wine, or the return cargo, or whatever is left of them) are to be shared equally between the lenders and the borrowers. The usual rule was that if a ship was lost, the borrowers need not repay the lenders.

[24] "Equal-tax man" (*isotelēs*) means that Theodotus was a metic who paid only the same taxes as citizens, without the additional tax normally paid by metics.

*Artemon, and that they know that they deposited the written agree-
ment with Archenomides of Anagyrus.*

[15] It was in accordance with that written agreement, men of the
jury, that I lent the money to Artemon, this man's brother. It was this
man who urged me to lend it, and undertook that everything would
be done for me honestly and in accordance with the agreement under
which I made the loan; and it was this man who actually wrote it, and
joined in sealing it after it was written. For his brothers were still quite
young, just lads, whereas this man was Lacritus of Phaselis, a big shot,
a pupil of Isocrates. [16] He was the man who arranged it all and told
me to listen to him. He said he would stay in Athens and do everything for me honestly, while his brother Artemon would make the
voyage in charge of the goods. At that time, men of the jury, when
he wanted to get the money from us, he declared that he was both the
brother and the partner of Artemon, and he spoke in a wonderfully
convincing manner. [17] But as soon as they got control of the cash,
they divided it between them and did what they liked with it. They
did nothing, large or small, in accordance with the maritime agreement under which they got the money, as the actual events showed.
And this man Lacritus was the ringleader of it all. On each clause in
the written agreement I shall prove that their actions have been utterly
dishonest.

[18] First, it is written that they borrowed the 30 minas from us on
security of 3,000 jars of wine, on the basis that they already had security of another 30 minas,[25] so that the cost of the wine amounted to a
talent of silver, including the expenses incurred in procuring the
wine;[26] and these 3,000 jars were to be taken to the Pontus in the
twenty-oared ship skippered by Hyblesius. [19] That's what is written
in the agreement, which you have heard, men of the jury. But these
men, instead of the 3,000 jars, didn't put even 500 jars on board the
boat. Instead of having purchased the correct quantity of wine, they

---

[25] The meaning is that Artemon and Apollodorus already possessed 30 minas
to contribute to the total cost of 60 minas (1 talent) of the wine which would be
the security for the loan.

[26] This shows that one jar of Mendaean wine cost somewhat less than 2 drachmas. However, the size of a jar (*keramion*) is uncertain.

did what they liked with the money, and they had no thought or intention of putting the 3,000 jars on board the boat in accordance with the written agreement. [*To the clerk*] To show that I'm telling the truth, take the testimony of the men who sailed with them in the same boat.

[20] [DEPOSITION] *Erasicles testifies that he was the helmsman of the ship skippered by Hyblesius, and he knows that Apollodorus*[27] *conveyed in the boat 450 jars of Mendaean wine and no more, and that Apollodorus conveyed no other wares in the boat to the Pontus.*

Hippias son of Athenippus of Halicarnassus testifies that he also sailed in Hyblesius' ship as the ship's commander, and that he knows that Apollodorus of Phaselis conveyed in the boat from Mende to the Pontus 450 jars of Mendaean wine, and no other cargo.

He gave his testimony out of court to the following:[28] *Archiades son of Mnesonides of Acharnae, Sostratus son of Philippus of Hestiaea, Eumarichus son of Euboeus of Hestiaea, Philtades son of Ctesias of Xypete, Dionysius son of Democratides of Cholleidae.*

[21] So that was what they actually did with regard to the quantity of wine which they were required to put on board the boat; they began straightaway to depart from the first clause of the agreement and not to do what is written in it. Next, it's in the written agreement that they pledge these goods free from encumbrance and owing nothing to anyone, and that they will not obtain any further loan from anyone on this security. That is written explicitly, men of the jury. [22] And what did these men do? They ignored what is written in the agreement and borrowed money from a certain young man; they lied to him that they owed nothing to anyone. They cheated us, by obtaining a loan on the security of our goods without telling us, and they lied to that young man, the lender, that they were borrowing on the security of unencumbered goods. Such is the evil-doing of these men. And all these are sophistries devised by this man Lacritus. To prove that I'm telling the

---

[27] Artemon seems to have ceased to be active in the business. Possibly he began to be affected by an illness which eventually caused his death.

[28] Hippias is not present in court to confirm his testimony, but the five men listed confirm that he confirmed it previously in their presence. All five are shown by their demes to be Athenian citizens.

truth and they did obtain a further loan, contrary to the written agreement, the testimony of the lender himself will be read to you. [23] [*To the clerk*] Read out the testimony.

[DEPOSITION] *Aratus of Halicarnassus testifies that he lent to Apollodorus 11 minas of silver on the security of the merchandise which he was conveying in Hyblesius' ship to the Pontus, and of the goods purchased there with the proceeds; and that he did not know that he had borrowed money from Androcles, or he would not have lent Apollodorus the money himself.*

[24] Such are the villainies of these people. Next, it's written in the agreement, men of the jury, that, after selling in the Pontus what they have brought, they are to use the proceeds to make further purchases as a return cargo and convey the return cargo to Athens, and after reaching Athens they are to repay us in good silver within twenty days; until they pay, we are to have control of the goods, and they are to hand these over intact until we receive payment. [25] This is written quite exactly in the agreement. But in this matter especially, men of the jury, these men displayed their own insolence and shamelessness, and they showed that they took not the least notice of what was written in the agreement, but considered the agreement to be just stuff and nonsense. They neither made any purchases with the proceeds in the Pontus nor loaded a return cargo to take to Athens; and because they arrived from the Pontus without it, we, the lenders of the money, had nothing to lay our hands on and take under our control until we obtained what belonged to us, for they didn't import anything at all into your harbor. [26] What has happened to us is quite extraordinary, men of the jury: in our own city, though we've done nothing wrong and haven't been condemned to pay them any penalty, we've been robbed of our property by these men, who are Phaselites—as if Phaselites had been granted rights of seizure against Athenians! For, since they refuse to repay what they received, what else can one call such men but violent misappropriators of other men's possessions? I've never even heard of any action more wicked than the one these men have perpetrated against us, even though they admit receiving the money from us. [27] Whereas any disputed points in contracts require a trial, men of the jury, the points that are accepted by both parties, and are written in maritime agreements, are considered by everyone to be valid, and it's right to abide by the documents. Yet they have done

nothing at all in accordance with the agreement, but right from the beginning they were plotting to swindle and defraud; that's proved quite plainly, both by the testimonies and by their own statements.

[28] But you must hear the most terrible thing of all that this man Lacritus did—for he was the one who arranged all this. When they arrived here, they didn't put in to your port but anchored in Thieves' Cove,[29] which is outside the boundary signs of your port. Anchoring in Thieves' Cove is like anchoring at Aegina or Megara; you can sail off from that harbor wherever you wish and whenever you like. [29] The boat lay at anchor there for more than twenty-five days, while these men walked around in the sample-market,[30] and we approached them and spoke to them, telling them to make sure we got our money as soon as possible. They agreed and said that was just what they were arranging. We kept on approaching them, and at the same time we were watching to see if they were unloading anything from a boat anywhere or paying the two-percent tax.

[30] When they had been in Attica for a good many days, and we found that nothing whatever had been unloaded or taxed in their name, we then began to press them harder with our demands. And when we were badgering them, this man Lacritus, Artemon's brother, answered that they wouldn't be able to pay, but all the goods were lost; and Lacritus said he could give a good explanation of that. [31] We became annoyed at what he said, men of the jury, but we didn't gain anything by our annoyance, because they didn't care in the least. Nonetheless, we asked them how the goods had been lost. This man Lacritus said the boat was wrecked while sailing along the coast from Panticapaeum to Theodosia,[31] and when the boat was wrecked, his

---

[29] Thieves' Cove was a creek on the coast west of Piraeus, near modern Perama. It was used by traders who wanted to evade the customs duties or harbor dues at Piraeus. Isager and Hansen (1975: 171–172) plausibly suggest that the Phaselite captain of the ship put in there because he was conveying to Chios (cf. 52–53) a cargo of grain which he would have been compelled to unload if he had put in at Piraeus (cf. *Ath. Pol.* 51.4).

[30] An area of the port where samples of cargoes were displayed to prospective buyers.

[31] Panticapaeum was the principal city in Bosporus, at the eastern extremity of what is now called the Crimea, and Theodosia was about 100 kilometers further west.

brothers lost the goods which were in the boat at the time. It contained salt fish, Coan wine, and some other things, and they said that all these were the return cargo which they intended to convey to Athens, if they hadn't been lost in the boat. [32] That's what he said; but it's worth hearing what disgusting liars these people are. They had no agreement concerning the boat that was wrecked,[32] but it was someone else who had lent money on the security of the freight from Athens to the Pontus and of the actual boat; the lender's name was Antipater, a Citian by birth.[33] The Coan plonk[34] was eighty jars of wine which had gone off, and the salt fish was being transported for a farmer in the boat from Panticapaeum to Theodosia for the use of his farm laborers. So why do they make these excuses? They're irrelevant.

[33] [*To the clerk*] Please take first Apollonides' testimony that it was Antipater who lent on the security of the boat, and the shipwreck was of no concern to these men; and then Erasicles' and Hippias' testimony that only eighty jars were being transported in the boat.

[DEPOSITIONS] *Apollonides of Halicarnassus testifies that he knows that Antipater, a Citian by birth, lent money to Hyblesius for a voyage to the Pontus on the security of the ship skippered by Hyblesius and the freight to Pontus; and that he himself shared ownership of the ship with Hyblesius, and his own slaves sailed on the ship; and that, when the ship was damaged, his own slaves were there, and they reported it to him; and that the ship was empty[35] when it was damaged while sailing along the coast to Theodosia from Panticapaeum.*

[34] *Erasicles testifies that he sailed with Hyblesius as helmsman of the ship to the Pontus, and that he knows that, when the ship was sailing along the coast to Theodosia from Panticapaeum, the ship was sailing empty, and that there was in the boat no wine belonging to Apollodorus himself, the defendant in this case,[36] but about eighty Coan jars of wine were being conveyed for one of the men from Theodosia.*

---

[32] The meaning is that no loan had been obtained on the security of the ship for the return journey (but merely for the outward journey).

[33] Citium was a city in Cyprus.

[34] The Greek word used here for the wine seems to be disparaging.

[35] "Empty" evidently means "without a full cargo," not contradicting the statement that there was on board some salt fish, Coan wine, and other things (31).

[36] This testimony (and perhaps also those in 20 and 23) seems to have been written for the prosecution of Apollodorus, but it is relevant to the present case too.

Hippias son of Athenippus of Halicarnassus testifies that he sailed with Hyblesius as the ship's commander, and that, when the ship was sailing along the coast to Theodosia from Panticapaeum, Apollodorus put on board the ship one or two bags of wool, eleven or twelve jars of salt fish, and some goat-skins—two or three bundles—but nothing else.

He gave his testimony out of court to the following:[37] *Euphiletus son of Damotimus of Aphidna, Hippias son of Timoxenus of Thymaetadae, Sostratus son of Philippus of Hestiaea, Archenomides son of Straton of Thria, Philtades son of Ctesicles of Xypete.*

[35] Such is the shamelessness of these people. But just think to yourselves, men of the jury, whether you know or have heard that any people ever imported wine to Athens from the Pontus by way of trade—especially Coan! Quite the contrary, surely: wine is exported to the Pontus from our part of the world—from Peparethos and Cos, Thasian[38] and Mendaean and every sort of wine from various other cities—but the goods imported here from the Pontus are different.

[36] We held on to them and pressed them to say whether any of the goods were saved in the Pontus. This man Lacritus replied that 100 Cyzicene staters[39] were saved, and his brother had lent that gold in the Pontus to a Phaselite skipper, a fellow-citizen and friend of his own, and was unable to recover it, so that this too was as good as lost. [37] That's what this man Lacritus said. But it's not what the written agreement says, men of the jury. It instructs these men to purchase a return cargo and bring it back to Athens, not to lend our property in the Pontus to anyone they like without our consent but to produce it intact for us in Athens until we get back all the money we lent. [*To the clerk*] Please read the written agreement again.

[WRITTEN AGREEMENT][40]

[38] Does the written agreement, men of the jury, instruct these men to lend our money—and that to a person we don't know and have never seen—or to purchase a return cargo and bring it to Ath-

---

[37] See above, 20n.

[38] Thasos is an island in the north Aegean.

[39] Cyzicene staters, each worth about 28 drachmas, were often used in international trade (cf. above, Isoc. 17.35). The sum of 100 staters was not much less than the 3,000 drachmas which Androcles and Nausicrates had lent.

[40] The document read out in 10–13 is now read out again.

ens and produce it for us and hand it over intact? [39] The agreement lays down that nothing is to prevail over what is written in it, and no law or decree or anything else is to be brought to bear against the agreement. But right from the beginning these men didn't care about this agreement, but used our money as if it were their own; they're such criminal sophists and dishonest people. [40] As far as I'm concerned—by Zeus the Lord and all the gods!—I've never made any objection or criticism, men of the jury, if anyone wants to be a sophist and pay cash to Isocrates; I'd be crazy to bother about that. But, by Zeus, I don't think that conceited people who think themselves clever should covet other people's property and deprive them of it, relying on making a speech. That's what a rascally damned sophist does.

[41] This man Lacritus, men of the jury, has come to this trial not relying on the justice of his case but well aware of what they've done with regard to this loan. He believes that he's clever and will easily find words for talking about dishonest activities, and he thinks he'll mislead you in any way he wishes. He claims to be clever at this; he charges money and takes pupils because he claims to give training on this very subject. [42] And first of all he gave his own brothers this training—you can see it's wicked and dishonest, men of the jury—training them to obtain maritime loans in the port and misappropriate them and not repay them. How could there be anyone wickeder than either the teacher or the learners of such skills? Anyway, since he is clever and relies on his speaking and on the 1,000 drachmas which he paid his tutor, [43] tell him to explain to you either that they did not receive the money from us, or that since receiving it they have repaid it, or that written maritime agreements should not be valid, or that it's right to make any other use of the money than the ones for which they received it according to the written agreement. Let him convince you of whichever of those he prefers, and I myself concede that he's a very clever man if he convinces you who give judgments concerning mercantile contracts. But I know very well that he can't explain or convince you of any of those things.

[44] Apart from that, tell me this, by the gods, men of the jury: if the opposite had happened—if it had not been this man's dead brother who owed me money, but I had owed his brother a talent or 80 minas or more or less—do you think, men of the jury, that this man Lacritus

would be using the same words as the ones he's been throwing about now, saying that he's not the heir and disclaiming his brother's estate? Wouldn't he be relentlessly demanding payment from me, as he has from all the other people who owed anything to his dead brother either in Phaselis or anywhere else? [45] And if any of us, when prosecuted by him, had dared to bring a counter-indictment claiming that the case was not admissible, I'm quite sure he would have been indignant, and he would have protested to you that it was outrageous and illegal treatment if his case, which was a mercantile one, was voted to be inadmissible. Then, Lacritus, if that seems just for you, why won't it be just for me? Don't we all have the same inscribed laws and the same rights with regard to mercantile cases? [46] But he's such a disgusting person, he beats everyone at dishonesty: he's attempting to persuade you to vote that this mercantile case is not admissible, although you are trying mercantile cases at this time.[41]

What is it you're demanding, Lacritus? That it should not be sufficient to deprive us of the money we lent you, but that we should also be thrown into prison by you if we fail to pay the penalty which we incur in addition?[42] [47] Surely it would be dreadful and scandalous and a disgrace to you, men of the jury, if men who make maritime loans in your port and are defrauded were taken off to prison by the borrowers who defraud them. That, Lacritus, is what you are urging to the jury.

Where else should justice concerning mercantile contracts be obtained, men of the jury? Before which official, or at what time?[43]

---

[41] During the winter. Trials of mercantile cases were held during the winter, so as not to keep merchants in Athens during the summer sailing season; cf. Dem. 33.23.

[42] For the penalty of *epōbelia* (1 obol per drachma), see above, Dem. 27.67n. A litigant in any mercantile case could be imprisoned until he paid; otherwise, it might have been too easy for a skipper or merchant to slip away from Athens without paying.

[43] The series of suggestions and answers which follows, with the speaker conducting virtually a dialogue with himself, is a striking example of the figure of speech called *hypophora*. It is intended to show that the present case has correctly been brought before the Thesmothetae, because no other magistrates would be appropriate for it.

Before the Eleven?[44] But they bring into court burglars and thieves and other malefactors liable to the death penalty. [48] Before the Archon?[45] The Archon, though, is instructed to look after heiresses and orphans and parents. Well, someone might say, before the Basileus.[46] But we aren't gymnasiarchs,[47] nor are we prosecuting anyone for impiety. Well, the Polemarch will bring us into court.[48] Oh yes, for defection and lack of a sponsor![49] Then the generals are left.[50] But they appoint trierarchs;[51] they never bring a mercantile case into court. [49] I am a merchant, and you are the brother and heir of one of the merchants who received the mercantile loan from us. Where, then, ought this case to come into court? Tell us, Lacritus—only say something that's just and in accordance with law. But there's no human being clever enough to justify that sort of behavior.

[50] That's not the only dreadful treatment I've had from this man Lacritus, men of the jury. Besides being defrauded of the money, I would have fallen into a very dangerous position as a result of his activities, if my written agreement with these men hadn't protected me by attesting that I lent the money for a voyage to the Pontus and back to Athens. You know, men of the jury, how severe the law is on any Athenian who imports grain to any place other than Athens or lends

---

[44] The Eleven arranged and presided at trials for certain crimes; see further the Introduction to Ant. 5, n. 1.

[45] The Archon (Introduction, IVA) was responsible especially for trials concerning family and inheritance disputes.

[46] For the Basileus, see the Introduction to Ant. 6.

[47] A gymnasiarch supported the runners in a torch race at a festival.

[48] The Polemarch was responsible for certain trials involving those who were not Athenian citizens (e.g., Dem. 59.40; Isoc. 17.12).

[49] These were accusations which could be brought only against metics. A case of defection (*apostasiou*) was probably one in which a slave who had been freed and given metic status was accused of failure to observe the conditions laid down by the owner who had freed him. A case of sponsorlessness (*aprostasiou*) was one in which a metic was accused of not having an Athenian citizen as his sponsor (*prostatēs*).

[50] The generals (*stratēgoi*), besides commanding in war, were responsible for arranging trials and taking various decisions concerning military and naval matters.

[51] A trierarch maintained and captained a trireme (Introduction, IVC).

money for trade to any port other than the Athenian port, and what heavy and fearful penalties there are for those offenses. [51] [*To the clerk*] You'd better read them the actual law, to inform them more exactly.

[LAW] *And it is not to be permitted for any of the Athenians or the metics residing in Athens or those whom they control*[52] *to advance money for any ship which is not going to bring grain to Athens—and the other provisions about each of them.*[53] *If anyone does advance money in contravention of this, there may be showing* (phasis) *and listing* (apographē)[54] *of the money to the supervisors,*[55] *in the same way as has been specified concerning the ship and the grain.*[56] *He may not raise an action to recover any money which he advances for any destination other than Athens, nor may any magistracy bring an action into court for it.*

[52] That's how strict the law is, men of the jury. But these men— the wickedest men in the world!—although it was explicitly written in the agreement that the money was to come back to Athens, allowed what they borrowed from us in Athens to be taken to Chios.[57] The Phaselite skipper wanted to borrow a further sum in the Pontus from a Chian, and because the Chian refused to lend it unless he was given as security the whole of what the skipper had on board with the consent of the previous lenders, they did consent that this money of ours should become security for the Chian and gave him control of everything. [53] On those terms they sailed away out of the Pontus with the Phaselite skipper and with the lender from Chios, and they anchored

---

[52] This expression covers women, children, and slaves. Here the reference must be primarily to slaves used as agents.

[53] The words following the dash seem to mean that the text here omits a part of the law which is not relevant to the present case. But the wording is strange, and there may be some corruption in the text.

[54] *Phasis* and *apographē* were procedures for initiating prosecution in public cases.

[55] Ten supervisors of the port (*epimelētai emporiou*) were appointed by lot each year.

[56] This may refer to something in the omitted portion of the law.

[57] Chios is an island in the eastern Aegean, which had long had friendly relations with the Phaselites.

at Thieves' Cove,[58] without anchoring in your port. And now, men of the jury, the money lent in Athens for a voyage to the Pontus and back from the Pontus to Athens has been transported to Chios by these men! [54] So, as I stated at the beginning of my speech, you are victims just as much as we who lent the money. Just consider, men of the jury: aren't you victims, when someone attempts to get the better of your laws, and makes written maritime agreements invalid and void, and has dispatched to Chios the money borrowed from us? Isn't such a man doing wrong to you too?

[55] My case, men of the jury, is against these men, because it was to these men that I lent the money. It will be for them to proceed against that skipper from Phaselis, their own fellow-citizen, to whom they say they lent the money, without our consent and contrary to the written agreement. We don't know what dealings they had with their own fellow-citizen, but they know that themselves. [56] That's what we consider to be just. We ask you, men of the jury, to support us, who are wronged, and to punish those who use tricks and sophistries, as these men do. If you do that, you will have voted for what is advantageous to yourselves, and you will get rid of all the crimes of these wicked people, crimes which some men commit concerning maritime contracts.

---

[58] See above, 28n.

BIBLIOGRAPHY

Andrewes, Antony, 1961: "Philochoros on Phratries," *Journal of Hellenic Studies* 81: 1–15.

Bers, V. 1985: "Dikastic *thorubos*," in *Crux: Studies Presented to G. E. M. de Ste. Croix on His 75th Birthday*, ed. Paul Cartledge and David Harvey. Exeter: 1–16.

Boegehold, Alan L., 1995: *The Lawcourts at Athens: Sites, Buildings, Equipment, Procedure, and Testimonia*. Princeton.

Burkert, Walter, 1987: *Ancient Mystery Cults*. Cambridge, MA.

Cantarella, Eva, 2005: "Gender, Sexuality, and Law," in *The Cambridge Companion to Ancient Greek Law*, ed. Michael Gagarin and David Cohen. Cambridge: 236–253.

Carawan, Edwin, 2001: "What the Laws Have Prejudged: *Paragraphē* and Early Issue-Theory," in *The Orator in Action and Theory in Greece and Rome*, ed. Cecil W. Wooten. Leiden: 17–51.

Carey, Christopher, 1989: *Lysias: Selected Speeches*. Cambridge.

Carey, Christopher, 1990: "Structure and Strategy in Lysias 24," *Greece & Rome* 37: 44–51.

Carey, Christopher, 1992: *Greek Orators VI: Apollodorus Against Neaira: [Demosthenes] 59*. Warminster.

Carey, Christopher, 1995a: "The Witness' *Exomosia* in the Athenian Courts," *Classical Quarterly* 45: 114–119.

Carey, Christopher, 1995b: "Rape and Adultery in Athenian Law," *Classical Quarterly* 45: 407–417.

Christ, Matthew, 1998: *The Litigious Athenian*. Baltimore.

Cohen, David, 1991: *Law, Sexuality and Society*. Cambridge.

Cohen, David, 1995: *Law, Violence and Community in Classical Athens*. Cambridge.

Cohen, Edward E., 1992: *Athenian Economy and Society: A Banking Perspective*. Princeton.

Cohen, Edward E., 1994: "Status and Contract in Fourth-Century Athens: A Reply to S. C. Todd," in *Symposion 1993: Vorträge zur griechischen und hellenistischen Rechtsgeschichte*, ed. Gerhard Thür. Cologne: 141–152.

Cox, Cheryl A., 1998: *Household Interests: Property, Marriage Strategies, and Family Dynamics in Ancient Athens*. Princeton.

Davies, John K., 1971: *Athenian Propertied Families 600–300 B.C.* Oxford.

Dover, Kenneth J., 1968: *Lysias and the Corpus Lysiacum*. Berkeley.

Edwards, Michael, 1994: *The Attic Orators*. London.

Edwards, Michael, and Stephen Usher, 1985: *Greek Orators, I, Antiphon and Lysias*. Warminster.

Fisher, Nicolas R. E., 1992: Hybris*: A Study in the Values of Honour and Shame in Ancient Greece*. Warminster.

Forster, E. S., trans., 1927: *Isaeus*. Cambridge, MA.

Foxhall, Lin, 1996: "Feeling the Earth Move: Cultivation Techniques on Steep Slopes in Classical Antiquity," in *Human Landscapes in Classical Antiquity*, ed. Graham Shipley and John Salmon. London: 44–67.

Gagarin, Michael, 1990: "*Bouleusis* in Athenian Homicide Law," in *Symposion 1988*, ed. Guiseppe Nenci and Gerhard Thür. Cologne: 81–99.

Gagarin, Michael, 1996: "The Torture of Slaves in Athenian Law," *Classical Philology* 91: 1–18.

Gagarin, Michael, 2002: *Antiphon the Athenian: Law and Oratory in the Age of the Sophists*. Austin.

Gagarin, Michael, 2007: "Background and Origins: Oratory and Rhetoric before the Sophists," in *A Companion to Greek Rhetoric*, ed. Ian Worthington. Oxford: 27–36.

Hamel, Debra, 2003: *Trying Neaira: The True Story of a Courtesan's Scandalous Life in Ancient Greece*. New Haven.

Hansen, Mogens Herman, 1976: Apagoge, Endeixis *and* Ephegesis *against* Kakourgoi, Atimoi *and* Pheugontes. Odense.

Hansen, Mogens Herman, 1991: *The Athenian Democracy in the Age of Demosthenes*. Oxford.

Harris, Edward M., 1988: "The Date of Aeschines' Birth," *Classical Philology* 83: 211–214.

Harris, Edward M., 1990: "Did the Athenians Regard Seduction as a Worse Crime than Rape?," *Classical Quarterly* 40: 370–377.

Harris, Edward M., 1995: *Aeschines and Athenian Politics.* Oxford.

Harrison, A. R. W., 1968–1971: *The Law of Athens.* Vol. 1: *The Family and Property.* Vol. 2: *Procedure.* Oxford.

Herman, Gabriel, 2006: *Morality and Behaviour in Democratic Athens: A Social History.* Cambridge.

Isager, Signe, and Mogens Herman Hansen, 1975: *Aspects of Athenian Society in the Fourth Century B.C.* Odense.

Johnstone, Steven, 1999: *Disputes and Democracy.* Austin.

Jones, Nicholas F., 1999: *The Associations of Classical Athens.* Oxford.

Kapparis, Konstantinos, 1999: *Apollodoros "Against Neaira" [D.] 59.* Berlin.

Kennedy, George A., 1963: *The Art of Persuasion in Greece.* Princeton.

Lambert, Stephen D., 2001: "Ten Notes on Attic Inscriptions," *Zeitschrift für Papyrologie und Epigraphik* 135: 51–62.

Lanni, Adriaan, 1997: "Spectator Sport or Serious Politics: *Hoi Periestēkotes* and the Athenian Lawcourts," *Journal of Hellenic Studies* 117: 183–189.

Lipsius, Justus Herman, 1905–1915: *Das attische Recht und Rechtsverfahren.* Leipzig.

MacDowell, Douglas M., 1978: *The Law in Classical Athens.* London.

Millet, Paul, 1991: *Lending and Borrowing in Ancient Athens.* Cambridge.

Mirhady, David C., 2000a: "Demosthenes as Advocate," in *Demosthenes: Statesman and Orator,* ed. Ian Worthington. London: 181–204.

Mirhady, David C., 2000b: "The Athenian Rationale for Torture," in *Law and Social Status in Classical Athens,* ed. Virginia Hunter and Jonathan Edmondson. Oxford: pp. 53–74.

Parke, H. W., 1939: "The Pythais of 355 B.C. and the Third Sacred War," *Journal of Hellenic Studies* 59: 80–83.

Parke, H. W., 1977: *Festivals of the Athenians.* London.

Rhodes, Peter J., 1972: *The Athenian Boule.* Oxford.

Rhodes, Peter J., trans., 1984: *Aristotle, The Athenian Constitution.* Harmondsworth.

Rubinstein, Lene, 1993: *Adoption in IV. Century Athens.* Copenhagen.

Rubinstein, Lene, 2000: *Litigation and Cooperation: Supporting Speakers in the Courts of Classical Athens*. Stuttgart.

Scafuro, Adele C., 1994: "Witnessing and False Witnessing," in *Athenian Identity and Civic Ideology*, ed. Alan L. Boegehold and Adele C. Scafuro. Baltimore: 156–198.

Schaps, David, 1977: "The Woman Least Mentioned: Etiquette and Women's Names," *Classical Quarterly* 27: 323–330.

Thür, Gerhard, 2005: "The Role of the Witness in Athenian Law," in *The Cambridge Companion to Ancient Greek Law*, ed. Michael Gagarin and David Cohen. Cambridge: 146–169.

Todd, Stephen C., 1993: *The Shape of Athenian Law*. Oxford.

Todd, Stephen C., trans., 2000: *Lysias*. Austin.

Todd, Stephen C., 2005: "Law and Oratory at Athens," in *The Cambridge Companion to Ancient Greek Law*, ed. Michael Gagarin and David Cohen. Cambridge: 97–111.

Todd, Stephen C., 2007: *A Commentary on Lysias: Speeches 1–11*. Oxford.

Trevett, Jeremy, 1992: *Apollodorus, the Son of Pasion*. Oxford.

Usher, Stephen, 1974: *Dionysius of Halicarnassus, Critical Essays*, Vol. 1. Cambridge, MA.

Usher, Stephen, 1976: "Lysias and His Clients," *Greek, Roman and Byzantine Studies* 17: 31–40.

Usher, Stephen, 1999: *Greek Oratory: Tradition and Originality*. Oxford.

Wallace, Robert W., 1989: *The Areopagus Council*. Baltimore.

Whitehead, David, 1986: *The Demes of Attica, 508/7–ca. 250 B.C.* Princeton.

Wolff, Hans Julius, 1943: "The *dikē blabēs* in Dem. 55," *American Journal of Philology* 64: 316–324.

Wyse, William, 1904: *The Speeches of Isaeus*. Cambridge.

INDEX